Financial and Monetary Policy Studies

Volume 55

The book series 'Financial and Monetary Policy Studies' features the latest research in financial and monetary economics. Books published in this series are primarily monographs and edited volumes that present new research results, both theoretical and empirical, on a clearly defined topic. All books are published in print and digital formats and disseminated globally.

Ioanna T. Kokores

Monetary Policy in Interdependent Economies

The Task Ahead

Springer

Ioanna T. Kokores
Department of Economics
University of Piraeus
Piraeus, Greece

ISSN 0921-8580 ISSN 2197-1889 (electronic)
Financial and Monetary Policy Studies
ISBN 978-3-031-41957-7 ISBN 978-3-031-41958-4 (eBook)
https://doi.org/10.1007/978-3-031-41958-4

This Springer imprint is published by the registered company Springer Nature Switzerland AG
The registered company address is: Gewerbestrasse 11, 6330 Cham, Switzerland

Acknowledgments

I am particularly grateful to Professor John H. Wood for his insightful suggestions early on in my endeavor, and passing on his scientific stand in his highly educated, rightly fitting, implicit manner; I owe him a great debt of gratitude. I need to extend my gratitude to Springer's *Financial and Monetary Policy Studies* series editor, Professor Farrokh K. Langdana; his expertise and aptly suited comments have been instrumental in shaping the direction toward current, as well as future, policy implication of this work. I would like to thank Taxiarchis Kokores, Ph.D., for his invaluable scientific guidance, support, and encouragement throughout the entire project. I am immensely grateful to my Commissioning editor, Niko Chtouris, and the editorial team in Springer, for their sincerely dedicated efforts and collaboration; this project would have never reached the stage of publication, if it were not for their unfailing support and consideration.

About this Book

Economies worldwide face an environment of recently heightened uncertainty due to non-economic factors, such as the COVID-19 pandemic, the war in Ukraine, and even from a rather long-term perspective, climate changes. In response to the COVID-19 pandemic, policymakers quickly activated a broad range of monetary and fiscal instruments to provide exceptional support to counter the deep impact on output and incomes, even though policy instruments were already stretched uncomfortably close to their limits. Economies worldwide experienced a massive increase in the growth rate of broad money and, eventually, a noticeable rise in inflation, which remains, nevertheless, a monetary phenomenon. After almost four decades of low and stable inflation, people have started talking about inflation again. Inflation is bound to remain a major challenge in the years ahead as we embark on a significant reallocation of resources. In their quest to fight inflation effectively, policymakers need to eliminate, whenever possible, surprises in both monetary and fiscal policies. *This book provides* an analytical framework in the context of intense globalization and increased interdependence across economies (irrespective of the recent re-examining of supply chains and trade relationships), as well as a policy framework thoroughly amended after the global financial crisis and the crises that followed it. The book presents policy proposals useful to central banking practitioners, monetary and fiscal policymakers, and academic researchers and students, emphasizing how policymakers must strive to build a set of policies that the public has faith in and will take into account when forming expectations of future inflation and spending.

Contents

List of Figures

List of Tables

Chapter 1
Introduction

> . . .Economic history suggests – it can never prove anything – that going the route of isolationism and autarky hurts rather than helps the trend of average national affluence and of average real wages.
> —*Paul A. Samuelson (1997), p. 8*
> . . .History suggests the path to taming inflation is through more international trade – not less.
> —*Harold James (2023), p. 64*

Over the last four decades, intense globalization has increased the interdependence across economies worldwide. The developments that "coin" the term "globalization" refer to the significantly increased intensity and span of both global trade flows and financial links. These developments similarly trigger the global co-movement of macroeconomic and financial variables, such as GDP growth, inflation, and equity prices, and promote the (at times even competitive) exchange of innovation in terms of pertinent institutional design and implementation among countries and jurisdictions worldwide.

Globalization, thus, raises a set of vital questions for central banks worldwide, and especially in major advanced economies, such as the European Central Bank (ECB), the US Federal Reserve System, the Bank of England, the Bank of Japan, the Bank of Canada, the Reserve Bank of Australia, and the Swiss National Bank (SNB). Such questions include the following: (1) To what extent do monetary policy actions in one jurisdiction spill over to real and financial variables among advanced economies? (2) What are the underlying transmission channels? (3) How do the concerns as in (1) and (2) refer to the question of whether there is a case for international monetary policy coordination?

It is, thus, rendered vital for central banks to understand how globalization affects the monetary transmission mechanism. Due to the rapid increase in cross-border exchange of goods, services, technology, capital, and information that has occurred over the past few decades, globalization has led to greater integration between individual economies. Trade and financial globalization change the dynamic interdependencies of economies, such as the increased exposure to foreign shocks, and facilitate international risk-sharing. A central bank's understanding of how

I. T. Kokores, *Monetary Policy in Interdependent Economies*, Financial and Monetary Policy Studies 55, https://doi.org/10.1007/978-3-031-41958-4_1

globalization affects monetary policy is crucial since it affects how monetary policy is transmitted. As a result of the global financial crisis (GFC) and the emergence of unconventional monetary policies, the *international dimension of national economic policy* has gained renewed interest.

Obstfeld and Rogoff (2002) argued in a seminal paper at the turn of the century that despite a fully integrated world, national monetary policy cross-border spillovers and externalities were likely to be small, thus dispensing with international coordination. The focus of national monetary policy should therefore be on purely domestic objectives. At least under normal circumstances (namely, in the absence of evidently prevailing financial instability), national monetary policies that were optimal from a purely domestic perspective would also be (fairly) optimal from a global perspective, according to this pre-GFC view. Since then, however, events have highlighted the risks of shocks spreading across borders and revived the debate over international monetary policy coordination (see, for example, Draghi, 2016; Kokores, T., 1989, for an early thorough account). Particularly, these events showed how financial linkages propagate and amplify spillovers across borders, as well as how new policy instruments have international side effects. As Brunnermeier (2023) argues, also fiscal expansion seems to have been a primary driver of inflation in the United States but has contributed to inflation in Europe as well (Brunnermeier, 2023, p. 7). As a result, several central banks were forced to coordinate their policies under various pertinent occasions.

Due to the COVID-19 pandemic that emerged and amplified during 2020 and the quarantine measures employed by most countries worldwide to counter it, the world faced a new crisis, resulting in massive downturns in production, cutbacks in consumption, and fragility or even breakdown in supply chains, thus eventually putting pressure on public finances. To prevent that economic crisis from amplifying into a financial one, monetary, fiscal, and prudential policy measures were initially implemented to safeguard the financial sector. As the pandemic broke out, the European Central Bank, the US Federal Reserve, and the Bank of Japan provided monetary easing to cushion the economic blow by unleashing the power of their balance sheets. Remarkably, they all refrained from the hesitation observed in previous (recent) crisis events, when interest rate policy was hampered by the interest rate effective lower bound. The eventual backstop protected government securities and private assets from a financial market meltdown, enabling a fiscal expansion in these central banks' countries and jurisdictions, which was deemed essential at the time.

Evidently, economies worldwide are rendered vulnerable to macroeconomic and financial instability, as well as disruptive crises like the COVID-19 pandemic, as public and private debt levels are high and policy rates are near their effective lower bound. In both advanced and developing economies, smaller disturbances can also activate perverse loops that can adversely affect activity without a convincing and sufficient policy response. Under such a persistent state of uncertainty and anxiety, households continue to save in order to protect themselves from illiquidity, while firms discourage investment, slowing down growth and pushing equilibrium interest rates down to zero or even negative levels. The eminent "tail risk" of consequent extreme output contractions, job losses, and financial instability cannot be protected by either monetary or fiscal policy alone in this context. Both monetary and fiscal policies need to boldly act together, which at times may also blur the distinction between the two.

For example, when the COVID-19 pandemic emerged, policymakers around the world stepped up to provide exceptional support by activating a broad range of fiscal and monetary instruments to counter lockdowns and social distancing measures which had a profound impact on output and incomes. Globally, this policy mix had been significantly congruent. As a result of disruptions in cash flows, monetary authorities began using unconventional instruments to alleviate liquidity stress. A variety of targeted lending programs were implemented, often backed by state guarantees in either an explicit or even an implicit manner. There were also exceptional fiscal policy responses; the latter bolstered automatic stabilizers through generous short-term work schemes, as well as check provision to households, small- and medium-sized enterprises, and self-employed individuals, in addition to tax cut and deferrals with carrybacks to buffer income losses (see, for example, BIS, 2020, for a discussion on these measures).

In many advanced or developing countries, public debt levels had already reached unprecedented levels in peace time before the emergence of the COVID-19 pandemic. Such policies had been implemented against the backdrop of policy instruments already stretched uncomfortably close to their limits. Notably, in several economies, conventional policy rates were at or near their effective lower bound, and at the same time, interest rates were historically low.

When aggregate demand falls below aggregate supply, monetary stimulus is deemed appropriate. This is the case under a recession, when the output gap widens, as—*in a typical business cycle*—demand falls while potential supply remains largely unaltered; it is monetary policy that is called to offset the opened up output gap. However, as, for example, King (2022, p. 6) remarks, the economic downturn caused by the COVID-19 pandemic and the measures employed to address it do not reflect the workings of an ordinary typical business cycle downturn; quoting the March 2021 report of the UK Office for Budget Responsibility (OBR), he recognizes that with reference to the United Kingdom, "[the chart] shows only a small margin of spare capacity since the start of the pandemic, reflecting our judgement that most of the fall in output during 2020 should be thought of as a simultaneous contraction in demand and supply" (OBR, 2021, p. 55).

King (2022), nevertheless, is hesitant to accept that additional monetary stimuli were deemed appropriate either during 2020 or the time of publication. He further accepts that quantitative easing (QE) constitutes an expansion of the money supply and recognizes the reluctance of most central bank officials and practitioners to describe it as such, eventually rendering difficult and seemingly arbitrary the calibration of changes to quantitative easing policies. King (2022, p. 7) further highlights that the implementation of QE monetary policy measures in the aftermath of the GFC aimed at preventing a *fall* in broad money, while in the aftermath of the COVID-19 pandemic it created a substantial *monetary overhang*; namely, a part of the money supply that people are holding only because they have not been able to spend it triggered, for example, by the shortages in real goods and services induced by the quarantine measures employed worldwide in conjuncture with the vast QE programs applied in most major economies. When the conditions that keep spending repressed are removed, monetary overhang typically tends to produce a burst of open inflation. This has been the case as the COVID-19 pandemic unfolded, when a substantial increase in the growth rate of broad money effectuated in most major economies and a noticeable rise in inflation, highlighting the eternal verities of David Hume[1] and most subsequent economists that inflation is a monetary phenomenon (King, 2022, p. 9).

In the seminal words of Milton Friedman (1980):

> Inflation is blamed on many things. But it has only one cause: It is a monetary phenomenon. *Inflation occurs when the quantity of money increases faster than the quantity of goods.* [emphasis added] Why does the money supply increase? Very often, it does so to enable the government to pay its bills without raising taxes. There's only one real cure for inflation. It is a cure that's easy to describe but difficult to apply: The government must reduce spending and print less money. The alternatives are *both* recession and double-digit inflation. [emphasis as in the original]. . . . Printing money is a very attractive device because inflation, from the point of view of a person sitting in Congress or in the Senate, is a wonderful tax. He doesn't have to vote for it. (par. 6)

As such, after almost four decades of low and stable inflation, namely, during the period of the so-called "Great Moderation" and the deflation years triggered by the GFC and the euro area crisis, people have started talking about inflation again. The effective implementation of monetary policy relies heavily on the expectations of inflation formed by financial market participants and the public. A central bank has a greater chance of achieving their inflation goal if they can secure the long-term inflation expectations of economic agents near their target for inflation. Since inflation expectations influence the current inflation rate by affecting wage and price levels, they tend to be critical in the monetary policy transmission (Bernanke et al., 2001). Therefore, central banks must strive to comprehend how domestic and global shocks influence inflation expectations, given their significance in monetary policy.

Additionally, since central banks are deemed to be "the voice of price stability" (King, 2022, p. 10), they need to form a narrow mandate that will enable them to preserve their independence, which remains critical to the effective design and implementation of monetary policy. Central bank independence relies on monetary policy decisions remaining insulated from short-term political considerations. Brunnermeier (2023, p. 6) distinguishes de jure from de facto independence, defining the latter as the central bank's setting its policy rate while not having to worry

[1]Hume (1752) claims that "it is only in the intermediate situation between the acquisition of money and the rise of prices that the increasing quantity of gold and silver is favourable to industry" (quoted in Hayek, 1939, p. 49, that highlights the clear similarities in Hume's belief on the long-run neutrality of the *level* of the money stock with respect to real variables, with the arguments expressed in Henry Thornton, 1802; also quoted in Friedman, 1987, p. 3, in his account on "The Quantity Theory of Money" in *The New Palgrave: A Dictionary of Economics*).

about whether higher interest rates (to potentially tame inflation) will increase government indebtedness or default risk.

The benefits of central bank independence have been well documented since the 1980s by extensive research contributions, using both theoretical and empirical constructs. For example, Rogoff (1985) and Debelle and Fischer (1994) provide a discussion of the distinction between different types of central bank independence, namely, the so-called operational or instrument independence and goal independence, while, for example, Alesina and Summers (1993) and Crowe and Meade (2008) give empirical evidence on the benefits of central bank independence. Bernanke (2010) and Tucker (2018a, 2018b) provide overviews of the development of central bank independence.

Powell (2023, Jan 10) constitutes a recent fervent reiteration, also highlighting the significance of a form of central bank independence with respect to bank regulation. The later helps ensure that the public can be confident that the central bank's supervisory decisions, let alone its potential responsibilities regarding climate-related financial risks (see, for example, Board of Governors, 2022), are not influenced by short-term political considerations. Furthermore, as Rogoff (2022) remarks, while central bank independence remains the bedrock of modern inflation targeting, it has been challenged over the past decade due to the zero-bound on nominal interest rates. Viewing that the effectiveness of monetary policy has been reduced, he accepts that the political economy pressure on central banks has increased significantly. He states that such novel pressure emerged since, in the aftermath of the GFC, fiscal policy has been responsible for much more of the burden of routine macroeconomic stabilization. Rogoff (2022) further highlights that, in a global low interest rate environment, to restore the efficacy of monetary policy, innovations in policy measures are required.

As economies worldwide emerged from the COVID-19 pandemic, a greater focus on resilience has been undertaken both by governments and by supervisory authorities, stirring a significant reallocation of resources, and also reinforced by the resurgent political pressures to raise public spending, the confrontation of a worldwide energy crisis due to the war in Ukraine, and the restructuring required to meet climate change targets. Such a reallocation of resources implies significant changes in relative prices and wages and as King (2022) remarks that, in view of the latter, inflation is bound to remain a major challenge over the years to come.

In the fight against inflation, to decrease the growth rate of money and to cut the federal budget deficit have been traditionally viewed as effective ways to combat inflation, as such policies will slow down real economic growth, leading to lower capacity utilization rates in factories and plants and potentially causing higher levels of unemployment. While some analysts support this approach, irrespective of the higher unemployment it causes, others purport that policy authorities should employ measures to fight inflation without causing significant increases in unemployment, such as economic controls on wages, prices, or credit.

In almost five decades ago, inflation in most advanced economies had been fought with the exploitation of abrupt cuts in money and debt growth that reduced real economic activity. These policies had been effective in slowing inflation, yet since because unemployment rose substantially, these policies (eventually labeled the "stop-go policies") had soon been abandoned. It thus became well recognized and documented at the time that to *permanently* reduce inflation policymakers must avoid politically intolerable increases in unemployment, and to achieve this policy, authorities must undertake gradual and pre-announced cuts in money and debt growth (see, for example, Federal Reserve Bank of Minneapolis, 1978, p. 1). This postulate not only gained credence in the years leading to the Great Moderation but also framed the effective implementation of monetary policy to such an extent that it became indispensable.

Nevertheless, the apparent "familiarity" with this type of monetary policy implementation forced monetary authorities in most major economies to render it promptly obsolete under the major worldwide economic turmoil caused by the 2007/2009 GFC and remained so as the consecutive crises unfolded. Avid fiscal stimuli in addition to pertinent monetary policy measures have been implemented to address the significant economic downturn due to the COVID-19 pandemic. Such policies had been effective to stimulate demand, yet this had been effected while the shift in demand from services to goods at a time when abrupt wide supply chain disruptions took place in addition to a withdrawal of workers from the labor force eventually caused a reduction of aggregate supply, which in combination lead to a surge in inflation in most advanced and emerging economies. This adverse effect has been further exacerbated by the unanticipated increases in energy prices during the first quarter of the year 2022 associated with the war in Ukraine, thus downgrading the forecasts for global economic growth. As Walsh (2022) argues, the reaction to the rising inflation by major advanced economies' central banks (namely, in the United States, the United Kingdom, and the euro area, which he addresses) has been rather slow.[2]

Nevertheless, in an environment where real rates remained rather subdued, central banks have been taught by the experience yielded in the aftermath of the GFC that they can execute policies altering the size and composition of their balance sheet, thus effectively substituting for interest rate policies. In direct equivalence to QE, central banks may implement unconventional monetary policies also to contain the surges of inflation. Such policies, labeled as quantitative tightening (QT), employ a shrinking of the size of a central bank's balance sheet instead of raising interest rates.

However, according to the Multivariate Core Trend (MCT) model for inflation persistence, namely, the dynamic factor model estimated by the Federal Reserve Bank of New York for the United States on monthly data for the 17 major sectors of the Personal Consumption Expenditure Index based on Stock and Watson (2016), released on April 6, 2023, the MCT showed a modest decline to 4.5% in February from (the revised value of) 4.6% in January 2023 (Almuzara et al., 2023). The model also demonstrated *increased uncertainty* on inflation dynamics, resulting in a 68%

[2]The Bank of England started raising its policy rate in November 2021 while the US Federal Reserve in March 2022, and the European Central Bank (ECB) started raising its key interest rate in July 2022.

probability band for MCT, namely, from 4.0% to 5.2%. This result may, at an initially minor extent, provide some solace to the concerns raised, for example, in Walsh (2022), that "the challenge now is to prevent transitory surges in inflation from increasing trend inflation" (p. 43), in view of the lessons learned half a century ago, by the major monetary policy mistake during the 1960s and 1970s of focusing on the volatility of inflation caused by the oil price shocks and erroneously allowing inflation to have a decades-long upward trend during the "Great Inflation" era.

The current analysis advances in three Parts. *Part I* focuses on the monetary theory and policy after the 2007/2009 GFC. It assesses what policymakers and academic economists have learned about monetary policy strategy and argues on the extent that we should change our thinking in this regard in the aftermath of the GFC. The part begins with a discussion of where the science of monetary policy stood before the crisis and how central banks viewed monetary policy strategy and then argues on how the crisis has changed the thinking of both macro and monetary economists, as well as central bankers, and, finally, examines the implications of this change in thinking for monetary policy science and strategy (see, for example, Mishkin, 2011, who provides a concise comprehensive analysis of the state of monetary policy analysis before the crisis).

Part II provides a critical analysis on the monetary considerations of the European sovereign debt crisis, also termed as the "Eurozone" crisis. As Portes (2014) remarks, "creditor countries have been unwilling to let their banks suffer the consequences of bad loans – rather, they have managed to put the entire burden on the taxpayers of the debtor countries." (p. 425). However, as recognized by Fisher (2012), "...we are where we are, the eurozone is where it is, and looking backward isn't going to get the zone out of its difficulties without diagnosing the current situation" (p. 493). The two decades that followed the launch of the Euro, eventually, witness a varied economic and financial landscape. Other than a vast expansion, the Eurozone faced two severe financial crises and has recently tried to address a severe adverse economic shock (*due to a pandemic*). The euro area has been facing economic stagnation, which rendered obvious the shortcomings of the initial monetary union. Furthermore, policy responses have included a (rather weak) fiscal backstop, an expansion on the ECB balance sheet, an imperfect bank union, and a progressing integration of capital markets. Since such shifts in monetary, fiscal, and macroprudential policy stance were effected under several sovereign debt runs and stagnating income growth, several dimensions of the "euro project" have been called into question (see, for example, Gerba, 2019).

The distinct long-term effects on European Union member countries' growth and fiscal stability stemming from the 2007/2009 GFC and the subsequent economic and Eurozone sovereign debt crisis have been accentuated by the inherent weaknesses in the European Union financial system, the apparent inadequacy of the policy tools, and the regulatory and surveillance environment in place, in addition to the overall incomplete Eurozone institutional architecture. During the early phase of the GFC, in an effort to stabilize the economy, fiscal stimuli were exercised in addition to state aid measures to support the banking sector. These led to a significant accumulation of public debt, which in addition to the overarching uncertainty of market participants about the resilience of the institutional architecture of the Eurozone created huge pressure on both sovereign yields and credit ratings assigned by rating agencies to distinct Eurozone member states. In this manner, the effect of the sovereign debt crisis fed back to the banking sector and the economy overall.

As remarked by the European Court of Auditors (2020) in a pertinent "Review," the European Union further proceeded in taking bold steps to "break the bank-sovereign nexus (also known as the 'doom-loop') by reducing the dependency of banks on public funds when facing the risk of failure, and developing the necessary instruments for their orderly resolution [; in addition to] EU member states' ... important fiscal and economic measures to avoid excessive deficits, thereby improving their fiscal position" (p. 5). Other sectors also affected include insurance, pensions, and nonbank financial intermediaries.

In addition to the retrospective assessment of the above measures, the effects of the adverse shock due to the COVID-19 pandemic and the measures adopted to battle it have formed an important testing procedure to assess the resilience of the European Union economic and financial architecture. The unfortunate timing of the pandemic shock (as the European Union was just recovering from the concomitant effects of the 2007–2012 GFC and "Eurozone" crises) resulted in its far larger global adverse impact on both the size of the economic effect and the scale of public response. Ample evidence is provided by the fiscal measures undertaken and the monetary and regulatory interventions employed. These measures vary in both their type and extent, including temporary exemptions for state aid rules, as well as the activation of the "general escape clause" of the Stability and Growth Pact, which eventually allow EU member states to implement immediate support to business and fiscal policies. Nevertheless, the European Court of Auditors (2020) further assesses the following: "a member state's fiscal health prior to the COVID-19 crisis has an important bearing on the ability to deploy policies and, therefore, on the economic impact of the pandemic. Phased reforms will need to be implemented, particularly in member states with low potential economic growth and/or high debt. *The COVID-19 crisis risks widening economic divergencies in the EU* [emphasis added]" (p. 6).

Nevertheless, as highlighted in Whelan (2019), the euro project has proven to be popular with the public since economic and monetary union has brought some important gains for European citizens, in that it managed to counter adverse events such as sovereign defaults, the imposition of capital controls, haircuts for depositors, and a slump that has taken almost a decade to recover from. However, even Whelan (2019) claims that to conclude that the worst has passed and the euro is now bound to succeed may be too prompt a remark, let alone "overly optimistic" (p. 29). Since the advent of the GFC and the subsequent crises, Eurozone member-state governments agreed and urged to implement a number of changes regarding crisis management and financial regulation. The open question still holds of whether the current institutional framework remains too fragile and insufficient to manage the next crisis or whether the context has improved considerably enough compared to the case (facing the euro area) over 10 years ago, encouraging the potential of devising a strategy that might actually work.

Part III, titled "The Task Ahead," summarizes the major conclusions. As Hicks (1969) stresses, since economics is about the history of economic thought, sometimes it is worth revisiting past debates in economics (reiterated in, for example, Cecchetti et al., 2009a, 2009b, p. 4). The unwinding of financial bubbles and the consequent episodes of financial stress are eventually too frequent and costly to be addressed as mere adverse shocks (exogenous to the system of economic interactions), which, according to Lucas (2009), are of little consequence to forward-looking stabilization policy. As argued, for example, in Cecchetti et al. (2009a, 2009b), academic researchers and central bank practitioners should ask whether policy should intervene to make financial stress both less likely and less damaging when it inevitably arises. The task to understand how to deliver economic stability should include a firm grasp of how to avoid financial instability.

Arbitrage in many segments of the market broke down as markets froze and market participants were hit by panic during the GFC. Existing economic and financial models immediately evidenced their serious limitations. Models of the macroeconomy were uncapable of predicting the crisis or explaining convincingly the events that most economies were facing worldwide. It is true that all models that central banks and international financial institutions had been frequently (and quite uncontestably) using to base their forecasting and policy or strategic design viewed the GFC as an improbable contingency. Indeed, the "global financial crisis was not supposed to happen" (White, 2011, p. 124). Modern macro models, such as the New Classical, New Keynesian, and dynamic stochastic general equilibrium (DSGE) models, exclude by assumption extended economic disequilibria. Indeed, it is challenging to implement unconventional monetary policy. Central banks must assume greater risks on their balance sheets if they plan to counter the nominal interest rate zero lower bound. The large-scale asset purchases that unconventional monetary policy entails have uncomfortable fiscal and distributional consequences. As, for example, Orphanides (2018, p. 35) remarks monetary policy is further hindered by a lack of clarity on the definition of price stability, as well as concerns about the legitimacy of large balance sheet expansions. As a result, central banks have been urged to accommodate too low inflation instead of undertaking decisive quantitative easing measures needed to stimulate the economy. Due to their being exceptional by nature, unconventional monetary policy measures tend to discourage solid explanations of their effectiveness by traditional models and frameworks. In this context and with the benefit of hindsight, it is imperative that new benchmarks are constructed for effective policy responses and new informative tools before academic and central bank research can examine and evaluate alternative policy responses.

Similar to other aspects of good economic governance in democratic societies, turning to the case for central bank independence, one recognizes, however, that it is not incontestable. It is not always clear what the boundaries of such independence are. Institutional design challenges include maintaining democratic legitimacy while achieving and sustaining economic efficiency with delegated discretionary power. Over time, greater independence does not necessarily result in better macroeconomic performance. A thorough understanding of the practical problems and challenges is crucial for establishing proper boundaries for central bank independence and promoting policies that are most beneficial to society.

As Tucker (2018a, 2018b) argues in the wake of the GFC, major central banks accumulated much more power, which is questioned whether it is compatible with our democratic values. He further contends that if we are to maintain central bank independence, as well as the confidence we have in our system of government as a whole, it is imperative that legislatures delegate power. Evidently, central banks—on an almost worldwide scale—led the way in reviving the economy and redesigning the international financial system this time, as opposed to elected politicians doing the "heavy lifting" during the Great Depression of the twentieth century. In ways that blurred the line between them and the elected fiscal authorities, central banks used their balance sheets to influence credit conditions, steer resource allocations, and take risk on a huge scale. In addition, major central banks have also been granted extensive microprudential and macroprudential regulatory powers. Tucker (2018a, 2018b) further recognizes that "central bankers have, indeed, become the poster boys and girls of *unelected power* [emphasis added]. . .[making it] hardly surprising, then, that more people have been asking whether the insulation of the monetary authorities from day-to-day political influence can still be justified" (para. 5).

A greater recovery of output and employment has been achieved than would otherwise have occurred as a result of unconventional expansionary monetary policies, which have eased financial conditions. However, macroeconomic performance has been rather disappointing despite policy action taken since the GFC was neither strong enough nor fast enough to avoid it. Much of the world remains far from full employment almost 15 years after the GFC, as recovery has evidently been sluggish compared to recoveries from past deep recessions.

The new crisis as a result of the COVID-19 pandemic that emerged in 2020 impacted most economies worldwide, affecting production, supply chains, and consumption and putting pressure on public finances. As an initial reaction monetary, fiscal and prudential policy measures had been undertaken to safeguard the financial sector from the economic impacts, in order to prevent the economic crisis from being amplified into a financial one. In fact, at the onset of the pandemic, the European Central Bank (ECB), the US Federal Reserve, and the Bank of Japan (BoJ) exploited the powers of altering the size and composition of their balance sheets without the hesitation that was seen in past encounters, when interest rate policy was hindered by the effective zero lower bound. By providing vast monetary easing, they cushioned the blow to the economy, and by facilitating the financing of an essential fiscal expansion, these banks prevented a financial market meltdown. In fact, as Orphanides (2021, p. 36) highlights between March and June 2020, the US Federal Reserve expanded its balance sheet by 3 trillion dollars, namely, issuing as much high-powered money as it did from 1913 to 2013 (the first 100 years of its history); the ECB and the BoJ undergone similar massive balance sheet expansions. Under normal times, unprecedented money printing of such extent would be alarming as the power of central bank balance sheets, when misused, can wreak havoc on the economy.

The headline consumer price index (CPI) has been increasing in both advanced and emerging market economies since the start of 2021. This rise is due to factors such as increased demand, shortages of inputs, and rapid increases in commodity prices (IMF, 2021). Although there is uncertainty about the impact of the COVID-19 pandemic on the measurement of output gaps (McMorrow et al., 2021), there is still a connection between economic slack and inflation.[3] However, long-term inflation expectations have remained stable, and as stated in the IMF World Economic Outlook publicized by October 2021, there is no evidence that the policy measures undertaken to address the pandemic shock have affected these expectations. In fact, the IMF projection at the time was that headline inflation would reach its highest point toward the end of 2021 and would return to pre-pandemic levels by mid-2022 in both advanced and emerging markets. Long-term inflation expectations have been projected to remain anchored in the baseline forecast, irrespective of the increased uncertainty, particularly relating to the assessment of economic slack. Nevertheless, even though at their time of writing the war in Ukraine and its worldwide adverse effects via the concomitant energy price shock did not seem of high possibility, they accepted that there are risks that could push global inflation even higher, such as commodity price shocks, longer-term expenditure commitments, and a de-anchoring of inflation expectations (IMF, 2021, p. 45), which could be contained through effective communication, and pertinent monetary and fiscal policies can help prevent inflation expectations from becoming unhinged.

A lesson learned through hard experience by monetary authorities during the "Great Inflation" era has been that to effectively combat inflation, policymakers need to reduce unexpected changes in their monetary and fiscal policies. They should establish a set of policies that the public has faith in and can rely on when forming expectations about future spending and inflation. This means that policies must be perceived as credible. The best way to achieve credibility is by announcing policies, executing them consistently, and avoiding sudden shifts.

It has been over 3 years since the COVID-19 outbreak began in spring 2020, and despite the occasional appearance of new variants, the worldwide economy has slowly been recovering. However, a new source of political instability has emerged after the burst of the war in Ukraine in late February 2022. Inflation rates have been on the rise globally since the second half of 2021 as economic activity picked up again after the pandemic. The recent increase in commodity prices following the crisis in Ukraine is expected to further fuel inflationary pressures worldwide (Kuroda, 2022).

It became evident due to the GFC that economic analysis should place greater attention to its international dimension, especially in light of the contemporary

[3] Several temporary adjustments to the European Union's Commonly Agreed Methodology (EUCAM) on the estimating output gaps and potential growth were required as a result of the COVID-19 pandemic (see, for example, Thum-Thysen et al., 2022). Almost all of the reduction in GDP due to the pandemic went into the output gap estimate as a result of these adjustments. Providing the policy response was robust and the recovery was rapid, the "frozen" capital and labor components of the EU's supply-side capacity could emerge from the pandemic largely unscathed.

highly integrated international financial systems and the intensively more tightly integrated production processes (e.g., via global supply chains). As, for example, Kokores, T. (1989) indicates it has become a truism to accept that due to the extent of international interdependencies and the prospect of further cross-border interconnections among financial markets and intermediaries, public policy addressing banking and finance practices can no longer be formulated and implemented in a purely national context. Indeed, in his early remark, he views that the "international dimension has probably become the most important policy parameter in a large and growing number of areas" (p. 31). As Praet (2022) eloquently remarks, monetary policy is now "walking on thin ice... and thin ice is ok if you are walking alone maybe, but when everybody goes the same direction may not be the same, so; if all central banks move towards the same direction it may be too much – this is one of the discussions we have internationally" (remarks, November 9, 2022).

The book is organized in nine *chapter*s clustered in three parts as follows: Chap. 1 is the introduction and then *Part I* follows, which presents an overview of the state of monetary theory and policy after the GFC and in view of the unprecedented over the Great Moderation years' recent increase on inflation; it consists of three chapters, Chaps. 2–4. Then *Part II* analyzes and critically reviews the challenges posed to the design and conduct of monetary policy in interdependent economies; it uses as an analytical example the paradigm of the European Unification and the hazards aroused by the recent sovereign debt crisis in the euro area, often dubbed the "Eurozone crisis." *Part II* includes two chapters, Chap. 5, titled "Monetary Policy Crisis in the Eurozone," and Chap. 6, titled "A Critical Assessment of the Euro-Project in Retrospect"; it presents an analytical critical review of the relevant literature. The final *Part III*, titled "The Task Ahead: Monetary Policy in Uncharted Waters," includes three chapters, namely, Chap. 7, titled "Monetary Theory and Policy: The Implications of Radical Uncertainty"; Chap. 8, titled "Monetary Policy in Interdependent Economies: The Task Ahead"; and Chap. 9, titled "Looking to the Future: Monetary Policy in Uncharted Waters" that summarizes the major conclusions while looking to the future amid radical uncertainty due to the recent crises trigged by economic and noneconomic factors as the COVID-19 pandemic, the war in Ukraine, and even (in a rather long-term perspective) climate changes. This part addresses potential future challenges to both academic researchers and central bank practitioners.

References

Alesina, A., & Summers, L. H. (1993). Central Bank independence and macroeconomic performance: Some comparative evidence. *Journal of Money, Credit and Banking, 25*, 151–162.

Almuzara, M., Kocaoglu, B., & Sbordone, A. (2023). MCT update: Inflation persistence declined modestly in February. Federal Reserve Bank of New York. *Liberty Street Economics*.

Bernanke, B. S. (2010). Central Bank Independence, transparency, and accountability. *Speech* delivered at the Institute for Monetary and Economic Studies International Conference, Bank of Japan, Tokyo, Japan, May 25.

Bernanke, B. S., Laubach, T., Mishkin, F. S., & Posen, A. S. (2001). *Inflation targeting: Lessons from the international experience*. Princeton University Press.

BIS—Bank for International Settlements. (2020). Annual economic report, Basel, Switzerland.

Board of Governors of the Federal Reserve System. (2022). Federal Reserve Board Invites Public Comment on Proposed Principles Providing a High-Level Framework for the Safe and Sound Management of Exposures to Climate-Related Financial Risks for Large Banking Organizations. *Press release*, December 2.

Brunnermeier, M. K. (2023). Rethinking monetary policy in a changing world. *Finance & Development 'New Directions for Monetary Policy'*, 60(1), International Monetary Fund, March, pp 6–9.

Cecchetti S.G., Disyatat, P., & Kohler, M. (2009a). Integrating financial stability: New models for a new challenge. Proceedings joint BIS-ECB workshop on "Monetary Policy and Financial Stability", Basel, Switzerland, 10–11 September.

Cecchetti, S. G., Disyatat, P., & Kohler, M. (2009b). Integrating financial stability: New models for a new challenge. Proceedings of the joint BIS-ECB workshop on *'Monetary policy and financial stability'*, Basel, Switzerland, 10–11 September.

Crowe, C., & Meade, E. E. (2008). Central Bank Independence and transparency: Evolution and effectiveness. *European Journal of Political Economy, 24*, 763–777.

Debelle, G., & Fischer, S. (1994). How independent should a Central Bank be? *Proceedings* of the conference on '*Goals, Guidelines, and Constraints Facing Monetary Policymakers*', North Falmouth, Massachusetts, in June 1994 (pp. 195–221). Boston: Federal Reserve Bank of Boston.

Draghi, M. (2016). The international dimension of monetary policy. *Speech* at the European Central Bank - ECB forum on central banking, Sintra, 28 June.

European Court of Auditors. (2020). How the EU took account of lessons learned from the 2008-2012 financial and sovereign debt crises. *Review* no 5, European Court of Auditors, European Union, Luxembourg.

Federal Reserve Bank of Minneapolis. (1978). Eliminating policy surprises: An inexpensive way to beat inflation. Federal Reserve Bank of Minneapolis. *Annual Review*, 1–8.

Fisher, S. (2012). *Global policy perspectives. Proceedings Jackson hole economic summit* (pp. 492–498). Jackson Hole, WY: A symposium sponsored by the Federal Reserve Bank of Kansas City.

Friedman, M. (1980). *Milton Friedman speaks: 15 videotaped lectures (with questions and answer sessions)*. Harcourt Brace Jovanovich, Inc.

Friedman, M. (1987). Quantity theory of money. In J. Eatwell, M. Milgate, & P. Newman (Eds.), *The new Palgrave: A dictionary of economics* (Vol. 4, pp. 3–20). Stockton Press/Macmillan.

Gerba, E. (2019). Euro project, 20 years on: A critical assessment and the road ahead. *Report* European Parliament's Committee on Economic and Monetary Affairs. Available online: http://www.europarl.europa.eu/committees/en/econ/monetary-dialogue.html

Hayek, F.A. V. (1939). Introduction. In Reprint of Henry Thornton (1802). *An enquiry into the nature and effects of the paper credit of Great Britain.* London: George Allen and Unwin.

Hicks, J. R. (1969). *A theory of economic history*. Oxford Clarendon Press.

Hume, D. (1752). Of money. In *Essays, moral, political and literary*, vol. 1 of *essays and treatises*, a new edition, Edinburgh: Bell and Bradfute, Cadell and Davies, 1804.

IMF—International Monetary Fund. (2021). *World economic outlook: Recovery during a pandemic—health concerns, supply disruptions*. Price Pressures.

James, H. (2023). In defense of globalisation. Finance & Development 'New Directions for Monetary Policy', vol. 60(1), International Monetary Fund, pp. 64–66.

King, M. (2022). Monetary policy in a world of radical uncertainty. *Conference Paper* 1, Institute of International Monetary Research, University of Buckingham, UK, January.

Kokores, T. (1989). *Euro-banking innovations and EEC monetary coordination (studies 4)*. Institute of European Civilization. Papazisis.

Kuroda, H. (2022). *Japan's inflation dynamics and the role of monetary policy* (p. 22). Speech at Columbia University.

Lucas, R. (2009). In defence of the dismal science. *The Economist.*

McMorrow, K., Thum-Thysen, A., Maier, C., Hristov, A., Döhring, B., D'Auria, F., & Blondeau, F. (2021). Output gaps, potential output and the Covid-19 crisis: Policymaking under uncertainty. *VoxEU, CEPR.*

Mishkin, F. S. (2011). Monetary policy strategy: Lessons from the crisis. In M. Jarociński, F. Smets, & C. Thimann (Eds.), *Approaches to monetary policy revisited—lessons from the crisis, sixth ECB central banking conference proceedings* (pp. 67–118).

OBR—Office for Budget Responsibility. (2021). *Economic and fiscal outlook—March 2021 (CP 387).* Office for Budget Responsibility.

Obstfeld, M., & Rogoff, K. (2002). Global implications of self-oriented national monetary rules. *Quarterly Journal of Economics, 117*(2), 503–535.

Orphanides, A. (2018). The boundaries of Central Bank independence: Lessons from unconventional times. *Bank of Japan Monetary and Economic Studies*, 35–56.

Orphanides, A. (2021). The power of central Bank balance sheets. Keynote Speech, Bank of Japan Institute of Monetary Studies Conference on 'Adapting to the New Normal: Perspectives and Policy Challenges after the COVID-19 Pandemic', May 24–25. *Monetary and Economic Studies*, Bank of Japan, November.

Portes, R. (2014). The Eurozone crisis. In D. D. Evanoff, C. Holthausen, G. G. Kaufman, & M. Kremer (Eds.), *The role of central banks in financial stability: How has it changed?* (30th world scientific studies in international economics) (pp. 423–432). World Scientific Publishing Co. Pte. Ltd.

Powell, J. H. (2023). *Panel* on 'Central Bank Independence and the Mandate—Evolving Views'. Remarks. Symposium on Central Bank Independence, Sveriges Riksbank, Stockholm, Sweden, January 10.

Praet, P. (2022). *Remarks. Seminar in 'Financial Stability and Policy Risks in the Euro area'.* Peterson Institute for International Economics.

Rogoff, K. S. (1985). The optimal degree of commitment to an intermediate monetary target. *Quarterly Journal of Economics, 100*(4), 1169–1189.

Rogoff, K. S. (2022). Institutional innovation and central Bank Independence 2.0. *Monetary and economic studies*, (vol 40, pp. 25–38) Institute for Monetary and Economic Studies, Bank of Japan.

Samuelson, P. A. (1997). Wherein do the European and American models differ? *Banca d'Italia Temi di Discussione*, *320*, Banca d' Italia.

Stock, J. H., & Watson, M. W. (2016). Core inflation and trend inflation. *The Review of Economics and Statistics, 98*(4), 770–784.

Thornton, H. (1802). *An enquiry into the nature and effects of the paper credit of Great Britain* (p. 1939). George Allen and Unwin.

Thum-Thysen, A., Blondeau, F., d'Auria, F., Döhring, B., Hristov, A., & McMorrow, K. (2022). Estimation of output gaps and potential output against the backdrop of the COVID-19 pandemic: The EUCAM approach. *Quarterly Report on the Euro Area.* Directorate General Economic and Financial Affairs, European Commission, *21*(1):21–30.

Tucker, P. (2018a). *Unelected power: The quest for legitimacy in central banking and the regulatory state*. Princeton University Press.

Tucker, P. (2018b). The governance of monetary and financial stability policy. Banking perspectives. *The Clearing House. Quarter, 2*, 50–57.

Walsh, C. E. (2022). Inflation surges and monetary policy. *Monetary and Economic Studies*, 40, Institute for Monetary and Economic Studies, Bank of Japan, pp. 39–66.

Whelan, K. (2019). The euro at 20: Successes, problems, progress and threats. Monetary dialogue, January. In-depth analysis PE 631.039 requested by the ECON Committee, Policy Department for Economic, Scientific and Quality of Life Policies Directorate-General for Internal Policies, European Parliament, January.

White, W. R. (2011). Comment on Mishkin, Frederic S. (2011). Monetary policy strategy: Lessons from the crisis. In M. Jarociński, F. Smets, & C. Thimann (Eds.), *Approaches to monetary policy revisited—lessons from the crisis, sixth ECB central banking conference proceedings* (pp. 124–132).

Part I
Does the Science of Monetary Policy Need to be Altered?

Chapter 2
New Challenges on the Science of Monetary Policy

> Now, a resurgence of inflation requires yet another shift in emphasis in monetary policy. The predominant intellectual framework central banks have followed since the global financial crisis that began in 2008 neither stresses the most pressing looming issues nor mitigates their potential dire consequences in this new climate.
> —*Markus K. Brunnermeier (2023), p. 6*

2.1 Introduction

Central banking theory and practice had been based, up to not a very distant past, on a firm belief that monetary policymakers assume both the power and the ability to exert considerable influence on the real interest rate and the real volume of credit. In this respect, the belief further held that the private sector may occasionally develop cumulative, endogenous expansions or contractions of credit.[1] The latter would directly affect real activity, moving it above or below the equilibrium employment level. Therefore, a central bank's ability to regulate the price and availability of credit would prove significantly to be a vital tool in an effort to stabilize real activity.

Over almost the past few decades, such concepts of belief have been rendered obsolete and have hardly been expressed since, not until the advent of the global financial crisis (GFC). Instead, in common pertinent scientific parlance—even well before the GFC became apparent—a near consensus emerged in that the only useful thing that monetary policy can accomplish is nominal stability. According to the eloquent early remark as in Leijonhufvud (2001), "either a great many of the heretofore distinguished figures of our monetary past were sadly deluded – or perhaps the world has changed even more than meets the eye?" (p. 22); he further accepts that "two closely related *monetarist hypotheses* [emphasis added] have

[1] The intellectual tradition follows Wicksell's contribution on the so-called cumulative process to inflation as in Wicksell (1898) and reflects the workings of a bank lending channel of monetary transmission (Bernanke & Blinder, 1988; Bernanke & Gertler, 1995; Hubbard, 1995, p. 64; Kashyap & Stein, 1995; Stein, 1998; Ehrmann et al., 2001).

I. T. Kokores, *Monetary Policy in Interdependent Economies*, Financial and Monetary Policy Studies 55, https://doi.org/10.1007/978-3-031-41958-4_2

played a crucial part in this change in the collective system of beliefs, [namely] the 'vertical Phillips curve' [2] and ... the invariance of the real rate of interest to monetary policy[3]" (p. 23). Nevertheless, labor market flexibility and the absence of (unanticipated) nominal policy shocks are not sufficient conditions to guarantee strong stability of (un)employment at its natural rate.

Avid fluctuations of the real interest rate (too high or too low a level of real interest reflecting failures of intertemporal coordination) may result in keeping employment below or above the natural rate persistently.[4] In addition, monetary authorities will be able to influence real interest rates and credit conditions through a monetary regime which is more or less designed to guarantee mean reversion to the trend of the price level. Addressing the monetary policymakers' choice between rules and discretion (another issue associated with monetarism), we recognize that *even within a rule-bound* framework, *it is possible to construct regimes that allow for some discretion.* One such example is provided in Leijonhufvud (2001), which however, in the author's claim, draws its inspiration from the—by now rather old—monetary history, yet expressing little doubt that better, more suited, proposals may be designed currently.

However, crucial aspects of monetary policy remain on which views still diverge. The most relevant of those open issues, with the hindsight of the GFC, seems to be the so-called "lean versus clean" debate. The latter refers to the issue of whether an asymmetric monetary policy reaction to asset price bubbles, opposed to busts, is warranted. Furthermore, the undisputed broad consensus remains on the benefits

---

[2]The Phillips curve is the economic theory—formally proposed in Phillips (1958)—stating that inflation and unemployment have a stable and inverse relationship. According to this principle, economic growth triggers inflation, which in turn should lead to more jobs and less unemployment. The change in unemployment within an economy has a predictable effect on price inflation. A vertical Phillips curve assumes full employment and the unemployment level to be fixed at its "natural" rate; it shows that there is no trade-off between unemployment and inflation in the long run. As highlighted in Laidler (2000, pp. 522–523) referencing Phillips' own LSE inaugural lecture in 1961, what interested Phillips himself about his curve had not been what the curve revealed about a trade-off between inflation and unemployment, nor did he ever presented the curve himself as a policy menu, but his intended focus had rather been on what the curve revealed about the unemployment rate that would rule when the economy reaches and maintains an inflation-free steady state.

[3]Even though monetary policy may reduce interest rates in the short run, it may have the opposite effect over a longer time horizon. A monetary expansion, for example, by adding more liquidity to the economy, causes a reduction of both the nominal and the real (inflation-adjusted) interest rate, a result often termed as the "liquidity effect." However, income also increases when the money supply expands, thus boosting the demand for credit and imposing an increase in interest rates, a result often termed the "income effect." Furthermore, the monetary expansion stirs the anticipation of (higher) inflation, forcing lenders to raise rates, a result often termed "the Fisher effect." See, for example, Hummel (2017).

[4]Leijonhufvud (2001) remarks that "Such a deviation of employment from the natural rate may persist for quite some time without producing a deflation (or inflation) enough to trigger corrective monetary action by a central bank cueing on a constant low inflation target. Consider, for example, the course of the price-level in Japan over several years before as well as after the collapse of the stock market and real estate booms" (p. 25).

yielded by price stability. However, the overall approach to potential risks to price stability differed considerably across major central banks. For example, Greenspan advocated the doctrine dubbed the "risk management approach to monetary policy," according to which policymakers should "consider not only the most likely future path of the economy, but also the distribution of possible outcomes about that path" (Greenspan, 2004, p. 37). According to this doctrine, policymakers need then to judge the costs and benefits of various possible outcomes under alternative policy choices to avoid significantly adverse outcomes. As Greenspan highlights, in 2003, it had been such considerations that led the US Federal Reserve to adopt an easier monetary policy stance to contain deflation risk triggered by the bursting of the "dotcom bubble," even though baseline forecasts did not foresee such an outcome. In fact, Greenspan (2004) stresses that the "risk management paradigm," even though it is seemingly discretionary and judgmental, is still better suited for policymaking than simple rules, since the latter are difficult to take into account significant and shifting uncertainties about the economic environment. In a similar manner, the European Central Bank (ECB) maintained its second "monetary" pillar of its monetary policy design and conduct to identify medium-term risks to price stability. Jürgen Stark, while an ECB Executive Board Member, argued (see, for example, Stark, 2011, p. 184) that the monetary analysis in the ECB[5] did not aim to detect financial imbalances per se but to highlight the extent of a long-term relationship between money and price developments. Nevertheless, the link between money and asset prices[6] provided complementary information about the role of money in the economy. As a result, in his view, the ECB monetary policy strategy constituted a suitable and a robust framework for an occasional but appropriate "leaning-against-the-wind" approach.[7]

Policymakers in major advanced economies faced an unprecedented policy challenge during the GFC and the subsequent sluggish recovery. All major central banks engaged in bold and innovative monetary policy actions in the aftermath of the GFC and the euro area sovereign debt crisis that followed, confirming their openness to innovation and willingness to break from established practices when necessary to

[5]ECB's "monetary analysis" encompasses a broad set of tools and instruments that are being continuously refined and expanded. The developments of the monetary aggregates including their components and counterparts, and even as of 2011, in particular the broad aggregate M3, had been playing a central role. At the time of publication (2022), the ECB publishes its stance on its "monetary and financial analysis" explaining how monetary policy in the euro area is transmitted to the member states' economies through credit, bank lending, risk-taking, and asset pricing channels, assigning an important role to monetary and financial indicators (https://www.ecb.europa.eu/mopo/strategy/monan/html/index.en.html). In August 2012, the ECB amended its statistical measurement of broad money to adjust for repurchase agreement (repo) transactions with central counterparties (see ECB, 2012, Box 3).

[6]The results in Greiber and Setzer (2007), as well as Adalid and Detken (2007), demonstrate a significant positive relationship between broad money and future house price growth.

[7]In fact, the absence of the ECB's monetary pillar to estimate the monetary policy reaction function of the ECB and to run the counterfactual exercise would suggest (see, for example, Fahr et al., 2011) that the euro area economy as a whole would have been more volatile in this case.

fulfill their mandates. Yet, still all major central banks continue to implement monetary policy frameworks which emphasize price stability, as well as the awareness that there is unlikely a trade-off between the level of real economic activity and the rate of inflation. In parallel, academic monetary policy research never ceases to evaluate policy developments in view of current economic and financial challenges. The experience of high and untamed inflation in most advanced economies during the 1970s triggered an extensive amount of research at the time and the decades that followed, focusing on the monetary policymakers' efforts to contain upward price pressures. The adverse experience of Japan with the protracted period of deflation over the past three decades (see, for example, IMES, 2001), in addition to the fact that all major central banks in the years that followed the GFC had inevitably been forced to operate close to interest rates near their effective lower bound, stimulated the academic research focus to the challenges of designing, communication, and conducting monetary policy under a type of a "liquidity trap" environment. In particular, policy frameworks that apply a higher weight on the evolution of the price level over the medium term seem to cater (at least in theory) more robust explanations on how to increase the effectiveness of the transmission of monetary policy in view of the recent crisis episodes including and after the GFC. Such monetary policy frameworks thus attract more academic research attention while also retaining their focus on the well-established paradigm of sound monetary policy based on the attainment and preservation of price stability. Furthermore, in view of the lessons learned from the GFC, the so-called "leaning-against-the-wind" monetary policy has gained wide acceptance, and the quest for the appropriate level and operational framework of such policy is reflected in pertinent research among academics and central banking practitioners, as well as in the actual conduct of monetary policy.

2.2 Has the Global Financial Crisis Changed Our Thinking?

Many commentators believe the 2007–2009 GFC not only flattened the economy but also flattened monetary policy, necessitating a complete rethink. We can now evaluate whether our earlier analysis needs to be modified in light of the events that unfolded during the GFC, armed with an understanding of where monetary policy science stood prior to the crisis. According to a timely account by Mishkin (2011a, pp. 82–91), a reading of the crisis leads one to the conclusion that there are *five lessons* that should alter our way of thinking about the *science of monetary policy* and *monetary policy strategy*:

1. *Developments in the financial sector have a far greater impact on economic activity than we previously realized*: Despite the general recognition by central bankers that financial frictions can have a significant impact on business cycles, the 2007–2009 financial crisis revealed that advanced economies could suffer far

worse adverse effects from financial disruptions than originally anticipated. As the advent of the GFC in August 2007, central bank actions to contain it seemed to be effective. Despite being concerned about the disruption to financial markets, many central bank officials hoped that the worst had passed and that the financial system was beginning to recover (see Mishkin, 2011a, 2011b). As the substantial financial fragility became evident in the subprime mortgage sector, which were (legitimately) perceived as a small part of the overall capital market, it seemed manageable at the time to policymakers to contain the adverse financial shock. As, for example, Wessel (2009) highlights, during the summer of 2008 (almost a year after the initial credit crunch in August 2007), monetary policymakers were focusing on the elevated inflation at the time, evidenced in the US Federal Reserve's discussions on reversing the easing monetary policy phase accordingly to contain inflation. Yet as Mishkin (2011a, 2011b) remarks, successive financial shocks emerged that "sent the financial system and the economy over the cliff," escalating the financial crisis into a global crisis. On September 15, 2008, Lehman Brothers declared bankruptcy; on September 16, 2008, AIG collapsed; on the same day, the Reserve Primary Fund faced a run as clients sought to withdraw their funds (due to concerns on its holdings of Lehman-issued commercial paper and the effect on its share price after Lehman bankruptcy); the Fund declared these assets as worthless (also announcing a share price of 0.97USD), leading other money market funds to experience similar runs; while by the end of the month, the Fund announced liquidation; and over the following few weeks, the US Treasury struggled to get approval by the US Congress on the Troubled Asset Relief Program (TARP) plan.[8]

The global financial crisis of 2007–2009 thus demonstrated that financial frictions should be front and center in macroeconomic analysis: they could not be ignored in the macroeconometric models that central banks used for forecasting and policy analysis, as were the case before the GFC.

Therefore, a resurgence of interest emerged in the interaction of macroeconomics with finance. Both academic researchers and central banking practitioners had by then actively been trying to effectively incorporate financial frictions into their general equilibrium models. A novel body of literature thus emerged based on the exploration of how financial frictions would modify the prescriptions provided by the science of monetary policy (for seminal accounts, see, for example, Gertler & Karadi, 2011; Cúrdia & Woodford, 2010).

[8]US economic activity faced a sharp downturn due to the eventual global crisis, namely, it experienced a decline in real GDP by an annual rate of −1.3% in the fourth quarter of 2008, −5.4% in the first quarter of 2009, and −6.4% in the second quarter of 2009. Similar sharp economic downturns were experienced in the rest of the world as well with an overall drop in real GDP by −6.4% in the fourth quarter of 2008 and by −7.3% in the first quarter of 2009. In the United States and several other advanced economies, unemployment rate raised to more than 10%, and it persisted in such increased levels even after the apparent recovery of the world economy. The worldwide recession that resulted from the financial crisis was evidently proven to be the most severe economic contraction since the worldwide depression of the 1930s (Mishkin, 2011a, p. 83).

2. *The macroeconomy is highly nonlinear*: Economic downturns typically result in increased uncertainty about asset values, so such episodes may result in an adverse feedback loop where financial disruptions lead to a decline in consumer and investment spending, leading to a contraction in economic activity. As a result, this contraction increases uncertainty about assets' values, worsening the financial disruption. This, in turn, causes economic activity to contract further.

   An important flaw lies in the theory of optimal monetary policy that was in general use prior to the crisis. This flaw is reflected in the role of nonlinearities in the macroeconomy in the presence of a financial disruption, namely, the theory of optimal monetary policy antecedent to the GFC was based on the assumption that linear dynamic equations can describe the macroeconomy. As demonstrated by the 2007–2009 GFC, the linear quadratic framework is a reasonable approximation of how optimal monetary policy operates under reasonably normal circumstances. However, it cannot be used to analyze monetary policy in the presence of financial disruptions when the economy is hit by adverse financial shocks.[9] Additionally, the extensive use of a quadratic objective function by assumption eliminates ambiguity aversion and the strong preference (demonstrated by most individuals) for minimizing the incidence of worst-case scenarios, like the one experienced during the GFC initially and the crises that succeeded it. Therefore, as the central bank's ultimate goal is to maximize public welfare, its monetary policy must reflect the public's preferences, especially in terms of avoiding particularly adverse economic outcomes.
3. *The zero lower bound (ZLB) is more problematic than pre-GFC realized*: Antecedent to the emergence of the GFC, central bankers broadly accepted that the nominal interest rates ZLB would require monetary policy to use unconventional measures in the event of a contractionary shock triggering a fall of nominal interest rates toward zero. Even since the late 1990s, academic research applied a certain focus to the challenge of conducting monetary policy at the ZLB, due to the adverse unfortunate experience in the Japanese economy struggling to counter the consequences of the collapse in its property price bubble that begun to rapidly unwind during the start of the decade in 1991 (for an extensive thorough early account, see IMES, 2001). As demonstrated, for example, in Krugman (1998), when risk-free short-term nominal interest rates are at or near zero, high-powered money increases impose a minor effect on broad monetary aggregates since banks in this case are indifferent between holding base money or other assets.[10] To escape such a "liquidity trap," the economy must face higher inflation through sufficiently negative real interest rates, to induce the vital investment growth

[9] Research antecedent to the GFC that recognized the existence of nonlinearities with respect to the dynamic behavior of the economy, at least in response to some shocks, includes, for example, Hamilton (1989), Kim and Nelson (1999), and Kim et al. (2005).

[10] As suggested by Milton Friedman (1969) in his famous illustration, a central bank could bypass financial intermediaries to avoid a liquidity trap and stimulate consumption just by "dropping money from a helicopter" (for a brief overview, see, for example, Ball et al., 2016, Chap. 3.3; and for a further discussion, see current Chap. 8.3).

needed to close the negative output gap. Therefore, due to the central bank's addressing the "liquidity trap," a credibility (time consistency) problem arises; the central bank needs to convince economic agents that it will in fact allow prices to rise sufficiently in the future, namely, it needs to "credibly promise to be irresponsible" (Krugman, 1998, p. 161) in order to bootstrap the economy out of the liquidity trap.

The ZLB problem had proven to be more challenging than originally contemplated as the effectiveness of nonconventional monetary policy employed during the GFC and the subsequent crises varied. Mishkin (2011a, p. 85) seems to strongly disagree with this view that is based on the claim of the ineffectiveness of unconventional monetary policy measures. He contends that the shock to the financial system resulting from the GFC was in several ways more complicated than the shock that produced the Great Depression of the 1930s, and yet the economic contraction turned out to be far less severe. He accepts that one key factor, which appreciably lessened the severity of the recent GFC economic downturn, had been that monetary policy in the United States and in coordination with other major advanced economies' central banks (maybe with the exemption of the ECB) was very aggressive and that it was indeed effective. Taylor (2009) presents a counterargument in that the United States erroneously attributed the credit market seize-up during August 2007 and further culminating to September 2008 to a lack of liquidity. He assigns blame to counterparty risk and even further to US government policymakers' erroneous assumptions and lack of a predictable strategy. *The unconventional monetary policy measures that have been exploited may be clustered in the following four types* (Mishkin, 2011a, p. 85): (1) liquidity provision in which central banks expanded lending to both banks and other financial institutions; (2) asset purchases of both government securities and private assets to lower borrowing costs for households; (3) quantitative easing, in which central banks greatly expanded their balance sheets; and (4) management of expectations, which involved central banks committing to keeping their policy rate at very low levels for a long period of time.[11]

[11]Early accounts on liquidity provision view such programs as lacking effectiveness; for example, Taylor and Williams (2009) report that lending from the "Term Auction Facility" had been ineffective to ease credit markets, while, for example, McAndrews et al. (2008), Wu (2008), Christensen et al. (2009), and Sarkar and Shrader (2010) base their argument on the broader premise that financial markets would react to the announcements of programs rather than the actual lending, contending that the dependent variable in the analysis should use changes in spreads and not levels, thus reporting the conclusion that the "Term Auction Facility" and other credit facilities actually helped lower interest rates. Furthermore, research on the effectiveness of US dollar swap facilities report that they actually improved the performance of the dollar swap markets (see, for example, Baba & Packer, 2009; McAndrews, 2009; Goldberg et al., 2010). Aït-Sahalia et al. (2010) use an event study methodology to eventually report that liquidity provision by US policy, as well as in Japan and the United Kingdom, actually helped lower interbank risk premia. Therefore, even from such early research accounts, liquidity provision is deemed effective to stabilize financial markets during the GFC.

Skepticism on the ability of quantitative easing to impose, by itself, any effect on stimulating the economy has been stressed at the advent of the exploitation of such policies during the GFC. Cúrdia and Woodford (2010) and Mishkin (2011a), for example, remained skeptical and wondered whether and why an expansion of the monetary base should trigger higher aggregate demand while unable to lower interest rates further or stimulate bank lending. Additionally, as Kuttner (2004) reports, ample evidence catered from the Japanese experience with deflation does not strongly support the theory that a pure central bank balance sheet expansion may be effective in stimulating aggregate demand.

It is well established that managing expectations stimulates spending when the policy rate hits the zero lower bound. The argument is based (as, for example, in Eggertsson & Woodford, 2003, 2004; Woodford, 2003) on the fact that a central bank's credibly committing to reduce short-term interest rates for an extended period of time lowers long-term interest rates and raises inflation expectations, thereby lowering real interest rates. In fact, Eggertsson and Woodford (2003) expand the analysis in Krugman (1998) and demonstrate that open market operations are effective when nominal interest rates have hit the zero lower bound, only on the occasion that they also alter expectations regarding future interest rate policy or the path of total nominal government liabilities (termed the "irrelevance proposition"). Furthermore, as argued in Eggertsson (2006), the inability of a central bank to commit to future policy may trigger excessive deflation when the natural rate of interest is temporarily *negative*. Therefore, in a liquidity trap instance may arise the *deflation bias of discretionary policy*; the latter lays in contrast to the inflation bias under a *positive* natural rate of interest as argued in Kydland and Prescott (1977). In this manner, deflation is not attributed to an inept central bank and the choice of bad policy rules but forms a direct consequence of the central bank's policy constraints and inability to commit to the optimal policy when faced with large negative demand shocks.

According to Brunnermeier (2023), the intellectual framework adopted by central banks after the GFC does not yet appear to have de-anchored inflation expectations. He, nevertheless, further remarks that it would be costly to wait until de-anchoring begins to alter the framework as the warning signals have already emerged in recent data on inflation expectations. Mishkin (2009a, 2011a) argues that during the GFC even measures of conventional monetary policy were effective, emphasizing that this had been the case to a greater extent during the GFC than at normal times.[12] He views the main shortcoming of using

[12]To support the argument, Mishkin (2009a, 2011a) addresses the counterfactual of "what would have happened to the interest rates relevant to spending decisions by households and businesses, if the Federal Reserve had *not* lowered the federal funds rate by over 500 basis points starting in September 2007" (p. 86). He values that *default-free* Treasury securities' interest rates in that occasion would have been higher; however, credit spreads would have also widened by a greater extent during the GFC, as financial fragility would have increased under a weaker economy. In fact, it would have been the increased macroeconomic risk that would increase credit spreads, in addition to default-free interest rates. Households and firms would then face significantly higher interest

conventional monetary policy tools during the GFC in that the contractionary shock from the GFC had been so severe that it exhausted the ability of conventional monetary policy to counteract it. Mishkin (2011a) argues that the fact that both conventional and unconventional monetary policy had been effective does not render the zero lower bound problem less severe. Indeed, *the lesson that* Mishkin (2011a) *takes from the crisis is that it is a more serious problem than central bankers anticipated.* Research antecedent to the GFC (see, for example, Reifschneider & Williams, 2000; Coenen et al., 2004) accepted that a 2% inflation objective, the zero lower bound problem, would be infrequent and short-lived and thus not pose too serious a problem for monetary policymakers.[13] Mishkin (2011a) identifies the flaw with this strand of research in that it used models that were essentially linear, which post-GFC evidence renders obsolete as it had been accepted that the macroeconomy is likely to be *very nonlinear* (see Sect. 2.2 above). Additionally, the fact that contractionary shocks to the economy can be far greater than previously anticipated—as during the GFC—provides further clear evidence that the zero lower bound problem poses a more serious problem than previously thought.[14]

4. *The cost of cleaning up after financial crises is very high*: The GFC suggests that as a result of the worldwide recession, there are likely to be three additional costs besides the obvious cost of a huge loss of aggregate output, which all lead to an increase of the total cost far higher. These may be clustered, following Mishkin (2011a), into the following: (1) very slow growth tends to be a typical sequel of financial crises, (2) a sharp deterioration in governments' budgets tends to occur, and (3) the exit strategy for central banks from the unconventional monetary policy implemented to address the "cleaning up" after the crisis may be intricate to implement and furthermore hinder the central bank's ability to successfully manage the economy in the future. Economies that fall into deep recessions tend to typically experience V-shaped recoveries (Reinhart & Reinhart, 2010), namely, very strong recoveries, which nevertheless may not be the characteristic pattern following post-financial crisis recessions due to the long duration of the pertinent deleveraging process, which results in strong headwinds for the

---

rates, causing household and firm spending to decline even more precipitously, leading to a far deeper recession.

[13]In fact, Mishkin (2011a) highlights that the zero lower bound problem appears to be far more prevalent than earlier research suggested and certainly not short-lived at all. Evidence is provided by US monetary policy conduct, in that the US Federal Reserve was forced to resort to unconventional monetary policy twice during the first decade of the twenty-first century, namely, during 2003–2004, making a commitment to keep interest rates low for a considerable period, and during the 2009–2010 period, addressing the GFC shock.

[14]The presence of nonlinearities and significant tail risks can lead to a situation where the costs of the zero lower bound constraint become very significant if there are big contractionary shocks. In such cases, conventional policy measures may not be effective enough to counteract the shocks and may require the central bank to make large interventions in credit markets and expand its balance sheet. However, these interventions could come at a very high cost for central banks in the future.

economy.[15] However, the GFC had more intense adverse outcomes that the average crisis episode (for example, addressed in Reinhart & Reinhart, 2010) producing massive cumulative output losses.

To address to GFC central banks (with varying degrees of promptness) proceeded in huge expansions of their balance sheets.[16] A far more serious concern is the expansion of the balance sheet that stems from asset market purchases, as it is not self-liquidating and concerns remain that the resulting expansion of the monetary base will lead to high inflation in the future. Mishkin (2011a) provides a detailed explanation, which, nevertheless, viewed at the time of publication that it "would be of greater concern if the expansion in the monetary base was closely linked to inflation, but this is unlikely to be the case in the current environment" (p. 88).

However, from the initial stages of the unconventional monetary policy implementation, of greater concern had been the potential drawbacks of central bank asset market purchases that such purchases can expose the central bank to interest and credit risks when the assets absorbed are either long-term or private securities, which can be subject to price fluctuations. If the central bank experiences losses on these securities, it could erode its capital and subject it to parliamentary criticism, which could weaken its ability to conduct an independent monetary policy. Additionally, the presence of private securities (such as mortgage-backed securities (MBSs)) on the central bank's balance sheet could be seen as encroaching on the realm of fiscal policy and make its political position more precarious, potentially leading to a loss of independence.[17]

In purchasing long-term government securities, the central bank can create the impression that it is accommodative of irresponsible fiscal policy. In the euro area, where the ECB had purchased government securities issued by governments with large fiscal imbalances, this was of particular concern. Furthermore,

[15] Reinhart and Reinhart (2010) examined 15 major financial crises that occurred after World War II, as well as the Great Depression, the 1973 oil shock period, and the Great Recession in the advent of the GFC, and reported that the real GDP growth rates were significantly lower in the decade that followed each of these events. On average, the decline in GDP growth was approximately 1%. Additionally, unemployment rates remained persistently high for 10 years after the crises, with a median increase of five percentage points in advanced economies.

[16] The increase in the size of central bank balance sheets due to liquidity provision can be easily reversed (Mishkin, 2011a) because most liquidity programs offer loans at rates above the market rates at normal times. Hence, these liquidity facilities are self-liquidating because as financial markets return to their usual state, market participants are no longer willing to borrow at above-normal-time-market rates, so the use of these facilities diminishes. Therefore, this source of balance sheet expansion naturally reverses itself as the financial system recovers, and this had been evidenced at the initial stage of the GFC (Wood, 2015).

[17] A particular problem for the Federal Reserve is that its holdings of MBSs on its balance sheet directly involve it in the most politicized financial market in the United States. As discussed in Mishkin (2011a), this could lead to politicians viewing the Federal Reserve as personally responsible for developments in the housing markets, which made it possible to expose it to increased political criticism and pressure on its policy decisions, thereby further weakening its independence.

long-term government asset purchases may unhinge inflation expectations and make it harder for the central bank to control inflation in the future.[18]

5. *Price and output stability do not ensure financial stability*: The common view shared both by academics and by central banking practitioners antecedent to the GFC had been that to achieving price and output stability is enough to also foster financial stability (Bernanke et al., 1999; Bernanke & Gertler, 2001). If monetary policy optimally stabilizes inflation and output, then it may potentially stabilize asset prices, making asset price bubbles less likely. Indeed, during the Great Moderation era, when central banks succeeded in stabilizing inflation and faced the dampened business cycle fluctuations, policymakers were made complacent about the risks from financial disruptions. Evidently, the benign economic environment during the Great Moderation not only failed to protect the economy from financial instability but also have fostered the later by masking the development of financial imbalances. In an economic regime of low volatility of both inflation and output fluctuations, market participants perceived there was less risk in the economic system than was really the case. As a result, at the time, credit risk premia reached significantly low levels, and underwriting standards for loans were considerable loose. Gambacorta (2009) demonstrates that excessive risk-taking may be fuelled by benign economic environments, thus rendering the financial system more fragile. The events and policy outcomes during the GFC demonstrated that monetary policy focusing only on price and output stability may not be enough to produce good economic outcomes.

2.3 Does the Science of Monetary Policy Need to Be Altered?

As in the early fervent remarks in Krugman (2009), an article in *The New York Times* titled "How Did Economists Get It So Wrong?" and The Economist (2009, July 16), due to the advent of the GFC, the deep flaws in the modern field of macroeconomics and monetary economics developed over roughly the last 40 years emerged, thus necessitating a thorough reassessment and amendment.[19] However, does this imply that the science of monetary policy as we knew it before the GFC should be abandoned and that policymakers and monetary economists should start all over, as Krugman (2009) seemed to imply? For an answer to this question, following the analysis as in, for example, Mishkin (2011a), we initially evaluate the elements of the science of monetary policy that have been repudiated by the lessons catered by the GFC (which have been presented and discussed in the previous section).

[18]Cochrane (2011b) gives an early discussion on how fiscal events during the Great Recession may have led to a rise in inflation expectations.

[19]For example, Lucas (2009) and Cochrane (2009, 2011a) provided prompt considerate replies to the articles in Krugman (2009) and The Economist (2009, July 16).

2.3.1 Basic Principles of the Science of Monetary Policy

The basic principles of the science of monetary policy and of the theory of optimal monetary policy can be summarized in the following nine premises of the so-called new neoclassical synthesis (as in Goodfriend & King, 1997), clustered as in, for example, Mishkin (2009b): (1) inflation is always and everywhere a monetary phenomenon; (2) price stability has important benefits; (3) expectations play a crucial role in the determination of inflation and in the transmission of monetary policy to the macroeconomy; (4) there is no long-run trade-off between unemployment and inflation; (5) real interest rates need to rise with higher inflation, as in the Taylor principle; (6) monetary policy is subject to the time-inconsistency problem; (7) central bank independence helps improve the efficiency of monetary policy; (8) commitment to a strong nominal anchor is central to producing good monetary policy outcomes; and (9) financial frictions play an important role in business cycles. Respectively, the lessons catered by the events during the GFC to academic researchers and central banking practitioners alike may be summarized in the following premises: (1) the impact imposed by the financial sector on economic activity may be significantly large; thus, (2) rendering the economy highly nonlinear; (3) the interest rate zero lower bound problem can be very serious, which is just one of the reasons why (4) cleaning up after financial crises can have very high costs; and (5) price and output stability do not suffice to ensure financial stability (see, for example, Mishkin, 2011a, pp. 67–91).

An extensive and meticulous examination of the theory and empirical work that supports the nine principles of the science of monetary policy justifies an evaluation of whether any of the lessons from the crisis refute the justification for those principles. Upon an analytical examination of the reasoning behind each of the nine principles, the answer that, for example, Mishkin (2011a) presents is very clear-cut, in that "none of the lessons from the financial crisis in any way undermine or invalidate the nine basic principles of the science of monetary policy developed before the crisis" (emphasis on the original) (p. 90). Indeed, each of the five lessons from the GFC, as analyzed in the previous section, is completely orthogonal to the theoretical and empirical research that supports the principles of the new neoclassical synthesis, emphasizing the great importance of the above conclusion. Rather, most of the elements of the science of monetary policy remain valid today as they had been before the GFC, which has important implications for how we view monetary policy strategy. As a consequence, the apparent lesson from the GFC that developments in the financial sector impose a large impact on economic activity renders the ninth principle concerning financial frictions both valid and even more relevant today than central bankers previously realized.

However, on the contrary, these five lessons from the GFC catered to academic researchers and monetary policymakers alike do also undermine two key elements of the theory of optimal monetary policy as postulated and evidenced antecedent to the GFC. Specifically, as Mishkin (2011a, p. 91) highlights, the lesson that the macroeconomy is inherently *nonlinear* undermines the linear quadratic framework that is a key element of that policy. The lesson that the developments in the financial sector can have a major impact on economic activity undermines the representative agent framework, another key element of the pre-crisis theory of optimal monetary policy. Such post-GFC doubts about both the linear quadratic and the representative agent framework have important implications for the strategy of monetary policy. The latter monetary policy strategy, as emerged from the initial eight principles of the new neoclassical synthesis, has been referred to as *flexible inflation targeting*. Mishkin (2011a, p. 91) argues that since none of the principles has been invalidated by the events of the GFC, the flexible inflation targeting approach to monetary policy strategy remains still equally valid. The arguments supporting central bank adherence to the principles of the new neoclassical synthesis are still as strong as they were before the GFC.

Therefore, even after the events that followed the emergence of the GFC, a strong support still holds for central banks pursuing flexible inflation targeting, in that they retain a strong, credible commitment to stabilizing inflation in the long run by announcing an explicit, numerical inflation objective yet also having the flexibility to pursue policies aimed at stabilizing output around its natural rate level in the short run. Even though the adherence to the flexible inflation targeting framework is not weakened by the lessons from the GFC, the lessons early on after the emergence of the GFC do suggest that the details of how flexible inflation targeting is conducted, and of what is meant by flexibility, need to be reconsidered.[20]

2.4 The Lean Versus Clean Debate After the Global Financial Crisis

The current section highlights the shift in the monetary policy literature in the aftermath of the GFC, indicating that the so-called "lean versus clean" debate has tilted in favor of the so-called "lean-against-the-wind" view. In particular, the pre-GFC "conventional" view eventually incorporated elements of the opposing view by addressing financial frictions in the models of the economy used as "workhorse" models for the design of monetary policy. In most models of the New Keynesian dynamic stochastic general equilibrium (DSGE) paradigm, which were widely used by central banks in most advanced economies, pre-GFC failed to include elements pertaining to frictions in the operation of the financial sector (from either the borrower's or the lender's side) and its interaction with the real sector (through, for example, alternative channels of the monetary transmission mechanism). Additionally, even the "lean-against-the-wind" view has post-GFC been advocating the merits of a coordination between monetary and macroprudential policies; the latter designed to promote and ensure financial stability. The underlying reason behind such coordination was the presence of complex interactions between

[20] See Mishkin (2011a), especially pp. 92–96, for a concise analysis and extensive bibliography.

monetary and macroprudential policies (for a concise account, see, for example, Dunstan, 2014; Beyer et al., 2017) and the potential for material spillover effects between them.

The debate labeled as the "lean versus clean" debate primarily focused on the justification of a potential reaction of monetary policy to asset price bubbles. It is elementary initially to distinguish between the prevailing two types of asset price bubbles, in order to evaluate the policy options catered by the debate. As, for example, Mishkin (2010, 2011a, 2014) identifies, not all asset price bubbles are alike, and financial history, let alone the events during the GFC, indicate that one distinctive type of bubble may be referred to as a *credit-driven bubble* and may trigger highly adverse economy-wide effects. A further second type of bubble may also be distinguished, which is considered far less dangerous, and may be labeled as an *irrational exuberance bubble*. The latter type of bubble is driven solely by overly optimistic expectations and poses much less risk to the financial system than a credit-driven bubble.[21]

The GFC has provided the lesson that the bursting of credit-driven bubbles may not only be extremely costly but also very hard to "clean up" after the bursting (as the "conventional" view of the "lean versus clean" debate advocated—see, for example, Schwartz, 1995; Greenspan, 2002; Bordo et al., 2002). Moreover, such bubbles may build up even under (extensive) periods of price and output stability. Indeed, the experience antecedent to the GFC evidenced that a period of price and output stability may actually encourage credit-driven bubbles, as it leads market participants to underestimate the amount of risk in the economy. The case for "leaning against" potential bubbles (for early accounts, see, for example, Kent & Lowe, 1997; Cecchetti et al., 2000, 2003; Bordo & Jeanne, 2002a, 2002b; Borio & Lowe, 2002, 2003; Farooq-Akram et al., 2007; Barrett et al., 2008) rather than "cleaning up" after them has therefore become much stronger.[22]

However, as White (2009) indicates, the distinction between the two types of bubbles, where one of the two (the credit-driven bubble) is much more costly than the other, suggests that the lean versus clean debate may have been misguided. Instead of leaning against potential asset price bubbles (of either type), a much stronger case stands for only leaning against credit-driven bubbles, and not irrational exuberance bubbles. White (2009) and Mishkin (2010, 2011a) argue that it is much easier to identify credit-driven bubbles, rather than it is to distinguish whether asset prices are deviating from their fundamental values; they, thus, contend that the argument holding that it is hard to identify asset price bubbles is not a valid argument against leaning against credit bubbles.

[21] The technology stock bubble during the late 1990s had not fuelled by a feedback loop between bank lending and rising equity values. Therefore, when that bubble burst, the economy did not face a marked deterioration in bank balance sheets, avoiding a significantly severe impact on the economy (see, for example, Mishkin, 2011a, p. 97). The resulting recession had also been rather mild.

[22] See Kokores (2022) Chap. 6 for an extensive discussion of the debate.

2.4.1 The Postcrisis Shift in the Literature

With the advent of the GFC, it became imperative to reevaluate the macroeconomic policy framework that has proven successful during the Great Moderation years in light of the unexpectedly acute adverse consequences of the GFC and the inability of monetary authorities to contain it in a timely manner in most affected economies. Explicit financial stability considerations have been incorporated in the conduct of monetary policy in major advanced economies, and central bank communication has been modified accordingly. The merits of macroprudential policies have also been widely accepted among both academic economists and central banking practitioners, as such policies incorporate a system-wide approach to ensuring financial stability (see, for example, Galati & Moessner, 2011, for a review). The dire necessity of their implementation has also been highlighted and accepted, in addition to microprudential policies passed over in most developed economies before the GFC so as to ensure a financial institution-based approach to safeguarding the stability of the financial system. At the advent of the GFC, a de facto realization emerged that to ensure the soundness and safety of individual financial institutions may not suffice to guarantee the system-wide financial stability. The objectives of macroprudential policies include the reduction of potentially adverse asset and credit-boom events and, additionally, the increase in the scope for banks to maintain lending provision following a period of financial stress. Early contributions antecedent to the GFC constitute, for example, Crockett (2000), Borio (2003), and Knight (2006), and it is worth noting that in New Zealand, for example, prudential policies have had a strong system-wide focus even before the GFC (see, for example, Dunstan, 2014; Kokores, 2015).

In the aftermath of the GFC, a research shift emerged in the literature addressing the so-called "lean versus clean" debate, and it has been in favor of the "lean-against-the-wind" view. In particular, the pre-GFC conventional view has eventually incorporated elements of the opposing view in that it addressed thereon several aspects of financial frictions in the models of the economy used for the design and conduct of monetary policy. Furthermore, the "lean-against-the-wind" view has also been altered accordingly, advocating the merits of further coordination between monetary and macroprudential policies due to, apparently, the presence of complex interactions between the implementation of each policy and an inherent potential for material spillover effects between them.

As monetary policy since the Great Moderation years, in essence, involved the conduct of "interest rate policy," we may distinguish the inherent interdependence between the monetary policymaker's decision-making process and the corresponding financial sector participants' strategic choices.

Thus, it may not suffice simply to incorporate financial frictions in the models of the economy that central banks use when designing the operational framework of "lean-against-the-wind" monetary policy. The experience catered to central banking practice since the GFC warrants a thorough and/or thoughtful improvement of the models describing the monetary transmission mechanism and how these may alter during the events of crisis or bubble formation. However, the latter still remain a challenge for future research.

References

Adalid, R., & Detken, C. (2007). Liquidity shocks and asset price boom-bust cycles. *ECB Working Paper* No 732, European Central Bank, Frankfurt Am Main, Germany.

Aït-Sahalia, Y., Adnritzky, J., Jobst, A., Nowak, S., & Tamirisa, N. (2010). Market response to policy initiatives during the global financial crisis. *NBER working paper*, no 15809, National Bureau of Economic Research, Cambridge MA, USA, March.

Baba, N., & Packer, F. (2009). From turmoil to crisis: Dislocations in the FX swap market before and after the failure of Lehman brothers. *Journal of International Money and Finance, 28*(8), 1350–1374.

Ball, L., Gagnon, J., Honohan, P., & Krogstrup, S. (2016). *What Else can central banks do?* Geneva reports on the world economy 18, International Centre for Monetary and Banking Studies, Geneva Switzerland & CEPR-Centre for Economic Policy Research, London, UK.

Barrett, C.R., Kokores, I.T., & Sen, S. (2008). Bubbles, instability and monetary policy games. Proceedings of the public choice society annual meeting 2008, San Antonio, Texas, USA.

Bernanke, B. S., & Blinder, A. (1988). Credit, money, and aggregate demand. *American Economic Review, 78*, 435–439.

Bernanke, B. S., & Gertler, M. (1995). Inside the black box: The credit channel of monetary policy transmission. *Journal of Economic Perspectives, 9*(4), 27–48.

Bernanke, B. S., & Gertler, M. (2001). Should central banks respond to movements in asset prices? *American Economic Review: Papers and Proceedings, 91*(2), 253–257.

Bernanke, B. S., Gertler, M., & Gilchrist, S. (1999). The financial accelerator in a quantitative business cycle framework. In J. B. Taylor & M. Woodford (Eds.), *Handbook of macroeconomics* (Vol. 1, part 3, pp. 1341–1393). North-Holland.

Beyer, A., Nicoletti, G., Papadopoulou, N., Papsdorf, P., Runstler, G., Schwarz, C., Sousa, J., & Vergote, O. (2017). The transmission channels of monetary, macro-and microprudential policies and their interrelations. ECB *occasional paper series* no 191, May, European Central Bank, Frankfurt Am Main, Germany.

Bordo, M. D., & Jeanne, O. (2002a). Boom-busts in asset prices, economic stability, and monetary policy. *NBER Working Paper* 8966, National Bureau of Economic Research, Cambridge, MA, USA.

Bordo, M. D., & Jeanne, O. (2002b). Monetary policy and asset prices: Does benign neglect make sense? *International Finance, 5*(2), 139–164.

Bordo, M. D., Dueker, M. J., & Wheelock, D. C. (2002). Aggregate price shocks and financial stability: A historical analysis. *Economic Inquiry, 40*(4), 521–538.

Borio, C. (2003). Towards a macroprudential framework for financial supervision and regulation. *CESifo Economic Studies, 49*(2), 181–216.

Borio, C., & Lowe, P. (2002). Asset prices, financial and monetary stability: Exploring the nexus. *BIS Working Papers* 114, Bank for International Settlements, Basel, Switzerland.

Borio, C., & Lowe, P. (2003). Imbalances or 'Bubbles'? Implications for monetary and financial stability. In W. C. Hunter, G. Kaufman, & Pomerleano (Eds.), *Asset price bubbles: The implications for monetary, regulatory, and international policies* (pp. 247–270). MIT Press.

Brunnermeier, M. K. (2023). Rethinking monetary policy in a changing world. *Finance & Development 'New Directions for Monetary Policy'*, 60(1), International Monetary Fund, March, pp 6–9.

Cecchetti, S. G., Genberg, H., & Wadhwani, S. (2003). Asset prices in a flexible inflation targeting framework. In W. C. Hunter, G. Kaufman, & M. Pomerleano (Eds.), *Asset price bubbles: Implications for monetary, regulatory, and international policies* (pp. 427–444). MIT Press.
Cecchetti, S. G., Genberg, H., Lipsky, J., & Wadhwani, S. (2000). *Asset prices and central Bank policy*. Geneva reports on the world economy, no. 2, International Centre for Monetary and Banking Studies, Geneva, Switzerland, and Centre for Economic Policy Research, London, UK.
Christensen, J. H. E., Lopez, J. A., & Rudebusch, G. D. (2009). Do Central Bank liquidity facilities affect interbank lending rates? *Federal Reserve Bank of San Francisco Working Paper*, no 2009–13, June.
Cochrane, J. H. (2009). How did Paul Krugman get it so wrong?. University of Chicago *manuscript*, 10 September, available at: https://www.johnhcochrane.com/news-op-eds-all/why-did-paul-krugman-get-it-so-wrong
Cochrane, J. H. (2011a). How did Paul Krugman get it so wrong?, *Economic Affairs*, Institute of Economic Affairs. Oxford: Blackwell.
Cochrane, J. H. (2011b). Understanding policy in the great recession: Some unpleasant fiscal arithmetic. *European Economic Review, 55*(1), 2–30.
Coenen, G., Orphanides, A., & Wieland, V. (2004). Price stability and monetary policy effectiveness when nominal interest rates are bounded at zero. *Advances in Macroeconomics, 4*(1), 1–25.
Crockett, A. (2000). Marrying the micro- and macro-Prudential dimensions of financial stability. *Remarks* before the eleventh international conference of banking supervisors, Basel, Switzerland, September 20–21.
Cúrdia, V., & Woodford, M. (2010). Credit spreads and monetary policy. *Journal of Money, Credit and Banking, 42*(s1), 3–35.
Dunstan, A. (2014). The interaction between monetary and macro-prudential policy. Reserve Bank of New Zealand Bulletin, 77(2), Reserve Bank of New Zealand, .
ECB—European Central Bank. (2012). Box 3 'The adjustment of monetary statistics for repurchase agreement transactions with central counterparties'. *ECB Monthly Bulletin*, (pp. 28–31) September, ECB—European Central Bank, Frankfurt Am Main, Germany.
The Economist. (2009). The other-worldly philosophers. 16 July.
Eggertsson, G. B. (2006). The deflation bias and committing to being irresponsible. *Journal of Money, Credit and Banking, 38*(2), 283–321.
Eggertsson, G. B., & Woodford, M. (2003). The zero bound on interest rates and optimal monetary policy. *Brookings Papers on Economic Activity, 2003*(1), 139–211.
Eggertsson, G. B., & Woodford, M. (2004). Policy options in a liquidity trap. *American Economic Review, 94*(2), 76–79.
Ehrmann, M., Gambacorta, L., Martínez-Pagés, J., Sevestre, P., & Worms, A. (2001). Financial systems and the role of banks in monetary policy transmission in the euro area. *ECB Working Paper* No. 105, European Central Bank, Frankfurt Am Main, Germany.
Fahr, S., Motto, R., Rostagno, M., & Smets, F. (2011). Lessons for monatary policy: Strategies from the recent past. In M. Jarociṅki, F. Smets, & C. Thimann (Eds.), *Approaches to monetary policy revisited – lessons from the crisis, sixth ECB central banking conference proceedings* (pp. 26–66).
Farooq-Akram, Q., Bårdsen, G., & Lindquist, K.-G. (2007). Pursuing financial stability under an inflation-targeting regime. *Annals of Finance, 3*(Special Issue), 131–153.
Friedman, M. (1969). *The optimal quantity of money and other essays*. Aldine.
Galati, G., & Moessner, R. (2011). Macroprudential policy: A literature review. *BIS Working Paper* 337, Basel, Switzerland: Bank for International Settlements.
Gambacorta, L. (2009). Monetary policy and the risk-taking channel. *BIS Quarterly Review*, 43–53.
Gertler, M., & Karadi, P. (2011). A model of unconventional monetary policy. *Journal of Monetary Economics, 58*(1), 17–34.
Goldberg, L., Kennedy, C., & Miu, J. (2010). Central Bank Dollar swap lines and overseas Dollar funding costs. *National Bureau of economic research working paper*, no 15763, February.

Goodfriend, M., & King, R. G. (1997). The new neoclassical synthesis and the role of monetary policy. In B. S. Bernanke & J. J. Rotemberg (Eds.), *NBER macroeconomics annual* (pp. 231–282). MIT Press.
Greenspan, A. (2002). Opening remarks. In Federal Reserve Bank of Kansas City (Ed.), *Rethinking stabilization policy* (pp. 1–10). Kansas City Fed.
Greenspan, A. (2004). Risk and uncertainty in monetary policy. *American Economic Review, 94*(2), 33–40.
Greiber, C., & Setzer, R. (2007). Money and housing: Evidence for the euro area and the US, Deutsche Bundesbank discussion paper, no 12/2007, Deutsche Bundesbank.
Hamilton, J. D. (1989). A new approach to the economic analysis of nonstationary time series and the business cycle. *Econometrica, 57*, 357–384.
Hubbard, R. G. (1995). Is there a 'Credit Channel' for monetary policy? *Federal Reserve Bank of St. Louis Review, 77*, 63–74.
Hummel, J. R. (2017). Central Bank control over interest rates: The myth and the reality. *Mercatus working paper*, Arlington, VA: Mercatus Center at George Mason University.
IMES. (2001). *The role of monetary policy under low inflation: Deflationary shocks and policy responses*. Bank of Japan Monetary and Economic Studies (special edition), Institute of Monetary and Economic Studies—IMES, vol 19, no S-1, February.
Kashyap, A. K., & Stein, J. C. (1995). The impact of monetary policy on bank balance sheets. *Carnegie Rochester Conference Series on Public Policy, 42*, 151–195.
Kent, C., & Lowe, P. (1997). Asset-price bubbles and monetary policy. Reserve Bank of Australia, Research Discussion Paper 97–09.
Kim, C.-J., & Nelson, C. (1999). Has the U.S. economy become more stable? A Bayesian approach based on a Markov-switching model of the business cycle. *Review of Economics and Statistics, 81*, 608–616.
Kim, C.-J., Morley, J., & Piger, J. (2005). Nonlinearity and the permanent effects of recessions. *Journal of Applied Econometrics, 20*(2), 291–309.
Knight, M. D. (2006). Marrying the micro- and macroprudential dimensions of financial stability: Six years on. Speech at the 14th international conference of banking supervisors, Mérida, 4–5 October.
Kokores, I. T. (2015). Lean-against-the-wind monetary policy: The post crisis shift in the literature. *SPOUDAI Journal of Economics and Business, 65*(3–4), 66–99.
Kokores, I. T. (2022). *Monetary policy and financial stability: Challenges before and after the global financial crisis*. Cambridge Scholars Publishing.
Krugman, P. R. (1998). It's Baaack: Japan's slump and the return of the liquidity trap. *Brookings Papers on Economic Activity, 29*(2), 137–206.
Krugman, P. R. (2009). *How did economists get it so wrong?* (p. 2). The New York Times.
Kuttner, K. N. (2004). Comment on 'Price stability and Japanese monetary policy' by Robert Hetzel. *Monetary and economic studies*, no 22, Bank of Japan Institute for Monetary and Economic Studies (pp. 37–46).
Kydland, F. E., & Prescott, E. C. (1977). Rules rather than discretion: The inconsistency of optimal plans. *Journal of Political Economy, 85*(3), 473–492.
Laidler, D. (2000). Phillips in retrospect. In R. Leeson (Ed.), *A.W.H. Phillips, collected works in contemporary perspective* (pp. 515–517). Cambridge University Press.
Leijonhufvud, A. (2001). Monetary theory and central banking. In A. Leijonhufvud (Ed.), *Monetary theory as a basis for monetary policy* (pp. 1–27). Palgrave, in association with the International Economic Association.
Lucas, R. (2009). In defence of the dismal science. *The Economist*.
McAndrews, J. (2009). Segmentation in the U.S. Dollar money markets during the financial crisis. *Paper* presented at the international conference of the Bank of Japan's Institute for Monetary and Economic Studies, Tokyo.
McAndrews, J., Sarkar, A., & Wang, Z. (2008). The effect of the term auction facility on the London inter-Bank offered rate. *Federal Reserve Bank of New York Staff Report, 335*.

Mishkin, F. S. (2009a). Is monetary policy effective during financial crises. *American Economic Review, 99*(2), 573–577.

Mishkin, F. S. (2009b). Will monetary policy become more of a science? In D. Bundesbank (Ed.), *Monetary policy over fifty years: Experiences and lessons* (pp. 81–107). Routledge.

Mishkin, F. S. (2010). Monetary policy strategy: Lessons from the crisis. Paper presented at the ECB central banking conference 'Monetary Policy Revisited: Lessons from the Crisis', Frankfurt, Nov. 18–19.

Mishkin, F. S. (2011a). Monetary policy strategy: Lessons from the crisis. In M. Jarociňki, F. Smets, & C. Thimann (Eds.), *Approaches to monetary policy revisited—lessons from the crisis, sixth ECB central banking conference proceedings* (pp. 67–118).

Mishkin, F. S. (2011b). Over the cliff: From the subprime to the global financial crisis. *Journal of Economic Perspectives, 25*(1), 49–70.

Phillips, A. W. (1958). The relationship between unemployment and the rate of change of money wages in the United Kingdom, 1861-1957. *Economica, 25*(100), 283–299.

Reifschneider, D., & Williams, J. C. (2000). Three lessons for monetary policy in a low-inflation era. *Journal of Money, Credit and Banking, 32*(2), 936–966.

Reinhart, C. M., & Reinhart, V. R. (2010). After the fall. In *Macroeconomic challenges: The decade ahead, proceedings—economic policy symposium—Jackson Hole* (pp. 17–60). Federal Reserve Bank of Kansas City Symposium.

Sarkar, A., & Shrader, J. (2010). Financial amplification mechanisms and the federal reserve's supply of liquidity during the crisis. *Federal Reserve Bank of New York Staff Report, 431.*

Schwartz, A. J. (1995). Why financial stability depends on price stability. *Economic Affairs, 15*(4), 21–25.

Stark, J. (2011). In search of a robust monetary policy framework. In M. In Jarociński, F. Smets, & C. Thimann (Eds.), *Approaches to monetary policy revisited: Lessons from the crisis* (pp. 176–189). European Central Bank.

Stein, J. C. (1998). An adverse selection model of bank asset and liability management with implications for the transmission of monetary policy. *RAND Journal of Economics, 29*(3), 466–486.

Taylor, J. B. (2009). *Getting off track: How government actions and interventions caused, prolonged and worsened the financial crisis.* Hoover Institution Press.

Taylor, J. B., & Williams, J. (2009). A Black swan in the money market. *American Economic Journal: Macroeconomics, 1*(1), 58–83.

Wessel, D. (2009). *In fed we trust: Ben Bernanke's war on the great panic.* Crown Business.

White, W. R. (2009). Should monetary policy 'Lean or Clean'?. *Federal Reserve Bank of Dallas Working Paper*, no. 34, August.

Wicksell, K. (1898). *Interest and prices. A study of the causes regulating the value of money.* Translated in English by R. F. Kahn (1936). London: Macmillan.

Wood, J. H. (2015). *Central banking in a democracy: The Federal Reserve and its alternatives* (Routledge explorations in economic history). Routledge.

Woodford, M. (2003). *Interest and prices: Foundations of a theory of monetary policy.* Princeton University Press.

Wu, T. (2008). On the effectiveness of the Federal Reserve's new liquidity facilities. Federal Reserve Bank of Dallas *Working Paper* No. 0808, May, Federal Reserve Bank of Dallas, USA.

Chapter 3
New Lessons for Macroeconomics and Finance Theory

3.1 Modeling the Monetary Transmission Mechanism

The global financial crisis (GFC) revealed the limitations of modern macroeconomic analysis, specifically its failure to accurately include financial intermediaries as important factors in the monetary transmission mechanism. To improve the *effectiveness* and *efficiency* of monetary policy and to understand how it affects the real economy, namely, to address the monetary transmission mechanism, alternative models that emphasize the role of financial frictions arising from borrower behavior, such as the broad credit channel, are being explored.[1] A range of surveys of the credit channel, as well as other key channels used in traditional macroeconomic analysis, are available.[2]

The impact of the incentives faced by financial intermediaries on credit supply was previously overlooked. However, in the aftermath of the financial crisis, three additional monetary transmission channels have been identified, which were previously neglected. These channels are believed to increase the effectiveness of monetary policy during periods of financial expansion. According to Detken et al. (2010), these channels are related to (a) *risk-taking behavior*, where low interest rates during economic expansions can lead to increased risk-taking, creating vulnerabilities in the financial sector; (b) *the signaling effects of monetary policy*, where small policy rate increases may lead to significant effects on investment behavior through efficient investment and better coordination among investors; and (c) *herd-*

[1] The consensus antecedent to the GFC had been founded in the theoretical propositions of models that consider variants of financial frictions only on the borrowers' side of the credit markets as in, for example, Bernanke and Gertler (1999, 2000, 2001), Filardo (2000), Cecchetti et al. (2000), Batini and Nelson (2000), Gilchrist and Leahy (2002), and Iacoviello (2005).

[2] Surveys of this channel and early empirical results (mainly for the United States) include among others Gertler (1988), Bernanke (1993), Ramey (1993), Gertler and Gilchrist (1993), Kashyap and Stein (1994), Bernanke and Gertler (1995), Cecchetti (1995), Hubbard (1995), Bernanke et al. (1996), and Kashyap and Stein (1997).

I. T. Kokores, *Monetary Policy in Interdependent Economies*, Financial and Monetary Policy Studies 55, https://doi.org/10.1007/978-3-031-41958-4_3

breaking behavior, where raising policy rates can effectively influence entrepreneurs' cost of resources, leading to a reduction in herding behavior and encouraging investors to rely on their own information. These findings were already highlighted in earlier research such as Borio and Zhu (2008) and Adrian and Shin (2010a) for risk-taking and Hoerova et al. (2009) and Loisel et al. (2012) for signaling and herding behavior, respectively.

Jimenez et al. (2007) provide empirical evidence supporting the existence of the risk-taking channel, showing that riskier loans tend to be issued during periods of low interest rates. However, the other two channels—signaling and herd-breaking behavior—have yet to be empirically tested, mainly because few central banks have implemented policies similar to lean-against-the-wind (LATW) in the past. Adrian and Liang (2014) argue that the growing body of research on the risk-taking channel, coupled with the interdependence of monetary and macroprudential channels, calls for greater consideration of the effects on financial conditions and stability when setting monetary policy. Smets (2014) highlights the balance sheet aspect of the monetary transmission mechanism and argues for a focus on both the asset- and liability-side vulnerabilities, accepting that a focus on credit and asset prices ignores the important link with increasing fragility stemming from a shortening and much more complex liability side (Smets, 2014, p. 287). He also suggests that the effectiveness of standard monetary policy instruments in containing financial imbalances and affecting the risk-taking capacity of intermediaries may necessitate an active, preventive role for monetary policy in maintaining financial stability.[3] Several studies have investigated the link between the monetary policy stance and risk-taking behavior of banks and other investors,[4] including Rajan (2005),[5] Adrian and

[3]Detken et al. (2010) build their argument on propositions similar to Assemacher-Weche and Gerlach (2010) and the verity of "Lucas critique"; the latter is a criticism of econometric models used for policy evaluation which do not qualify for optimal decision rules of economic agents varying systematically with policy alterations. The "Lucas critique" addresses the use of past data to estimate relevant statistical relationships to forecast the effects of novel policy implementation, since the estimated regression coefficients are not invariant, but will change along with agents' decision rules in response to the new policy (Ljungqvist, 2008). In this vein, Detken et al. (2010) recognize the inability to defend the empirical evidence seemingly supporting the argument that "LATW monetary policy is too blunt an instrument" (since the negative effects to the real economy are of a greater magnitude than the effects on asset prices). They accept that "only in a policy regime in which the principle of LATW has explicitly been adopted could a test be conducted regarding the effectiveness of the signalling and herd-breaking channels" (p. 322).

[4]See, for example, Ioannidou et al. (2009), Altunbas et al. (2010), Buch et al. (2010), Delis and Brissimis (2010), Delis and Kouretas (2011), Maddaloni and Peydró (2011), Delis et al. (2017), Paligorova and Santos (2012), and Dell'Ariccia et al. (2013).

[5]Rajan (2005) identifies an institutional factor-driven search for yield that results in higher risk-seeking behavior by to maintain yields after rates on safer asset decline.

Shin (2009, 2010b),[6] Borio and Zhu (2008),[7] and Agur and Demertzis (2012).[8] Holmström and Tirole (1998) and De Nicolò et al. (2010) also provide insights on the impact of liquidity injection and monetary policy on financial stability. Smets (2014, p. 282) discusses the evidence for the euro area, suggesting that loose monetary policy during the boom most recent before the advent of the GFC contributed to the buildup of imbalances.

3.2 The Conventional View Revisited

The monetary policy framework reevaluation after the advent of the GFC primarily focused on maintaining price stability, as the events after the GFC culmination justified that at times price stability may not suffice to guarantee financial stability. Additionally, ample evidence gained during the countering of the GFC adverse effects had proven that lack of financial stability can also have large negative feedback effects on price stability.[9]

Conventional skepticism about LATW tended to relate to the costs of asset price boom-bust cycles. In theory, the welfare consequences of bubbles tend to be ambiguous (Farhi and Tirole, 2012), urging, for example, Miao (2014) to remark that with reference to the economic theory of bubbles "many issues still remain ... [as] for example, ... what are the welfare effects of bubbles?" (p. 135). Additionally, theoretical models (for a seminal account, see Tirole, 1985) propose that certain paths of bubble behavior can be consistent with individual optimizing behavior in general equilibrium (for a survey on rational bubbles, see Martin & Ventura, 2018).[10] The counterargument proposed is that most theoretical models rely on their imposing restrictive assumptions that can explain the growth of bubbles and allow for the existence of the latter in general equilibrium. They mainly refrain from encompassing elements of bubble behavior that make them costly in the real world (Santos & Woodford, 1997). However, the global financial crisis proved that boom-

[6]They contend that relatively small short-term interest rate changes can lead to large risk-taking effects from financial intermediaries.

[7]In Borio and Zhu (2008), different valuation effects lead to riskier profiles, as, for example, the use of collateral that gains value from an expansive monetary policy.

[8]As in Dell'Ariccia et al. (2010), cheaper short-term debt due to accommodative monetary policy raises levering incentives of financial intermediaries, in addition to asset risk incentives through interaction with banks' limited liability.

[9]See, for example, Smaghi (2009), Blanchard et al. (2010), Mishkin (2011a, 2011b), Eichengreen et al. (2011), Baldwin and Reichlin eds. (2013), and Smets (2014).

[10]Ikeda (2022) recognizes that "the advancement of the literature on monetary policy in asset price bubbles lags far behind the literature on rational bubbles, ... [and] monetary policy analyses in asset price bubbles in a New Keynesian framework—a standard workhorse of monetary policy analyses for many central banks—remain scarce" (p. 1570).

bust cycles with the potential to trigger systemic crises do exist and, therefore, constitute a significant hazard to global economic growth.

Even though central banking practitioners realized the damaging effects of financial disruptions to the economy even before the crisis,[11] the macroeconomic models used for forecasting and policy analysis (belonging either to the dynamic stochastic general equilibrium paradigm (DSGE), as, for example, Christiano et al. (2005) and Smets and Wouters (2003), or be it more traditional macroeconometric models such as FRB/US, used at the Federal Reserve) did not allow for the impact of financial frictions and disruptions on economic activity. As Goodhart and Tsomocos (2011) point out, the main limitation of standard Walrasian models, from which the DSGE model is directly descended, is a failure to incorporate the possibility of default, including that of banks, into the core of the analysis. They further remark that if incidents of default are not incorporated in the workings of the model, there remains no role for financial intermediaries, for financial disturbances, or even for money.

The link between business cycle fluctuations and financial frictions is supported, for example, by theoretical research that stresses the effect of asymmetric information to the obstruction of the efficient functioning of the financial system (as in Akerlof, 1970; Myers & Majluf, 1984; Greenwald et al., 1984; and the growing literature that followed). The roughly concurrent (with the abovementioned strand of research) rediscovery of Fisher (1933), as Mishkin (2011a, p. 75) points out, led to the recognition that financial instability played a central role in the collapse of economic activity during that Great Depression years (see Calomiris, 1993, for a survey), and it generated a vast amount of research on the role of financial frictions in business cycle fluctuations.

Some recent theoretical research even suggests that benign economic environments may promote excessive risk-taking and may actually make the financial system more fragile (Gambacorta, 2009). As Mishkin (2011a) (member of the US Federal Reserve Board of Governors from September 2006 until August 2008) points out, "although price and output stability are surely beneficial, the recent crisis indicates that a policy focused solely on these objectives may not be enough to produce good economic outcomes" (Mishkin, 2011a, p. 90). Additionally, empirical research (Gilchrist et al., 2009; Adrian & Shin, 2010a; Ciccarelli et al., 2015) highlights the effect of loose credit conditions in several advanced economies to the amplification of the business cycle prior to the global financial crisis, as well as of the tightening of lending standards after the collapse of Lehman Brothers Holdings Inc. investment bank, to the strong decline in US output during the years end of 2008 and 2009. Therefore, theoretical research shifted focus on the implications of the credit supply channel for the conduct of monetary policy (see, for example, Meh &

[11] Evidence to this point is given by the extraordinary unconventional actions that central banks took during the GFC to support the functioning of financial markets (the US Troubled Asset Relief Program (TARP) is an early vivid example) (see Wood, 2015, and also Oda & Okina, 2001, for an early account on central bank actions to support the functioning of segmented markets at times of a crisis).

Moran, 2010; Woodford, 2011a, 2011b; Gertler & Karadi, 2011; Gambacorta & Signoretti, 2014).

Woodford (2011a, 2011b), who considers financial frictions on the side of lenders, points out that "decisions about interest-rate policy should take account of changes in financial conditions" (p. 39).[12] Cúrdia and Woodford (2010), for example, formally treat this aspect and introduce an ad hoc financial intermediation friction which creates a spread between the loan and the policy rate in a standard New Keynesian model and demonstrate that credit-augmented rules outperform the standard Taylor rule for a number of different shocks. Woodford (2012) also builds on Cúrdia and Woodford (2011) in order to analyze the implications of financial imbalances for monetary policy, in a model where endogenous state variables (like leverage) affect the probability of a crisis, and considers the effects on optimal monetary stabilization policy. The implication for the latter is that (while price stability remains the primary policy objective over the medium term) financial stability concerns should also be taken into account in the adjustment path. According to this model, it may be appropriate to use monetary policy to "lean against" a credit boom, even if this requires both inflation and the output gap to be below their medium-run target values for a time.

An agency consideration of the monetary transmission mechanism is introduced in Acharya and Naqvi (2012), who accept bank loan officers to be compensated on the basis of new loans issued. An asset price bubble is thus generated, which calls for a LATW monetary policy. Angeloni and Faia (2013), Angeloni et al. (2015), and Gertler and Karadi (2011) introduce a risk-taking channel in a DSGE framework and make quantitative comparisons of welfare under different central bank objectives, testing thus the validity of financial policy objectives. See Gertler and Kiyotaki (2010) for an early review of a growing literature that uses the framework in Bernanke et al. (1999) to introduce financial frictions in DSGE models. The focus is on the monetary policy effect on the buildup of financial sector risks and the presence of a negative relationship between the interest rate and risk-taking.

Central banks in their effort to design and implement LATW policies tend to face additional trade-offs, which necessitate increased credibility of the price stability target, and even though they complicate the design of monetary policy, they do not alter its setup (Smets, 2014, p. 273). As central banks are the first in line to clean up when the bubble bursts, they need the right incentive to lean against the building up of the bubble ex ante. Smets (2014, p. 266) nevertheless recognizes that a main

[12] Woodford (2011a, 2011b) introduces banks' leverage target levels, which give rise to a positively sloped loan supply curve that shifts procyclically with banks' profitability and capital, as well as with changes in the policy rate. He contends that such a loan supply curve may arise due, for example, to intermediaries' facing costs for originating and servicing loans, with marginal costs increasing with the volume of lending, or to regulatory limits or market-based constraints restraining leverage. Similarly, Woodford (2011a) introduces a risk-taking channel of monetary policy by applying a regime as in Stein (2012), where fire sales during a financial crisis distort the behavior of financial intermediation, into an otherwise traditional New Keynesian model of monetary policy.

counterargument is that the central bank's involvement in financial stability may undermine the credibility of its pursuit of price stability.[13] LATW monetary policy may shift the trade-off between price and output-gap stability inward and thus result to an overall improvement of macroeconomic performance, as in Fahr et al. (2013), who include financial frictions in a model of the euro area.

As Barrett et al. (2016) demonstrate, LATW monetary policy (where financial stability is an explicit policy objective of an inflation-targeting central bank) is not optimal when the financial sector is uncertain as to whether the central bank will conduct such a policy, raising issues of transparency of monetary policy. In their model without a clear commitment to LATW, central banks will be expected to conduct this style of policy only when large inflationary shocks are likely. Yet, for a central bank to consider LATW, inflation forecasts should not signal any threat, and, therefore, this type of policy is sustainable only when the central bank credibly commits to it. Barrett et al. (2008), Diamond and Rajan (2009), Farhi and Tirole (2009), Ueda and Valencia (2012), and Smets (2014) formally treat certain additional aspects of time-inconsistent monetary policy addressing separate elements of the "financial cycle." Borio (2014) identifies the latter in that "... policies that are too timid in leaning against financial booms but are then too aggressive and persistent in leaning against financial busts, may end up leaving the authorities with no further ammunition over successive financial and business cycles"[14] (Borio, 2014, p. 16).

The end result of a downward trend in policy rates across cycles and the essential incessant resort to balance sheet policies (yet with minor gains in terms of financial and macroeconomic stability) is reinforced in a global level as the stance of monetary policy is transmitted from core economies to the rest of the world.

In the presence of credit supply effects, a response to financial variables allows the central bank to achieve a better trade-off between inflation and output stabilization, as in, for example, Gambacorta and Signoretti (2014) who combine frictions in both borrowers' and lenders' side (with loan spreads endogenously depending on banks' leverage) and show that LATW monetary policy is indeed desirable when the economy is driven by supply-side shocks and the central bank is concerned with output stabilization. They use a model similar to Gerali et al. (2010) (who estimate a medium-scale model for the euro area) and focus on aggregate supply shocks, which create a trade-off for a central bank that aims at stabilizing output and inflation

[13] Smets (2014) distinguishes two main channels for this effect to hold: (1) a need for a stronger involvement in distributional policies (see, for example, Brunnermeier & Sannikov, 2013) and a resort to quasi-fiscal operations (see, for example, Pill, 2013), which call for both a greater monetary policy accountability and a political involvement that both jeopardize central bank independence and give rise to political pressure, and (2) the presence of time inconsistency problems for monetary policy as the monetary authorities may end up providing more liquidity than needed for long-run price stability if the fundamental problems of debt overhang following a financial crisis are not addressed.

[14] Borio (2012, 2013) stress that the adverse outcome of that form of inconsistency applies also to prudential, as well as fiscal policies, while Smets (2014) formally addresses the concept with respect to the macroprudential authority's setting its policy, taking the monetary policy reaction into account in a context similar to Barrett et al. (2008).

(since, conditional on the shocks, the two variables tend to move in opposite directions). They thus demonstrate how the presence of financial frictions may amplify financial cycle fluctuations (thus, affecting macroeconomic stability) during a benign economic outlook. In addition, they run simulations that demonstrate a "LATW" rule to outperform a standard rule in terms of macroeconomic stabilization, suggesting, thus, that compared to output fluctuations, financial variables are better indicators of the procyclical effects stemming from financial frictions (see also Kokores & Kanas, 2021). They argue that these gains from a LATW approach to monetary policy are shown to be amplified under a high degree of private sector indebtedness and tend to be larger if financial stability were also of explicit concern to policymakers.

An account of shocks on expected future economic conditions and their effect on a LATW monetary policy, yet without a credit supply channel, is also given by Lambertini et al. (2011) and Christiano et al. (2010). In addition, Agur and Demertzis (2013) demonstrate that financial stability objectives render monetary policy more aggressive, since in reaction to negative shocks policy rate cuts are deeper but shorter-lived than otherwise in an effort also to achieve standard objectives. A rather extensive strand of research highlights that prolonged accommodative monetary policy increased risk-taking incentives of financial intermediaries that (among other reasons) spurred the GFC (see, for example, Dell'Ariccia et al., 2008; Calomiris, 2009; Brunnermeier, 2009; Brunnermeier et al., 2009; Allen et al., 2009; Diamond & Rajan, 2009; Adrian & Shin, 2011; Kannan et al., 2012; Borio & Zhu, 2008).

Benes and Kumhof (2012) add a calibrated model of the banking system in a DSGE model of the US economy in an effort to reaffirm the so-called "Chicago Plan" proposal for monetary reform passed over during the Great Depression envisaging the separation of the monetary and credit functions of the banking system (through a 100% reserve requirement over deposits). They reiterate the four main advantages of this plan as in Fisher (1936) as follows: (1) much better control of a major source of business cycle fluctuations, sudden increases, and contractions of bank credit and of the supply of bank-created money, (2) complete elimination of bank runs, (3) dramatic reduction of the (net) public debt, and (4) dramatic reduction of private debt, as money creation no longer requires simultaneous debt creation. They find support for all four of Fisher's claims, while output gains amount a 10 percent, and steady-state inflation can drop to zero without posing problems for the conduct of monetary policy.

Bofinger et al. (2013) suggest that a standard Taylor rule is not well-suited to maintain macroeconomic stability in the wake of monetary policy shocks. As persistent boom-bust cycles cannot be explained in a standard DSGE model with rational expectations, they address the question of whether monetary policy can cause pronounced boom-bust cycles in house prices and create persistent business cycles by introducing heuristics into a standard DSGE model. Their model, thus, accounts for cognitive limitations of agents, waves of optimism and pessimism (animal spirits) that drive house prices, which, in turn, have repercussions on the real economy. Their results demonstrate that an augmented rule that incorporates house prices or debt is superior to the standard Taylor rule.

It is worth noting the shortcomings in the forecasting methods used by most central bank economists concurrently with the advent of the GFC and their effect in policy design and conduct, as Goodhart and Tsomocos (2011) point out. Additionally, similar to Mishkin (2011a), Trichet (2011), and Smets (2014) (after reviewing an extensive literature, pertaining especially to the euro area) stresses that the existing empirical analysis is mostly performed using linear regression methodologies, while it is deemed necessary to acquire nonlinear approaches capturing the possibly time-varying nature of interest rate changes on credit and house prices and their effect on the probability of a crisis as in the early accounts of, for example, Hubrich and Tetlow (2012) and Hartmann et al. (2013).

Smets (2014, p. 269) distinguishes a view termed as the "modified Jackson Hole consensus" (as in, for example, Bean et al., 2010; Gerlach, 2010; Svensson, 2012, 2013) which postulates that monetary authorities should address financial stability concerns only to the extent that they affect the outlook for price stability and economic activity, while it is a task for macroprudential authorities to pursue financial stability, with each policy having distinct instruments. This view argues that the objectives, the instruments, and the transmission mechanisms of monetary and macroprudential policy can easily be separated, that the interaction between the two policies is limited, and that the effectiveness of the short-term interest rate to deal with financial imbalances is limited. Even though this view remains to be supported by the pertinent empirical research, central banking practitioners tend to advocate in favor of the "separability" between financial stability and monetary stability accepting that there is no conflict between the central bank's raising rates to combat recent protracted increases in inflation and financial stability (see, for example, a synopsis of central banking officials' remarks in Posen, 2023).[15] ECB President Christine Lagarde (2023, March 16) stated in a press conference on the ECB monetary policy statement that "I believe there is no trade-off between price stability and financial stability," and the latter can be dealt with using specific tools, in that interest rates are assigned to price stability, and the various tools on liquidity policy are assigned to financial stability (see Kokores, 2022, Chap. 8). Nevertheless, for example, Yi Gang Governor of the People's Bank of China states that under normal situations, these two decisions may be separable, but he accepts that in periods of significant or even systemic risk evidently jeopardizing financial stability, thus impacting on credit stability, and the assets that financial institutions are holding, for "practical reasons [central banks] have to consider them jointly" (referring also to the twin mandate on price and financial stability of the People's Bank of China) (Yi, 2023).

[15] Adam S. Posen (2023, April 15) hosting the annual "Macro Week" in Peterson Institute for International Economics (PIIE) in Washington (a series of speeches and onstage discussions by central bankers and finance officials) reiterates the above statement claimed by most central banking officials (especially European ones) during the annual Macro Week.

As highlighted in the next subsection, a growing empirical and theoretical research strives to provide evidence on the room for cooperation between monetary and macroprudential policies mainly based on the premise of a complex interaction between the two (in terms of both effectiveness of instruments used and attainment of primary objectives). The counterargument is based in the premise that if macroprudential policies are well-targeted, they may not only contain the undesirable effects of monetary policy, and create additional room for maneuver for monetary policy, but also reduce policy dilemmas (Antipa & Matheron, 2014, p. 227). Justifications of the latter counterargument include the limits on debt-to-income ratios attenuating the impact on defaults from a tightening of monetary policy (Igan & Kang, 2011); capital requirements or leverage ratios possibly containing increases in bank leverage in response to low policy rates and eliminating risk-taking incentives (Farhi & Tirole, 2012); limits on loan-to-value ratios reducing asset price booms, when accommodative monetary policy inflates asset prices (IMF, 2011); as well as limits on foreign exchange lending reducing the systemic risk associated with capital flows (Hahm et al., 2012). Gilchrist and Zakrajšek (2015), for example, demonstrate that the interaction of customer markets with financial frictions in their calibrated DSGE model implies a significant attenuation of the response of inflation to demand shocks and a strong negative co-movement between inflation and output in response to financial disruptions. The latter creates a major policy dilemma for monetary authorities that aim to stabilize both inflation and output fluctuations. Their results highlight the challenge of applying a specific interest rate rule in a world where financial market distortions influence firms' pricing behavior.

3.3 The Lean-Against-the-Wind View Revisited

In an early account, Trichet (2005) described the LATW principle in the following terms:

> ... [it] describes a tendency to cautiously raise interest rates even beyond the level necessary to maintain price stability over the short to medium term when a potentially detrimental asset price boom is identified ... It should be mentioned that LATW has the advantage that it can to some degree ameliorate the moral hazard problem of the purely reactive approach to asset price boom-bust cycles. By reacting more symmetrically—i.e. being tighter in booms as well as looser in busts—the central bank would discourage excessive risk-taking and thereby reduce over-investment already during the boom. This in turn would lead to a lower level of indebtedness and less severe consequences of a possible future bust. (p. 7)

In support to the conventional view, Assenmacher-Wesche and Gerlach (2010) offer a skeptical view regarding LATW monetary policy. They use quarterly data between years 1986 and 2008 from 18 countries and argue that deviations of credit and asset prices from trend used to capture financial imbalances contain little information useful for forecasting the future economic conditions, which casts doubts on the LATW view. They also argue that tightening monetary policy in response to such imbalances is likely to depress real growth substantially, accepting, however, that their finding is subject to the Lucas critique.[16] It is worth highlighting the remarks in Smets (2014) that accepts that a concern for financial stability may lead to the so-called financial dominance and views price stability's remaining a primary objective for monetary policy to be enough to mitigate these risks, provided a lexicographic ordering with financial stability is maintained. He views such a policy to allow the central bank to LATW, when deemed necessary (if necessary, for example, macroprudential policies fail), while also maintaining its primary focus on price stability in the medium term[17] (Smets, 2014, p. 267, 292).

In the current regime of high inflation and high levels of both private and public debt, Brunnermeier (2023, p. 8) views financial dominance to depend on private banks having sufficient buffer capital to withstand losses and on private bankruptcy proceeding smoothness; he contends that a well-functioning insolvency law may insulate the system from spillover effects from the failure of an individual institution and make it less likely that a central bank would feel compelled to bail it out.

According to the LATW view, concerns about financial stability should be part of the secondary objectives in the monetary policy strategy, which lead to a lengthening of the policy horizon of the monetary authorities. This argument is mainly based on the financial cycle (see Borio, 2012, for a definition and analysis on the financial cycle and Drehmann et al., 2012, for empirical evidence on the latter argument). Apart from the complex interactions in their implementations, financial stability and monetary policies can coexist (Caruana & Cohen, 2014), so long as monetary policy maintains a longer-term price stability perspective avoiding conflict with financial stability objectives and accepting the premise that the financial cycle tends to be longer in duration than the business cycle. They remark that:

> This longer-term perspective, in fact, relieves some of the possible tensions between *monetary policy* and *macroprudential decisions*. . .Since financial crises can generate huge disinflationary pressure, a tightening of monetary policy will promote longer-run price stability. Moreover, if macroprudential considerations do call for a different calibration of a policy instrument (such as the policy rate) than would be derived solely from monetary policy considerations, the size of this deviation need not be large. . .if a build-up of credit pressures calls for macroprudential policy measures, the appropriate response could be to LATW through a small but persistent increase in the policy rate as long as these pressures continue. This is unlikely to impose much of a burden on price stability which would continue to be the main driver of movements in the policy rate. (p. 20)

[16]For a brief elaboration on the "Lucas critique," see footnote 28.

[17]It is contended (Mishkin, 2011a; Smets, 2014) that a lexicographic ordering may protect the central bank from an inflationary bias stemming from its involvement with financial stability; such an ordering implies that the central bank assigns primary focus to the price stability objective than the financial stability one (while also ensuring the attainment of financial stability concerns). Nevertheless, as Barrett et al. (2008) propose, modeling the trade-off between price and financial stability such an inflation bias may be addressed by rule-based LATW monetary policy. Smets (2014) additionally asserts that "such a credible mandate of the monetary authorities will also give the right incentives for the macroprudential policymakers to lean against the build-up of leverage and growing imbalances and not rely on inflation to solve their problems" (p. 291).

Furthermore, as in the International Monetary Fund (IMF) (2013), in view of the macroeconomic framework at the time, both macroprudential and monetary policy measures had been exploited for countercyclical management, *with monetary policy focused primarily at price stability and macroprudential policies primarily at financial stability,*[18] aiming to prevent, or at least to contain, the buildup of financial imbalances and to ensure that the financial system may withstand the unwinding of such financial imbalances and be resilient to shocks. An answer pertaining to the relative importance of the twin objectives of smoothing the financial cycle and improving the resilience of the financial system in response to shocks depends in part on how effective macroprudential policies are expected to be in LATW.

In general, the introduction of macroprudential policies can improve the trade-offs for monetary policy and increase its room for maneuver (Smets, 2014). Maintaining financial stability can help ensure a well-working financial system and an effective transmission mechanism that render achieving price stability more efficient. Moreover, macroprudential policies, by managing the financial cycle and increasing the resilience of the financial sector, may reduce the probability of systemic stress. It can also reduce trade-offs that may arise when exiting accommodative monetary policies (as, for example, Bernanke, 2013, that discusses an exit from the expansionary Federal Reserve policies implemented to address the GFC). To ensure financial stability instruments other than the policy interest rate should better be implemented and in the context of a broader framework of macroprudential supervision. Nevertheless, central banks should actively monitor asset prices and credit flows, so that policymakers promptly extract useful information that enables them to "better calibrate the course of monetary policy and to avoid the risk of being 'behind the curve'" (Smaghi, 2009, p. 1).

Nevertheless, as distinguished by Smets (2014), a certain strand in the postcrisis literature, which he terms as *financial stability is price stability* (Whelan, 2013; Brunnermeier & Sannikov, 2014), "is based on the premise that price and financial stability are so intimately intertwined due to financial frictions that it is impossible to make a distinction, and therefore, both standard and non-standard monetary policies are in the first place attempts at stabilizing the financial system, as well as addressing segmented financial markets, and unclogging the monetary transmission process" (p. 274) and thus calls for a more radical change in the monetary policy objectives. *It is argued, for example, in* Blinder (2010) and Duff (2014), *that since the objectives of financial and price stability seem to be closely interlinked, a central bank is legitimately motivated to ensure financial stability.*

On the other hand, a certain strand of literature contends that price stability concerns may undermine the attainment of macroprudential policy objectives, and

[18] See, for example, De Bandt et al. (2009), Brunnermeier et al. (2009), and European Systemic Risk Board (2011) for accounts on macroprudential policy objectives and definitions of systemic risk.

vice-versa, since monetary and macroprudential objectives may, at times, diverge.[19] Similarly, as remarked in Cihák (2010), poor macroprudential policy performance may possibly damage central bank reputation, thus raising concerns about central bank independence. Nevertheless, Blinder (2010) argues, on the opposite direction, that central bank reputation may actually be enhanced by an effective handling of a financial crisis.

Time inconsistency issues may also arise when central bank monetary policy and financial stability concerns need to be coordinated because of the prevailing threats of financial dominance. Similarly, as argued in Whelan (2013), time inconsistency concerns arise when most efficient monetary policy trade-offs take place in central banks with mandates encompassing financial stability objectives in addition to the traditional price and output-gap stability ones.

It is in such a context that it has been proposed to embed macroprudential policymaking in central banks. Nier et al. (2011) stress that central bank practitioners' expertise may enhance the efficiency of the conduct of macroprudential policies, while, also, Lim et al. (2013) propose that central bank involvement may improve the timeliness of macroprudential policy responses. Also, Berger and Kißmer (2013) build a model where the degree of central bank independence influences the optimal choice of monetary policy strategy during potentially unsustainable asset price booms and demonstrate that the more independent central bankers are, the more likely it is that they refrain from implementing preemptive monetary tightening to maintain financial stability. Beyer et al. (2017) analyze the interactions between monetary and prudential policies (both micro and macro) and suggest that to achieve better policy outcomes (let alone to avoid conflicting effects), a constant sharing of information among the three polices is essential; thus, extra cooperation between the two policy authorities is necessary.

Nevertheless, Kamber et al. (2015) point out a tension associated with the consolidation of power in a single institution in that it increases the possibility of groupthink, while conversely they admit that spreading policymaking power across institutions may complicate coordination and communication but may also foster greater diversity in views, providing healthy checks and balances on the implementation of policy. They, also, distinguish another problem arising if macroprudential policies were to reside in central banks, in that it increases the influence and power of central bank officials in determining macroeconomic outcomes and also giving rise to agency relationships. De Paoli and Paustian (2013), however, show in a dynamic context using a welfare-based criterion that, if faced with cost-push shocks (as, for example, an increase in VAT), policy authorities should cooperate and commit to a given course of action. However, in a regime where monetary and macroprudential tools are set independently and under discretion, their findings suggest that

[19] See, for example, Buiter (2009), as well as Svensson (2015a, 2015b) who argues that the Swedish experience of macroprudential concerns having adversely affected the conduct of monetary policy is an example of this problem.

coordination problems can be mitigated by assigning conservative mandates (as in Rogoff, 1985) and one of the authorities acting as a leader.

A still growing literature addresses the issue of cooperation between macroprudential and monetary policy by incorporating the former in monetary models (see, for example, Angeloni & Faia, 2009; Darracq-Paris et al., 2010; Angelini et al., 2011, 2014; Lambertini et al., 2011; Baillu et al., 2012; Cecchetti & Kohler, 2012; Collard et al., 2012; Gelain et al., 2012; Kannan et al., 2012; Brzoza-Brzezina et al., 2013; Quint & Rabanal, 2014; Farhi & Werning, 2016; Lagarde, 2020; Powell, 2020; Van der Ghote, 2021; and references in Laeven et al., 2022; Beau et al., 2012; Galati & Moessner, 2011). As highlighted in Smets (2014, p. 271), the conclusions of this strand of research can be classified in the following: (1) introducing macroprudential policies is useful in leaning against the financial cycle driven by overoptimistic expectations or expectations of reduced volatility and risk premia and increase welfare; (2) there are potential coordination problems due to the "push-me, pull-you" nature of both policy instruments; and (3) the introduction of macroprudential policies does not change the optimal reaction function of the monetary authorities very much.

3.4 Macroprudential and Monetary Policies

Vital though it may be for monetary policymakers to address credit bubbles, to determine the most effective policies still remains a challenge. The key factor to consider when designing policies is whether they address market failures, which are often the root cause of credit bubbles (Mishkin, 2014). Given that credit extension necessarily entails risk-taking, it is only when market failures lead to excessive risk-taking that credit bubbles become a concern. To address this issue, prudential regulatory measures can be implemented to limit the development of credit bubbles. These measures include standard elements of a well-functioning prudential regulatory and supervisory system, such as adequate disclosure and capital requirements, liquidity requirements, prompt corrective action, risk management monitoring, close supervision of financial institutions to ensure compliance, and adequate resources and accountability for supervisors. These latter measures focus on promoting the safety and soundness of *individual* firms and are termed as *microprudential* policies. Nevertheless, the hazard of systemic risk still remains even if individual financial intermediary institutions are operating prudently. Due to the interactions between financial firms that promote externalities, the danger remains for excessive risk-taking. When the regulatory approach addresses these interactions between financial firms in a system-wide level, it falls in the cluster of *macroprudential* policies. Hanson et al. (2011) point out the partial equilibrium approach of microprudential policies, which aim at preventing the costly failure of individual financial institutions, in contrast to the macroprudential approach that highlights the importance of general equilibrium effects (Bernanke, 2018), and seek to safeguard the financial system as a whole.

Macroprudential policies can be used to mitigate the impact of asset price bubbles on credit provision. As asset values increase during a boom, financial institutions accumulate higher capital buffers, which can support more lending without impacting their capital adequacy ratios. However, during a bust, the value of these capital buffers can drop significantly, potentially necessitating a reduction in lending (Kashyap & Stein, 1994; Adrian & Shin, 2009). An ongoing strand of research evaluates the effectiveness of bank capital requirements in promoting financial stability, including whether these requirements should be adjusted over the business cycle. Theoretical work stresses the importance of ex ante measures, such as capital buffers that reduce the need to rely on ex post policy intervention (Lorenzoni, 2008; Martinez-Miera & Suarez, 2014; Clerc et al., 2015; Begenau, 2020; Malherbe, 2020). Macroprudential policies to address credit bubbles also include dynamic provisioning by banks, lower loan-to-value ratios, higher haircut requirements for repo lending during credit expansions, and Pigouvian taxes on certain liabilities of financial institutions (Bank of England, 2009; French et al., 2010; Beyer et al., 2017). While some policies can be a standard part of the regulatory system, discretionary prudential policies may be necessary to address market failures driving a particular credit bubble. For instance, discretionary policies may be required during periods when risks across institutions are highly correlated in order to reduce systemic risk.

Financial instability may have been promoted by overly easy monetary policy, considering the fact that low interest rate policies from 2002 to 2005 were followed by excessive risk-taking.[20] Even though the Federal Reserve monetary policy is not clearly to blame for the housing bubble, a growing body of microeconomic research, both theoretical and empirical, supports the hypothesis that monetary policy is involved in creating credit bubbles (see Mishkin, 2011a; Wood, 2015, especially Chap. 6). Borio and Zhu (2008) label this mechanism as the *risk-taking channel of monetary policy.*

Pertinent research provides two basic reasons why low interest rates might promote excessive risk-taking. The first strand contends that increased risk-taking is induced by financial institution asset managers' search for yield triggered by low interest rates (Rajan, 2005, 2006; Summers, 2014).[21] Another mechanism through

---

[20]Using aggregate data, Taylor (2007) has argued that excessively low policy rates led to the housing bubble, while contrary arguments are provided in Posen (2009), Bernanke (2010), Bean et al. (2010), and Turner (2010).

[21]Summers (2014, p. 69) views the regime of low real interest rates combined with low inflation (at the time) leading to low nominal interest rates, to stir risk-seeking activities by investors and greater reliance on Ponzi finance (leading to increased financial instability). These risk-seeking incentives may arise from behavioral aspects like money illusion, as a result of which the managers believe that low nominal rates indicate that real returns are low, encouraging them to purchase riskier assets to obtain a higher target return (Mishkin 2011a, p. 99). Typically, incentives to search for yield arise either from contractual arrangements or from fixed rate commitments. The former compensate asset managers for returns above a minimum level, and when nominal interest rates are low, high-risk investments may be the ones that lead to high compensation. The latter (often present in insurance companies) force the firm to seek out higher-yielding, riskier investments.

which low interest rates could promote risk-taking stems from income and valuation effects. Under low interest rates, financial firms tend to increase their net interest margins, thus increasing their value, and therefore expand their capacity to increase their leverage and assume more risk (Adrian & Shin, 2009, 2010a) and Adrian et al., 2010). Additionally, low interest rates can boost collateral values, further expanding lending capacity.[22]

Furthermore, risk-taking incentives tend to affect interconnected economies. With reference to the United States, since the dollar is a global funding currency, Surti (2021) asserts that the search-for-yield incentives arising from long periods of low interest rates in the United States are not limited to financial firms in the United States but also affect firms operating in other countries, which may undertake a carry trade of borrowing in the United States and investing locally at a higher rate of return. The riskiness of the latter arises from the fact that any tightening of monetary policy in the United States (or a domestic shock) may result in a loss-inducing dollar appreciation. An example of the latter is the 2013 "taper tantrum" when large financial firms operating in emerging markets experienced significant carry trade losses due to the dollar appreciation; these financial firms' market valuations were sharply decreased, and such losses even led to increased volatility in the domestic financial markets.[23]

Additionally, monetary policy can enhance risk-taking in two other ways. More predictable monetary policy can reduce uncertainty and cause asset managers to underestimate risk, even though it is desirable from a standpoint of building credibility and strengthening the nominal anchor, which helps stabilize the economy (Gambacorta, 2009). When monetary policy lowers interest rates to clean up after financial disruptions, it may lead to moral hazard in a manner that financial intermediaries expect that the central bank will assist them in recovering from bad investment choices through the design and implementation of monetary policy (see, for example, Farhi & Tirole, 2012; Keister, 2016; Wilson & Wu, 2010). This type of monetary policymaking has been termed as the "Greenspan put" after then

[22]With the exception that this mechanism stems from lender-originated financial frictions (rather than from borrowers), it is closely related to the financial accelerator of Bernanke and Gertler (1999, 2000) and Bernanke et al. (1999).

[23]In spring 2013, US Federal Reserve Chairman Ben Bernanke gave an initial statement that he expected QE asset purchases to be tapered off in a staggered manner to eventually wean the economy off the extra support, which was referred to as the "taper tantrum" illustrating the impact of effective central bank communication. The statement prompted strong reactions ("tantrums") in financial markets not just in the United States but also worldwide, which were probably unintentional and undesired. The US market fell by 4% following the announcement, setting off an international chain reaction. A policy statement that should have ideally been factored in started causing global markets to react negatively as investors, digitally apt to disseminate information, overreacted promptly. Several advanced economies experienced a sharp reversal of capital flows and currency depreciation at the time, while several emerging economies (like India, Indonesia, Brazil, and Turkey) experienced a sharp decline in stock markets and higher sovereign yields. Global economies cushioned the shock in 2013, while the Fed tapered its asset purchases in January 2014.

Chairman of the US Federal Reserve Alan Greenspan, who communicated and implemented this type of policy at the time. Such type of monetary policy may actually trigger systemic risk since it is implemented when several financial institutions are in unison facing the hazard of not meeting their liquidity or even solvency constraints and are encouraged to pursue similar investment strategies, thereby increasing the correlation of returns.[24,25]

Macroprudential policies, which aim to prevent credit bubbles, are more vulnerable to political pressure compared to monetary policies because they directly impact the financial institutions' profits. As a result, these institutions have a greater motivation to persuade politicians against implementing macroprudential policies. Additionally, financial institutions may try to find creative ways to evade these policies. The fact that macroprudential policies can be bypassed raises doubts about their effectiveness, which means that monetary policy may also need to be used. However, using monetary policy to counter credit bubbles may not be successful, which presents another challenge (Mishkin, 2014, p. 417). We are sympathetic to the view discussed by Mishkin (2014) that tightening monetary policy may be ineffective in restraining a particular asset bubble because market participants expect such high rates of return from purchasing bubble-driven assets. On the other hand, based on the evidence regarding the risk-taking channel of monetary policy, it appears that there is a stronger argument for increasing interest rates to curb lending growth and excessive risk-taking. Additionally, the theoretical analysis presented earlier suggests that if the general public believes that the central bank will raise interest rates when a credit bubble seems to be forming, then credit market expectations will make this policy more successful. Expectations that interest rates will increase with higher risk-taking would decrease the profitability of such activities, making them less likely to occur. This would result in less of a need to raise interest rates significantly to achieve the desired effect.

Nevertheless, to utilize monetary policy to counter credit bubbles may lead to an economic slowdown that the monetary authorities did not intend, as well as to lower inflation rates. This implies a trade-off in monetary policy between achieving financial stability and achieving price and output stability. Furthermore, to assign

---

[24]For research supporting the risk-taking channel of monetary policy both antecedent to the GFC and after its emergence see, for example, Jiménez et al. (2008), Ioannidou et al. (2009), Adrian and Shin (2009, 2010b); Maddaloni and Peydró (2011), Buch et al. (2014), Jimenez et al. (2014), Heider et al. (2019), Bubeck et al. (2020), and ECB (2021).

[25]If monetary policy is used to lean against credit bubbles and therefore aiming at stabilizing the financial sector, in addition to the real sector, a main objection refers to the issue of asking one policy instrument to do two "jobs," thus violating the Tinbergen (1939) principle. Ensuring stability in the financial sector is closely related to stabilizing the overall economy, as financial instability can lead to economic instability and inflation. However, since the nature of financial instability is distinct from the dynamics of inflation and economic activity, it can be considered a separate policy goal under the Tinbergen principle. This is because macroprudential supervision (a distinct tool) can be used to stabilize the financial sector. It thus considered preferable to utilize macroprudential supervision for maintaining financial stability while leaving monetary policy to concentrate on maintaining price and output stability (Lagarde, 2023).

an additional objective to monetary policy might cause confusion about the central bank's dedication to price stability, potentially weakening the nominal anchor and having unfavorable effects on economic outcomes (Mishkin, 2011a, pp. 99, 101). There is a risk associated with using monetary policy to promote financial stability, which is the possibility of making decisions to tighten monetary policy even when it is not necessary to control credit bubbles, a situation of low interest rates does not always indicate that monetary policy is encouraging excessive risk-taking. Policymakers, particularly those involved in monetary policy, need tools to evaluate the development of credit bubbles. Ongoing research is exploring measures that can indicate the likelihood of credit bubble forming,[26] such as high credit growth, increasing leverage, low-risk spreads, surging asset prices, and surveys that evaluate whether credit underwriting standards are being relaxed. These data points can assist central banks in determining if there is an imminent risk of credit bubbles. Frederic S. Mishkin (appointed at the US Federal Reserve Board of Governors on September 5, 2006, and resigning on August 31, 2008) suggests in Mishkin (2014) that the "monitoring of credit market conditions will become an essential activity of central banks in the future, and research on the best ways of doing so will have a high priority in the future" (p. 418). Furthermore, with the benefit of hindsight, he further suggests that "monetary policy and financial stability policy are intrinsically linked to each other, and so the dichotomy between them is a false one" (Mishkin, 2014, p. 419). On the one hand, monetary policy can affect financial stability, while on the other macroprudential policies implemented to safeguard financial stability can

[26]In a seminal account, Borio and Lowe (2002) argue on the buildup of financial imbalances under low inflation regimes, in that sustained rapid credit growth combined with large increases in asset prices appears to increase the probability of an episode of financial instability. Adrian and Shin (2010a) show that marked-to-market leverage is strongly procyclical. They demonstrate that changes in dealer repos (the primary margin of adjustment for the aggregate balance sheets of intermediaries) forecast changes in financial market risk as measured by the innovations in the Chicago Board Options Exchange Volatility Index (VIX), thus showing that aggregate liquidity can be seen as the rate of change of the aggregate balance sheet of the financial intermediaries. Similarly, several methodologies rely on specific asset price processes using time series price data. Asset price process may be assumed to follow a simple diffusion model as in Jarrow et al. (2011a, 2011b), according to whom to detect bubbles, a Feller's test for explosions is applied, which is estimated using a kernel method. A stochastic disorder model is specified in Shiryaev et al. (2014, 2015) that constitutes a more complex diffusion process where the drift and volatility parameters jump at change points. Phillips et al. (2015a, 2015b) develop bubble tests that look for explosive dynamics in long time series of asset prices using variants of an augmented Dickey-Fuller test, under an autoregressive framework.

Another strand of research exploits option-price cross-sectional data, which contain useful information about the state-price distribution (SPD) of the underlying asset which is related to the risk-neutral measure; the risk-neutral distribution and density function are identified by the partial derivative of a European option price with respect to the strike price (Breeden & Litzenberger, 1978). For nonparametric methods that recover the SPD from option data, see, for example, Aït-Sahalia and Lo (1998), Aït-Sahalia and Duarte (2003), Yatchew and Härdle (2006), Fan and Mancini (2009), Kitsul and Wright (2013), Song and Xiu (2016), Jarrow and Kwok (2021), and Lu and Qu (2021). In principle, estimates of the asset price bubble are obtained by deducing the fundamental asset value (proxied by the mean of the SPD).

affect monetary policy. Since macroprudential policies aim at restraining a credit bubble, they result in slowing credit growth and the growth of aggregate demand. In such a context, more accommodative monetary policy may potentially be warranted, in order to offset weaker aggregate demand.

Alternatively, if policy rates are kept low to stimulate the economy, then a credit bubble might occur at a greater risk. Therefore, tighter macroprudential policies are required to ensure that a credit bubble does not develop. Gadea Rivas et al. (2020) show that intermediate levels of credit growth maximize long-term growth while limiting volatility, suggesting that there is a trade-off between the pace of credit growth and the level of risk associated with it. The trade-off posed for the policymaker implies that to limit the buildup of financial risk to avoid a deep recession can negatively affect the cumulation of economic growth during the expansion. When the objectives of price stability, output stability, and financial stability are to be pursued simultaneously, then the coordination of monetary and macroprudential policies becomes of greater value. The GFC provides strong support for the vital task that a systemic regulator undertakes and that central banks tend to be a primary natural choice for this role (in addition to their being fitted for the valid coordination between monetary policy and macroprudential policy) (Mishkin, 2009; French et al., 2010). At the advent of the GFC monetary and macroprudential policy coordination was perceived to be more effective when executed under one government agency being in charge of both.[27]

In sum, the aftermath of the GFC altered the perception about prudential and monetary policies by both academics and central banking practitioners. This evolution rendered the task of a central bank much more complicated since it needs to focus not only on the appropriate design and conduct of monetary policy to stabilize inflation and economic activity but also on the effective design and interaction of macroprudential and monetary policies to make financial crises less likely.

3.5 Monetary Policy and Financial Stability

The use of monetary policy to promote financial stability has been a topic of intense debate. The financial crisis served as a reminder that maintaining price stability alone is insufficient to ensure financial stability and that dealing with the aftermath of financial crises is costly. Therefore, policy should aim to decrease the likelihood of financial crises, not just react to them after they occur. It is apparent that prudential policies, including both microprudential and macroprudential regulation and supervision, should be implemented actively to mitigate the accumulation of financial

[27] Agur (2018) demonstrates in a game theoretic context that the coordination problem vanishes only when the unconstrained player (monetary authority) is so similar to the constrained player (macroprudential authority—in terms of the imprecision of macroprudential policy) that he prefers the same equilibrium.

risks. The question that arises is whether monetary policy should be modified to address financial stability risks. Should interest rates be temporarily raised more than necessary to achieve price and output stability objectives? Alternatively, keeping rates persistently high is another option, but it is more expensive.

Based on the knowledge accumulated in the aftermath of the GFC and the subsequent euro area sovereign debt crisis and antecedent to the current resurgence of inflation post the COVID-19 pandemic, the answer has been generally no (see, for example, IMF, 2015). It yet has been asserted that "the door should remain open as our knowledge of the relationship between monetary policy and financial risks evolves and circumstances change [, and] in principle, monetary policy should deviate from its traditional response only if costs are smaller than benefits (the principle of doing no harm on net)" (p. 1). Since costs, which are associated with lower output and inflation, accumulate over the short term, and the benefits, which are associated with the mitigation of financial risks, materialize mainly in the medium term and their broad effects tend to be more uncertain, any deviation in monetary policy is a challenging task. As the GFC and the euro area crisis emerged, "leaning-against-the-wind" monetary policy had been considered to bare, in most circumstances, costs that outweighed benefits. In practice, several central banks have incorporated financial stability considerations in their monetary policy frameworks and generally view macroprudential measures as a first-best option to mitigate systemic risks, subject to the effectiveness of the macroprudential tools (let alone their availability).

However, our understanding of the channels through which monetary policy affects financial stability domestically, across borders, and over the business cycle is rapidly evolving (Kashyap & Stein, 2023; Grimm et al., 2023), rendering further research a key priority. As consecutive crises unfolded and novel policy contexts had been revealed, a call for deviations from traditional policy responses had been warranted. Additionally, central banks never ceased to monitor and communicate potential risks to financial stability and their forecasted effects and also cautiously consider the costs and benefits of further policy implementation.

Prior to the GFC, the consensus that had emerged accepted that different policy tools should have distinct roles and responsibilities. Consequently, most central banks adopted a so-called "benign neglect" approach to asset prices and credit booms. Policymakers acknowledged the risks associated with financial imbalances. However, in the period leading up to the crisis, financial stability risks grew unnoticed under the guise of seemingly stable inflation and output gaps. This contradicted the beliefs held prior to the crisis, which underestimated the costs of dealing with its aftermath, particularly in countries where financial imbalances were most pronounced. The severity of such crises necessitated exceptional monetary policy measures, especially when fiscal policy was limited by high and increasing public debt burdens. These events have caused the so-called "lean versus clean" debate to resurface.

Policymakers right in the aftermath of the GFC acknowledged the need to proactively mitigate the risk of crises, rather than solely relying on postcrisis cleanup efforts. There is a growing consensus that price stability is no longer enough to

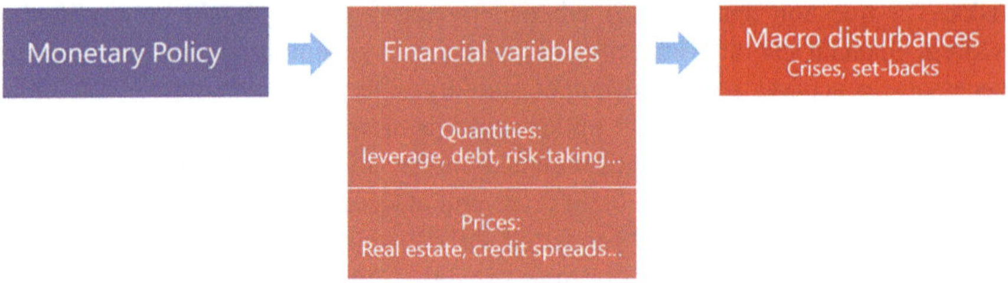

Fig. 3.1 Transmission between monetary policy and financial stability: from interest rates to macroeconomic conditions. Source: IMF (2015), p. 13

ensure macroeconomic stability, and attention has shifted toward containing systemic risk by complementing microprudential policies aimed at individual institutions with macroprudential policy frameworks. This approach is, for example, advocated in Viñals (2013), which points to a strong inaction bias of macroprudential policies, IMF (2013, 2014, 2015), and Freixas et al. (2015)[28] and includes cyclical instruments such as countercyclical capital buffers, loan-to-value limits, or dynamic loss provisioning, as well as permanent measures to enhance the structural resilience of the financial system. Nevertheless, there are concerns that even with the combination of stronger microprudential and macroprudential policies, it may still be insufficient to mitigate financial stability risks.

Therefore, the case remains whether monetary policy should be designed and implemented to pursue a further financial stability objective, in addition to its price stability mandate. Given the lack of an accepted theoretical framework, the question of leaning against the wind remains contested. The Bank for International Settlements (BIS) has been actively involved in this discussion, advocating for a more significant role for monetary policy in promoting financial stability. The debate has taken on added urgency in the current economic environment experiencing a stream of bank liquidations of threat toward the latter.

The exposition of the key issues on the debate as in, for example, IMF (2015) and Lagarde (2023), aims to help policymakers assess the value and implications of using monetary policy to support financial stability. Three distinct ways have been identified, namely, by (1) providing a framework to conceptualize and clarify the channels of transmission and policy trade-offs, (2) advancing initial policy guidance based on the most recent empirical findings, and (3) emphasizing the gaps that still need to be filled before more definitive policy advice can be formulated. The IMF (2015) asks: "what do we know and can be quantified, what should we do based on what we know, and how much do we really know?" (p. 10).

The transmission between monetary policy and financial stability entails two links as illustrated in Fig. 3.1, initially between interest rates and key financial variables, and second between these latter financial variables and the probability of large disturbances to macroeconomic conditions.

[28] For surveys, see Claessens et al. (2013), Galati and Moessner (2014), and Kokores (2022).

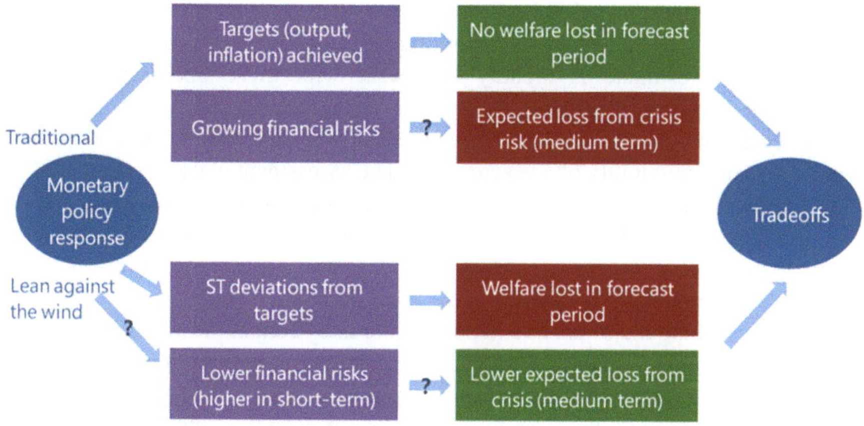

Fig. 3.2 To lean or not to lean: such are the trade-offs. Source: IMF (2015), p. 23

A rough guide for policy deliberations is provided by a simpler framework for cost-benefit analysis, as in Svensson (2015a, 2015b). Such framework is useful to build intuition, highlight interactions among variables, and explore rough magnitudes. In particular, the implementation of a "leaning-against-the-wind" policy involves paying a short-term cost in terms of lower output or higher unemployment; the cost is assumed in exchange for a medium-term benefit in the form of lower expected costs from a financial crisis.[29] As illustrated in Fig. 3.2, there is less of an inter-temporal trade-off with respect to the role of monetary policy in stabilizing inflation, since inflation and output over shorter horizons demonstrate strong correlations, where bringing inflation to target typically also implies bringing output toward its target.[30]

A vital parameter in the illustrative cost-benefit analysis is the unemployment loss from interest rate increases in the short run, which can be approximated by using a standard dynamic stochastic general equilibrium (DSGE) model used for policy analysis. The GIMF model proposed and used by the IMF, as well as several central

[29]Following Svensson (2015a, 2015b), at the initial period, the central bank moves to an interest rate increase that reduces financial vulnerabilities and leads to higher unemployment for 3–4 years. Once unemployment reaches its steady-state level, the second period begins by defining the probability whether the economy is hit by a crisis, which is lower provided that interest rates were raised at the initial period. If a crisis emerges, the economy faces significantly higher unemployment, for a period equal to, or longer than, the initial period. In the end, to estimate the effect on welfare, unemployment is squared over both periods. In fact, it is the deviations of unemployment from the natural rate, which can be assumed to be zero to simplify computations, that is actually squared.

[30]Blanchard and Galí (2007) referred to "a divine coincidence" demonstrated by many models, namely, the fact that to bring inflation to target coincided with bringing output to target as well; most models introduced wage rigidities or cost-push shocks and thus have exhibited some (rather not substantial) trade-offs (see Blanchard, 2006, for a discussion, or Goodfriend, 2004). Bayoumi et al. (2014) argue on the indications that the trade-off may be weakening.

banks, demonstrates that a 100 basis point increase in short-term interest rates leads to an increase in unemployment by approximately less than ½ percentage point as for a year.[31] This estimate is broadly consistent with those obtained by vector autoregressive models estimating the monetary transmission process.[32]

The costs associated with leaning against the wind exceed the benefits, unless there is a strong possibility of a severe crisis. The assessment of costs and benefits is highly dependent on the strength of the connections between the policy rate and the risk of a crisis and the predicted severity of the crisis. To justify leaning against the wind, these factors need to be close to the upper range of existing empirical estimates. It is important to note, however, that such calculations only consider the benefits of escaping major crises and do not take into account the additional benefits of mitigating minor economic setbacks. Three considerations are relevant: the impact of leaning against the wind on the probability of setbacks, in addition to crises, effects on central bank credibility, and open economy implications. Further research is also warranted to investigate the implementation of leaning-against-the-wind policy in cases other than a full-fledged crisis.

However, there is a lack of sufficient and conclusive evidence to support the notion that this added advantage exists. Furthermore, taking actions to counteract economic headwinds may have negative consequences, such as damaging the central bank's reputation and the efficacy of monetary policies, which could lead to inflation expectations becoming unhinged. In the case of large economies with significant cross-border financial interconnectedness, the benefits and costs of lean-against-the-wind policies may be more pronounced, particularly when considering potential spillover effects. Nevertheless, when addressing smaller open economies, the justification for taking this approach may be less compelling.

3.6 Concluding Thoughts

Taking everything into account while considering the recent circumstances and understanding, limited reasons still remain to bluntly support "leaning-against-the-wind" monetary policy. Under macroeconomic slack due to consecutive crises and an evidently rather weak transmission from interest rates to financial risks, the costs of this monetary policy stance often seem to outweigh the benefits. It also remains too challenging a policy to put into practice. Instead, to use macroprudential policies that include both structural and cyclical measures is essential to prevent financial

[31] By averaging two model variants, namely, one being a proxy of a large, closed economy, with another of a small open economy, we yield that effects peak after 1–2 years, while unemployment returns to steady-state peak after 3–4 years.

[32] For a survey, see Altavilla and Ciccarelli (2009). Other models used by central banks—each with distinct particular features—are rather tailored to small open economies; an example is the model used by Sweden's Riksbank, labeled the "Ramses" model, that estimates unemployment to react to monetary policy shocks in a more sluggish manner.

instability caused by a crisis. These policies can effectively target imbalances and market imperfections much more precisely than monetary policy can. They also have the potential to enable monetary policy to concentrate on its primary objective of maintaining price stability, thus simplifying communication and increasing accountability.

Monetary policymakers would certainly benefit from further research as, first, our comprehension of how monetary policy impacts financial stability is restricted. By gathering new data and conducting further analysis, we may be able to identify new monetary transmission channels, which could enhance the argument for leaning against the wind. Second, although not very common, in some specific situations, the benefits of LATW policy may outweigh the costs, even based on our current understanding. These situations can arise from a combination of both initial conditions related to the current economic cycle and structural conditions unique to specific countries. These conditions may include the following:

- *Initial conditions. B*enefits relative to costs may arise due to the following: low unemployment (as due to LATW monetary policy interest rate increases may lead to smaller macroeconomic costs), rapid credit growth (if interest rate increases impose a stronger effect on credit growth and discourage (Shiller, 2000), type of exuberant, self-fulfilling behavior, thus diminishing the probability of a crisis occurring), and when balance sheets of both financial intermediaries and borrowers are strong enough to thus withstand the initial interest rate shock.
- *Structural conditions. B*enefits of LATW monetary policy may also outweigh costs under the following: severity of crisis events is likely to be intense, for example, due to the absence of well-targeted macroprudential measures in a large and interconnected financial system and large financial spillovers among systemically interconnected countries with open capital accounts, and when potential financial risks may be reliably identified ex ante and in a timely manner, so that early interest rate hikes may be able to avoid a large buildup of risks.

References

Acharya, V. V., & Naqvi, H. (2012). The seeds of a crisis: A theory of bank liquidity and risk-taking over the business cycle. *Journal of Financial Economics, 106*(2), 349–366.

Adrian, T., & Liang, N. (2014). Monetary policy, financial conditions, and financial stability. *Federal Reserve Bank of New York Staff Reports* 690, New York, USA.

Adrian, T., & Shin, H. S. (2009). Money, liquidity and monetary policy. *American Economic Review: Papers and Proceedings, 99*(2), 600–605.

Adrian, T., & Shin, H. S. (2010a). Liquidity and leverage. *Journal of Financial Intermediation, 19*, 418–437.

Adrian, T., & Shin, H. S. (2010b). Financial intermediation and monetary economics. Federal Reserve Bank of New York Staff Report, 398 (Revised May), New York, USA.

Adrian, T., & Shin, H. S. (2011). Financial intermediaries and monetary economics. In B. M. Friedman & M. Woodford (Eds.), *Handbook of monetary economics 3A*. Elsevier.

Adrian, T., Moench, E., & Shin, H. S. (2010). Macro risk premiums and intermediary balance sheet quantities. In *Federal Reserve Bank of New York Staff Report* (Vol. 428).
Agur, I. (2018). Monetary and macroprudential policy coordination among multiple equilibria. *IMF Working Paper* No. 235, International Monetary Fund, Washington DC, USA.
Agur, I., & Demertzis, M. (2012). Excessive Bank risk-taking and monetary policy. *ECB working paper* 1457, European Central Bank, Frankfurt Am Main, Germany.
Agur, I., & Demertzis, M. (2013). Lean-against-the-wind and the timing of monetary policy. *Journal of International Money and Finance, 35*, 179–194.
Aït-Sahalia, Y., & Duarte, J. (2003). Nonparametric option pricing under shape restrictions. *Journal of Econometrics, 116*, 9–47.
Aït-Sahalia, Y., & Lo, A. W. (1998). Nonparametric estimation of state-price densities implicit in financial asset prices. *Journal of Finance, 53*(2), 499–547.
Akerlof, G. A. (1970). The market for 'Lemons': Quality, uncertainty and the market mechanism. *Quarterly Journal of Economics, 84*, 488–500.
Allen, F., Babus, A., & Carletti, E. (2009). Financial crises: Theory and evidence. *Annual Review of Financial Economics, 1*, 97–116.
Altavilla, C., & Ciccarelli, M. (2009). The Effects of Monetary Policy on Unemployment Dynamics under Model Uncertainty: Evidence from the United States and the Euro Area. *Journal of Money, Credit and Banking, 41*(7), 1265–1300.
Altunbas, Y., Gambacorta, L., & Marquez-Ibanez, D. (2010). Bank risk and monetary policy. *Journal of Financial Stability, 6*, 121–129.
Angelini, P., Neri, S., & Panetta, F. (2011). Monetary and macroprudential policies'. *Banca d Italia Working Paper* 801, Bank of Italy, Rome, Italy.
Angelini, P., Neri, S., & Panetta, F. (2014). The interaction between capital requirements and monetary policy. *Journal of Money, Credit and Banking, 46*(6), 1073–1112.
Angeloni, I., & Faia, E. (2009). A tale of two policies: Prudential regulation and monetary policy with fragile banks. *Kiel Institute for the World Economy Working Paper* 1569.
Angeloni, I., & Faia, E. (2013). Capital regulation and monetary policy with fragile banks. *Journal of Monetary Economics, 60*(3), 311–324.
Angeloni, I., Faia, E., & Lo Duca, M. (2015). Monetary policy and risk taking. *Journal of Economic Dynamics and Control, 52*(C), 285–307.
Antipa, P., & Matheron, J. (2014). Macroprudential policies: Implementation and interactions. *Banque de France Financial Stability Review, 18*, 225–239.
Assenmacher-Wesche, K., & Gerlach, S. (2010). Monetary policy and financial imbalances: Facts and fiction. *Economic Policy, 25*(63), 437–482.
Baillu, J., Meh, C., & Zhang, Y. (2012). Macroprudential rules and monetary policy when financial frictions matter. *Bank of Canada working paper* 2012-06.
Baldwin, R., & Reichlin, L. (Eds.). (2013). Is Inflation Targeting Dead? Central banking after the Crisis. VoxEU.org e-book. *Centre for Economic Policy Research.*
Bank of England. (2009). The role of macroprudential policy. Bank of England *Discussion paper*, November.
Barrett, C.R., Kokores, I.T., & Sen, S. (2008). Bubbles, instability and monetary policy games. Proceedings of the public choice society annual meeting 2008, San Antonio, Texas, USA.
Barrett, C. R., Kokores, I. T., & Sen, S. (2016). Monetary policy games, financial instability and incomplete information. *Annals of Finance, 12*(2), 161–178.
Batini, N., & Nelson, E. (2000). When the bubble bursts: Monetary policy rules and foreign exchange market behavior. Working Paper No. 2000-01, University of Sydney, School of Economics, Sydney, Australia.
Bayoumi, T., Dell'Ariccia, G., Habermeier, K., Mancini-Griffoli, T., & Valencia, F. (2014). Monetary policy in the new normal. IMF Staff Discussion Note, April, International Monetary Fund, Washington DC, USA.

Bean, C., Paustian, M., Penalver, A., & Taylor, T. (2010). Monetary policy after the fall. In *Macroeconomic challenges: The decade ahead. Proceedings of the Federal Reserve Bank of Kansas City economic policy symposium* (pp. 26–28). Jackson Hole.

Beau, D., Clerc, L., & Mojon, B. (2012). Macro-prudential policy and the conduct of monetary policy. *Banque de France working paper* 390, Banque de France, Paris, France.

Begenau, J. (2020). Capital requirements, risk choice, and liquidity provision in a business-cycle model. *Journal of Financial Economics, 136*(2), 355–378.

Benes, J., & Kumhof, M. (2012). The Chicago plan revisited. IMF working paper 202, International Monetary Fund, Washington, DC, USA.

Berger, W., & Kißmer, F. (2013). Central Bank Independence and financial stability: A tale of perfect harmony? *European Journal of Political Economy, 31*, 109–118.

Bernanke, B. S. (1993). Credit in the macroeconomy. *Federal Reserve Bank of New York, Quarterly Review, 18*(1), 50–70.

Bernanke, B. S. (2010). Monetary policy and the housing bubble. Speech at the American Economic Association Annual Meeting, Atlanta, GA, January 3.

Bernanke, B. S. (2013). Long-term interest rates. Speech at the annual monetary/macroeconomics conference: The past and future of monetary policy, Federal Reserve Bank of San Francisco, San Francisco, CA, March 1.

Bernanke, B. S. (2018). The real effects of the financial crisis. Brookings Papers on Economic Activity, Fall.

Bernanke, B. S., & Gertler, M. (1995). Inside the black box: The credit channel of monetary policy transmission. *Journal of Economic Perspectives, 9*(4), 27–48.

Bernanke, B.S., & Gertler, M. (1999). Monetary policy and asset price volatility. *Economic review of the Federal Reserve Bank of Kansas City*, 4th Quarter, also published at (2000) *NBER Working Papers* 7559 [the response by Cecchetti, S. G., *et al.*, 2000, "Asset prices and central bank policy," Geneva Reports on the World Economy No. 2, London: Centre for Economic Policy Research, July].

Bernanke, B. S., Gertler, M., & Gilchrist, S. (1996). The financial accelerator and the flight to quality. *Review of Economics and Statistics, 78*, 1–15.

Bernanke, B. S., Gertler, M., & Gilchrist, S. (1999). The financial accelerator in a quantitative business cycle framework. In J. B. Taylor & M. Woodford (Eds.), *Handbook of macroeconomics* (Vol. 1, part 3, pp. 1341–1393). North-Holland.

Beyer, A., Nicoletti, G., Papadopoulou, N., Papsdorf, P., Runstler, G., Schwarz, C., Sousa, J., & Vergote, O. (2017). The transmission channels of monetary, macro-and microprudential policies and their interrelations. ECB *occasional paper series* no 191, May, European Central Bank, Frankfurt Am Main, Germany.

Smaghi, L. B. (2009). Monetary Policy and Asset Prices. *Opening Address*, University of Freiburg, Freiburg. *Germany*. 14 October.

Blanchard, O. (2006). European unemployment: The evolution of facts and ideas. *Economic Policy, 21*(45), 5–59.

Blanchard, O., & Galí, J. (2007). Real wage rigidities and the new Keynesian model. *Journal of Money, Credit and Banking, 39*(02, s1), 35–65.

Blanchard, O., Dell'Ariccia, G. & Mauro, P. (2010). Rethinking macroeconomic policy. *IMF staff position note*, no 10/03, February, International Monetary Fund, Washington, DC, USA.

Blinder, A. S. (2010). How central should the Central Bank be? *Journal of Economic Literature, 48*(1), 123–133.

Bofinger, P., Debes, S., Gareis, J., & Mayer, E. (2013). Monetary policy transmission in a model with animal spirits and house price booms and busts. *Journal of Economic Dynamics and Control, 37*, 2862–2881.

Borio, C. (2012). The financial cycle and macroeconomics: What have we learnt? *BIS Working Paper* 395, Bank for International Settlements, Basel, Switzerland.

Borio, C. (2013). On time, stocks and flows: Understanding the global macroeconomic challenges. *National Institute Economic Review, 225*, R3.

Borio, C. (2014). Monetary policy and financial stability: What role in prevention and recovery? *BIS Working Paper* 440, Bank for International Settlements, Basel, Switzerland, 2014.

Borio, C., & Lowe, P. (2002). Asset prices, financial and monetary stability: Exploring the nexus. *BIS Working Papers* 114, Bank for International Settlements, Basel, Switzerland.

Borio, C., & Zhu, H. (2008). Capital regulation, risk-taking and monetary policy: A missing link in the transmission mechanism? *BIS Working Paper* 268, Bank for International Settlements, Basel, Switzerland.

Breeden, D., & Litzenberger, R. (1978). Prices of state contingent claims implicit in option prices. *Journal of Business, 51*, 621–657.

Brunnermeier, M. K. (2009). Deciphering the liquidity and credit crunch 2007–2008. *Journal of Economic Perspectives, 23*, 77–100.

Brunnermeier, M. K. (2023). Rethinking monetary policy in a changing world. *Finance & Development 'New Directions for Monetary Policy'*, 60(1), International Monetary Fund, March, pp 6–9.

Brunnermeier, M. K., & Sannikov, Y. (2013). Reviving money and banking. In R. Baldwin & L. Reichlin (Eds.), *Is inflation targeting dead?* VoxEU e-book.

Brunnermeier, M. K., & Sannikov, Y. (2014). A macroeconomic model with a financial sector. *American Economic Review, 104*(2), 379–421.

Brunnermeier, M. K., Crockett, A., Goodhart, C., Persaud, A. D., & Shin, H. S. (2009). The fundamental principles of financial regulation. Geneva reports on the world economy 11, International Centre of Monetary and Banking Studies, Geneva, Switzerland, and Centre for Economic Policy Research, London, UK.

Brzoza-Brzezina, M., Kolasa, M., & Makarski, M. (2013). *Macroprudential policy instruments and economic imbalances in the euro area.* National Bank of Poland.

Bubeck, J., Maddaloni, A., & Peydró, J.-L. (2020). Negative monetary policy rates and systemic banks' risk-taking: Evidence from the euro area securities register. *Journal of Money, Credit and Banking, 52*(S1), 197–231.

Buch, C. M., Eickmeier, S., & Prieto, E. (2010). Macroeconomic factors and micro-level bank risk. CESifo Working Paper 3194.

Buch, C. M., Eickmeier, S., & Prieto, E. (2014). In search for yield? Survey-based evidence on bank risk taking. *Journal of Economic Dynamics and Control, 43*(C), 12–30.

Buiter, W. H. (2009). The proposed European systemic risk board is overweight central bankers. *FT.com-comment-blogs*, Oct. 28. Available online: http://blogs.ft.com/maverecon/2009/10/the-proposed-european-systemic-risk-board-is-overweight-central-bankers/#axzz3qRh4bzMM

Calomiris, C. W. (1993). Financial factors in the great depression. *Journal of Economic Perspectives, 7*(Spring), 61–85.

Calomiris, C. W. (2009). The subprime crisis: what's old, what's new, and what's next? *Journal of Structured Finance, 15*(1), 6–52.

Caruana, J., & Cohen, B. H. (2014). Five questions and six answers about macro-prudential policy. *Banque de France Financial Stability Review, 18*, 15–23.

Cecchetti, S. G. (1995). Distinguishing theories of the monetary transmission mechanism. *Federal Reserve Bank of St. Louis Economic Review, 77*, 83–97.

Cecchetti, S. G., & Kohler, M. (2012). When capital adequacy and interest rate policy are substitutes (and when they are not). *BIS Working Paper* 379, Bank for International Settlements, Basel, Switzerland.

Cecchetti, S. G., Genberg, H., Lipsky, J., & Wadhwani, S. (2000). *Asset prices and central Bank policy.* Geneva reports on the world economy, no. 2, International Centre for Monetary and Banking Studies, Geneva, Switzerland, and Centre for Economic Policy Research, London, UK.

Christiano, L. J., Eichenbaum, M., & Evans, C. (2005). Nominal rigidities and the dynamic effects of a shock to monetary policy. *Journal of Political Economy, 113*, 1–45.

Christiano, L.J., Ilut, C., Motto, R., & Rostagno, M. (2010). Monetary policy and stock market booms. NBER Working Paper 16402.

Ciccarelli, M., Maddaloni, A., & Peydro, J.-L. (2015). Trusting the bankers: A new look at the credit channel of monetary policy. *Review of Economic Dynamics, 18*(4), 979–1002.
Cihák, M. (2010). Price stability, financial stability, and central Bank Independence. In Oesterreichische National-Bank (Ed.), *Central Banking after the Crisis*. Oesterreichische National-Bank.
Claessens, S., Ghosh, S. R., & Mihet, R. (2013). Macro-prudential policies to mitigate financial system vulnerabilities. *Journal of International Money and Finance, 39*(C), 153–185.
Clerc, L., Derviz, A., Mendicino, C., Moyen, S., Nikolov, K., Stracca, L., Suarez, J., & Vardoulakis, A. P. (2015). Capital regulation in a macroeconomic model with three layers of default. *International Journal of Central Banking, 11*(3), 9–63.
Collard, F., Dellas, H., Diba, B., & Loisel, O. (2012). Optimal monetary and prudential policies. *Banque de France Working Paper* 413, Banque de France, Paris, France.
Cúrdia, V., & Woodford, M. (2010). Credit spreads and monetary policy. *Journal of Money, Credit and Banking, 42*(s1), 3–35.
Cúrdia, V., & Woodford, M. (2011). The Central-Bank balance sheet as an instrument of monetary policy. *Journal of Monetary Economics, 58*(1), 54–79.
Darracq-Paris, M., Soerensen, C. K., & Palenzuela, D. R. (2010). Macroeconomic propagation under different regulatory regimes: Evidence from an estimated DSGE model for the euro area. *ECB working paper* 1251, European Central Bank, Frankfurt Am Main, Germany.
De Bandt, O., Hartmann, P., & Peydró, J.-L. (2009). Systemic risk in banking: An update. In A. N. Berger, P. Molyneux, & J. O. S. Wilson (Eds.), *The Oxford handbook of banking* (pp. 633–672). Oxford University Press.
De Nicolò, G., Dell'Ariccia, G., Laeven, L., & Valencia, F. (2010). Monetary policy and Bank risk taking. *IMF staff position note* 10/09, International Monetary Fund, Washington, DC, USA.
De Paoli, B., & Paustian, M. (2013). Coordinating monetary and macroprudential policies. *Federal Reserve Bank of New York Staff Reports, 653*.
Delis, M.D., & Brissimis, S.N. (2010). Bank Heterogeneity and Monetary Policy Transmission. ECB Working Paper 1233.
Delis, M. D., & Kouretas, G. P. (2011). Interest rates and Bank risk taking. *Journal of Banking and Finance, 35*(4), 840–855.
Delis, M. D., Hasan, I., & Mylonidis, N. (2017). The risk-taking channel of monetary policy in the U.S.: Evidence from corporate loan data. *Journal of Money, Credit and Banking, 49*(1), 187–213.
Dell'Ariccia, G., Igan, D., & Laeven, L. (2008). Credit booms and lending standards: Evidence from the subprime mortgage market. *IMF Working Paper* 08/106, International Monetary Fund, Washington, DC, USA.
Dell'Ariccia, G., Laeven, L., & Marquez, R. (2010). Monetary policy, leverage, and Bank risk-taking. *IMF Working* Paper 10/276, International Monetary Fund, Washington, DC, USA.
Dell'Ariccia, G., Laeven, L., & Suarez, G. (2013). Bank leverage and monetary Policy's risk-taking channel: Evidence from the United States. *IMF Working Paper* 13/143, International Monetary Fund, Washington, DC, USA.
Detken, C., Gerdesmeier, D., & Roffia, B. (2010). Interlinkages between money, credit and asset prices and their implications for consumer price inflation: Recent empirical work. In L. Papademos & Stark (Eds.), *Enhancing monetary analysis* (pp. 307–327). ECB.
Diamond, D. W., & Rajan, R. G. (2009). The credit crisis: Conjectures about causes and remedies. *American Economic Review, Papers and Proceedings, 99*(2), 606–610.
Drehmann, M., Borio, C., & Tsatsaronis, K. (2012). Characterizing the financial cycle: Don't lose sight of the medium term!. *BIS Working Papers* 380, Bank for International Settlements, Basel, Switzerland.
Duff, A. W. (2014). Central Bank Independence and macroprudential policy: A critical look at the U.S. financial stability framework. *Berkeley Business Law Journal, 11*(4), 182–220.
ECB—European Central Bank. (2021). The role of financial stability considerations in monetary policy and the interaction with macroprudential policy in the euro area. *Occasional Papers*,

No. 272, *ECB Strategy Review*, September, European Central Bank, Frankfurt Am Main, Germany.
Eichengreen, B., Prasad, E., & Rajan, R. (2011). Central Banks Need a Bigger and Bolder Mandate. *Financial Times Oct., 24.*
European Systemic Risk Board. (2011). Recommendation of the ESRB of 22 December 2011 on the Macro-Prudential Mandate of National Authorities. *ESRB* 2011/2.
Fahr, S., Motto, R., Rostagno, M., Smets, F., & Tristani, O. (2013). A monetary policy strategy in good and bad times: Lessons from the recent past. *Economic Policy, 28*(74), 243–288.
Fan, J., & Mancini, L. (2009). Option pricing with model-guided nonparametric methods. *Journal of the American Statistical Association, 104*(488), 1351–1372.
Farhi, E., & Tirole, J. (2009). Leverage and the central Banker's put. *American Economic Review, 99*(2), 589–593.
Farhi, E., & Tirole, J. (2012). Collective moral hazard, maturity mismatch and systemic bailouts. *American Economic Review, 102*(1), 60–93.
Farhi, E., & Werning, I. (2016). A theory of macroprudential policies in the presence of nominal rigidities. *Econometrica, 84*(5), 1645–1704.
Filardo, A. J. (2000). Monetary policy and asset prices. Federal Reserve Bank of Kansas City. *Economic Review, 85*(3), 11–37.
Fisher, I. (1933). The debt-deflation theory of great depressions. *Econometrica, 1*, 337–357.
Fisher, I. (1936). 100% money and the public debt. *Economic Forum*, 406–420.
Freixas, X., Laeven, L., & Peydró, J.-L. (2015). *Systemic risk, crises and macroprudential policy*. MIT Press.
French, K. R., et al. (2010). *The squam lake report: Fixing the financial system*. Princeton University Press.
Gadea Rivas, M. D., Laeven, L. A., & Perez-Quirós, G. (2020). Growth-and-risk trade-off. *ECB Working Paper* No. 2397, European Central Bank, Frankfurt Am Main, Germany, April.
Galati, G., & Moessner, R. (2011). Macroprudential policy: A literature review. *BIS Working Paper* 337, Basel, Switzerland: Bank for International Settlements.
Galati, G., & Moessner, R. (2014). What do we know about the effects of macroprudential policy? *DNB working papers 440*, Amsterdam: Netherlands Central Bank, Research Department.
Gambacorta, L. (2009). Monetary policy and the risk-taking channel. *BIS Quarterly Review*, 43–53.
Gambacorta, L., & Signoretti, F. M. (2014). Should monetary policy lean against the wind? An analysis based on a DSGE model with banking. *Journal of Economic Dynamics & Control, 43*, 146–174.
Gelain, P., Lansing, K., & Mendicino, C. (2012). House prices, credit growth, and excess volatility: Implications for monetary and macroprudential policy. *Norges Bank working paper* 2012/08, Norges Bank, Oslo, Norway.
Gerali, A., Neri, S., Sessa, L., & Signoretti, F. M. (2010). Credit and banking in a DSGE model of the euro area. *Journal of Money, Credit and Banking, 42*(6), 44–70.
Gerlach, S. (2010). Asset prices and monetary policy: Some sceptical observations. In M. Balling, J. M. Berk, & M. O. Strauss-Kahn (Eds.), *The quest for stability: The macro view* (pp. 45–60). SUERF.
Gertler, M. (1988). Financial structure and aggregate activity: An overview. Journal of Money, Credit and Banking, 20(3, Part 2), 559–588.
Gertler, M., & Gilchrist, S. (1993). The role of the credit market imperfections in the monetary transmission mechanism: Arguments and evidence. *Scandinavian Journal of Economics, 95*(1), 43–64.
Gertler, M., & Karadi, P. (2011). A model of unconventional monetary policy. *Journal of Monetary Economics, 58*(1), 17–34.
Gertler, M., & Kiyotaki, N. (2010). Financial intermediation and credit policy in business cycle dynamics. In B. Friedman & M. Woodford (Eds.), *The handbook of monetary economics* (Vol. 3). Elsevier.

Gilchrist, S., & Leahy, J. V. (2002). Monetary policy and asset prices. *Journal of Monetary Economics, 49*(1), 75–97.

Gilchrist, S., & Zakrajšek, E. (2015). Customer markets and financial frictions: Implications for inflation dynamics. Proceedings of the Federal Reserve Bank of Kansas City Jackson Hole Economic Policy Symposium, August 27–29.

Gilchrist, S., Yankov, V., & Zakrajšek, E. (2009). Credit market shocks and economic fluctuations: Evidence from corporate bond and stock markets. *Journal of Monetary Economics, 56*(4), 471–493.

Goodfriend, M. (2004). Monetary policy in the new neoclassical synthesis : A primer. *Economic Quarterly*, Federal Reserve Bank of Richmond, (Sum), 21–45.

Goodhart, C., & Tsomocos, D. (2011). The Mayekawa lecture: The role of default in macroeconomics. *Monetary and Economic Studies*. Bank of Japan IMES, *29*, 49–71.

Greenwald, B., Stiglitz, J. E., & Weiss, A. (1984). Informational imperfections in the capital market and macroeconomic fluctuations. *American Economic Review: Papers and Proceedings, 74*, 194–199.

Grimm, M., Jordà, Ò, Schularick, M., & Taylor, A. M. (2023). Loose monetary policy and financial instability. *NBER working paper*, no. 30958, Cambridge MA: National Bureau for Economic Research.

Hahm, J. H., Mishkin, F.S., Shin, H.S., & Shin, K. (2012). Macroprudential policies in open emerging economies. *NBER Working Paper* 17780, Cambridge, MA: National Bureau of Economic Research.

Hanson, S. G., Kashyap, A. K., & Stein, J. C. (2011). A macroprudential approach to financial regulation. *Journal of Economic Perspectives, 25*(1), 3–28.

Hartmann, P., Hubrich, K., Kremer, M., & Tetlow, R. (2013). *Melting down: Systemic financial instability and the macroeconomy*. European Central Bank.

Heider, F., Saidi, F., & Schepens, G. (2019). Life below zero: Bank lending under negative policy rates. *The Review of Financial Studies, 32*(10), 3728–3761.

Hoerova, M., Monet, C., & Temzelides, T. (2009). Money talks. *Federal Reserve Bank of Philadelphia Working Paper Series* 18.

Holmström, B., & Tirole, J. (1998). Private and public supply of liquidity. *Journal of Political Economy, 106*(1), 1–40.

Hubbard, R. G. (1995). Is there a 'Credit Channel' for monetary policy? *Federal Reserve Bank of St. Louis Review, 77*, 63–74.

Hubrich, K., & Tetlow, R. (2012). Financial stress and economic dynamics: The transmission of crises. *FEDS paper* no. 2012-82, Board of Governors of the Federal Reserve System (April).

Iacoviello, M. (2005). House prices, borrowing constraints and monetary policy in the business cycle. *American Economic Review, 95*(3), 739–764.

Igan, D., & Kang, H. (2011). Do loan-to-value and debt-to-income limits work? Evidence from Korea, *IMF working paper* 297, Washington, DC: International Monetary Fund.

Ikeda, D. (2022). Monetary policy, inflation and rational bubbles. *Journal of Money, Credit and Banking, 54*(6), 1569–1603.

IMF—International Monetary Fund. (2011). *Macroprudential Policy: an organizing framework*. International Monetary Fund, Washington DC., USA.

IMF—International Monetary Fund. (2013). Key aspects of macroprudential policies. IMF Policy Paper, Washington, DC: International Monetary Fund.

IMF—International Monetary Fund. (2014). Staff guidance note on macroprudential policy. IMF Policy Paper, Washington, DC: International Monetary Fund.

IMF—International Monetary Fund (2015). Monetary policy and financial stability. IMF *Staff Report*, International Monetary Fund, Washington, DC.

Ioannidou, V., Ongena, S., & Peydró, J. L. (2009). Monetary policy, risk taking and pricing: Evidence from a quasi-natural experiment. European Banking Center Discussion Paper 2009-04S.

Jarrow, R. A., & Kwok, S. S. (2021). Inferring financial bubbles from option data. *Journal of Applied Econometrics, 36*(7), 1013–1046.
Jarrow, R. A., Kchia, Y., & Protter, P. (2011a). How to detect an asset bubble. *SIAM Journal of Financial Mathematics, 2*, 839–865.
Jarrow, R. A., Kchia, Y., & Protter, P. (2011b). Is there a bubble in LinkedIn's stock price? *Journal of Portfolio Management, 38*(1), 125–130.
Jiménez, G., Ongena, S., Peydró, J. -L., & Saurina, J. (2008). Hazardous times for monetary policy: What do twenty-three million bank loans say about the effects of monetary policy on credit risk-taking?. Bank of Spain, Working Paper, No. 0833.
Jimenez, G., Ongena, S., Peydró, J.-S., & Saurina, J. (2014). Hazardous times for monetary policy: What do twenty-three million Bank loans say about the effects of monetary policy on credit risk-taking? *Econometrica, 82*(2), 463–505.
Jimenez, G., Ongena, S., Peydro-Alcalde, J. L., & Saurina, J. (2007). Hazardous times for monetary policy: What do twenty-three million bank loans say about the effects of monetary policy on credit risk? *CEPR discussion paper series* 6514, Centre for Economic Policy Research, London, UK.
Kamber, G., Karagedikli, O., & Smith, C. (2015). Applying an inflation targeting lens to macroprudential policy 'Institutions'. *Federal Reserve Bank of New Zealand discussion paper* DP2015/04.
Kannan, P., Rabanal, P., & Scott, A. (2012). Monetary and macroprudential policy rules in a model with house price booms. *B.E. Journal of Macroeconomics*, Contributions, *12*(1).
Kashyap, A. K., & Stein, J. C. (1994). Monetary policy and bank lending. In N. G. Mankiw (Ed.), *Monetary policy* (pp. 221–256). University of Chicago Press.
Kashyap, A. K., & Stein, J. C. (1997). The role of banks in monetary policy: A survey with implications for the European Monetary Union. Federal Reserve Bank of Chicago. *Economic Perspectives, 21*, 2–19.
Kashyap, A. K., & Stein, J. C. (2023). Monetary policy when the central Bank shapes financial-market sentiment. *Journal of Economic Perspectives, 37*(1), 53–76.
Keister, T. (2016). Bailouts and Financial Fragility. *The Review of Economic Studies, 83*(2 (295)), 704–736.
Kitsul, Y., & Wright, J. H. (2013). The economics of options-implied inflation probability density functions. *Journal of Financial Economics, 110*(3), 696–711.
Kokores, I. T. (2022). *Monetary policy and financial stability: Challenges before and after the global financial crisis*. Cambridge Scholars Publishing.
Kokores, I. T., & Kanas, A. (2021). Monetary policy and systemic risk: U.S. evidence. In I. T. Kokores, P. Pantelidis, T. Pelagidis, & D. Yannelis (Eds.), *Money, trade and finance: Recent trends and methodological issues* (pp. 131–140). Palgrave Macmillan.
Laeven, L., Maddaloni, A., & Mendicino, C. (2022). Monetary policy, macroprudential policy and financial stability. ECB Discussion Paper No 2647, European Central Bank, Frankfurt Am Main, Germany.
Lagarde, C. (2020). The monetary policy strategy review: some preliminary considerations. *Speech* at the "ECB and Its Watchers XXI" (Vol. 30) conference organized by the European Central Bank, Frankfurt am Main (Vol. 30).
Lagarde, C. (2023). Press Conference on ECB Monetary Policy Statement, European Central Bank, Frankfurt am Main, March 16.
Lambertini, C., Mendicino, M., & Punzi, T. (2011). Leaning against boom-bust cycles in credit and housing prices. Banco de Portugal Working Paper 8.
Lim, C.H., Krznar, I., Lipinsky, F., Otani, A., & Wu, X. (2013). The macroprudential framework: Policy responsiveness and institutional arrangements. *IMF working papers* 166, Washington, DC: International Monetary Fund, 13, i.
Ljungqvist, L. (2008). Lucas critique. In N. Durlauf & L. E. Blume (Eds.), *New Palgrave dictionary* (2nd ed.).

Loisel, O., Pommeret, A., & Portier, F. (2012). Monetary policy and herd behavior: Leaning against bubbles. Banque de France Working Paper 412.

Lorenzoni, G. (2008). Inefficient credit booms. *Review of Economic Studies, 75*(3), 809–833.

Lu, J., & Qu, Z. (2021). Sieve estimation of option-implied state price density. *Journal of Econometrics, 224*(1), 88–112.

Maddaloni, A., & Peydró, J.-L. (2011). Bank risk-taking, securitization, supervision, and low interest rates: Evidence from the euro-area and the U.S. lending standards. *The Review of Financial Studies, 24*(6), 2121–2165.

Malherbe, F. (2020). Optimal capital requirements over the business and financial cycles. *American Economic Journal: Macroeconomics, 12*(3), 139–174.

Martin, A., & Ventura, J. (2018). The macroeconomics of rational bubbles: A user's guide. *NBER working paper* 24234, National Bureau of Economic Research, Cambridge, MA.

Martinez-Miera, D., & Suarez, J. (2014). *A macroeconomic model of endogenous systemic risk taking*. CEMFI.

Meh, C., & Moran, K. (2010). The role of Bank capital in the propagation of shocks. *Journal of Economic Dynamics and Control, 34*, 555–576.

Miao, J. (2014). Introduction to the economic theory of bubbles. *Journal of Mathematical Economics, 53*, 130–136.

Mishkin, F. S. (2009). The financial crisis and the Federal Reserve. *NBER Macro Annual*, 495–508.

Mishkin, F. S. (2011a). Monetary policy strategy: Lessons from the crisis. In M. Jarociñki, F. Smets, & C. Thimann (Eds.), *Approaches to monetary policy revisited—lessons from the crisis, sixth ECB central banking conference proceedings* (pp. 67–118).

Mishkin, F. S. (2011b). Over the cliff: From the subprime to the global financial crisis. *Journal of Economic Perspectives, 25*(1), 49–70.

Mishkin, F. S. (2014). Macrorpudential and monetary policies. In D. D. Evanoff, C. Holthausen, G. G. Kaufman, & M. Kremer (Eds.), *The role of central banks in financial stability: How has it changed?. 30th world scientific studies in international economics* (pp. 409–422). World Scientific Publishing.

Myers, S. C., & Majluf, N. S. (1984). Corporate financing and investment decisions when firms have information that investors do not have. *Journal of Financial Economics, 13*, 187–221.

Nier, E. W., Osiński, J., Jácome, L. I., & Madrid, P. (2011). Towards effective macroprudential policy frameworks: An assessment of stylized institutions. *International monetary fund working paper* 250.

Oda, N., & Okina, K. (2001). Further monetary easing policies under the non-negativity constraints of nominal interest rates: Summary of the discussion based on Japan's experience. Bank of Japan, Institute of Monetary and Economic Studies. *Monetary and Economic Studies (special edition), 19*(S-1), 323–360.

Paligorova, T., & Santos, J. (2012). When is it less costly for risky firms to borrow? Evidence from the bank risk-taking channel of monetary policy. *Bank of Canada working paper* 2012-10.

Phillips, P. C. B., Shi, S., & Yu, J. (2015a). Testing for multiple bubbles: Historical episodes of irrational exuberance and collapse in the S&P 500. *International Economic Review, 56*(4), 1043–1077.

Phillips, P. C. B., Shi, S., & Yu, J. (2015b). Testing for multiple bubbles: Limit theory of real-time detectors. *International Economic Review, 56*(4), 1079–1133.

Pill, H. (2013). Central banking after the crisis: Challenges for the ECB. In R. Baldwin & L. Reichlin (Eds.), *Is inflation targeting dead?* VoxEU e-book.

Posen, A. S. (2009). Finding the right tool for dealing with asset price booms. Speech to the MPR Monetary Policy and the Markets Conference, London, December 1.

Posen, A. S. (2023). Discussion on Yi Gang—Governor of the People's Bank of China presentation "China's Monetary Policy: Practice and Rationale", Peterson Institute for International Economics Macro Week 2023, Washington, DC, USA, April 15.

Powell, J. H. (2020). Index, F.M.V.E., & Room, F.T. New economic challenges and the Fed's monetary policy review, Federal Reserve Chair Jerome H. Powell, At 'Navigating The Decade

Ahead: Implications For Monetary Policy', an economic policy symposium sponsored by the Federal Reserve Bank of Kansas City, Jackson Hole, Wyoming.
Quint, D., & Rabanal, P. (2014). Monetary and macroprudential policy in an estimated DSGE model of the euro area. *International Journal of Central Banking, 10*(2), 169–236.
Rajan, R. G. (2005). Has financial development made the world riskier? The Greenspan era: Lessons for the future, proceedings of the Federal Reserve Bank of Kansas City Economic Symposium (pp. 313–369), Wyoming: Jackson Hole, August 25–27.
Rajan, R. G. (2006). Has finance made the world riskier? *European Financial Management, 12*(4), 499–533.
Ramey, V. (1993). How important is the credit channel in the transmission of monetary policy? *Carnegie-Rochester Conference Series on Public Policy, 39*, 1–45.
Rogoff, K. S. (1985). The optimal degree of commitment to an intermediate monetary target. *Quarterly Journal of Economics, 100*(4), 1169–1189.
Santos, M. S., & Woodford, M. (1997). Rational asset pricing bubbles. *Econometrica, 65*(1), 19–58.
Shiller, R. J. (2000). *Irrational exuberance*. Princeton University Press.
Shiryaev, A. N., Zhitlukhin, M. V., & Ziemba, W. T. (2014). When to sell apple and the NASDAQ? Trading bubbles with a stochastic disorder model. *Journal of Portfolio Management, 40*(2), 54–63.
Shiryaev, A. N., Zhitlukhin, M. V., & Ziemba, W. T. (2015). Land and stock bubbles, crashes and exit strategies in Japan circa 1990 and in 2013. *Quantitative Finance, 15*(9), 1449–1469.
Smets, F. (2014). Financial stability and monetary policy stability: How closely interlinked? *International Journal of Central Banking, 10*(2), 263–300.
Smets, F., & Wouters, R. (2003). An estimated stochastic general equilibrium model of the euro area. *Journal of the European Economic Association, 1*, 1123–1175.
Song, Z., & Xiu, D. (2016). A tale of two option markets: Pricing kernels and volatility risk. *Journal of Econometrics, 190*(1), 176–196.
Stein, J. C. (2012). Monetary policy as financial stability regulation. *Quarterly Journal of Economics, 127*(1), 57–95.
Summers, L. H. (2014). U.S. Economic Prospects: Secular stagnation, hysteresis, and the zero lower bound. Keynote address at the NABE policy conference, National Association for Business Economics, February 24, 2014. *Business Economics, 49*(2), 65–73.
Surti, J. (2021). Risk and return: The search for yield. *Finance & Development* (pp. 48–49), Washington, DC: IMF—International Monetary Fund.
Svensson, L. E. O. (2012). The relation between monetary policy and financial stability policy. *International Journal of Central Banking, 8*(S1), 293–295.
Svensson, L. E. O. (2013). Some lessons from six years of practical inflation targeting. Proceedings Riksbank conference 'Two Decades of Inflation Targeting: Main Lessons and Remaining Challenges', Stockholm, Sweden, June 3.
Svensson, L. E. O. (2015a). Forward guidance. *International Journal of Central Banking, 11*(S1), 19–64.
Svensson, L. E. O. (2015b). Inflation targeting and leaning against the wind. In South African Reserve Bank (Ed.), *Fourteen years of inflation targeting in South Africa and the challenge of a changing mandate: South African Reserve Bank conference proceedings*. South African Reserve Bank.
Taylor, J. B. (2007). Housing and monetary policy. In *Housing, housing finance and monetary policy* (pp. 463–476). Federal Reserve Bank of Kansas City.
Tinbergen, J. (1939). Business cycles in the United States of America: 1919–1932. Statistical testing of business cycle theories, vol 2. Geneva, Switzerland: League of Nations.
Tirole, J. (1985). Asset bubbles and overlapping generations. *Econometrica, 53*(6), 1499–1552.
Trichet, J. C. (2005). Asset price bubbles and monetary policy. *MAS Lecture*.
Trichet, J. C. (2011). Reflections on the nature of monetary policy non-standard measures and finance theory. In M. Jarociński, F. Smets, & C. Thimann (Eds.), *Approaches to monetary policy revisited: Lessons from the crisis* (pp. 12–22). European Central Bank.

Turner, P. (2010). *Central Banks and the Financial Crisis* (*Bank for International Settlements Paper* No 51, pp. 21-25). Bank for International Settlements.

Ueda, K., & Valencia, F. (2012). Central Bank Independence and macro-prudential regulation. *IMF Working Paper* 12/101, Washington, DC: International Monetary Fund.

Van der Ghote, A. (2021). Interactions and coordination between monetary and macroprudential policies. *American Economic Journal: Macroeconomics, 13*(1), 1–34.

Viñals, J. (2013). *Making macroprudential policy work.* Speech given at the Brookings Institution.

Whelan, K. (2013). A broader mandate: Why inflation targeting is inadequate. In R. Baldwin & L. Reichlin (Eds.), *Is inflation targeting dead?* VoxEU e-book.

Wilson, L., & Wu, Y. W. (2010). Common (stock) sense about risk-shifting and bank bailouts. *Financial Markets and Portfolio Management, 24*(1), 3–29.

Wood, J. H. (2015). *Central banking in a democracy: The Federal Reserve and its alternatives* (Routledge explorations in economic history). Routledge.

Woodford, M. (2011a). Monetary policy and financial stability. In *Columbia University working paper presented at the 2011 NBER Summer Institute.*

Woodford, M. (2011b). Financial intermediation and macroeconomic analysis. *Journal of Economic Perspectives, 24*(4), 21–44.

Woodford, M. (2012). Inflation targeting and financial stability. *Sveriges Riksbank Economic Review, 1*, 7–32.

Yatchew, A., & Härdle, W. (2006). Nonparametric state price density estimation using constrained least squares and the bootstrap. *Journal of Econometrics, 133*(2), 579–599.

Yi, G. (2023). Governor of the People's Bank of China *Speech* on "China's Monetary Policy: Practice and Rationale", at the Peterson Institute for International Economics Macro Week 2023, Washington, DC: Peterson Institute for International Economics, April 15.

Chapter 4
In Search for a New Monetary Policy Framework

4.1 Introduction

It is worth to refer here that as Mishkin (2011a) stresses:

> The bad news is that we have just been through a once-in-a-century credit tsunami that has had a devastating impact on the economy, one that will last for years to come. The good news is that macro/monetary economists and central bankers do not have to go back to the drawing board and throw out all that they have learned over the last forty years. Much of the science of monetary policy remains intact. The case for the basic monetary policy strategy, which for want of a better name I have called flexible inflation targeting, is still as strong as ever, and in some ways more so. (p. 103)

More specifically, the global financial crisis (GFC) has prompted a significant reconsideration of the fundamental framework for monetary policy strategy. It is now widely acknowledged that the financial sector has a significant impact on the overall macroeconomy, which can cause nonlinear effects. As a result, the linear quadratic framework for monetary policy is insufficient when addressing financial disruptions. Instead, there is now a stronger case for a risk management approach that considers the possibility of tail risks leading to adverse outcomes for the economy. Another lesson learned is that it is preferable for monetary policy to lean against credit bubbles rather than merely cleaning up after a bubble has burst, though this is not an easy task. Research will focus on how to monitor credit conditions effectively to make informed decisions regarding the use of monetary policy to limit excessive risk.

Since the advent of the GFC, the interdependence between the financial sector and the overall economy has been highlighted, emphasizing the close connection between monetary policy and financial stability policy. The financial crisis has resulted in significant lessons for macroeconomic and financial analysis, and the current situation continues to be challenging. Policy decisions are crucial for the well-being of our economies and citizens. These decisions rely heavily on two crucial factors in the economic field: the credibility of central banks and

I. T. Kokores, *Monetary Policy in Interdependent Economies*, Financial and Monetary Policy Studies 55, https://doi.org/10.1007/978-3-031-41958-4_4

governments. The credibility of central banks is based on their ability to achieve price stability over the medium term according to their definition of it, which solidly anchors inflation expectations. On the other hand, the credibility of governments is determined by their ability to maintain and strengthen their creditworthiness, which requires, among other things, the consolidation of public finances, which contributes to sustainable growth in the long run (Trichet, 2011, p. 20).

As Mishkin (2011a, 2011b, p. 104) points out, there is one other piece of good news that has emerged from the GFC, pertaining to the field of macroeconomics/ monetary economics which has become considerably more exciting. The current situation has presented a new research agenda that will keep experts in the field occupied for a long time. Furthermore, the work of central bankers has become more interesting as they must now consider a broader range of policy issues than before. While this may be challenging, it makes central banking a more exciting profession.

4.2 The New Monetary Framework

The question of whether the policy actions of monetary authorities have an impact on economic activity is a valid one. While time and resources are expended in implementing such policies, it is essential to evaluate their effectiveness. To answer this question, it is useful to understand how monetary authorities typically influence economic activity in discretionary, fiat currency regimes. In most countries, a nation's money supply consists of two components: paper currency and deposits at banking organizations. While paper currency was once the larger component, deposits at banks have come to dominate in recent years. Banks' deposits are subject to minimum reserve requirements, and the total deposit liabilities of banks make up a multiple of reserve balances (which includes vault cash and deposits at the central bank). As a result, the banking system as a whole is "reserve-constrained," meaning that there is a limit to the total deposits that individuals and businesses can hold unless the central bank provides additional reserves. Therefore, if the central bank fails to increase the total supply of reserves available to private banks while currency outstanding increases, there will be a corresponding reduction in deposit money. Historically, these reserve constraints have given monetary authorities the power to control a nation's money supply and, in turn, affect economic activity, for better or worse. In accordance with traditional theory, the transmission mechanism works as follows:

The traditional interest rate or money perspective of monetary policy transmission concentrates on the liability side of bank balance sheets. The important role of banks in this transmission mechanism comes from the reserve requirement limitations that banks face. Since banks usually do not keep considerable extra reserves, the reserve requirement limitation is usually considered to be binding at all times. Thus, changes in monetary policy that affect the amount of outside money cause changes in the quantity of inside money in the form of reservable deposits that can be generated by the banking system. When the monetary authority takes open market operations to tighten monetary policy (by selling securities), the banking industry experiences a decrease in reserves. Then, the fractional reserve system compels banks (as a whole) to reduce reservable deposits to meet the reserve requirement. Therefore, this exogenous shock restricts bank behavior. To encourage households to hold fewer reservable deposits (transaction accounts), interest rates on other deposits and non-deposit alternatives must increase. That is, since the supply of transaction deposits has decreased relative to that of alternative assets, interest rates on these alternative assets will have to rise to clear the market for transaction deposits. When the increase in short-term interest rates is transmitted to longer-term interest rates, aggregate demand drops.

4.3 The Role of Banks in Monetary Policy: An Overview

The conventional theory of monetary policy has a major limitation, in that it is based on a simplistic two-asset model that fails to take into account the growing number of financial assets that behave like checking accounts but are not under the control of the central bank. These non-reservable transaction-type accounts (mutual funds with check writing privileges being an early example) are becoming more widespread, reducing the relevance of the central bank's power over currency and transaction deposits in determining interest rates (Kashyap & Stein, 1997). This does not mean that the central bank will be unable to affect interest rates, but it suggests that the traditional model is becoming increasingly less valid. In fact, given the limitations of the traditional monetary policy theory, a strand of research has emerged that includes three key assets: money, bonds, and bank loans. Unlike the traditional theory, this new approach considers the role of banks not only as deposit creators but also as *lenders*. The focus is on the lending response of banks to changes in monetary policy, rendering the definition of money in this model less important. In order for this mechanism to be effective, it is necessary that there is no perfect substitute for bank loans in terms of financing a fraction of spending. Based on this assumption, the sensitivity of bank loan supply to monetary policy and the dependence of some spending on bank lending generate several predictions about how monetary policy will operate.

The literature suggests that an important prediction of the three-asset model is that borrowers with poor credit ratings are more dependent on banks for funding. Such borrowers face higher costs to raise funds from third parties and are sensitive to the composition of their liabilities. Banks have an advantage in lending to these borrowers because they can specialize in gathering information to determine creditworthiness and maintain relationships with their customers. As demonstrated in Diamond (1984), banks are more apt to make more efficient prudent lending decisions than lenders who do not have access to such information. However, banks that lend to relatively unknown borrowers have collections of assets that are difficult to value, making it difficult for individual investors to assess the bank's existing assets. This may create an adverse selection problem, where some banks prefer to make fewer loans than to pay the rates required to attract funds. Deposit insurance can help overcome this problem by allowing banks to issue insured deposits, which do not require account holders to worry about the bank's lending decisions. To fund insured deposits, banks typically must allow the deposit guarantee provider to oversee their lending decisions and put aside reserves against the insured deposits. This link between deposit insurance and reserve requirements gives the monetary authorities a powerful lever. The assumption of imperfect price adjustment tends to underpin the pertinent literature (for seminal accounts, see Bernanke & Gertler, 1995; Cecchetti, 1995; Hubbard, 1995; Stein, 1995; Kashyap & Stein, 1994, 1997, 2000).

The conventional textbook model of monetary policy overlooks an important consequence of a reduction in reserves: it forces banks to resort to more expensive forms of financing. After the reserve outflow, there is a decrease in the number of loans that banks can offer (because of the extra premium that banks will have to pay to bring in noninsured deposits), potentially causing a drop in spending levels. To hedge against this risk, banks and firms hold buffer stocks of liquid assets, but these can be costly and may not fully offset the impact of contractionary monetary policy. Banks typically prefer making loans instead of holding securities, which offer returns that are similar to the rates they pay on deposits. Furthermore, holding these types of assets is inefficient due to double taxation on the bank's shareholders, as is the case for any equity financed corporation.

To summarize, the traditional theory of monetary policy focuses on households' preference for money over other assets, while the newer theory emphasizes the crucial role of the banking sector in the monetary policy transmission. Two factors are important in determining how monetary policy works: firstly, how much banks rely on reservable deposits for financing and adjust their loan schedules when there are changes in bank reserves and, secondly, how dependent certain borrowers are on banks and are unable to offset changes in bank loan supply. Extensive literature assesses this bank-centric stand on the theory of the transmission of monetary policy.[1] Early proponents of this view accept that these findings strongly support the view that "banks play an important role in the transmission of monetary policy ... [and] the factors that determine the significance of this role are the degree of bank dependence on the part of firms and consumers and the ability of banks to offset

[1] Although relatively little of this research has been done using European data, the existing results suggest there may be powerful effects in Europe; see Borio (1996) and Berran et al. (1996) for two exceptions. The work (which mostly focuses on the United States) can be summarized by the following picture of monetary policy transmission. When the Federal Reserve tightens policy, aggregate lending by banks gradually slows down, and there is a surge in nonbank financing, such as commercial paper. When this substitution of financing is taking place, aggregate investment is reduced by more than would be predicted solely on the basis of rising interest rates. Small firms that do not have significant buffer cash holdings are most likely to trim investment (particularly inventory investment) around the periods of tight money. Similarly, small banks seem more prone than large banks to reduce their lending, with the effect greatest for small banks with relatively low buffer stocks of securities at the time of the tightening (Kashyap & Stein, 1997, pp. 4–5).

monetary-policy-induced deposit outflows" (Kashyap & Stein, 1997, p. 8, 13). Based on research conducted across different countries and time periods, there is evidence to suggest that when monetary policy is restrictive, banks tend to reduce their supply of loans, and as a result, spending also decreases. This indicates that the effects of monetary policy extend beyond the standard interest rate effects and can have significant real consequences; for detailed reviews of this evidence, see Kashyap and Stein (2000) and also Peek and Roesengren (2010).

4.4 The Role of Banks in the Transmission of Monetary Policy

Over the past two decades, both theoretical and empirical research have underscored the crucial role played by banks in the transmission of monetary policy. This body of work has identified the impact of changes in bank assets, in addition to the conventional interest rate channel on the liability side of bank balance sheets, in response to monetary policy shocks. The empirical evidence strongly supports the notion that banks facing liquidity constraints and borrowers dependent on bank loans can suffer adverse effects when monetary policy is tightened. Furthermore, the research suggests that the bank lending channel is particularly important in international settings, particularly in countries where financial markets are less accessible to banks and firms. Additionally, a significant amount of research indicates that during periods of credit crunches, the bank lending channel may not operate as expected, necessitating more substantial regulatory and policy interventions in monetary policy instruments to achieve the desired impact on aggregate demand.

Furthermore, evidence from the international context suggests that banks with limited capital can impede the effectiveness of monetary policy, compared to banks without such constraints. *Looking forward*, the bank lending channel could become more significant as it may become more challenging to access off-balance sheet and nonbank financing, given the credit and liquidity shocks during the GFC and the crises that followed. As the government and institutional support for banks and credit provision remains extensive, Peek and Roesengren (2010) argued in the aftermath of the GFC that "the extent of the recent problems indicates that banks are likely to continue to play an important, although changing, role as financial markets continue to evolve" (p. 275). Yet, Jordan (2016) claims that the conventional understanding is no longer valid and "[since] the commercial banking system has ceased to be reserve constrained, … *monetary authority actions to change the size of the central bank balance sheet do not affect the nation's money supply*" (p. 368). Presently, banks are restricted not by the quantity of reserves furnished by central banks but rather by the availability of earning assets accessible to them. Within the confines of capital limitations, it is the supply of these earning assets that determines the total deposit liabilities of banks.

This shift poses several significant implications. Brunner and Meltzer (1972, p. 973) suggested that even though inflation or deflation may occur without an alteration in the monetary base, most events of inflation were in fact caused by an expansion of the monetary base. That conclusion indicated that the banking system was reserve-constrained, meaning that the money stock could not increase without an expansion in the central bank's balance sheet. However, given the existence of huge excess reserves in today's banking system, the model employed by Brunner and Meltzer implies that the creation of money is now dependent on the demand for loans and the availability of securities that banks can invest in. Jordan (2016) further remarks that the current version of the intermediate monetary theory textbook (which has not been written yet) will no longer suggest that the monetary authorities control the "money supply" and estimate the "money demand" to prevent inflation caused by an oversupply or a recession caused by a shortage. This theoretical framework has currently been rendered dysfunctional in such a way that monetary authorities cannot take actions that target the central bank balance sheet to impact overall economic activity.

4.4.1 Interest Rates and Monetary Stimulus

The intermediate-level course on monetary theory also presents an alternative theoretical approach to influencing the economy, which involves manipulating *nominal* market interest rates. The fundamental concept is that lower interest rates will encourage people to borrow more for consumption and investment, while higher interest rates will discourage borrowing for such purposes. The primary economic debate and empirical analysis have focused on whether individuals fully comprehend the inflation premium of nominal interest rates, as well as the pretax and posttax interest costs they will incur. The economic argument suggests that if people factor in anticipated inflation and taxation when considering interest rates, the actual market interest rates will be higher than the "real" interest rates that influence consumer and investor decisions.[2]

Despite theoretical arguments and evidence from past experiences, recent near-zero interest rates have not been correlated with domestic household consumption or

[2] Jordan (2016, p. 369) highlights that the central bank's zero interest rate policy (ZIRP) is effective by reducing bond yields and directing investors toward equities to achieve higher returns. This, in turn, leads to higher valuations in equity markets, resulting in a "wealth effect" where stockholders increase consumption spending. The idea is that increased consumption demand can boost investor confidence, leading to new projects and capacity expansions. However, this model only works in a closed economy. In an open, global economic system, it is not reasonable to expect that increased investment and output will be domestic, even if aggregate consumer spending responds to stock prices. This is particularly true in the presence of tax and regulatory policies hostile to capital formation. Policymaker would essentially refrain from arguing that the best way to promote prosperity via monetary policy is to increase the trade deficit ever as imports outpace export growth.

domestic private sector investment. Instead, the low interest rate environment may have actually decreased the demand for bank credit and increased demand for earning assets by nonbank lenders such as mutual funds, pension funds, and insurance companies (Jordan, 2014). This has resulted in slower growth of bank liabilities, namely, demand deposits. Therefore, the idea that low interest rates are expansionary conflicts with the notion that slow money growth is contractionary in terms of the channels through which monetary authorities influence the economy.

4.4.2 Central Banks and Economic Growth

According to the propositions of the "market monetarists" (a term coined by Christensen, 2011), central banks should focus on achieving a target growth rate for *nominal* GDP—namely, the size of the local economy in noninflation-adjusted local currency—to achieve their goals for real economic growth and inflation (Sumner, 2009; Lee, 2011). However, critics of this approach considered it unrealistic as the monetary policy tools available to central banks that are mandated inflation-targeters tend to be limited. Antecedent to the era of inflation-targeting interest rate policy, central banks had a range of tools at their disposal, including reserve requirements, interest ceilings, discount rates, and open market operations, but until the era on post-GFC implementation of unconventional monetary policy measures, central banks lacked effective tools to influence the pace of *nominal* GDP growth (see, for example, Taylor, 2016). Therefore, monetary authorities are viewed as desolate of any ability to give instructions to their trading desk to achieve faster or slower growth of nominal GDP. "Market monetarists" are also skeptical of the use of unconventional monetary policy tools as they are too discretionary by nature yet claim that policies such as quantitative easing, charging instead of paying interest on excess bank reserves, and having the central bank publicly commit to nominal income targets may have catered for an exit from the liquidity trap in the aftermath of the GFC when policy rates reached their zero lower bound (Sumner, 2011).

The concept behind both monetary and fiscal stimuli is that government actions aimed at "stimulating demand" will lead to economic growth by encouraging consumers to spend and businesses to invest. However, this is not actually how growth happens. Growth—in terms of rising standards of living—occur when opportunities for real cost reductions arise, often through *innovation* that lowers information and transactions costs. In these cases, people are naturally more prone to undertake the now-lower-priced activity, without the need for government to "promote demand." The insatiable nature of "wants" remains, and people will naturally increase consumption if the cost of a good or service decreases, however, as, for example, Taylor (2016) stresses the idea that government should stimulate demand is at best outdated.

4.4.3 *Monetary Policy and the Politics of Wealth Sharing*[3]

Reducing obstacles that hinder economic progress is crucial, and these obstacles can be both natural (such as information and transaction costs) and artificial. In contemporary societies, many of these artificial barriers are created by collusion between private interests and government officials who seek to protect their own interests and obtain campaign contributions. This collusion leads to the establishment and maintenance of barriers that prevent potential competitors from entering the market, resulting in fewer innovations, new businesses, and cost reductions in many industries. The increase in licensing and certification requirements during the latter half of the twentieth century has further exacerbated this issue.

Political parties have engaged in a competition to win voters by offering them a share of someone else's earnings, either immediately or at a later time. As a consequence, even tax systems that are highly efficient and effective will eventually fail to generate enough revenue to meet all of these promises, forcing politicians to make difficult choices. Modern central banks have contributed to this problem rather than providing a lasting solution (Jordan, 2016, p. 371).[4] As a result of political promises to distribute other people's money, the tax system became insufficient to meet those promises. To make up for the shortfall, central banks were forced to create new money, which led to inflation and a decrease in the value of the currency. Ultimately, voters who exchanged their votes for nominal money units were deceived because the money they received did not have the same purchasing power as before. This occurred because of a corrupt alliance between fiscal and monetary authorities influenced by the political cycle. Governments issue bonds and make "entitlement" promises to voters that are both reliant on future tax collections. Historical patterns indicate that these claims on the tax system created by the government tend to expand and surpass potential future tax revenues.

Jordan (2016) further recognizes *the recent experience of Greece to be significantly instructive.* Irrespective of a booming economy during the 1950s and 1960s, the Greek tax system did not collect enough revenue to fund all the promises

[3]This section draws significantly from Jordan (2016), pp. 370–372.

[4]During the 1960s in the United States, tax revenues had started to be outrun at a significantly accelerating rate promises made to individuals and households, in addition to rising government expenditures for the military. As Jordan (2016) highlights, instead of reining in spending, the Johnson administration and then the Nixon administration cut the US central bank loose from its specie anchor in three steps: (1) the "London Gold Pool" was suspended; (2) the "gold window" was closed, while the "gold cover" of US currency was removed by the Congress; and (3) the commitment to redeem foreign-held dollars for gold was eliminated in 1973. These steps striped any institutionalized discipline in the creation of new currency and bank reserves from the central bank and in turn removed any need for fiscal discipline. The concomitant result was accelerating inflation, which in fact constitutes a form of "taxation", that has been favored by politicians as an (abominate) law needs not to be passed to impose it. In this respect, the US experience in the 1960s and 1970s was no different from that of other developed and developing countries with central banks and a monopoly national currency (for a detailed argumentative account, see Wood, 2009, pp. 67–80).

politicians were making to voters. This led to a devaluation of the national currency in the early 1970s, leading to a path of consecutive depreciations for the next couple of decades until the country (already a member of the then European Economic Community since January 1, 1981) entered the European common currency area on January 1, 2001. Jordan (2016) further remarks that "*Once Greek politicians realized they could sell euro-denominated bonds to foreign investors in order to fund the promises they had made to voters, a frenzy of vote buying led to a national debt much larger than any tax system could service* [emphasis added]. Because inflation and devaluation were not possible once the Greek central bank was deprived of its power to create new money, default on the foreign-owned Greek government bonds became unavoidable" (p. 372). He further, highlights that ironically, the absence of a national currency, let alone the central bank's ability to issue more of it, in the case of Greece enabled politicians to assume extensive amounts of public debt much larger than had previously been possible. With the benefit of hindsight, we may recognize that this practice has been fuelled by the fact that foreign buyers of Greek euro bonds were confident that the central bank in charge of the issuing of euros, the European Central Bank, would be pressured by governments of lender countries in the euro area to create the additional euros needed by the Greek fiscal authority to make the interest payments to the non-Greek banks and other lenders that owned the Greek debt. Certainly, in fact, the holders of Greek government bonds do not care whether the euros necessary to pay them back with interest come from the ECB or loans from other governments to the Greek government. Nevertheless, some of those other countries had very large debts of their own, rendering as highly problematic the issue of even more bonds in order to finance loans to the Greek government. The moral of this story is that effective discipline in the fiscal decisions made by politicians cannot and will not be achieved as long as there are central banks empowered to create more of the money that politicians have promised to deliver.

Despite the negative consequences of central banking and monopoly currency, politicians continue to make guised promises to potential voters that, if elected or reelected, they will transfer taxpayers' money to their supporters. In many democratic nations, the "politics of wealth sharing" has overtaken the "politics of wealth creation." This is because elected representatives have little influence over the rate at which an economy generates wealth. It is not credible for a politician to promise that newly created national wealth will benefit any particular voter or group of voters (Jordan, 2016, p. 372). However, a single elected representative can facilitate the transfer of existing wealth to specific voters or constituents. A coalition or political party of politicians can facilitate this transfer on a larger scale. When the total amount of promises made by politicians exceeds the available funds for redistribution, no group of recipients will willingly abandon their entitlements to other people's money. While there may be some politicians who campaign on reducing certain beneficiary groups' payments from the government, they are rarely successful in being elected or reelected. Even if they do win, they often lack the power to implement their agenda while in office.

4.4.4 Learning and Unlearning from Experience[5]

The results of the past almost five decades of using discretionary monetary policies have been mixed. [6] As politicians became more experienced in using mandates and government guarantees to win voters' support, they believed it was their responsibility to promote home ownership. Thus, credit standards for obtaining mortgages were lowered, and government agencies guaranteed that investors in securities backed by home mortgages would not suffer losses. The main goal was to promote home ownership, while any wealth effects from rising house prices were considered a secondary objective. However, the phenomenon of "mortgage equity withdrawals," which involved refinancing as house prices increased, allowed households to spend trillions of dollars on consumption, driving the share of national output devoted to consumption spending to record levels.

Normally, when house prices collapse, there is usually a decrease in the consumption share of GDP. However, in this case, the government intervened and issued a large amount of debt in order to maintain demand at the same level as during the "bubblenomics" period. This was done without much concern for fiscal discipline and led to a reversal of decades of reducing the national debt relative to the economy's productivity. This decoupling of fiscal and monetary policies raised concerns that the "fiscal dominance hypothesis" had returned, which suggests that in a world where fiat currency is not anchored, monetary policy is ultimately a fiscal instrument.

Because the political process was unable to quickly reintroduce fiscal responsibility and correct the mistakes of 2008–2009, many believed that it was just a matter of time before monetary policy would be subordinated to fiscal policy, resulting in inflationary taxation. Meanwhile, those in charge of monetary policy began to

---

[5]This section draws heavily from Jordan (2016, pp. 373–383).

[6]*The first decade* during the 1960s saw soaring inflation and concurrent increases in unemployment; at the time, policymakers were left barren of a trade-off between inflation and unemployment (Phillips, 1958) to exploit, contrary to widespread economic opinion at that time. As policymakers, both politicians and central bankers, were facing this hugely adverse reality, monetary policy was accompanied by tax reductions and regulatory reforms, which in turn gave rise to unexploited supply-side opportunities. Prosperity thus flourished without monetary actions to stimulate consumption and investment demand. *The second and third of the past five decades* were pave on the belief that monetary discipline was a necessary condition—let alone potentially a sufficient one—for fiscal discipline. Politicians were deterred from incurring budgetary deficits to fund their political agenda attracting voters, and the alternative of raising tax rates was constrained by the political process. Meanwhile, e-commerce emerged as a practice and has been extensively used, while concurrent significantly large productivity increases effectuated throughout most advanced economies (especially the United States) during the 1990s. These enabled measured unemployment rate to fall below the level at which trade-off theorists claimed that inflation would begin to pose a threat. Jordan (2016) argues that "instead of questioning the validity of their model, these theorists simply kept revising down where they thought the noninflationary rate of unemployment might be encountered; the puncturing of the dot-com bubble cut short this experiment, so the model was not successfully rejected by actual experience" (p. 374).

express concern that inflation rates in the United States and other major economies were too low and argued that policies should be aimed at increasing inflation levels. [7]

There were two main reasons why there was a rush to use monetary pump priming. The first reason was the belief that the Great Depression of the 1930s could have been prevented if the central bank had expanded its balance sheet enough. Therefore, contemporary monetary authorities were determined not to make the same mistake. The second reason was the idea that there was a trade-off between inflation and employment, which policymakers could exploit. Although this belief had been discredited in the 1990s (see, for example, Wood, 2015, p. 108), it regained popularity among policymakers only a decade later. Policymakers defended their so-called "pedal-to-the-metal" monetary actions by arguing that there would be enough time to withdraw monetary stimulus as the unemployment rate approached the non-accelerating inflation threshold.[8]

Central banks have the ability to control the size of their balance sheets. However, as shown by Jordan (2016), recent attempts to increase consumer inflation rates have not been successful. Nevertheless, an even larger bond-buying program may be deemed necessary to achieve this goal. An alternative explanation is that the central bank's balance sheet is not directly linked to economic activity in the national economy. It is clear that the various measures of the country's money supply have

---

[7]Twenty years ago, it was considered unacceptable for central bankers or finance ministers to suggest that inflation rates were too low and needed to be raised. However, by the end of the first decade of the 2000s, the bond market vigilantes of the 1990s were no longer present. Monetary authorities worldwide made a commitment to take strong measures to speed up the devaluation of their currencies. This was not just a case of fiscal restraint being ignored; concepts and theories of monetary discipline were also disregarded.

[8]An unanticipated development has been the decline in the unemployment rate was not due to an increase in labor demand or employment, but, instead, it was caused by a substantial drop in the labor force participation rate. Even advocates of the trade-off theory were unsure of how to determine when a low unemployment rate would lead to inflation, as an increase in labor demand could be met with millions of people returning to the labor market. According to the theory, if labor force participation rates were already high and monetary stimulus led to increased labor demand, wages would rise rapidly, resulting in faster inflation. However, with the labor force participation rate at a 38-year low, even if monetary policies led to greater labor demand, wouldn't the result simply be a surge in labor supply? If there is no excess demand for labor, how can rising wages be expected to trigger higher consumer inflation? The unreliability of the trade-off model when the labor force participation rate was high suggests that policymakers should not rely on it when the participation rate is severely depressed.

A theory that economic slack can be used to gauge inflationary pressures also has its drawbacks. The concept suggests that an economy has a long-term sustainable potential output that depends on various factors, including the working age population, labor productivity, and technological innovation. If actual output falls below this potential, inflationary pressures are expected to be low, which means policymakers can safely encourage consumption and investment demand to increase actual output. However, there are several knowledge issues associated with pursuing such a strategy, especially in a global economy where capacity constraints are not limited to domestic markets. With the exception of non-tradable goods and services, sourcing of final goods and production inputs occurs in a global marketplace, making any estimate of domestic capacity irrelevant in determining potential price pressures.

not responded to the significant increase in the volume of central bank money. Additionally, the low interest rates prevalent worldwide can be attributed to factors other than central bank bond-buying, as demonstrated by Walker (2016).

At first glance, it may appear that central banks buying large amounts of any asset should raise its price and lower its current yield (in the case of bonds). However, central banks operate differently than other portfolio managers because they acquire more financial assets by creating liabilities or by essentially creating money from nothing, rather than selling other assets. *In an important sense, large-scale asset purchases (LSAP) by central banks involve a form of liability swap within consolidated government accounts—the duration, or maturity structure, of outstanding government liabilities is shortened by LSAP.*

It is crucial to note that when central banks buy government bonds, the effects are different from when they purchase private assets like mortgage-backed securities. Although both decrease the amount of earning assets available to commercial banks and other investors, only buying private assets transfers the risk of potential default to taxpayers. In contrast, when central banks buy Treasury bonds, it can be viewed as an "early retirement" of a type of national debt that is outstanding.[9]

In financial markets normally, government debt that is considered "riskless" is commonly used as collateral for various transactions. Therefore, a decrease in the supply of these securities available for use as collateral can result in tighter conditions in the wider financial intermediary system. In other words, when a central bank conducts LSAP, it generates a contractionary force throughout the financial system.[10] Williamson (2015) argues that the use of high-quality "riskless" securities as collateral in financial markets declined for several reasons following the financial crisis of 2008. Antecedent to the crisis, sovereign debts (in the United States and the euro area) were viewed as riskless, similar to the obligations of US government-sponsored enterprises (GSEs) (as, for example, Freddie Mac and Fannie May). Some privately issued mortgage-backed securities (MBS) were also considered safe enough to be used as collateral. In fact, however, eventually the GSEs failed and were eventually nationalized to be rescued, the MBS market seized up, *and some European countries found themselves on the brink of default.*

[9]Suppose, for example, that US Treasury bonds could be redeemed early, like many corporate bonds. Assuming that the Treasury issued $1 trillion of short-term securities with very low interest rates and then redeemed an equal amount of long-term debt, this would keep the total debt amount the same but would change the duration and interest costs of the debt. Lower-cost, short-term liabilities would replace higher-cost, long-term debt.

[10]Williamson (2015) states: "A Taylor-rule central banker may be convinced that lowering the central bank's nominal interest rate target will increase inflation. This can lead to a situation in which the central banker becomes permanently trapped in ZIRP. With the nominal interest rate at zero for a long period of time, inflation is low, and the central banker reasons that maintaining ZIRP will eventually increase the inflation rate. But this never happens and, as long as the central banker adheres to a sufficiently aggressive Taylor rule, ZIRP will continue forever, and the central bank will fall short of its inflation target indefinitely. This idea seems to fit nicely with the recent observed behaviour of the world's central banks" (p. 10).

Those developments resulted in a sharp decline in the stock of assets deemed to be of sufficiently high quality to serve as collateral in financial transactions. In addition to this, the central bank's acquisition of the US Treasury securities on a large scale, intended to provide a form of monetary stimulation, had the unintended consequence of further restricting the operation of capital markets. Quantitative easing (QE) was even considered a mistake due to such a result. Any analysis, however preliminary, as proposed by Jordan (2016) suggesting that "LSAP actually had a contractionary effect during the period of quantitative easing must be taken seriously" (Jordan, 2016, p. 381).

The end of large-scale asset purchases by central banks was certainly necessary. However, the issue of devising an efficient "exit strategy" had been crucial. Suggestions include that the central bank should have reduced its balance sheet to its pre-quantitative easing (QE) level and require commercial banks to hold more reserves. Nevertheless, this is unlikely to occur, especially after the massive expansions of central bank balance sheets to counter the effects of the COVID-19 pandemic. The traditional practice of using daily open market operations to control the overnight interbank lending rate, known as the federal funds rate, had not been viable in the interest rate zero lower bound. Policymakers can no longer rely on central bank purchases and sales of securities in the open market as their primary tool. Nevertheless, as Goodfriend (2002) argues, "open market operations are neither necessary nor sufficient to implement interest rate policy" (p. 12). He further highlights that they are not a necessary condition due to their restricting the supply of reserves in order to maintain a positive marginal liquidity services yield and an interest opportunity cost of reserves. By paying and varying interest on reserves, a central bank could exert leverage over market rates without maintaining an interest opportunity cost spread. Additionally, open market operations are not a sufficient condition to implement interest rate policy either, since they govern only the interest opportunity cost spread, while the level of the interbank rate is determined only if, in addition, the rate of interest paid on reserves is specified at zero or otherwise.

The central banks' new tools—namely, by *administering the interest rate paid on reserve (IOR) deposits and auctioning "reverse repurchase agreements" (RRP)*[11]—have not been tested in an accelerating inflation environment as the current regime (for earlier accounts on IOR and RRP, respectively, see Ennis & Weinberg, 2007; Frost et al., 2015). No matter how aggressively utilized, neither has any direct effect

[11]The Federal Reserve Bank of New York's Open Market Trading Desk (the Desk) carries out open market operations under the Federal Open Market Committee's (FOMC) direction. The Desk conducts reverse repurchase agreements (RRP) or "reverse repo" transactions, which involve selling a security to an eligible counterparty and agreeing to repurchase it at a predetermined price and time in the future. The difference in price, together with the time between the sale and the repurchase, results in an interest rate paid by the Federal Reserve on the transaction. During RRP open market operations, the Desk sells securities held in the System Open Market Account (SOMA) to eligible RRP counterparties, with an agreement to repurchase them on the specified maturity date. The size of the SOMA portfolio remains the same, but the transaction shifts some of the liabilities on the Federal Reserve's balance sheet from bank reserves to reverse repos. These operations may be for overnight maturity or a specific term (New York Fed, 2023).

on money creation (Jordan, 2016). IOR can be considered simply as central bank borrowing *from* private banks, while the latter RRP is central bank borrowing from GSEs and money market firms. In theory, market interest rates would be influenced by the rate the central bank offers for such borrowings. If higher rates paid by monetary authorities cause other interest rates to be higher, businesses and households will curtail some credit-financed purchases, aggregate demand for output will be moderated, and inflationary pressures will be mitigated. This theory depends on several restrictive assumptions, however, as, for example, that monetary policymakers must have considerable knowledge about the impact of their actions on other interest rates, about the lags involved before businesses and households respond to rising rates, and about whether and how much *real* interest rates—rather than just nominal rates—are changing. As there is no historical experience employing these tools, there is no basis for assessing their effectiveness. Central banks have demonstrably failed to achieve their objective of higher inflation during the decade after the advent of the GFC—their tools to contain any inflation that emerges untested (Jordan, 2016).

The risk posed by the enormous central bank balance sheet is that the willingness of commercial banks to hold idle balances (even those earning some administered rate of interest) will decline. While individual banks can take steps to reduce their excess reserves, the banking system as a whole cannot. Unless there is a corresponding decrease in the central bank's assets, excess reserves can only decline if they become required reserves. There are two possible ways to achieve this: Congress can authorize a significant increase in reserve requirement ratios, or commercial banks can dramatically increase their reservable deposit liabilities, which would result in a hyperinflationary surge in the money supply.

Commercial bank deposit liabilities are now linked to the supply of earning assets, both domestic and foreign, available to commercial banks. In simpler terms, the amount of "inside money" generated by the banking system depends on the demand for bank loans and the overall availability of government bonds, mortgage-backed securities, and other suitable financial instruments that banks can acquire. In order to predict the growth of deposits and the money supply, it is necessary to predict the availability and yields of these earning assets, as well as factors such as government budget deficits that require financing, and the prices of commercial and residential real estate that affect the creation of mortgage securities. It should be noted that the knowledge needed to make accurate forecasts cannot be obtained from past experiences alone. Furthermore, as Cheng and Wessel (2020) remark, since the crisis, the US Treasury (for example) has kept funds in the Treasury General Account (TGA) at the Federal Reserve rather than at private banks. As a result, when the Treasury receives payments, such as from corporate taxes, it is draining reserves from the banking system. The TGA has become more volatile since 2015, reflecting a decision by the Treasury to keep only enough cash to cover 1 week of outflows making it harder for the Fed to estimate demand for reserves.

To conclude, as stated by Jordan (2016, p. 382), although central banks have attempted to use massive quantitative easing as a means of increasing the inflation rate, this goal has not been achieved despite a significant increase in the size of the central bank balance sheet (quadrupling in the case of the United States). This is due to the fact that commercial banks are no longer constrained by reserves, so changes in the central bank's assets and liabilities no longer affect the amount of money in circulation. Therefore, central bank open market operations no longer have an impact on the rate of inflation, and changes in the federal funds rate have no implications for economic activity or inflation. If inflation were to occur, central banks would have no tools to counteract it. In the past, central banks mistakenly expanded their balance sheets in response to rising nominal interest rates, failing to recognize that this was an indication of rising inflation expectations. However, for the foreseeable future, this is unlikely to be a concern as ballooning central bank balance sheets alone can fuel extreme rates of inflation without further debt monetization. This is not a forecast of impending inflation but rather a statement that central banks have limited influence on inflation rates.

4.5 Conclusions on New Perspectives on Tools, Transmission, and the Effectiveness of Monetary Policy

To summarize, monetary policy operates through asset prices and the financial conditions faced by borrowers and lenders. This, in turn, affects the cost of capital, the household wealth, the balance sheets of firms and financial intermediaries, and the strength of the currency. In general, monetary policy operates through (1) setting short-term nominal rates, (2) managing expectations through various communication tools, (3) providing liquidity to financial intermediaries and markets when nonfundamental stress or panic poses significant risks to financial instability, (4) implementing regulatory/supervisory measures (when they have assumed responsibility), and (5) conducting foreign exchange interventions (when they have assumed responsibility).

Central banks manage the quantity and/or cost of the monetary base, consisting of currency in circulation and bank reserves, through several tools like open market operations, credit operations, standing facilities, and reserve requirements. By informing the public about its policy, the central bank can establish the trajectory of short-term market rates at the intended level. The movement of these safe, nominal rates, along with the corresponding communication from the central bank, affects the whole interest rate term structure, risk premia, and exchange rates.

Central banks indirectly manage macroeconomic risk and directly manage financial and liquidity risk by serving as a lender of last resort and providing a backstop to government debt (even if only implicitly). Following the global financial crisis (GFC), monetary authorities utilized unconventional tools that resulted in a significant increase in their balance sheets. However, managing risk depends on their capacity to leverage significantly and conduct maturity and liquidity transformation using their balance sheet.

4.5.1 Monetary Policy with Policy Rates at Their Lower Bound

The absence of interest on cash sets a limit on how low central banks can set policy rates without causing arbitrage opportunities. However, it is possible for central banks to set their policy rate below zero into negative territory (ultimately by up to 75 basis points, as warranted by recent negative interest rate policy experience) due to the expenses involved in storing and hoarding large amounts of cash. Therefore, academic researchers and central banking practitioners tend to refer to an *effective lower bound* (ELB) instead of the traditional term *zero lower bound* (ZLB). While eliminating the use of cash and switching to an entirely digital money system could in principle alleviate this constraint (see, for example, Ball et al., 2016; Rogoff, 2017; Lilley & Rogoff, 2020), it may compromise financial inclusion and increase the risk of systemic cyber threats and significant unpredictable events. Therefore, central banks consider it preferable to keep cash as a form of central bank money to maintain resilience in the face of such challenges. Additionally, the way negative interest rate policies are executed can have an impact on the expenses associated with holding central bank reserves. As Jobst and Lin (2016, p. 36) argue, the implementation of tiered reserve systems may enable central banks to reduce the effective policy rate by lowering the direct cost of negative rates on excess reserves. Through the exemption of a certain amount of excess reserves from the marginal policy rate, banks avoid the full impact of negative deposit rates. [12]

When policy rates are in their zero lower bound, monetary policy has not necessarily lost its efficacy. Unconventional instruments can be employed to compensate for the lack of conventional policy space. Unconventional policy has three distinct features (Bartsch et al., 2020, pp. 13–14): *Firstly*, central banks increase their balance sheets and broaden the range of assets they purchase. The aim is to influence credit, borrowing conditions, and risk-taking by directly influencing the portfolia of financial intermediaries. The aim is to flood them with reserves until they rebalance their composition in favor of loans. In fact, on October 15, 2008, the Eurosystem, for example, in response to the collapse of interbank markets after the Lehman failure, introduced fixed rate full allotment tender procedures in all refinancing operations, thus abandoning central bank reserve provision quantity controls. Under fixed *rate full allotment—a flexible and efficient measure (as stressed by members of the ECB Executive Board in* Gonzáles-Páramo, 2011*)—counterparties have their bids fully satisfied, against adequate collateral, and on the condition of financial soundness.*

[12] As highlighted in Jogst and Lin (2016, p. 36), the cost of a bank's holding central bank liabilities varies with the structure of reserves and their remuneration (see Bech & Malhozov, 2016). Tiering systems have been used in the past by central banks to ensure that excess reserves are distributed widely within the banking sector, as well as in an effort to protect the interests of domestic retail depositors and concurrently attempt to push as much of the costs onto wholesale (and especially foreign) investors whose deposits contribute mostly to excess reserves. Therefore, the ideal size of the exemption threshold is determined by the amount of domestic retail funding banks have at the time of the introduction of the system, namely, the level of deposits central banks want to protect.

Secondly, unconventional instruments enhance the credibility of a central bank's future policy measures. These enable central banks to develop more intricate strategies to manage expectations, such as forward guidance. The latter involves committing to keep interest rates at a particular level over a predetermined time period, even in cases where economic conditions would normally warrant an increase. Alternatively, they may be contingent on a set of predefined conditions, typically relating to inflation or unemployment rates. *Thirdly*, central banks can differentiate interest rates based on the lending and deposit behavior of financial intermediaries.

Central banks face legal and political limitations on the assets they are allowed to trade. However, these restrictions have been gradually eased over time. Prior to the COVID-19 pandemic, the US Federal Reserve primarily purchased government bonds or bonds issued by government-sponsored enterprises. The European Central Bank (ECB) encountered several challenges before being able to execute substantial purchases of government bonds starting in 2015. Nonetheless, the ECB has been able to operate on a more extensive range of assets compared to other central banks over the years.

4.5.2 *Is Unconventional Monetary Policy Effective at the Effective Lower Bound?*

The effectiveness of unconventional monetary policy remains controversial (for a survey, see, for example, Papadamou et al., 2020). When markets are significantly segmented, monetary authority asset purchases may be potentially more effective, because there is less scope for arbitrageurs to undo the effects of policy interventions on, for example, prices of bonds at different maturities (Bartsch et al., 2020). For this reason, empirical research finds central bank asset purchase programs to be relatively more effective during the peak of a financial crisis, when financial markets tend to be dysfunctional forcefully necessitating the central bank (varied) intervention so as to restore financial stability.

As suggested in Bernanke (2020), unconventional measures could be equivalent to a three percentage point cut in conventional policy interest rates. A helpful reference points toward the "shadow short-term rate" (Black, 1995; Krippner, 2012a, 2012b), which is a metric for the stance of monetary policy in a zero lower bound environment, thus providing an estimate of the conventional monetary policy equivalent when unconventional monetary policy measures are implemented. Even though it is widely accepted that unconventional monetary policy can lower the "shadow rate" (Wu & Xia, 2016), much less agreement holds with respect to the effectiveness of this lower rate in terms of the impact on aggregate demand and inflation (Debortoli et al., 2020; Bhattarai et al., 2021; Dash, 2023).

Negative interest rates may hinder financial stability despite their potential to increase credit demand from firms and households. Negative rates could affect the health of financial intermediaries, life insurance, and pension systems, leading to tighter financial and borrowing conditions. Although pushing interest rates into negative territory initially improves banks' equity position by raising the value of their assets, persistent negative rates can ultimately reduce banks' profits by squeezing their lending margins, with negative impacts on their net worth (Brunnermeier & Koby, 2019). Additionally, reducing rates below a certain threshold may actually reduce demand and encourage savings (in cases that the economic agents seek to preserve their future purchasing power), which is known as the "reversal rate" hypothesis.

4.5.3 Institutional Arrangements with the Treasury Matter

As stressed by the so-called unpleasant monetarist arithmetic described in Sargent and Wallace (1981), if the fiscal authority undertakes a stream of aggressive debt issue and fiscal deficit accumulation, then the monetary authority essentially needs to generate sufficient seigniorage income to foster sovereign solvency despite the inflationary consequences. Recent evidence highlights that under large shocks hitting the economy, fiscal rules may become procyclical and offset the direction of monetary policy (Bianchi & Melosi, 2019; Corsetti et al., 2019). Furthermore, a regime may arise in which the interest rate used as a tool for monetary policy implementation is close to the effective zero lower bound or the economy has been hit by a shock too abrupt that breaks down the flow of payments across sectors; a stark example of the latter is the experience during lockdowns in most advanced economies to address the spread of the COVID-19 pandemic during 2020 and 2021 (see, for example, Woodford, 2020). Therefore, if interest rate policy is rendered ineffective due to the above, fiscal policy proves to be a powerful tool to stabilize the economy. It thus tends to be exploited forcefully.

The interaction of the monetary with the fiscal authority is warranted by the general government budget constraint in affecting the price level (Cochrane, 2022; see also Barthélemy et al., 2021, highlighting the dynamic strategic interactions between the two authorities). However, the institutional balance between the central bank and the fiscal authority is inevitably altered when monetary policy is implemented in terms of quantities (rather than prices) and extensive asset purchase programs are implemented. A main reason refers to the fact that the central bank takes on risk by purchasing large amounts of risky assets, which could result in significant losses. These losses would then be passed on to the government in the form of reduced seigniorage. In addition, if the central bank needs to raise interest rates to combat inflation, it may have to retain long-term bonds at a loss. This loss, combined with a decrease in seigniorage revenue and raised interest payments, could result in the fiscal authority being unable to sustain its fiscal position.

The operating ability of the central bank to create money at will has led to institutional and scientific discussions about its potentially possessing an unlimited capacity to absorb losses, including the possibility of its operating negative capital. However, following Bartsch et al. (2020), we contend that the central bank's ability to absorb losses is actually limited by its mandated responsibility to control inflation. If the losses incurred by the central bank exceed the value of seigniorage (adjusted for any transfers to the fiscal authority) discounted based on the condition of maintaining inflation at the official target and without any fiscal assistance, the central bank would need to increase seigniorage and inflation, thereby losing control of its ability to maintain price stability and anchor expectations. In fact, it is the set of rules that govern the flow of dividends and net income that is of greater importance, as it ultimately determines whether the central bank needs to create money solely to meet its obligations. In essence, the central bank's loss absorption capacity is constrained by its mandate to maintain low inflation.

Provided the central bank receives fiscal assistance, this contingency may be eventually mitigated (see, for example, Stella, 1997; Del Negro & Sims, 2015). Several countries (as, for example, the United Kingdom and the United States) have implemented institutional arrangements to potentially maintain the Treasury's possibility to recapitalize the central bank. However, such institutional arrangements are highly regime-dependent, since in contexts, for example, of a currency union (not one fiscally unified) as the euro area, they bound to result in political and institutional tensions. Such arrangements may be perceived as an indirect bailout that yields asymmetric benefits to particular member states violating the union's democratic foundation (Buiter, 2020; Wood, 2020; Bartsch et al., 2020). Broadly reiterating Wood (2020) that argues on the effectiveness of institutional arrangements in the US liquidity management context (monetary authority and financial market participants), one may claim that "perhaps the best we can do is to identify the interests as well as the legislative and bureaucratic influences on markets in particular cases ... [;]the pair considered ... suggests that official influences may have been exaggerated, especially in comparison with the permanent forces of finance" (p. 13).

Reichlin et al. (2023), with reference to the euro area, study the monetary and fiscal authority interaction through the general government budget constraint and find it to depend on whether unexpected monetary policy affects the short-term interest rate (conventional) or the long end of the yield curve (unconventional). They recognize that, first, the effect on the return on the value of debt depends on the extent that yields at the relevant maturity change and, second, that the response of the primary surplus depends on fiscal policy. Their results demonstrate that unconventional monetary policy has a much larger effect on returns since, given the average debt maturity and duration adjustment, long-term yield changes have a higher impact on returns than short-term rates. The long-run price level is lower than in the conventional policy case. The primary surplus response is muted and even slightly positive in the long run, unlike in the conventional case (which they find to be negative both at business cycle frequency and in the long run). They thus argue that historical data (covering the period 1991–2019) suggest that the small effect of unconventional monetary policy on inflation is explained by an unresponsive fiscal policy calling for mechanisms to ensure monetary and fiscal policy coordination.

As Schnabel (2022) highlights that during the COVID-19 pandemic crisis the two policies reinforced each other, enabling the euro area economy to contain the major adverse shock, while in the current macroeconomic environment, of high inflation and high public and private debt levels, the risk emerges that monetary and fiscal policies may pull in opposite directions, leading to a suboptimal policy mix. She further adds that while fiscal policy needs to protect the most vulnerable parts of society from the consequences of the current energy and food price shocks, governments must avoid an overly expansionary stance that fuels inflationary pressures and adds to the historically high public debt burden. Benigno (2020) however, demonstrates that a central bank that is appropriately capitalized can succeed in controlling prices by setting the interest rate on reserves, holding short-term assets, and rebating its income to the Treasury from which it has to maintain financial independence.

Therefore, any level of success of central bank balance sheet policies (in terms of quantitative easing or tightening—as circumstances necessitate) is heavily dependent on the *institutional relationship* between the central bank and the Treasury. Pessoa and Williams (2012) stress that the central bank may supply a number of services to the Treasury, with the most vital one as a banker, but also providing services that fall under the general heading of debt and cash management, for example, fulfilling the roles of fiscal agent, settlement agent, and/or registrar/paying agent. At the same time, the Treasury may provide services to the central bank, notably, for example, cash flow forecasts. In view of the high inflation-high public and private debt environment, if there is no possibility of receiving fiscal assistance in case of losses, the central bank may be discouraged to expand its balance sheet to the extent necessary to stabilize the economy. On the other hand, if fiscal help is available but comes with conditions that threaten the central bank's independence, it could make monetary authorities hesitant to implement stabilizing measures in the first place. Thus, finding a balance between these extremes is essential for effective balance sheet policies.

References

Ball, L., Gagnon, J., Honohan, P., & Krogstrup, S. (2016). *What Else can central banks do?* Geneva reports on the world economy 18, International Centre for Monetary and Banking Studies, Geneva Switzerland & CEPR-Centre for Economic Policy Research, London, UK.

Barthélemy, J., Mengus, E., & Plantin, G. (2021). The central Bank, the Treasury, or the market: Which one determines the Price level?. *CEPR discussion paper* no. DP16679, October.

Bartsch, E., Benassy-Queré, A., Corsetti, G., & Debrun, X. (2020). It's all in the mix: How can monetary and fiscal policies work or fail together. *Geneva reports on the world economy* 23, International Centre of Monetary and Banking Studies, Geneva, Switzerland, and Centre for Economic Policy Research, London, UK.

Bech, M., & Malhozov, A. (2016). How have central banks implemented negative policy rates? BIS Quarterly Review, March, Bank for International Settlements, Basel, Switzerland.

Benigno, P. (2020). A Central Bank theory of price level determination. *American Economic Journal: Macroeconomics, 12*(3), 258–283.

Bernanke, B. S. (2020). The new tools of monetary policy. *American Economic Review, 110*(4), 943–983.

Bernanke, B. S., & Gertler, M. (1995). Inside the black box: The credit channel of monetary policy transmission. *Journal of Economic Perspectives, 9*(4), 27–48.

Berran, F., Coudert, V., & Mojon, B. (1996). The transmission of monetary policy in European countries. *CEPII working paper*, no 1996-03, *Centre D'Études Prospectives et D' Informations Internationales,* Paris, France, February.

Bhattarai, S., Chatterjee, A., & Park, W. Y. (2021). Effects of US quantitative easing on emerging market economies. *Journal of Economic Dynamics and Control, 122*, 104031.

Bianchi, F., & Melosi, L. (2019). The dire effects of the lack of monetary and fiscal coordination. *Journal of Monetary Economics, 104*(C), 1–22.

Black, F. (1995). Interest rates as options. *The Journal of Finance, 50*(5), 1371–1376.

Borio, C. (1996). Credit characteristics and the monetary transmission mechanism in fourteen industrial countries: Facts, conjectures, and some econometric evidence. In A. Koos, K. Kees, C. Kool, & C. Winder (Eds.), *Monetary policy in a converging Europe* (pp. 77–115). Kluwer Academic Press.

Brunner, K., & Meltzer, A. H. (1972). Money, debt, and economic activity. *Journal of Political Economy, 80*(5), 951–977.

Brunnermeier, M. K., & Koby, Y. (2019). The reversal interest rate. IMES Discussion Papers 2019-E6.

Buiter, W. H. (2020). The Eurosystem: An accident waiting to happen. VoxEU.org, 1 October.

Cecchetti, S. G. (1995). Distinguishing theories of the monetary transmission mechanism. *Federal Reserve Bank of St. Louis Economic Review, 77*, 83–97.

Cheng, J., & Wessel, D. (2020). What is the repo market and why does it matter? Up-Front *blog*, Hutchins Centre, Brookings Institution, Washington, DC, USA, Jan. 28.

Christensen, L. (2011). Market monetarism: The second monetarist counterrevolution. Available online: https://thefaintofheart.files.wordpress.com/2011/09/market-monetarism-13092011.pdf Accessed 12 September, 2020.

Cochrane, J. H. (2022). The fiscal roots of inflation. *Review of Economic Dynamics, 45*, 22–40.

Corsetti, G., Dedola, L., Jarociński, M., Maćkowiak, B., & Schmidt, S. (2019). Macroeconomic stabilization, monetary-fiscal interactions, and Europe's monetary union. *European Journal of Political Economy, 57*(C), 22–33.

Dash, P. (2023). The effects of conventional and unconventional monetary policy on the unemployment rate in the US. *Journal of Economic Studies.* https://doi.org/10.1108/JES-10-2022-0555

Debortoli, D., Galí, J., & Gambetti, L. (2020). On the empirical (ir)relevance of the zero lower bound constraint. *NBER Macroeconomics Annual, 34*(1), 141–170.

Del Negro, M., & Sims, C. (2015). *When does a central bank's balance sheet require fiscal support* (p. 701). Federal Reserve Bank of New York Staff Report.

Diamond, D. W. (1984). Financial intermediation and delegated monitoring. *Review of Economic Studies, 51*(166), 393–414.

Ennis, H. M., & Weinberg, J. A. (2007). Interest on reserves and daylight credit. *Federal Reserve Bank of Richmond Economic Quarterly, 93*(2), 111–142.

Frost, J., Logan, L., Martin, A., McCabe, P., Natalucci, F., & Remache, J. (2015). *Overnight RRP operations as a monetary policy tool: Some design considerations. Finance and economics discussion series 2015–010.* Board of Governors of the Federal Reserve System.

Gonzáles-Páramo, J. M. (2011). The ECB's monetary policy during the crisis. Closing speech by ECB's member of the executive board at the 10th economic policy conference, Malaga, Spain, October 11th.

Goodfriend, M. (2002). Interest on reserves and monetary policy. *Federal Reserve Bank of New York Economic Policy Review, 8*(1), 13–29.

Hubbard, R. G. (1995). Is there a 'Credit Channel' for monetary policy? *Federal Reserve Bank of St. Louis Review, 77*, 63–74.

Jobst, A., & Lin, H. (2016). Negative interest rate policy: Implications for monetary transmission and Bank profitability in the euro area. IMF Working Paper, 16/172.

Jordan, J. L. (2014). A century of central banking: What have we learned? *Cato Journal, 34*(2), 213–227.

Jordan, J. L. (2016). The new monetary framework. *Cato Journal, Special Issue Rethinking Monetary Policy, 36*(2), 367–383.

Kashyap, A. K., & Stein, J. C. (1994). Monetary policy and bank lending. In N. G. Mankiw (Ed.), *Monetary policy* (pp. 221–256). University of Chicago Press.

Kashyap, A. K., & Stein, J. C. (1997). The role of banks in monetary policy: A survey with implications for the European Monetary Union. Federal Reserve Bank of Chicago. *Economic Perspectives, 21*, 2–19.

Kashyap, A. K., & Stein, J. C. (2000). What do a million observations on banks say about the transmission of monetary policy? *American Economic Review, 90*, 407–428. Also as *NBER Working Paper* 6056, 1997.

Krippner, L. (2012a). Measuring the stance of monetary policy in zero lower bound environments. *Reserve Bank of New Zealand, discussion paper*, 2012/04, Reserve Bank of New Zealand, Wellington, New Zealand.

Krippner, L. (2012b). Modifying Gaussian term structure models when interest rates are near the zero lower bound. *Reserve Bank of New Zealand, discussion paper* 2012/02, Reserve Bank of New Zealand, Wellington, New Zealand.

Lee, T. (2011). The politics of market monetarism. *Forbes*.

Lilley, A., & Rogoff, K. (2020). The case for implementing effective negative interest rate policy. In J. H. Cochrane & J. B. Taylor (Eds.), *Strategies for monetary policy* (Vol. Chapter 2, pp. 27–69). Hoover Institution Press. Barnes & Noble.

Mishkin, F. S. (2011a). Monetary policy strategy: Lessons from the crisis. In M. Jarociński, F. Smets, & C. Thimann (Eds.), *Approaches to monetary policy revisited—lessons from the crisis, sixth ECB central banking conference proceedings* (pp. 67–118).

Mishkin, F. S. (2011b). Over the cliff: From the subprime to the global financial crisis. *Journal of Economic Perspectives, 25*(1), 49–70.

New York Fed. (2023). FAQs: Reverse repurchase agreement operations. Federal Reserve Bank of New York Markets and Policy Implementation, May 3. Available online: https://www.newyorkfed.org/markets/rrp_faq.

Papadamou, S., Siriopoulos, C., & Kyriazis, N. A. (2020). A survey of empirical findings on unconventional central bank policies. *Journal of Economic Studies, 47*(7), 1533–1577.

Peek, J., & Roesengren, E. (2010). The role of banks in the transmission of monetary policy. In A. N. Berger, P. Molyneux, & J. O. S. Wilson (Eds.), *The Oxford handbook of banking* (pp. 257–277). Oxford University Press.

Pessoa, M., & Williams, M. (2012). Government cash management: Relationship between the treasury and the Central Bank. *IMF technical notes and manuals* 12/02, Washington, DC: International Monetary Fund, Fiscal Affairs Department, November.

Phillips, A. W. (1958). The relationship between unemployment and the rate of change of money wages in the United Kingdom, 1861-1957. *Economica, 25*(100), 283–299.

Reichlin, L., Ricco, G., & Tarbé, M. (2023). Monetary–fiscal crosswinds in the European Monetary Union. *European Economic Review*, Elsevier, *151*(C), 104328.

Rogoff, K. S. (2017). Dealing with monetary paralysis at the zero bound. *Journal of Economic Perspectives, 31*(3), 47–66.

Sargent, T. J., & Wallace, N. (1981). Some unpleasant monetarist arithmetic. *Federal Reserve Bank of Minneapolis Quarterly Review*, 531.

Schnabel, I. (2022). Finding the right mix: Monetary-fiscal interaction at times of high inflation. Keynote speech by Isabel Schnabel, Member of the Executive Board of the ECB, at the Bank of England Watchers' Conference, London, 24 November.

Stein, J. C. (1995). An adverse selection model of bank asset and liability management with implications for the transmission of monetary policy. National Bureau of economic research working paper, no. 5217, Cambridge, MA: National Bureau of Economic Research

Stella, P. (1997). Do central banks need capital? IMF Working Paper No. 97/83, Washington, DC: International Monetary Fund.

Sumner, S. (2009). Misdiagnosing the crisis the real problem, was not real, it was nominal. *VoxEU Column—Macroeconomic Policy*, Centre for Economic Policy Research, UK.

Sumner, S. (2011). Re-targeting the Fed. *National Affairs, 9.*

Trichet, J. C. (2011). Reflections on the nature of monetary policy non-standard measures and finance theory. In M. Jarociński, F. Smets, & C. Thimann (Eds.), *Approaches to monetary policy revisited: Lessons from the crisis* (pp. 12–22). European Central Bank.

Taylor, J. B. (2016). The Staying Power of Staggered Wage and Price Setting Models in Macroeconomics. In J. B. Taylor & Harald Uhlig (eds.), *Handbook of Macroeconomics*, vol. 2 (pp. 2009–2042). Elsevier.

Walker, M. (2016). *Why are interest rates so low? A framework for modelling current global financial developments*. Fraser Institute.

Williamson, S. D. (2015). Current federal reserve policy under the lens of economic history: A review essay. Federal Reserve Bank of St. *Louis Working Paper* No. 2015-015A.

Wood, J. H. (2009). *A history of macroeconomic policy in the United States. Routledge explorations in economic history*. Routledge.

Wood, J. H. (2015). *Central banking in a democracy: The Federal Reserve and its alternatives* (Routledge explorations in economic history). Routledge.

Wood, J. H. (2020). *Who governs? Legislatures, bureaucracies or markets* (Palgrave studies in American economic history). Palgrave Macmillan, Springer Nature.

Woodford, M. (2020). Effective demand failures and the limits of monetary stabilization policy. *NBER working paper*, no. 27768, Cambridge MA: National Bureau of Economic Research.

Wu, C. J., & Xia, F. D. (2016). Measuring the macroeconomic impact of monetary policy at the zero lower bound. *Journal of Money, Credit and Banking, 48*(2–3), 253–291.

Part II
Challenges for Monetary Policy in Interdependent Economies: Lessons from the Eurozone Crisis

Chapter 5
Monetary Policy Crisis in the Eurozone

> Creditor countries have been unwilling to let their banks suffer the consequences of bad loans -rather, they have managed to put the entire burden on the taxpayers of the debtor countries. *[emphasis added]* This may seem clever, but it is short-sighted, not to say hypocritical. It also disregards the EU and Eurozone financial integration that policymakers have promoted.
>
> —*Portes, M. (2014), p. 425*
>
> Now, we could have a discussion of why didn't we see this crisis coming. That could be very interesting, particularly as a lot of people did see it coming. But we are where we are, the eurozone is where it is, and looking backward isn't going to get the zone out of its difficulties without diagnosing the current situation" *[emphasis added]*.
>
> —*Fisher, S. (2012), p. 493*

5.1 Background

The economic and monetary union (EMU) has been a highly significant monetary innovation for the European Union, since the Bretton Woods system. It has been a persistent goal for the EU, as it offers the promise of stability and an appropriate macroeconomic structure that would support growth and employment. The EU was established through the Treaty of Rome in 1957, with a focus on creating a "common market" for trade. The Treaty did not initially include provisions for a single currency, although it acknowledged the need for economic coordination (ECOFIN, 2008). However, over time, it became increasingly evident that closer economic and monetary collaboration was necessary for the internal market to continue to grow and prosper, as well as to enhance the overall performance of the European economy (see Kokores T., 1989, for a detailed analysis of the importance and benefits of economic coordination).

The EMU had its roots in the Werner Report (Werner, 1970), which proposed a plan to establish EMU within a decade. However, currency instability on global markets thwarted this effort. In 1979, the European Monetary System (EMS) was introduced, which aimed to limit fluctuations in exchange rates among EU member

I. T. Kokores, *Monetary Policy in Interdependent Economies*, Financial and Monetary Policy Studies 55, https://doi.org/10.1007/978-3-031-41958-4_5

states and coordinate their monetary policies. This system operated effectively for over 10 years. The project of a single currency was not pursued in the 1970s and was only revived at the end of the 1980s. In 1988, the European Council established a committee led by Jacques Delors, then President of the European Commission, to investigate economic and monetary union. The Delors Report, submitted in 1989, suggested a three-stage process for the introduction of EMU (Delors, 1989). In 1991, the Maastricht Treaty, which included these three stages, was approved by the member states, paving the way for a single currency for Europe in the twenty-first century. After a decade of preparation, decisions on the final stage of EMU were made in May 1998, and the euro was officially introduced on January 1, 1999.

The introduction of a single currency for Europe has been a significant step forward in the process of economic integration on the continent. Although the origins of this idea can be traced back to the 1970s, progress toward a single currency accelerated in the early 1990s. The lifting of the Iron Curtain and the subsequent political uncertainty highlighted the need for a stronger sense of solidarity and common purpose in Europe. Several political events in the early 1990s contributed to this perception, including the reunification of Germany. This event had significant macroeconomic implications and added to the turbulence in the European Exchange Rate Mechanism (ERM), causing tensions within the system (see, for example, Kokores, 1989, pp. 127–162). As established by the Maastricht Treaty signed in 1992, the approval for monetary union in Europe was granted. EU members willing to join the first wave of the euro area underwent a process of convergence toward the reference values specified in the Treaty, concerning factors such as price stability, exchange rate stability, interest rates, government net borrowing, and government indebtedness. To meet the necessary criteria for qualification, a country had to satisfy several requirements. These included keeping inflation at or below the average of the three countries with the lowest inflation rates plus 1.5 percentage points, maintaining a long-term interest rate below 2 percentage points above the average for those three countries, keeping the general government deficit below 3% of GDP and public debt below or approaching 60% of GDP and maintaining an exchange rate within the ERM II system of exchange rates for a continuous period of 2 years. The term "nominal convergence" has often been used to describe the fulfillment of these criteria, while "real convergence" typically refers to convergence of per capita GDP among member states. Ultimately, the 11 countries that were member states at the time met the necessary qualifications to participate in the first wave of the euro area.[1]

There was a lively debate before the creation of the monetary union in Europe, about whether such a union was viable or desirable. There were varying views on the matter, with some predicting a rough start or even a collapse, while others were more optimistic. However, a large number of individuals tended toward a pessimistic

[1] These included (in alphabetical order) Austria, Belgium, Finland, France, Germany, Ireland, Italy, Luxembourg, the Netherlands, Portugal, Spain, and, eventually, Greece, which entered on January 1, 2001.

view, which may have negatively influenced perceptions of the euro area's performance in its early years. This negative view was also affected by the global economic downturn in the early 2000s and the depreciation of the euro against the US dollar during the period leading up to and following the introduction of euro coins and notes in 2002.

Apart from the political motivations for creating a single currency for Europe, *the euro was designed to serve three economic goals*: *Firstly*, it was intended to promote macroeconomic stability by removing the volatility caused by exchange rates and monetary policy instruments, which had lost their efficacy in smaller countries. *Secondly*, it aimed to foster growth and jobs by reducing transaction costs and risk premia associated with different currencies. *Lastly*, it was hoped that the euro would enhance cohesion and convergence by encouraging integration and real economic convergence toward the best performers. However, the creation and management of the single currency in Europe posed a major challenge, primarily due to two reasons: Firstly, unlike federal monetary unions like the United States, the European economic and monetary union (EMU) comprised a single currency in combination with fiscal policies conducted at the national level. This meant that the euro area lacked a transfer mechanism for fiscal transfers between booming and slumping states, which could act as a stabilizer (Eichengreen, 1994). Secondly, alternative mechanisms of adjustment in the euro area were deemed comparatively weak, including low labor mobility within and across borders, weak responsiveness of prices and wages to the business cycle, and the limited degree of integration of financial markets. These factors increased the risk of tensions building up between participating countries if their economies failed to move in synchronization.

Fiscal policies were seen as a potential solution, but previous experience had given rise to growing skepticism. There was a risk of countries running budget deficits and neglecting longer-term considerations of fiscal sustainability, which would have a negative spillover effect and harm other participating countries' productive capital formation (ECOFIN, 2008, p. 18). This would also hinder the European Central Bank in maintaining price and macroeconomic stability. These concerns led to the development of the convergence criteria for inflation, exchange rate stability, interest rates, and public deficits and debt, which countries must comply with to qualify for euro area accession. The Stability and Growth Pact, which fixes rules for fiscal policy and penalties if those rules are breached, was also adopted in 1997 (Annett, 2006). Participating countries were to submit an annual Stability Programme, containing a record of current and expected fiscal outcomes and on which the assessment of compliance by the competent EU authorities were to be based.

5.2 Introduction: An Overview to Conceptualize the Overall Gains of the European Unification

In the decades leading up to the introduction of the single currency, it was widely recognized that membership in the European Union was advantageous for all participating countries. The establishment of the single market in Europe promoted greater economic integration and generated benefits for all parties involved. In order to address the economic stagnation and high unemployment rates prevalent in the early 1980s, the European Community (at that time) initiated a program of unification. In 1985, Jacques Delors, then president of the European Commission, along with his colleagues, introduced a plan to revive the European economy. This plan, known as "Completing the Internal Market," was outlined in a white paper[2] and aimed to eliminate internal trade barriers by the end of 1992. Referred to as "Europe 1992," this program consisted of around 300 directives that aimed to establish a unified European market. Despite the European Community being labeled as a common market, which suggests the absence of trade barriers, this term was proven inaccurate. While formal trade tariffs and quotas had been eliminated within the European Community, there were still regulatory obstacles impeding the movement of goods and factors of production. The acceptance of the proposals outlined in the white paper aimed to ensure unrestricted mobility for both goods and factors of production. If this were to occur, then the term common market would be more appropriate for the European Community.

In an effort to press for acceptance of the entire unification program, the European Commission had not set priorities on the white paper proposals. Nevertheless, four key measures played a crucial role in advancing the goal of achieving a unified Europe. These measures encompassed the removal of border controls, opening up of public procurement, harmonization of technical standards and regulations, and liberalization of capital movements and related financial services. By eliminating these restrictions on trade within then European Community, numerous distortions in the European marketplace would be eradicated. Estimates varied significantly, but the potential gains for Europe from becoming a unified market were substantial (for a survey, see Jonung & Drea, 2009). The removal of regulatory obstacles would not only result in immediate cost savings but also generate long-term benefits through increased competition and the exploitation of economies of scale by firms. However, it is important to note that the benefits of unification would not be evenly distributed among member countries. Research indicated that peripheral countries such as Portugal, Spain, and Greece would experience fewer advantages compared to countries located in the core of Europe, such as West Germany. Antecedent to the

[2]European Commission white papers are documents containing proposals for European Union action in a specific area aiming to launch a debate on the relevant topics with the public, stakeholders, the European Parliament, and the Council in order to arrive at a political consensus. They are currently published on the Commission's "Have Your Say" web portal (retrieved from https://eur-lex.europa.eu/EN/legal-content/glossary/white-paper.html).

launch of the common European currency, concerns have been raised by analysts regarding the possibility of these peripheral countries becoming discouraged and delaying the process of unification (Hunter, 1991).

The potential gains to the EU from removing the barriers have been derived from three types of cost savings: (1) there are immediate benefits resulting from the removal of barriers, (2) there are medium-term gains as firms become more efficient and take advantage of economies of scale, and (3) there are dynamic gains that arise from technological advancements as the economy expands. Research indicated (Van den Noord & Cournède, 2006) that the medium-term and dynamic gains outweigh the immediate benefits derived from integration. In fact, the mechanism through which integration affects a particular industry is as follows: The elimination of trade barriers within the industry represents a beneficial supply shock. By dismantling internal barriers, European companies experience reduced costs when engaging in trade with other EU nations. This reduction in costs leads to a decline in commodity prices as competition intensifies and firms take advantage of economies of scale. Increased competition also stimulates investment. As the price of goods decreases, sales and employment within the industry increase. Consequently, the removal of trade barriers promotes the expansion of specific industries. However, this shift in resources toward the newly liberalized industries results in the contraction of other sectors.

Nevertheless, whether this euro area pattern of production and trade leads to improvement in global welfare depends on whether unification leads to trade creation or trade diversion (Viner, 1950; Mattoo et al., 2022). As trade barriers diminish between countries within the European Union (EU), the volume of intra-EU trade is expected to rise. If this increased trade within the EU leads to countries sourcing goods from the most efficient producers, it can be classified as trade creation. On the other hand, trade diversion occurs when changes in regulatory regimes redirect trade away from more efficient producers toward less efficient ones. This phenomenon may benefit EU producers, but, from a global perspective (Johnson, 1994), it may generate and feed a system of disincentives that reduces world economic welfare.[3]

Figure 5.1 shows the effects of the dismantling of barriers on aggregate demand and supply (Dornbusch, 1989, pp. 344–345). The economy starts at an initial equilibrium point A. However, with the elimination of intra-EU trade barriers, the

---

[3]To illustrate trade diversion, consider a scenario where the most efficient producer of a certain good is located in the United States and sells its product to French buyers. Additionally, there is a higher-cost producer in Italy. However, due to the dismantling of intra-EU trade barriers, the Italian producer becomes the lowest-priced option for the French market. If there were no trade barriers, both within and outside the EU, the US firm would remain the lowest-priced producer for the French buyers. However, the combination of high external EU trade barriers and the removal of intra-EU barriers results in the Italian product being delivered to the French buyers at the lowest price (Viner, 1950). In this hypothetical example, the process of unification leads to a decrease in global welfare if the loss incurred from switching to the less efficient Italian producer outweighs the gain derived from removing intra-EU trade barriers (Hunter, 1991, p. 20).

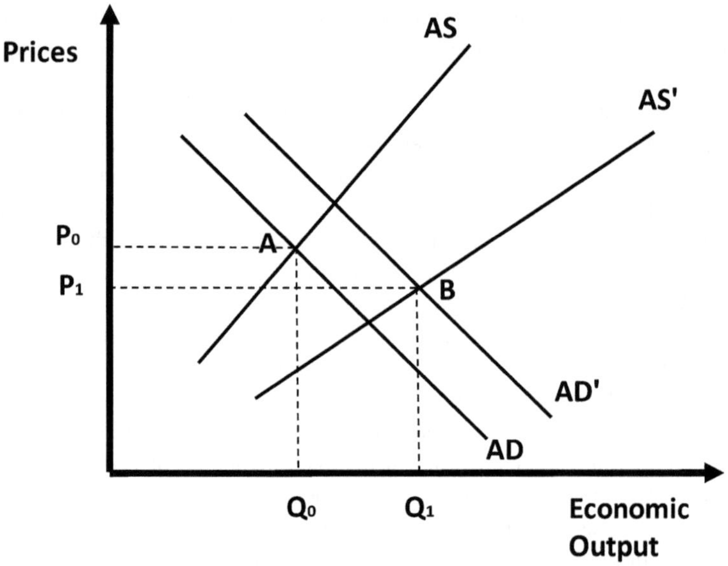

Fig. 5.1 The effects of unification on European aggregate demand and supply. Source: Dornbusch (1989), p. 344

cost of goods within the EU decreases, resulting in an increase in aggregate demand. This rise in demand, coupled with improved profitability, leads to higher levels of investment. Consequently, there is a shift in aggregate demand from AD to AD', indicating an increase in overall demand. Moreover, as firms take advantage of economies of scale and enhance their competitiveness, productivity experiences a boost. This improvement in productivity causes a shift in aggregate supply from AS to AS'. As a result of these changes, the economy transitions from the original equilibrium point A to a new equilibrium point B. In this new equilibrium, aggregate output in the economy expands, reflecting an overall increase in economic activity.

In general, the process of Europe becoming a fully unified market presents numerous advantages. The existence of trade barriers before the establishment of the European Union resulted in price distortions and inefficiencies. However, the removal of intra-EU barriers contributes to an increased demand for European goods. As a result, firms can expand their market beyond a single country and operate within the entire EU community, enabling them to capitalize on economies of scale. The heightened competition among EU firms stimulates profitability and investment, leading to an overall increase in aggregate supply.

Table 5.1 Variables affecting which member states will gain from European Unification

	Hourly labor costs	Inflation (percent)	Total exports	Net exports of capital goods (as % of GDP)	Current account
West Germany	100.0	2.3	32.6	3.9	5.4
Denmark	81.7	3.0	34.1	0.0	−1.1
Netherlands	81.4	2.1	54.8	−1.6	1.9
Belgium	79.3	3.2	69.0	−2.2	2.2
Italy	74.6	5.8	18.1	1.0	−1.4
France	68.1	3.2	21.5	−0.3	−0.4
Britain	59.5	9.4	23.3	0.2	−3.4
Ireland	55.7	4.2	72.0	6.3	1.4
Spain	43.0	7.0	19.5	[a]	−3.8
Greece	29.1	17.0	24.4	[a]	4.7
Portugal	18.1	12.8	33.0	[a]	−3.1

Source: The Economist (1990), p. 72
Note: these data are the latest available, except the current account, which is a 1990 forecast. The data refer to West Germany before the unification with East Germany
[a] Net importers

5.2.1 Distributional Effects Within Europe

Milton Friedman in an interview in May 2000 stated the following: "From the scientific point of view, the euro is the most interesting thing. I think it will be a miracle – well a miracle is a little strong. I think it's highly unlikely that it's going to be a great success. ... But it's going to be very interesting to see how it works" (Friedman, 2007, quoted in Jonung & Drea, 2009, p. 1). The benefits of European unification even before its creation were expected not to be distributed evenly across the European Union, with their variation depending on the region. Due to *existing regional disparities*, certain areas had been expected to experience greater advantages than others. Some countries may even witness job losses or the decline of industries as individuals and firms relocate to seek better employment opportunities or proximity to markets (Table 5.1). Countries situated in the periphery of Europe had been expected to receive the smallest benefits from European unification and even potentially face losses in certain cases (The Economist, 1990).[4]

[4]If these countries were to become discouraged, the process of unification may have slowed or even ceased. Many different economic variables were to determine potentially which areas were to be the greatest winners from unification and which areas might incur problems. An article in *The Economist* (1990, p. 72) ranked the then European Community (EC) member countries by estimated growth in the 1990s. The ranking included the effects of Europe 1992, German unification, and economic reforms in Eastern Europe. Table 5.1 lists the economic variables that determine the pattern of growth of EC member countries from Europe 1992. *The Economist* ranking which takes into account exports to West Germany as a share of total exports and exports to Eastern Europe as a share of total exports found West Germany to be the greatest winner in the 1990s and Spain the country with the lowest growth rates in the 1990s, according to the analysis.

According to The Economist (1990), increased trade and capital flows would likely result in investments flowing into areas with lower wages, particularly in labor-intensive industries. Net exporters of capital goods, such as West Germany, Ireland, and Italy, are well-positioned to capitalize on this surge in investment. On the downside, countries with high inflation rates (such as Portugal and Greece) and countries with large current account deficits (including Greece, Spain, and Britain) were viewed to potentially face supply constraints. These countries might be less capable of immediately increasing production in response to the expanded market-place. Based on a rough estimation by The Economist (1990), the countries least able to leverage the gains offered by unification had been expected to be Britain, Greece, Portugal, and Spain, all of which are located in the periphery of Europe. West Germany from the advent has stood out as the country likely to benefit the most from the process of unification (The Economist, 1990, p. 72).

One of the critical issues was whether unification would exacerbate the then existing regional disparities (see Calingaert, 1988, pp. 68–70; Begg, 1990; Bean et al., 1990, p. 14–16, for more detailed discussions of this issue). Begg (1990) argues that regional disparities were to increase with unification, particularly with respect to labor characteristics. In general, the periphery of Europe exhibited lower wage rates compared to the core. Countries such as Portugal, Greece, and Spain had the lowest wage rates, while West Germany, Denmark, and the Netherlands had the highest wages within the European Community. For instance, wages in Portugal were less than one-fifth of the wages in West Germany. The wage disparities can be attributed to two main factors: Firstly, wages tended to reflect the varying skill levels across different regions. The differences in skills contributed to wage differentials between the periphery and the core of Europe. Secondly, a combination of demographic pressures and obstacles to labor mobility had led to high unemployment rates in the periphery. As a result, wages for a given skill level had been lower in the periphery compared to the core. In the past, the migration of unskilled labor had partially addressed this imbalance, although it had not completely resolved the issue.

The white paper proposals, however, concentrated on increasing the mobility of skilled labor. Begg (1990) argues that the increased mobility of skilled, professional, and managerial workers may cause the peripheral regions to lose skilled labor, increasing the disparity in average skill levels across countries; for a comprehensive comparative study on the intra-European so-called brain drain, see Cavallini et al. (2018). The redistribution of gains from European unification is also influenced by the increased mobility of firms. According to Begg (1990), industries that experience increasing returns tend to relocate to central locations, while less dynamic sectors remain in the periphery. This concentration of production and distribution facilities in the core regions leads to the benefits of scale economies and proximity to markets outweighing the costs associated with higher wages and congestion. Begg (1990) concludes that the distribution of gains from European unification favors the core regions. This pattern emerges from the historical economic performance of the periphery, which indicates relatively low competitiveness. Consequently, countries with weaker competitive positions are likely to gain the least or potentially even experience losses from the integration into the European Union.

In conclusion, the EU had much to gain by becoming a unified market by the end of 1992. The barriers to trade that existed in Europe distorted markets and led to inefficiencies in production. By removing these restrictions, the EU had the opportunity to invigorate its economy and improve its position in the world economy. The elimination of trade barriers within the European Union directly reduces costs. As firms expand their markets, they gain competitiveness and take advantage of economies of scale, resulting in further cost reductions. These declining costs lead to lower prices and an increase in demand. The increased profitability that arises from this drives higher levels of investment. Consequently, this stimulates economic growth, which in turn attracts more investment, fuelling further growth. Conversely, while the elimination of intra-EU trade barriers can result in increased efficiencies in certain markets, it may also give rise to new inefficiencies in other markets. If the EU continued to uphold its high external trade barriers or even strengthen them, unification could potentially lead to trade diversion. This means that countries would shift their purchases from the most efficient producers outside the EU to less efficient producers within the EU. In such a scenario, the removal of intra-EU trade restrictions allows external EU trade barriers to distort markets. As Hunter (1991) remarks, "Europe 1992 [was] not an event; it was an ongoing process" (p. 26). Regardless, the European Community of 1992 has been considerably more integrated than that of 1985.

5.2.2 Entering the Monetary Union

Joining the Monetary Union was seen as the subsequent phase to further capitalize on international collaboration and economic integration. During the late 1990s and early 2000s, this anticipation was largely met for the majority of member states. Governments, businesses, and households experienced the benefits of reduced transaction costs, price stability, and low-risk premia. Nonetheless, this unification process involved countries with distinct monetary and economic policy backgrounds being merged into a single currency regime. Concurrently, Eurozone membership had vast implications for policymakers and economic institutions beyond the field of monetary policy alone (as, for example, fiscal policy, labor market regulation, wage setting): First, it is no longer possible to depreciate the national currency, so real exchange rate misalignments within the Eurozone are more difficult to correct. Second, governments are now indebted in a quasi-foreign currency, so they cannot (implicitly) guarantee the nominal value of issued government bonds (Gern et al., 2019, p. 7). The Maastricht Treaty (signed in February 1992) established the foundational legal and organizational framework for the European Central Bank. This Treaty was a response to the dissatisfaction of numerous EU member states with the outcomes of their monetary policies. Many countries experienced higher inflation rates than desired, and maintaining stable exchange rates proved challenging within the European Monetary System, which aimed to keep currencies within predetermined ranges.

Two areas of academic macroeconomics literature played a crucial role in inspiring the perceived necessity for a shared monetary policy and the subsequent design of the Eurosystem. The first area focused on exchange rate crises, and it coincided with the period following the establishment of the European Monetary System (EMS) in 1979. During this time, economists were developing intricate models that explained how difficulties with current accounts could ultimately result in exchange rate crises; key contributions include Krugman (1979), Flood and Garber (1984), and Obstfeld (1986). Fiscal and monetary policies that generated current account deficits would cause a decline in the foreign currency reserves. As a result, investors would anticipate that foreign exchange reserves would be expended from that state rendering it incapable of defending its fixed exchange rate. This anticipation would trigger a self-fulfilling cycle in which investors would sell off the currency, leading to a devaluation. The history of the EMS—which experienced frequent crises and realignments (Eichengreen, 1994, pp. 96–101)—aligned with the expectations of these models.

Indeed, shortly after the signing of the Maastricht Treaty, the EMS encountered its most severe crisis. This crisis was triggered by macroeconomic developments in Germany following its reunification. As a result, the United Kingdom exited the EMS's Exchange Rate Mechanism in September 1992 due to a speculative attack. In the following months, the majority of other EMS members also devalued their currencies in relation to the Deutsche Mark. Additionally, there was a notable expansion in the permissible fluctuation ranges for the currencies of the remaining EMS members.

From a present-day perspective, the EMS crisis of 1992–1993 could be interpreted as a warning sign that substantial asymmetric shocks were likely to impede the success of economic and monetary union (EMU). However, for numerous European leaders and academics, the events during that period actually bolstered the arguments in favor of monetary union (Whelan, 2019, p. 9). In the years leading up to this crisis, there had been a significant relaxation of restrictions on capital movements and financial deregulation. The substantial capital flows observed during the sterling crisis of 1992 convinced many individuals that the self-fulfilling speculative crises described in academic models would become increasingly severe, rendering a system of quasi-fixed exchange rates unworkable.

When European politicians made the decision to adopt a shared currency, the design of the European Central Bank was influenced by the academic theories prevalent in the 1980s and 1990s. The underwhelming macroeconomic performance of several countries in the 1970s, characterized by the undesirable combination of high unemployment and high inflation known as "stagflation" heightened the recognition of the importance of central banks in managing public expectations regarding policies. This period also emphasized the advantages associated with central banks committing to a policy of low inflation and being granted independence from political influence.[5] By the 1990s, these ideas were having a dramatic effect on monetary policy institutions around the world due to that decade's evidencing a number of central banks adopting explicit inflation targeting regimes and others, such as the Bank of England, be given far greater independence from political control.

The mandate of the ECB aligns with the prevailing ideas of that era. It is an extensively independent central bank with specific measures in place to safeguard against political interference in the monetary policy decisions made by its Governing Council. The primary objective of the ECB is to ensure price stability (Langarde, 2023). Other economic goals are pursued only as long as they do not jeopardize the primary goal of maintaining stable prices. The ECB has proven to be a rather successful institution based on its mandate and how it interprets that mandate. Its management of the euro area economy has resulted in a period of low inflation, with an average inflation rate (measured by the HICP (Harmonized Index of Consumer Prices)) of 1.75% from January 2000 to June 2021. This figure had been in close alignment with the ECB's own definition of price stability as "close to but below two percent." The achievement of this success was not predetermined. Despite having legal structures similar to the Bundesbank, some may have been concerned that the ECB's Governing Council, consisting of representatives from multiple countries with varying inflation histories, would struggle to match the Bundesbank's track record. However, the ECB has not only met but surpassed those expectations (see, for example, Whelan, 2019, p. 9).

5.3 Understanding the Key Drivers of the Eurozone Crisis

The GFC and the subsequent Great Recession of 2008–2009 strained government finances, triggering a confidence crisis in several Eurozone member states that was aggravated by the outcome of domestic malinvestments during the preceding boom. Although there were already indications of a slowdown in global economic growth toward the end of 2006 and early 2007, it is undeniable that financial factors played a crucial role in initiating and exacerbating the macroeconomic impact of the GFC. One of the primary factors was the surge in overall financing costs within the financial sector, which had a ripple effect on companies and households as demonstrated in Fig. 5.2. As conditions in the US housing market deteriorated significantly, there was a sharp increase in perceived risks related to defaults and lack of liquidity. The result was a worldwide revaluation of risk, causing a sudden outbreak of instability in global money markets in August 2007. This event served as a clear indication of the advent of a financial crisis.

[5]The advantages of committing to a policy of low inflation, rather than continuously setting policy in a discretionary manner, are demonstrated in seminal research antecedent to the signing of the Maastricht Treaty, such as Kydland and Prescott (1977) and Barro and Gordon (1983a, 1983b).

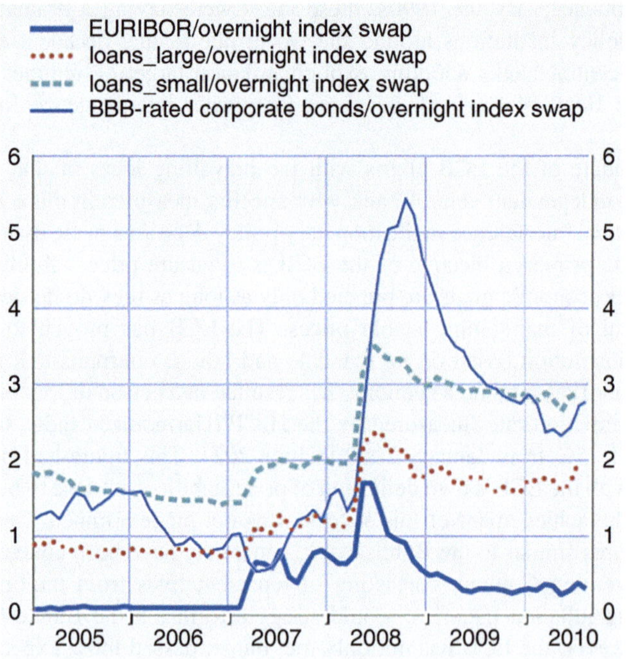

Fig. 5.2 Financial market spreads indicating the onset of the global financial crisis. Note: an overnight indexed swap (OIS) is an interest rate swap where the periodic floating rate of the swap is exchanged for an overnight index. In this chart, the 3-month OIS rate, which is based on the 3-month euro overnight index average (EONIA), is used to calculate the spreads. "EURIBOR" refers to the 3-month euro interbank offered rate. "loans_large" refers to the interest rates applied by monetary financial institutions (MFIs) to loans to nonfinancial corporations of over €1 million with a floating rate and an initial rate fixation period of up to 1 year. "loans_small" refers to MFI interest rates on loans to nonfinancial corporations of up to (and including) €1 million with a floating rate and an initial rate fixation period of up to 1 year. Meanwhile, "BBB-rated corporate bonds" refers to the euro-denominated nonfinancial corporate bond index calculated by Bank of America Merrill Lynch including maturities of over 1 year. Figures in basis points. Source: Kenny and Morgan (2011), p. 8; Reuters and the ECB

When considering the euro area, the financial nature of the global shock became evident in the form of widened money market spreads and increased spreads in bank lending rates for loans to households and nonfinancial businesses. This disparity became even more pronounced following the collapse of Lehman Brothers in September 2008. During this period, there was a significant surge in spreads and overall financing costs, which had a substantial impact on euro area growth, particularly on investment spending. Another financial factor was the general deterioration observed in asset markets beyond the US housing. Notable declines in stock prices as depicted in Fig. 5.3 and house prices in various countries contributed to weakened balance sheets for both firms and households, further intensifying the negative cycle caused by heightened risk perceptions and elevated financing costs. Together with a decline in confidence and deteriorating real economic conditions, these

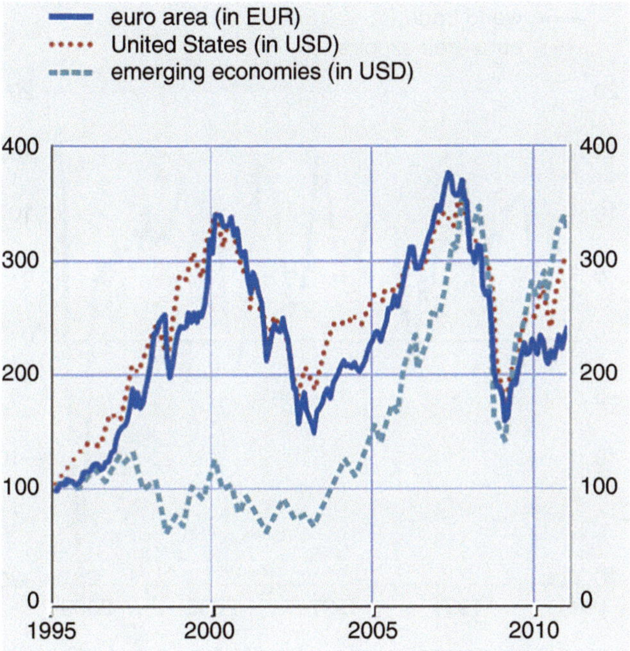

Fig. 5.3 Stock prices in the euro area, the United States, and emerging economies at the onset of the global financial crisis. Note: regional stock market index, January 31, 1995 = 100. Source: Kenny and Morgan (2011), p. 8; datastream (regional market indices)

developments ultimately led to a significant reduction in lending to firms and households in the euro area.

Although financial factors played a critical role in initiating and intensifying the recessionary trends, it is crucial to acknowledge the substantial nonfinancial aspects involved. One notable factor was the widespread decline in business and consumer confidence, which occurred simultaneously across major developed economies within the Organisation for Economic Co-operation and Development (OECD). Specifically in the euro area, this heightened uncertainty likely led to a delay in investment spending by firms. Additionally, households responded by adopting a cautious approach, as evidenced by a significant increase in the household saving rate in the euro area. This shift toward a precautionary behavior reflected the prevailing economic circumstances.[6] Furthermore, after the collapse of Lehman Brothers, global trade experienced a drastic decline as depicted in Fig. 5.4. This decline intensified the worldwide propagation of the shock and the synchronized nature of its consequences. The contraction in trade volumes had a significant effect on economies, including those in the euro area. Interestingly, the extensive

[6]For a discussion on the implications of such heightened uncertainty for economic prospects in the euro area during that era, see ECB Monthly Bulletin, August 2009, Box 6.

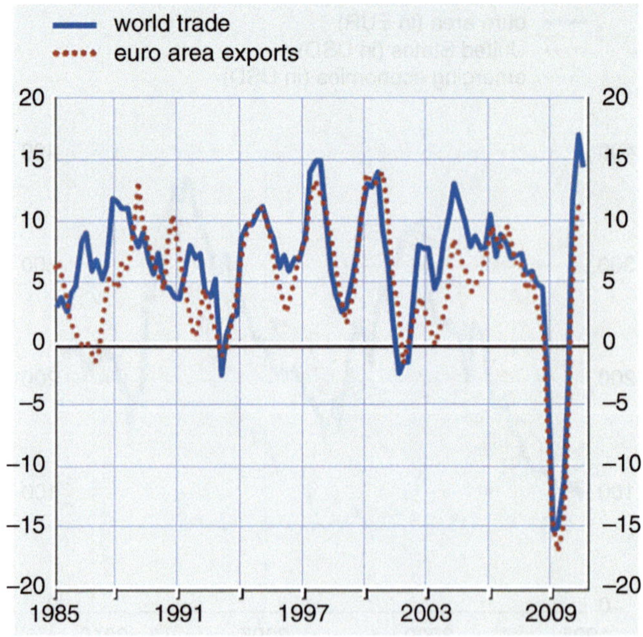

Fig. 5.4 World trade and euro area exports at the onset of the global financial crisis. Note: annual percentage change. Source: Kenny and Morgan (2011), p. 9; Eurostat, and the International Monetary Fund

international connections facilitated by the establishment of global supply chains, which had contributed to the robust expansion of global trade prior to the crisis, paradoxically may have exacerbated the downward spiral observed in the fourth quarter of 2008 and the first quarter of 2009. As a result of these strong international linkages, the quantity of goods exported by euro area member states experienced a substantial decline of more than 16% on average in 2009, compared to the previous year of 2008. In fact, the decline in euro area GDP was largely attributed to the weakness in exports, which was a key factor in causing a more pronounced contraction in economic output compared to previous systemic crises observed in OECD countries (ECB, 2009).

To conclude the analysis of the primary economic factors behind the crisis, Fig. 5.5 offers a visual summary specifically from the perspective of the euro area, highlighting the main elements that have been identified thus far (adapted from Kenny & Morgan, 2011, pp. 8–10). It is essential to note that this diagram primarily focuses on the key triggers, transmission channels, and amplification mechanisms, rather than providing a comprehensive explanation of what ultimately "caused" the crisis. Looking back with the benefit of hindsight, as highlighted by Fig. 5.5, it becomes evident that the financial sector served as the catalyst for the economic events during the GFC. This stands in contrast to traditional business cycle analyses of the three decades antecedent to the GFC, where the financial sector was typically

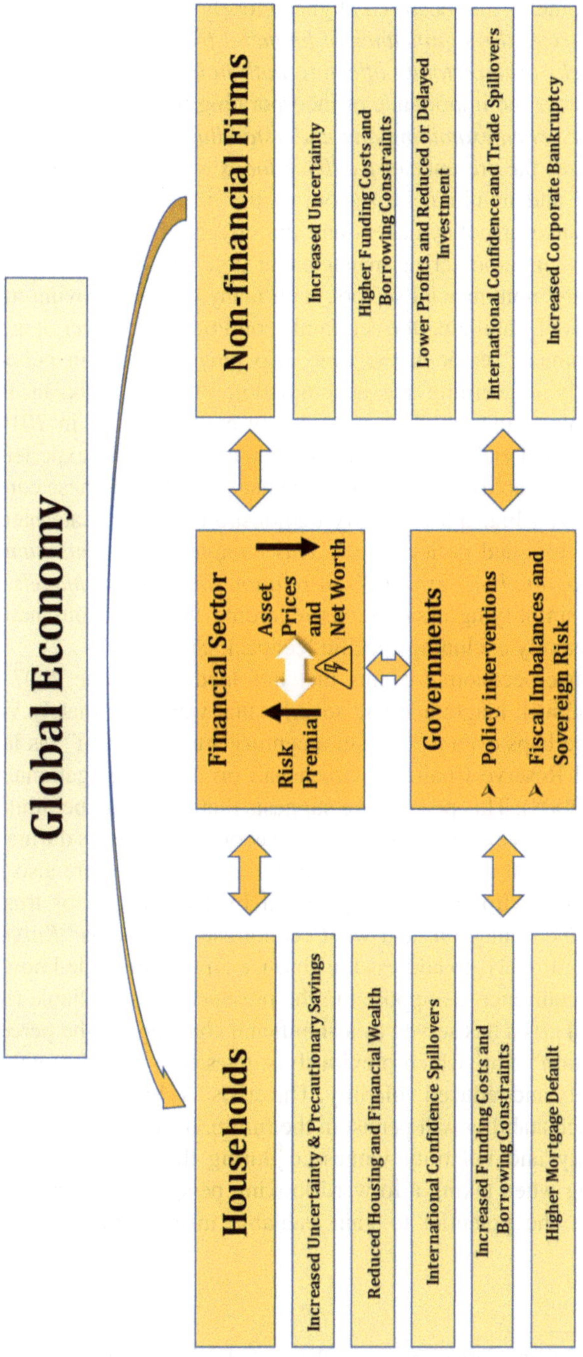

Fig. 5.5 The 2007–2010 financial crisis: key trigger, propagation, and amplification mechanisms. Source: Kenny and Morgan (2011), p. 11

perceived as more passive and not necessarily central to comprehending cyclical dynamics. The developments that occurred aligned closely with the particular body of research that *emphasizes the significance of financial frictions and nonfinancial factors, including shocks of uncertainty affecting both households and businesses*. These findings underscore the importance of incorporating financial considerations and nonfinancial factors *when examining and understanding economic fluctuations*.

Figure 5.5 emphasizes the presence of *feedback loops* within the financial sector and between financial and nonfinancial sectors of the economy. Additionally, it highlights the significance of policymakers and the effects of policy measures on private sector entities. Numerous crisis management policies were put into action within both financial and nonfinancial sectors, with many of them proving to have positive effects in terms of stabilizing the economic conditions. However, it is worth noting that the government sector at the time also played a role in generating uncertainty, particularly concerning the accumulation of fiscal imbalances and sovereign risk in certain countries. This was clearly evident when, in 2010, the long-term government bond yields of several euro area member states experienced a sharp increase following a rapid deterioration in the fiscal position of these euro area member states. Moreover, Fig. 5.5 explicitly demonstrates the intricate nature of interactions among sectors and policy actors. *This complexity presents numerous challenges for economic analysis, especially in relation to the use of models*. Such models often rely on simplifying assumptions regarding the exogenous nature of certain variables, effectively excluding specific feedback channels.

In summary, the macroeconomic events that unfolded during the 2007–2010 financial crisis were of such magnitude and severity that were legitimately viewed as a rare occurrence, perhaps even a "once-in-a-century credit tsunami" (as labeled by former US Federal Reserve Chairman Greenspan on his Congregational testimony on October 23, 2008). This perspective suggests that there may be limitations in applying lessons from this extraordinary period to economic analysis during more normal times. The extreme fluctuations observed during the crisis were also indicative of a panic-driven environment, characterized by the absence of trust, the manifestation of fear and contagion, and what economists refer to as "*Knightian*" *uncertainty* (after Knight, 1921; to address the absence any quantifiable knowledge about some possible occurrence, as opposed to the presence of quantifiable risk).

Indeed, the financial crisis has served as a significant challenge to the perception of the "Great Moderation" era,[7] which previously suggested a period of enhanced macroeconomic stability and reduced volatility. The crisis has brought into question the assumption that such stability will persist in the future. Instead, it suggested that the levels of instability and volatility witnessed during the GFC may be more prevalent and recurring when taking a forward-looking perspective. Consequently, research expanded on the potential to gain valuable insights by studying and

[7] The "Great Moderation," a term coined by Stock and Watson (2002), refers to the reduction in the volatility of the business cycles of many advanced economies that started in the mid-1980s.

Table 5.2 Overview of the main causes of the EU financial crisis

Area	Main causes
Financial system	• Weak corporate governance and risk management • Weak capital and liquidity buffers • Failures of large banks that were "too big to fail"
Regulatory and supervisory framework	• Inadequate microprudential oversight • Different rules between member states • No resolution and adequate winding-up mechanisms
Economic governance	• Low interest rates • Macroeconomic imbalances • High levels of debt

Source: adapted from European Court of Auditors—ECA (2020), pp. 10–11

comprehending these developments, aiming to advance our understanding of macroeconomic dynamics.

5.4 Weaknesses in the Policy Tools, Surveillance Systems, and Regulatory Environments

The 2008 global financial crisis had its roots in the US real estate market, specifically the collapse of the subprime housing bubble. This resulted in substantial losses for banks and had a spillover effect into the European Union (EU) in 2008, primarily through securitized loans. The crisis not only exposed vulnerabilities in the EU financial system but also revealed shortcomings in the surveillance systems, policy tools, and regulatory frameworks of both the EU and its individual member states (Stiglitz, 2017). Varied economic and financial conditions as well as differing policies among EU member states at the start of the Eurozone financial crisis resulted in varying impacts. Nevertheless, there were certain factors common to the EU financial system that contributed to the crisis, including regulatory and supervisory frameworks, as well as economic governance arrangements as summarized in Table 5.2.

Several circumstances pertaining to the three areas depicted in Table 5.2 created *pressures on sovereign bond yields, resulting in financial instability and making it challenging to secure financing from capital markets.* Consequently, assistance was necessary as the crisis unfolded. In particular, these circumstances are clustered as follows (ECA, 2020, pp. 10–11):

Financial system: (1) *Weak corporate governance and risk management.* Inadequate corporate governance and risk management practices were evident during the crisis, characterized by insufficient monitoring and internal control of risks, particularly in loan origination processes, concentration of exposure in specific assets (such as real estate in certain EU member states), and certain complex financial products that were largely unregulated at the time. (2) *Weak capital and liquidity buffers* compared to the level of risk incurred. Insufficient capital and liquidity buffers relative to the level of risk undertaken were observed, with several significant institutions having an equity capital base that represented less than 3% of their balance sheets during the crisis. (3) *Failures of large banks that were "too big to fail"* (such as Lehman Brothers in the United States) or risks of large bank failures in the EU caused the entire banking sector to experience systemic stress.

Regulatory and supervisory framework: (1) *Inadequate microprudential oversight* over the quality of internal risk management and capital and liquidity adequacy, (2) *different rules between member states* within the internal market and weak EU-level coordination for large financial institutions operating across borders and markets, and (3) *no resolution and adequate winding-up mechanisms* for financial institutions and no EU framework to deal with failures of cross-border financial institutions.

Economic governance: (1) *Low interest rates* prior to the crisis contributed to the formation of real-estate bubbles; (2) *macroeconomic imbalances* prior to the crisis remained largely unaddressed, with no EU macroprudential framework in place for systemic risks; and (3) *high levels of debt* accumulated prior or as a result of the crisis among financial institutions and the wider economy, with unbalanced growth in certain euro area member states.

Before the crisis, certain euro area member states exhibited weak monitoring and control over public finances, with low fiscal buffers. Additionally, coordination of economic policies at the EU level was weak (for a detailed analysis, see Kokores, T., 1989), as evidenced by the divergence of economic fundamentals, loss of competitiveness, inflexible labor markets, and product markets. Furthermore, the absence of a robust supranational banking supervision and resolution framework led to fragmentation and increased the risk of a bank-sovereign doom loop. The financial crisis had a significant impact on the banking sector, resulting in substantial losses. The subsequent bailouts of banks put pressure on sovereign debt markets, causing investors to question the stability of the euro area's structure and the sustainability of public debt levels. This spillover effect had wide-ranging consequences for the overall economy. While measures such as state aid for banks, fiscal stimulus, and automatic stabilizers helped stabilize the economy during the initial phase of the crisis, they also contributed to a significant increase in an already high level of public debt. Starting from 2009, the growing public debt created challenges in terms of sovereign yields and credit ratings for specific member states, which raised concerns among investors even about a potential dissolution of the euro area. Member states entered the crisis with varying fiscal and macroeconomic conditions, and capital outflows from certain countries exacerbated preexisting macroeconomic imbalances (Table 5.3).

Table 5.3 Years leading to full current account adjustment and cumulative output loss depending on the inflation rate

Inflation	Average wage growth	Core wage growth	Years to adjust	GDP loss
1	2	3	6.7	13.3
2	3	4.5	4.2	8.4
3	4	6	3.3	6.6
4	5	7.5	2.7	5.4

Source: Krugman (2014), p. 117, based on own calculations

5.5 Reflections on the Weaknesses of the Monetary Policy Environment in the European Union and Its Member Countries

The global financial crisis and the Great Recession led to significant government expenditure programs aimed at bailing out distressed banks and implementing countercyclical deficit spending across all euro area member states. This resulted in a sharp increase in public debt levels, leading investors to question the creditworthiness of economically weaker euro area member states. This skepticism was reflected in the substantial rise in risk premia on government bonds of countries such as Greece, Ireland, Portugal, Spain, Cyprus, and Italy, accompanied by multiple downgrades by rating agencies. Conversely, core countries like Germany enjoyed the benefits of being perceived as safe havens, allowing them to access funding at lower costs. The situation was exacerbated in countries where the preceding economic boom had created significant imbalances in the domestic capital stock and production structures, placing additional strain on government budgets (resulting in higher structural unemployment) and the financial sector (with a rise in nonperforming domestic financial claims).

The high levels of domestic public debt held by national banking sectors "revealed a problematic bank-sovereign loop," as the devaluation of these assets weakened the capital base of banks and undermined the credibility of national bailout efforts for banks in crisis-stricken countries. Consequently, the banking industry in the Eurozone faced an uneven playing field, as the solvency of banks became closely linked to the solvency of their respective sovereigns. These concerns, coupled with growing fears of distressed countries exiting the Eurozone, triggered capital and liquidity flight from the periphery to the core countries (Gern et al., 2019, p. 15). The Eurozone crisis that occurred in the autumn of 2011 was a direct consequence of the preceding financial crisis in 2008–2009. During this period, the government bond yields of several countries within the economic and monetary union reached levels that were not sustainable in the long run.[8]

[8] With the 10-year German bond (known as the Bund) yielding 2.26% at the time, the bond yields of other countries within the euro area reveal a significant spread. Italy, with a gross debt of 120% of GDP, had a bond yield of 7.28%. Spain's bond yield stood at 6.62%, Belgium's at 5.65%, and

Consequently, the Eurozone sovereign debt market became strained from buyers, with the exception of occasional purchases by the European Central Bank (ECB) and domestic financial institutions that faced either explicit or implicit pressure from their respective governments. This situation was further compounded by a shortage of liquidity in the market.[9]

The countries at the heart of the Eurozone crisis were located on the geographical periphery of the Eurozone and faced diverse sources of their predicaments. Crucially, these hazards were not primarily a result of their membership in the single currency or fiscal recklessness.[10] *The four countries, namely Greece, Ireland,*

France's at 3.63%. This indicated a spread of 137 basis points over the Bund. It is worth noting that prior to 2008, this spread was close to zero for most of the period from 1999 to 2008. Consequently, only Germany's Bund had been considered a risk-free "safe asset" among the Eurozone government bonds. However, even the credit default swap (CDS) premium for Germany had risen to 110 basis points, compared to 40 in July 2011. Even though the CDS market may not provide a reliable indicator of default risk, it does nevertheless offer insights into sovereign bond prices. The signal transmitted had been rather cautious over the next 3 years as Italy had a CDS spread of 535 basis points, Spain at 466, Belgium at 344, and France at 225.

[9]Euribor, although still below levels seen in 2008–2009, kept rising, making it difficult for banks to access market funding, particularly in dollars. Reports indicated evident shortcomings in the functioning of the repo market. The European Financial Stability Facility (EFSF) faced challenges in selling some of its bond issues and acknowledged limited leverage possibilities. France was at risk of losing its AAA rating, and all euro area banks were under review by rating agencies. Greek banks experienced a steady decline in deposits, and similar but slower trends were observed in other vulnerable countries, indicating concerns among depositors. The reliability of the sovereign CDS market itself was questioned as authorities sought to restructure Greek debt without triggering CDS contracts, raising doubts about the effectiveness of CDS as insurance. On a positive note, ECB monetary policy was still deemed credible based on market inflation expectations, with inflation projected at 1.79% over a 5-year horizon and 2.04% over a 10-year horizon. However, the underlying issue was that ECB policy rates had been too high. The prime ministers of Greece and Italy at the time were experienced and capable, understanding the necessary steps for restarting economic growth in their respective countries. However, as they were not elected politicians, their legitimacy and authority were limited (Portes, 2014, p. 424). Considering that implementing the necessary measures did remain challenging irrespective of popular support, indeed, the effectiveness of technocratic governments in carrying out such measures had been put into severe scrutiny.

[10]With the benefit of hindsight, we may concisely address the case of the main four euro area periphery countries that faced the major challenges from the Eurozone crisis, namely, Greece, Ireland, Portugal, and Spain.

Greece stood as an exception to the aforementioned general statement due to its significant fiscal imbalances, which were partially concealed from statisticians. However, the issues faced by Greece are not solely attributed to fiscal matters but also stem from profound structural weaknesses, particularly within its institutions (Jacobides et al., 2011), high levels of political polarization, and irresponsible capital inflows that masked these fundamental flaws for a considerable period. As Portes (2014) remarks, it would be incorrect to simplify these factors as merely a lack of "competitiveness" that could have been resolved through currency devaluation if Greece were not a member of the Eurozone (Portes, 2014, p. 424).

Ireland encountered significant difficulties due to an unprecedented increase in the housing market, characterized by an inflated housing bubble. In Ireland, this surge was driven by irresponsible capital inflows into property development and mortgage financing facilitated by domestic banks, along with a culture of favoritism toward capitalists (crony capitalism) (Allen, 2000).

Portugal, and Spain (the GIPS), initially had stable fiscal positions but were facing significant current account deficits within the Eurozone, which were financed by substantial capital inflows from surplus countries, particularly Germany. The result was a surge of capital flow into the periphery countries with predictable outcomes (see Reinhart & Reinhart, 2008). *Unlike the overall current account balance of the Eurozone with the rest of the world, which was relatively balanced, the imbalances were internal to the Eurozone* (Portes, 2014). Germany assumed a role similar to that of China in the global economy. However, unlike the United States, the GIPS were not characterized as "free spenders."

Although Ireland, Spain, and Greece experienced housing booms, their overall consumption as a percentage of GDP declined, while the investment share increased during the period from 2000 to 2007 (with a slight decrease in Portugal's investment share). Furthermore, as Portes (2014) highlights, "unlike China, *the capital flows from Germany (as well as some other countries like France)* came primarily from banks – *they were private*, not official, flows[emphasis added]" (p. 425). Therefore, the macroeconomic problem in the euro area had been *the fiscal consequence of the financial crisis in bank-based financial systems*. Portes (2014) further remarks: "Creditor countries have been unwilling to let their banks suffer the consequences of bad loans-rather, they have managed to put the entire burden on the taxpayers of the debtor countries. This may seem clever, but it is short-sighted, not to say hypocritical. It also disregards the EU and Eurozone financial integration that policymakers have promoted" (p. 425).[11]

However, the primary factor contributing to Ireland's current difficulties was not solely the housing boom, but rather the government's choice to guarantee the debts of the affected banks. This decision effectively transferred private debt onto the public sector, resulting in a substantial change in Ireland's debt dynamics and causing the country's public debt-to-GDP ratio to reach exceptionally high levels (Allen, 2009; Smyth, 2011).

Portugal faced several economic challenges, including inadequate education, an uncompetitive production system, and inflexible product and labor markets. However, Portugal's main error was failing to utilize the substantial capital inflow it received in the precrisis era to modernize its economy (Portes, 2014). *Spain* also experienced a housing boom and an influx of capital into the construction sector. These issues were worsened by the reckless actions of politically influenced regional banks which faced significant challenges when the housing bubble collapsed.

[11] As a result, Greece faced insolvency, while Ireland had excessive debt that needed restructuring (Portes, 2011). The IMF program in Portugal was deemed unworkable. Spain and Italy, on the other hand, were solvent under the condition that financial markets returned to normal and both countries implemented appropriate macroeconomic and structural policies. However, Spain, Italy, and even France faced market pressure. There were also concerns that Spanish banks would suffer further from the impact of bad real estate loans, leading to potential state bailouts. In Italy, political instability and indecisiveness exacerbated the contagion from weaker countries, resulting in a self-perpetuating vicious circle; rising costs of servicing debt weakened Italy's fiscal position (despite being close to primary fiscal balance), eroding market confidence and causing a rise in borrowing costs that made debt service increasingly unsustainable. Confidence in French banks also diminished in the eyes of the markets, despite assurances of their soundness from the banks and regulators (Portes, 2014).

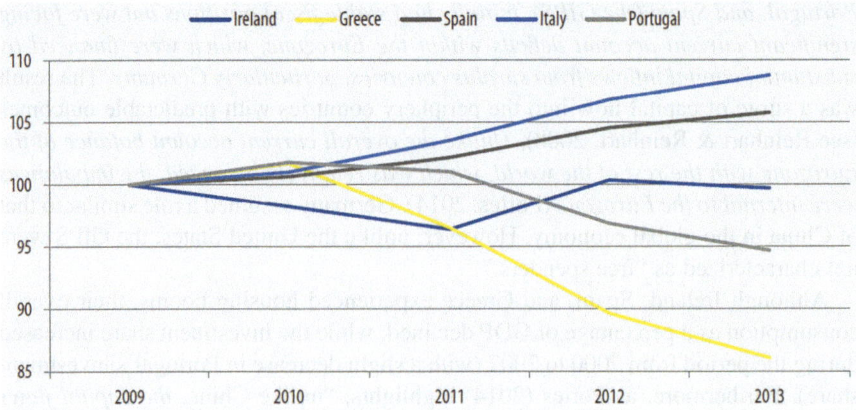

Fig. 5.6 Hourly compensation in manufacturing in the Eurozone periphery. Note: base year 2009: value 100. Source: Krugman (2014), p. 117; Eurostat

The presence of downward nominal wage rigidity is evident in the macroeconomic data within the euro area. The euro crisis, according to Krugman (2014), can be best understood as a classic sudden stop phenomenon. Peripheral European countries experienced substantial capital inflows that led to a significant real appreciation of their currencies. However, these capital flows abruptly ceased, leading these nations to undertake substantial internal devaluations by reducing wages relative to the core economies. Since internal devaluation is a time-consuming process, the intermediate-term effect is a need for current account adjustment through economic contraction and import reduction.

Remarkably, considering this narrative, the adjustment in nominal wages had been minimal. Figure 5.6 illustrates the nominal compensation in manufacturing for debtor nations in the euro area during the Eurozone crisis; the manufacturing sector is utilized by Krugman (2014) to mitigate compositional effects arising from the sharp decline in Spain's low-wage construction sector. *Except for Greece, none of the debtor countries have experienced a significant decline in compensation, despite having exceptionally high unemployment rates* (Krugman, 2014, p. 116). In fact, *according to the International Labour Organization (ILO) Global Wage Report 2018/2019, the nominal wage reduction in Greece during 2008–2017 had been at 31%, while also Eurostat reported a 23% income reduction.* Assigning responsibility for this lack of adjustment to structural rigidities is also challenging. Even countries like Ireland, which received recognition for their flexibility prior to the crisis, have shown resistance to wage cuts similar to Spain and Portugal. This pattern is observed in other countries that have been commended for their flexibility as well. Blanchard et al. (2014) report that private sector wages in Latvia have essentially not declined.

Within the context of the euro area, the presence of downward nominal wage rigidity creates challenges by complicating the process of internal devaluation. As a result, the period of significantly reduced output in debtor nations had been prolonged.[12] While it is uncertain how frequently we can anticipate occurrences similar to the euro crisis and its aftermath, this situation serves as an illustration that in a currency area with imperfect integration, lacking fiscal integration and sufficient labor mobility as recommended by traditional theories of optimal currency areas, moderate inflation can play a vital role in facilitating the adjustment process. Conversely, low inflation can lead to substantial losses. A common characteristic among all four member states' cases (GIPS) was the interdependence of a sovereign debt crisis and a banking crisis. The banks held substantial amounts of questionable sovereign debt, and the credibility of the sovereigns was undermined due to the potential need for them to bail out their banks (Portes, 2014, p. 425; Krugman, 2014, p. 118). In situations where an economy with low inflation faces a significant adverse shock to demand, its central bank may encounter challenges in preventing a self-perpetuating cycle that leads to a prolonged period of low inflation or deflation.

The concept of a self-reinforcing process, known as *debt deflation*, was originally introduced by Irving Fisher (1933). Despite being largely overlooked by the economics profession for many years, it has regained attention since the GFC. Figure 5.7 illustrates this phenomenon, demonstrating a transition from increasing leverage to deleveraging during the crisis. Deflation or lower-than-expected inflation can elevate real debt burdens compared to a scenario with stable inflation, resulting in an economic drag that further diminishes inflation. Similar to the challenge of downward nominal wage rigidity, this issue became particularly pronounced within the euro area during the sovereign debt crisis, where the repercussions of a debt bubble were needed to be addressed in an environment of imperfect integration. Figure 5.7 provides a comparison between debt levels (both public and private) and core inflation within the euro area. It is not surprising that countries burdened with high levels of debt, stemming from the housing and capital flow bubble between 2000 and 2007, also experienced low inflation or deflation due to the necessity of internal devaluation. Consequently, the impact of debt deflation within the euro area is more substantial than what is apparent when solely examining overall inflation in the region.

[12]To illustrate the rationale behind this, we may simplify the process of euro area adjustment using the following model: Initially, there is a significant decline in output in the peripheral countries, which is large enough to roughly balance their current accounts. This is followed by an internal devaluation that occurs solely through increasing wages in the core countries and a gradual recovery in peripheral output. The duration of this process depends on the magnitude of the required internal devaluation and the rate at which core wages rise, which is directly linked to the inflation rate of the currency area. Let us consider a stylized but reasonably realistic numerical example. We assume that the euro periphery represents one-third of the euro area GDP and needs to achieve a 20% internal devaluation relative to the core. Furthermore, we assume that the inflation rate in the euro area equals the average wage increase minus 1%. Lastly, we assume that the initial output loss in the periphery compared to its potential, before internal devaluation can take place, amounts to 12% of GDP or 4% of the entire area's GDP. As Table 5.3 depicts, the time required for adjustment and the cumulative output loss, measured in percentage years of GDP, are influenced by the underlying inflation rate. Evidently, a higher inflation rate smoothens the path of adjustment. Furthermore, this effect is significant even at between 3% and 4% inflation (Krugman, 2014, p. 117).

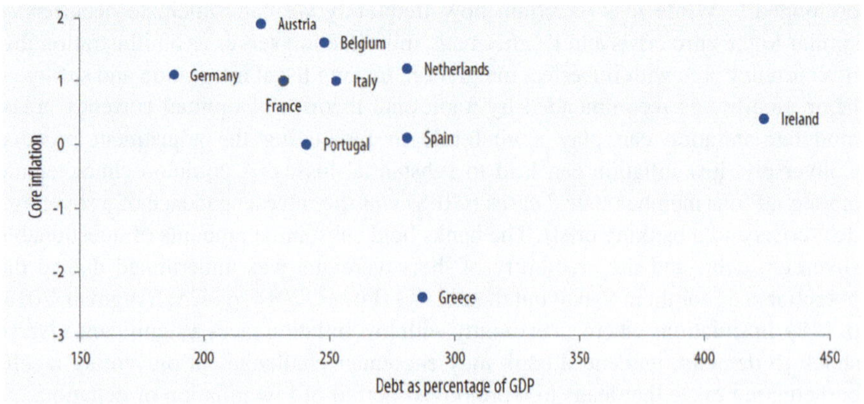

Fig. 5.7 Total (public and private) debt and core inflation in the euro area during the Eurozone crisis. Source: Krugman (2014), p. 119; Eurostat

Apart from the possibility of triggering debt deflation as in Fisher (1933), low inflation can exacerbate itself through expectational influences. When an economy reaches the zero lower bound, a decline in inflation leads to an increase in real interest rates, which can dampen economic activity and further decrease inflation. This self-reinforcing cycle of declining inflation and rising real interest rates can perpetuate the low inflation environment.[13] Therefore, *doom loops* arise as depicted in Fig. 5.8 and exacerbated by elements of Fisher (1933)-type debt deflation. The term *doom loop* describes a situation where risks associated with both weak banks and high levels of sovereign debt intensify each other. In some countries, the need to bail out banks resulted in elevated levels of government debt. Consequently, the assets held by banks, which largely comprised domestic sovereign debt, decreased in value, leading to a weakened banking system. In other countries, high levels of debt placed strain on the banking sector. Additionally, a significant number of euro area countries experienced negative GDP growth rates in 2012 and 2013, with nine countries in 2012 and eight countries in 2013.

The euro (monetary union) was not the cause of this crisis. It would have been much easier to contain and resolve had there been no global financial crisis, no deep recession in the advanced countries. It is therefore too facile, indeed wrong, to say that the Eurozone crisis was essentially or even mainly due to inherent faults in the monetary union. Nevertheless, the crisis had exposed genuine faults that were neither manifest nor life-threatening before 2008–2009 (Portes, 2014, p. 423). The ECB's handling of the crisis seemed to have also hindered a solution. The ECB has been reluctant to acknowledge the gravity of the situation, maintaining until as late

[13] Inflation can have a "stall speed," meaning that if inflation is too low during periods of economic stability, central banks may be unable to effectively counteract a downward spiral when faced with adverse shocks. The challenging task of combating such a downturn is often compounded by the political and economic dynamics associated with low inflation.

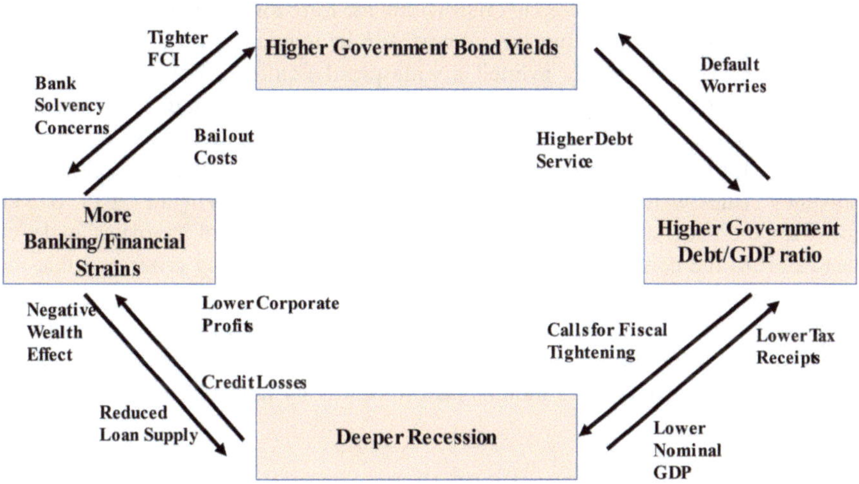

Fig. 5.8 Financial instability: doom loops. Source: Goldman Sachs, *Global Economics Weekly* 11/38, Nov. 2011; Portes (2014), p. 427

as May 2011 that it was unimaginable for a Eurozone country to default on its debt. The agreement reached in July 2011 to restructure Greek debt was essentially an admission of default, regardless of whether the restructuring was considered "voluntary" or not. In autumn 2008, the ECB informed Ireland that it was not permitted to consider debt default, backed by the threat of withdrawing repo facilities. It is unusual for a central bank to dictate to a government what it can or cannot do in fiscal matters.

The decision to provide support to banks placed additional pressure on strained government finances, causing concerns about the possibility of countries failing to meet their financial obligations and raising uncertainties about the stability of private banks. As funding from external sources decreased and banks encountered difficulties in meeting regulatory capital standards, lending by banks in peripheral economies experienced a sudden and severe decline, worsening economic downturns. The increased perception of risks linked to both governments and banks greatly contributed to the Eurozone entering a recession in 2012, while the rest of the world was enjoying a strong economic rebound.[14] The European Central Bank (ECB) played a

[14]The significance of the banking sector in pre-economic and monetary union (EMU) discussions was minimal, but it became apparent that euro area countries were particularly susceptible to systemic banking pressures. The European Union's free movement of capital allowed investors and depositors to withdraw their funds from struggling banks without incurring costs. Additionally, deposit insurance funding operated at a national level, meaning that concerns about a state's ability to handle failing banks could further trigger deposit withdrawals. This interplay between concerns about bank and state solvency was most pronounced in Ireland in 2010 when the government's attempt to rescue its banking sector raised concerns about potential sovereign default. Similar concerns have also impacted other countries, such as Cyprus and Greece, at different points over the past decade. Other issues related to the banking sector included the lack of harmonization in rules

key role in addressing the banking crisis within the Eurozone, although the outcomes were varied. By implementing full allotment in its regular monetary policy operations, the ECB successfully averted a widespread liquidity crisis throughout the banking system in the Eurozone; this measure prevented certain countries from facing the severe disruptions typically associated with "sudden stops" in financial markets. The ECB's interactions with different banks that encountered significant solvency issues were not very encouraging.[15] According to Whelan (2019, p. 19), however, the uncertainty surrounding the ECB's performance of its role as lender of last resort to the banking system has tended to worsen banking crises and that the politicization of this role has damaged the reputation of the ECB as an institution. Politicians share responsibility, however, with their indecision and endlessly repeated "too little, too late" measures—such as the agreement of July 21, 2011, which was recognized only 3 months later to be wholly inadequate.[16]

5.6 Policy Implications of the Eurozone Crisis

The euro is a political project, no less than an economic project (Fisher, 2012, p. 493). While it made significant progress in its initial years, the flaws of the project have become increasingly apparent over the past decade. These weaknesses manifest in the form of substantial budget deficits, some of which were revealed only after correcting previously inaccurate data. There are also cost disparities among countries, resulting in differences in competitiveness and balance of payments, as well as variations in the strength of banking systems. A notable distinction between the United States and Europe is that following the Lehman Brothers' collapse, the United States promptly addressed its banking crisis head-on. In contrast, European

governing the resolution of banks and the complexities involved in dealing with failing cross-border banking entities.

[15]The ECB's policies concerning collateral policies for refinancing operations and, specifically, Emergency Liquidity Assistance (ELA) to banks were deemed inadequate (Whelan 2014, 2015, 2016). There were instances of lending to banks with severe insolvency issues, a lack of transparency regarding the conditions for capping or withdrawing ELA by the Eurosystem, and a series of decisions where the provision or restriction of ELA seemed to be influenced by political developments in different countries (Whelan, 2019).

[16]As highlighted in Portes (2014), the French president and German chancellor have made two significant mistakes that have had a disastrous impact on the markets. The Deauville statement in October 2010 introduced, in a poorly thought-out manner, the possibility of involving the private sector in addressing the debt of Eurozone countries. This had a detrimental effect on market confidence. Additionally, a year later, the Cannes statement explicitly suggested the potential for an EMU member country to exit the euro, which went against established norms and was considered a taboo. This proposal lacked any legal basis. Some have drawn a parallel with the statement made by the president of the Bundesbank in early September 1992, which allowed for the immediate exit of Italy and the United Kingdom from the EMS after he mentioned that "devaluations cannot be ruled out" (quoted in Portes, 2014, p. 427).

countries were more optimistic about the condition of their banks and failed to act swiftly enough to recapitalize and restore their health. However, it is important to acknowledge that no banking system, no matter how robust or well-capitalized, can endure a prolonged recession. Moreover, the weaknesses are evident in the failure of both markets and political authorities to hold accountable countries that were clearly deviating from the right path. Discipline measures were lacking, highlighting the need for better oversight and enforcement mechanisms.

Fisher (2012) notably remarks the following: "Now, we could have a discussion of why didn't we see this crisis coming. That could be very interesting, particularly as a lot of people did see it coming. But we are where we are, the eurozone is where it is, and looking backward isn't going to get the zone out of its difficulties without diagnosing the current situation" (p. 493). The crisis has brought about a significant outcome by providing greater clarity on the necessary measures for the long-term survival of the euro and the eventual growth of the Eurozone. Fisher (2012) emphasizes three key aspects that have garnered increasing attention in the discussions: the establishment of a fiscal union, the formation of a banking union, and the identification of mechanisms for maintaining discipline, particularly fiscal discipline, within the system. These features are considered crucial for the future stability and progress of the euro and the Eurozone.[17]

The issue of discipline appears to be more significant than it has been acknowledged thus far. Doubt has been cast on the ability of club members to effectively enforce discipline on weaker members without creating tensions among countries, which goes against the original purpose of the European Union to prevent such conflicts. To understand this problem, one can observe the current pressure exerted by Germany on Greece and the resulting tensions. If we were to examine the root causes of the Eurozone's current difficulties, it would undoubtedly include the initial failure of financial markets to impose discipline on national governments by setting national risk premia to zero upon entry into the Eurozone (Fisher, 2012). This can be attributed to the assumption that countries would be rescued if they encountered difficulties, and some argue that the markets were correct, as countries were indeed

[17] Regarding the *fiscal union*, the establishment of a complete fiscal union would require a corresponding political union or, at the very least, a political structure capable of addressing economic interactions that necessitate central-level intervention. This does not necessitate an immediate full fiscal union but rather requires progress toward empowering a European authority with legal powers and sufficient funds to address issues that require transfers among member countries. This could be achieved through dedicated taxes that are significantly larger than the current contributions to Brussels. To ensure full legitimacy, greater involvement of national political entities in the process, potentially through national legislatures, would be necessary. As for the *banking union*, progress has been occurring at a faster pace than anticipated, with the ECB preparing itself for supervisory responsibilities at the zone level. However, there are doubts among certain elements in European national central banks and governments regarding the desirability of locating Eurozone bank supervision within the ECB, as well as the feasibility of initiating zone-wide regulation (beginning of 2013). Nonetheless, efforts to establish uniform banking standards in Europe, particularly for systemically important banks, gained momentum, and the necessary work is underway.

been bailed out. However, it is important to note that not all holders of Greek government debt received a full bailout. The bailouts have been partial, resulting in significant pain for certain bondholders. Fisher (2012) further argues in favor of market discipline to curb governments' inclination to maintain larger budget deficits than is prudent; rendering the concept of euro bonds contradictory to this objective as it eliminates a crucial source of market discipline. This is why to remain in the monetary union had been deemed at the time as (and remains) the most favorable outcome for Greece, after effectively defaulting. By doing so, it would be widely recognized—lasting as long as market participants remember—that default is possible within the monetary union and that their debts are not guaranteed by the central authority. Eventually, European politicians and dedicated policymakers grasped the fundamental issues and the ultimate solution, and they engaged in discussions aimed at implementing the necessary measures. However, while policymakers were demonstrating an increasing comprehension of the challenges and reasserting their commitment to safeguarding and sustaining the euro, a contrasting trend emerged among the general public in Europe.

As highlighted by Reinhart and Rogoff (2009), financial crises typically lead to a significant rise in government debt levels. This has been observed in the aftermath of the recent crisis, where extensive financial institution bailouts, fiscal stimulus measures, and economic contractions have adversely impacted the fiscal positions of many countries. Advanced economies like the United States have commonly experienced budget deficits exceeding 10% of GDP. Consequently, *concerns have emerged regarding the potential for sovereign debt defaults, particularly evident in Europe following the Greek debt crisis and the challenges faced by the Irish government in dealing with the escalating costs of bank bailouts. The necessary fiscal adjustments to restore sustainable fiscal balances are likely to have contractionary effects and further strain societal dynamics. In fact, there is even a possibility that the fiscal challenges arising from the crisis could ultimately lead to some countries exiting the euro* (Mishkin, 2011, p. 88).

Fisher (2012) wonders "What is not clear is what are believed to be the alternatives with regard to future developments in the eurozone" (p. 496), while Portes (2014, p. 428) acknowledges that various solutions have been proposed to address the situation. One option have been to recapitalize the banks if their capital is insufficient, even at the challenge of securing external funding for this purpose, especially if government involvement is excluded. The problem underlying bank recapitalization is exacerbated when the markets are reluctant to provide even short-term funding to banks. As a result, banks have resorted to deleveraging by selling assets and not renewing loans, which has had detrimental effects globally.

Another suggestion proposed had been to expand or leverage the European Financial Stability Facility (EFSF). However, in this case, non-euro countries have been unwilling to contribute, borrowing from the European Central Bank (ECB) was prohibited at the time of the Eurozone crisis, and Eurozone countries were reluctant to provide additional funds. The most drastic option proposed for Greece, for example, was to exit the Eurozone in an attempt to restore stability. However, this would likely trigger severe bank runs in other countries that could potentially be seen as next in line after Greece. It is reasonable to assume that businesses and households in Portugal, Ireland, Spain, or Cyprus would strive to protect their bank deposits, even if the probability of overnight devaluation were low (Portes, 2014). The probable outcome would have been multiple exits, potentially leading to the disintegration of the monetary union. Such a scenario would be disastrous not only for the departing "weaker" countries but also for those remaining, as they would experience substantial exchange rate appreciation and the resulting economic turbulence due to heightened contract uncertainty.

Nonetheless, a few potential options remained to be proposed at the time. The first was for all member countries to remain in the Eurozone, which had proven to be increasingly the desired outcome among European authorities. The second possibility, which was once considered, namely, for Greece to exit the monetary union, had been received with less enthusiasm, even among those who believed that it would serve as a valuable lesson for all countries and markets. The importance of adhering to the established rules had gained emphasis, and moreover, concerns about the extent of contagion have grown over the past year (Forbes, 2012). Another option that emerged had been for the stronger countries to form a smaller but more resilient Eurozone. While this may seem straightforward, the political dynamics of deciding which countries would be included and excluded required significant consideration. It was highly unlikely that those wishing to remain in the Eurozone would be willing to abandon others with a dismissive attitude, as this stance would undermine the process of European integration.

Therefore, the focus on a remaining potential viable solution had been cast to the crucial role of the ECB in preventing a complete breakdown of the system. Then ECB's President Mario Draghi's speech (July 26, 2012) in London—dubbed as the "whatever it takes" speech—marked a significant breakthrough by stating that the ECB would intervene when countries are engaged in supervised programs aimed at addressing their difficulties. This stand by the monetary authority had been a critical development, although it also presents significant challenges. During the crisis, many leaders of troubled countries initially denied the severity of their problems, which is evidently a common stage in any crisis as observed in the IMF. IMF's varied experience in crisis resolution highlights that, eventually, they come to realize the need for a program, but this process takes time, and valuable time is wasted while the problem worsens. Eventually, countries facing difficulties do request a program, and once it is established, the monetary authority can help them maintain reasonable interest rates.

Portes (2014), therefore, maintains that (at the time) "the only solution is for the ECB to accept explicitly, in some form, the role of lender of last resort (LLR) for the monetary union, [which] one might alternatively regard this as a form of quantitative easing, [and] this does come within the Maastricht Treaty mandate" (p. 428).[18] The

[18]In accordance with Article 105(1) of this Treaty, the primary objective of the ESCB shall be to maintain price stability. Without prejudice to the objective of price stability, it shall support the general economic policies in the Community.... The ESCB shall contribute to the smooth conduct

implication is that the ECB, under its Secondary Market Program, undertakes only ad hoc government debt purchases in its effort to normalize the monetary transmission mechanism that had been impaired by debt market instability. This represents a variation of the so-called constructive ambiguity that central bankers often employ, a negotiation technique first employed in the 1970s by Henry Kissinger, premised on the belief that ambiguously worded text can create opportunities for advancing the interests of both parties to a negotiation (Elgindy, 2014). However, in the case of the ECB addressing the effects of the Eurozone crisis, the approach could have been more detrimental than beneficial. The incremental and reactive approach, characterized by delayed action under pressure, has proven to be highly costly. Essentially, the ECB is engaged in a high-stakes game with both politicians and the markets, resembling a game of "chicken" (Portes, 2014), which is proven to be particularly hazardous for two reasons: firstly, there are three players involved, with no single decision-maker among them, and, secondly, the parameters that define the game are not well-defined. This lack of clarity makes it challenging to predict when a vicious downward spiral may transform into an uncontrollable crisis of confidence, beyond the authorities' ability to manage.

On the other hand, the ECB tends to require political support in order to openly assume the role of lender of last resort. It is crucial for the leaders of Germany and France to articulate the argument that this is the sole method of preserving the monetary union. Subsequently, the ECB should make a significant announcement regarding the new policy, aiming to reshape expectations, similar to the approach taken by the Swiss National Bank when it implemented a cap on the value of the Swiss franc. Drawing from this example, it is highly probable that if such a commitment were made, the financial markets would acknowledge that speculating

---

of policies pursued by the competent authorities relating to the prudential supervision of credit institutions and the stability of the financial system (*Treaty of Maastricht (1992), Article 2 and Protocols Art. 105.5 (numbering changes in Lisbon Treaty, but no change in text).* It would not violate the "no bailout clause" (which does exclude ECB purchases of Eurozone sovereign debt on the primary market). And in fact, the ECB has been purchasing member state bonds on the secondary market since May 2010, without any successful legal challenge. To stop self-fulfilling confidence crises, therefore, it has been suggested that the ECB should commit to capping yields for solvent countries through unlimited purchases in the secondary markets. This approach would lead to a decrease in primary issue yields as arbitrage brings them down to the capped level. Notably, this commitment would apply to solvent countries, as opposing such purchases for insolvent countries, like Greece in May 2010, would be justified (as proposed by then governor of the Bundesbank). Portes (2014) argues that this policy does not pose any significant inflation risk, as is the case for quantitative easing, as demonstrated in the case of the United States, the United Kingdom, and Japan. The ECB can always adjust its measures to tighten monetary policy as needed, retaining as its primary concern, however, the risk of incidents of moral hazard. The ECB strongly believed and still does that "market discipline" is the most effective way to encourage desired macroeconomic policies. This is evidenced by instances such as Berlusconi's departure and the appointment of Mario Monti as Italy's Prime Minister, as well as the technocratic government in Greece led by former ECB Vice President Lucas Papademos, which was willing to implement the stringent austerity measures demanded by the IMF-ECB-EC troika. Financial market pressures are intentionally utilized to compel governments to adopt austerity measures and reforms.

against bonds (engaging in a speculative attack) would prove futile because the ECB possesses the unrestricted capacity to resist. Consequently, the ECB may not need to purchase substantial amounts of bonds or perhaps not purchase any at all.

More important, Blinder (2012, p. 490) emphasizes that while it is significant to maintain anti-inflation credibility, the latter encompasses more than just this aspect. It is equally crucial for a central bank to make promises, such as Ben Bernanke's commitment to prevent a financial crisis in the United States in 2008 or Mario Draghi's pledge to preserve the euro in 2012, and vitally to follow through on those promises. Successfully handling a financial crisis requires not only effective policy measures but also a high level of transparency and extensive communication. The public, the markets, and the politicians deserve comprehensive, clear, and coherent explanations of any unconventional or unprecedented policy actions. It is important to remember that credibility is established by aligning actions with words. Although Montagu Norman (Bank of England's longest-serving Governor from 1920 to 1944) famously advocated for a central bank to "never explain, never apologize" (Boyle, 1967, p. 217), for example, Krugman (2009) and Blinder (2012) argue that this approach is mistaken.

Ideally, in addition to implementing short-term measures for stabilization, it is important to have long-term strategies for fiscal stability and integration, along with the introduction of Eurobonds that carry joint and varied liability at the Eurozone level. This approach creates a "convergence play" similar to what facilitated a smooth transition into the EMU in the late 1990s. Although there were several proposals for Eurobonds being discussed during the Eurozone crisis, the leaders of the major countries have subsequently rejected them (yet accepting them in the subsequent crisis). In the meantime, while the ECB's suggested policy could provide a temporary respite for economic reforms to take effect, achieving long-term debt sustainability ultimately relies on economic growth. However, implementing fiscal contraction measures tends to have a contractionary effect on the economy (Guajardo et al., 2011). The sole exception to this is observed in the case of Ireland during the 1980s. Ireland, being a relatively less developed nation, experienced significant progress in catching up with technological advancements. Additionally, it benefited from an economic boom in its major trading partners, particularly the United Kingdom, and successfully attracted foreign direct investment due to its highly advantageous conditions. Moreover, Ireland capitalized on the contributions of a well-educated diaspora who were willing to return and contribute to the country's growth.

At that stage, the contest gets under way (Fisher, 2012). The challenge lies in whether politicians can effectively convey to their respective populations the reasons why they should embrace the euro. This includes explaining how surplus countries benefit from the euro due to their superior productivity and the subsequent strengthening of their export markets as they become low-cost producers. However, this task is not easy, as it implies acknowledging that deficit countries may be at a disadvantage. It becomes the responsibility of deficit country politicians to justify to their own populations why this is still a favorable situation for them. This is the task that lies ahead for politicians. The crucial question is whether politicians can successfully convince their constituents and whether their political processes can support this endeavor within a timeframe that outpaces the rapid actions of the ECB and the programs that countries may undertake under each pertinent crisis occasion. This presents a challenging issue that needs to be addressed.

As the authors Blinder et al. (2017, p. 40) point out, just when it seemed that the ECB was moving past the hazards caused by the global financial crisis, the European sovereign debt crisis erupted in spring 2010. In the case of Greece, the ECB's involvement, alongside the European Commission and the IMF, introduced a completely new dimension to the situation. The ECB's role within this troika was to provide specialized expertise and advice to the European Commission (Coeuré, 2014), although it is not a signatory to the agreements made with governments. Nonetheless, it was important for all three institutions to present a unified front in order to effectively negotiate with the Greek government. The arrangement has raised concerns about the political independence of the ECB, with several observers questioning its autonomy (ECB President Draghi's press conference 7 March 2013). This unease was further exacerbated when the ECB decided not to increase the ceiling of Emergency Liquidity Assistance (ELA) to Greek banks in the summer of 2015 after the breakdown of negotiations between the troika and the Greek government. These developments, as discussed by Wyplosz (2015) and highlighted in the *Financial Times* article "ECB ensnared in politics as it faces vote on Bank of Greece loans" (19 May 2015), have generated doubts about the ECB's political independence. At present, it remains difficult to predict the long-term consequences of these events. However, it is worth noting that *support for populist parties in Europe, which generally oppose central bank independence and advocate for exiting the EMU and returning to national currencies or even following the United Kingdom in leaving the EU, has been on the rise.*

As Portes (2014) further remarks: "The austerity policies championed by Germany and other apostles of fiscal rectitude, implemented enthusiastically by the European Commission, are not the solution, but rather a major part of the problem. They are driving the Eurozone into a new recession. The debt of several Eurozone countries is not sustainable if they contract" (p. 430).[19] Within the Eurozone, the countries with fiscal capacity are the ones with external surpluses. Unless these surplus countries are willing to acknowledge that the others need the freedom to generate surpluses, there will be no escape from the current cycles of debt and economic stagnation. This can be achieved either by relaxing fiscal policies or by implementing measures to reduce private net savings. Furthermore, the overall situation would benefit from a significant depreciation of the euro, which further underscores the need for monetary easing. Mishkin (2011) emphasizes the significance of the international aspect and how policies implemented in one country can impact others. He disagrees with the notion of comparing the quantitative easing

[19]Moreover, fiscal contraction together with private sector deleveraging is not feasible without a current account surplus $[CA = (Sp - Ip) + (T - G)]$. The current account must equal the sum of private sector net saving and government net saving (Portes, 2014).

undertaken appropriately in the United States to beggar-thy-neighbor policies. Mishkin also *acknowledges the international dimension of policies within Europe, specifically noting the forced adoption of highly contractionary fiscal measures by countries like Ireland and Greece.* In light of this situation, Mishkin argues *at an early stage on the Eurozone crisis that the ECB should adopt a more accommodative monetary policy to support these countries and offset the fiscal contraction* (Mishkin 2011, p. 134). It is important to note that this does not imply that implementing "competitive quantitative easing" at the zero lower bound for interest rates is ineffective or constitutes beggar-thy-neighbor policies, as, for example, argued in Portes (2012).

As Portes (2014) further remarks: "Germany and France have benefited greatly from the single currency over its first decade. Their business communities see this. One must still hope that the core Eurozone countries will eventually act in their own best interests. The global financial crisis need not lead to the demise of the single currency through a Eurozone crisis that could be resolved successfully if policymakers were to change course" (p. 430). Furthermore, Buiter (2014), for example, asserts: "I expect that by the time the European sovereign and banking crises are over, the financial stability role of the ECB will have been enhanced to a scale not seen elsewhere since the crisis started in 2011. If it is not, there will at most be a rump euro area left, consisting essentially of a 'greater Deutschmark zone', when the dust of history settles on the euro area crises" (p. 12). Fisher (2012) further wonders "What will happen and on what horizon?" and answers "We don't know," but we would like to conclude by quoting Jean-Claude Trichet at this podium [at the Jackson Hole symposium], "I think a year ago. When he was pushed to the wall on the future of the euro, he eventually said, look, the European project is a project in process. It was not set up with this particular aim of getting to a monetary union. We've had crisis after crisis since we started. At every stage of the process, we have heard the same story from Americans. He must have been thinking about the people sitting in this room a year ago. 'You Europeans don't know how to make decisions. You're always slow. What phone number should I call if I want to speak to Europe?' This dream is bound to collapse. We have heard that every time, and we have been slow. But, in the end we have emerged stronger from every crisis" (p. 497). The statement made regarding the history of modern Europe was highly impactful and thought-provoking, capable of challenging mainstream skepticism. Upon reconsideration, it becomes apparent that European policymakers have made surprisingly rapid progress in their thinking, surpassing previous expectations. Since the advent of the GFC and especially the burst of the Eurozone crisis, they have been actively working toward establishing a sustainable framework to ensure the survival of the euro.

5.7 A Corollary of the Eurozone Crisis

By the late 1980s, there was growing support for the concept of economic and monetary union, which was later formalized in the Maastricht Treaty. This entailed the establishment of a single market where capital controls would be eliminated, as well as the pursuit of fixed exchange rates as a crucial step toward a common currency. The countries destined to join the euro area embraced a *monetary policy trilemma*[20] that balanced capital mobility and exchange rate stability among themselves while maintaining jointly floating exchange rates with nonmember currencies. The European approach to capital controls and its impact on global practices are thoroughly examined by Abdelal (2007). However, similar to the previous oversight in the Bretton Woods Treaty that neglected financial stability concerns, the Maastricht Treaty also failed to address such issues, albeit in a different context and for different reasons, leading to significant destabilizing effects later on. *The euro lacked mechanisms to handle persistent and substantial trade imbalances between countries. There was no common framework for prudential banking and financial regulation, let alone any pooling of risks associated with bank failures (such as deposit insurance).* As subsequent crises in the euro area revealed, both banks and governments could face liquidity shortages despite sharing a single currency, intensifying risks to financial stability. Unlike the relatively restrictive global financial environment of the 1950s and 1960s, which mitigated the consequences of overlooking these issues under Bretton Woods, the disregard for financial stability within the euro's architecture during a period of rampant financialization proved to be a costly oversight.

The original Maastricht Treaty operated under the assumption, as advocated in neoclassical economics, that the private sector is inherently robust and always seeks to maximize profits. Consequently, the Treaty did not consider the possibility of balance sheet recessions, nor did it anticipate the destabilizing capital flows within the Eurozone emerging right upon its creation. However, when the private sector is actively reducing its debt despite zero interest rates—a scenario not hugely discussed in business schools or economic literature—it indicates significant distress and necessitates assistance. This assistance can only come from the public sector. The mandatory withdrawal of this support, as dictated by the Maastricht Treaty, resulted

---

[20]The classic trilemma of monetary policy emphasizes that when exchange rates are flexible and there is capital mobility, monetary policy can prioritize domestic goals. However, the trilemma does not directly address concerns regarding financial stability. In fact, relying solely on monetary policy may not be very effective in dealing with potential financial stability issues (Obstfeld & Taylor, 2017). In such cases, countries could face significant challenges from global financial shocks and economic cycles, which may be caused by monetary or other developments in the financial markets of industrialized countries. These challenges can overwhelm countries even if they have flexible exchange rates. If the latter outcome poses a risk, countries may wish to implement a combination of financial regulations or restrictions on international capital movement to better protect their economies. Rey (2013, 2016) forms the latter core argument, and on global financial cycles, see also Borio and Disyatat (2015), Avdjiev et al. (2016), and Reinhart et al. (2016).

in detrimental policy reactions in numerous member countries, ultimately leading to self-destructive outcomes (Koo, 2014). The primary objective of establishing the Eurozone was not to provide member state governments with increased leeway to engage in irresponsible deficit spending.

However, the Eurozone can address the requirement for enhanced fiscal discipline *and* acquire the necessary flexibility to combat balance sheet recessions while also controlling volatile capital flows. This can be achieved by initially declaring that member states will restrict the sale of government bonds to their own citizens after a specified transition period, followed by the development of a gradual plan for individual countries to reach this goal. In countries experiencing balance sheet recessions like Ireland and Spain, a two-stage approach is necessary. Initially, fiscal policy must be implemented to facilitate the recovery of private sector balance sheets. Once the private sector shifts its focus from minimizing debt to maximizing profit, the public sector can initiate the process of fiscal consolidation. In the case of Greece, where private sector deleveraging has been limited, the government will need to gradually reduce its fiscal deficit during the transition period to a level that can be covered by domestic financing.

While the Eurozone crisis unfolded, the European Union and European Central Bank needed to adhere to explicit processes declaring their readiness to provide assistance during the transitional phase. It had been crucial for these organizations to endorse the new roadmap, as without their support, the capital flight from distressed countries was only to intensify. Once the comprehensive plans were to be announced, backed by the EU, ECB, and ideally the International Monetary Fund, it was and had been bound to instill greater confidence in private investors, as the risk of an endless destructive cycle would be eliminated. In hindsight, the Maastricht Treaty should have originally included provisions limiting the sale of government bonds to citizens. If this rule had been adopted by all member countries in 2000 instead of the 3% deficit limit, the current problems would not have arisen (Koo, 2014, p. 407). Even though to revise the Maastricht Treaty would remain challenging, it would be worth trying to make it more responsive to balance sheet recessions while ending destabilizing capital flows.

References

Abdelal, R. (2007). *Capital rules: The construction of global finance*. Harvard University Press.

Allen, K. (2000). *The Celtic Tiger: The myth of social partnership in Ireland*. Manchester University Press.

Allen, K. (2009). *Ireland's economic crash: A radical agenda for change*. The Liffey Press.

Annett, A. (2006). Enforcement and the stability and growth pact: How fiscal policy did and did not change under Europe's fiscal framework. *IMF working papers*, no. 06/116, International Monetary Fund, Washington DC, USA, May.

Avdjiev, S., McCauley, R. N., & Shin, H. S. (2016). Breaking free of the triple coincidence in international finance. *Economic Policy, 31*(87), 409–451.

Barro, R. J., & Gordon, D. B. (1983a). A positive theory of monetary policy in a natural rate model. *Journal of Political Economy, 91*(4), 589–610.

Barro, R. J., & Gordon, D. B. (1983b). Rules, discretion and reputation in a model of monetary policy. *Journal of Monetary Economics, 12*(1), 101–121.

Bean, C., Malinvaud, E., Bernholz, P., Giavazzi, F., & Wyploz, C. (1990). Policies for 1992: The transition and after. In *The macroeconomics of 1992*. Centre for European Policy Studies.

Begg, I. (1990). European integration and regional policy. *Oxford Review of Economic Policy, 5*(2), 90–104.

Blinder, A., Ehrmann, M., de Haan, J., & Jansen, D.-J. (2017). Necessity as the mother of invention: Monetary policy after the crisis. *ECB working paper series* no 2047, April, European Central Bank, Frankfurt Am Main, Germany.

Blinder, A. S. (2012). Global policy perspectives: Central bank independence, and credibility during and after a crisis. Proceedings Jackson hole economic summit (pp. 483–491). A symposium sponsored by the Federal Reserve Bank of Kansas City, Jackson Hole, Wyoming.

Borio, C., & Disyatat, P. (2015). Capital flows and the current account: Taking financing (more) seriously. *BIS Working Paper* 525, Bank for International Settlements, Basel, Switzerland.

Boyle, A. (1967). *Montagu Norman: A biography*. Cassell.

Buiter, W. H. (2014). The role of central banks in financial stability: How has it changed. In D. D. Evanoff, C. Holthausen, G. G. Kaufman, & M. Kremer (Eds.), *The role of central banks in financial stability: How has it changed?* (30th world scientific studies in international economics) (pp. 11–56). World Scientific Publishing Co. Pte. Ltd.

Calingaert, M. (1988). *The 1992 challenge from Europe: Development of the European Community's Internal Market*. National Planning Association.

Cavallini, S., Soldi, R., Di Matteo, L., Utma, M. A., & Errico, B. (2018). *Addressing 'brain drain': Local and regional dimensions. Report to the Commission for Social Policy, Education, Employment, Research and Culture*. European Committee of the Regions.

Coeuré, B. (2014). Exchange of views of Benoît Cœuré with ECON on troika matters. Brussels, 13 February. Available online at: https://www.ecb.europa.eu/press/key/date/2014/html/sp140213.en.html

Delors, J. (1989). Regional implications of economic and monetary integration. In Committee for the Study of the Economic and Monetary Union (Ed.), *Report on economic and monetary union in the European Community*. Office for Official Publications of the European Communities.

Dornbusch, R. (1989). Europe 1992: Macroeconomic implications. *Brookings Papers on Economic Activity, 2*, 341–381.

ECOFIN. (2008). EMU @10: Successes and challenges after ten years of economic and monetary union. *European Economy* 2, Directorate General for Economic and Financial Affairs, European Commission, Luxembourg.

The Economist. (1990). Europe's horn of plenty (pp. 71–72). 2 June.

Eichengreen, B. (1994). Fiscal policy and EMU. In B. Eichengreen & J. Frieden (Eds.), *The political economy of European Monetary Unification*. Routledge.

Elgindy, K. (2014).When ambiguity is destructive. *Op-Ed Brookings*. Brookings Institution, Washington, DC, USA. January 22.

Fisher, I. (1933). The debt-deflation theory of great depressions. *Econometrica, 1*, 337–357.

Fisher, S. (2012). *Global policy perspectives. Proceedings Jackson hole economic summit* (pp. 492–498). Jackson Hole, WY: A symposium sponsored by the Federal Reserve Bank of Kansas City.

Flood, R. P., & Garber, P. M. (1984). Collapsing exchange-rate regimes: Some linear examples. *Journal of International Economics, 17*, 1–13.

Forbes, K. J. (2012). *The 'Big C': Identifying and mitigating contagion. Proceedings Jackson hole economic summit* (pp. 23–87). Jackson Hole, WY: A symposium sponsored by the Federal Reserve Bank of Kansas City.

Friedman, M. (2007). An interview with Milton Friedman. Interviewed by John B. Taylor, May 2000. In P. Samuelson & W. Barnett (Eds.), *Inside the Economist's mind. Conversations with eminent economists (Ch. 6)*. Blackwell.

Gern, K. J., Kooths, S., & Stolzenburg, U. (2019). Euro at 20: The monetary union from a bird's-eye view. In *Depth analysis*, PE 631.038, European Parliament, January.

Guajardo, J., Leigh, D., & Pescatori, A. (2011). Expansionary austerity: New international evidence. *IMF working paper*, no. 11/158, International Monetary Fund, Washington DC, USA.

Hunter, L. (1991). Europe 1992: An overview. *Federal Reserve Bank of Dallas Economic Review*, 17–27.

Jacobides, M., Portes, R., & Vayanos, D. (2011). Greece: The way forward. White paper, October 27, summarized at www.voxeu.org, November 30.

Johnson, K. H. (1994). International dimension of European monetary union. Board of Governors of the Federal Reserve System, International Finance Discussion Papers, no. 469.

Jonung, L. & Drea, E. (2009). The euro: It can't happen. It's a bad idea. It won't last. US economists on the EMU, 1989-2002. *Economic papers*, no. 395, December, European Commission—Economic and Financial Affairs Directorate General.

Kenny, G., & Morgan, J. (2011). Some lessons from the financial crisis for economic analysis. ECB occasional paper no. 130, October, European Central Bank, Frankfurt Am Main, Germany.

Knight, F. H. (1921). *Risk, uncertainty and profit*. Hart, Schaffner & Marx; Houghton Mifflin Company.

Kokores, T. (1989). *Euro-banking innovations and EEC monetary coordination (studies 4)*. Institute of European Civilization. Papazisis.

Koo, R. C. (2014). The Eurozone crisis: Causes, remedy and misperceptions. In D. D. Evanoff, C. Holthausen, G. G. Kaufman, & M. Kremer (Eds.), *The role of central banks in financial stability: How has it changed?* (30th world scientific studies in international economics) (pp. 391–408). World Scientific Publishing Co. Pte. Ltd.

Krugman, P. (1979). A model of balance-of-payments crises. *Journal of Money, Credit and Banking, 11*(3), 311–325.

Krugman, P. R. (2009). The curse of Montagu Norman. *New York Times Blog*.

Krugman, P. R. (2014). Inflation targets reconsidered. Proceedings ECB forum on central banking 'Monetary Policy in Changing Financial Landscape', (pp 110–132), Sintra, Portugal.

Kydland, F. E., & Prescott, E. C. (1977). Rules rather than discretion: The inconsistency of optimal plans. *Journal of Political Economy, 85*(3), 473–492.

Langarde, C. (2023). Press Conference on ECB Monetary Policy Statement, European Central Bank, Frankfurt Am Main, March 16.

Mattoo, A., Mulabdic, A., & Ruta, M. (2022). Trade creation and trade diversion in deep agreements. *Canadian Journal of Economics/Revue canadienne d'économique, 55*(3), 1598–1637.

Mishkin, F. S. (2011). Monetary policy strategy: Lessons from the crisis. In M. Jarociñki, F. Smets, & C. Thimann (Eds.), *Approaches to monetary policy revisited—lessons from the crisis, sixth ECB central banking conference proceedings* (pp. 67–118).

Obstfeld, M. (1986). Rational and self-fulfilling balance-of-payments crises. *American Economic Review, 76*(1), 72–81.

Obstfeld, M., & Taylor, A. M. (2017). International monetary relations: Taking finance seriously. *Journal of Economic Perspectives, 31*(3), 3–28.

Portes, R. (2011). Restructure Ireland's debt. Available at www.voxeu.org, April 26.

Portes, R. (2012). Monetary policies and exchange rates at the zero lower bound. *Journal of Money, Credit and Banking, 44*, 157–163.

Portes, R. (2014). The Eurozone crisis. In D. D. Evanoff, C. Holthausen, G. G. Kaufman, & M. Kremer (Eds.), *The role of central banks in financial stability: How has it changed?* (30th world scientific studies in international economics) (pp. 423–432). World Scientific Publishing Co. Pte. Ltd.

Reinhart, C. M., Reinhart, V., & Trebesch, C. (2016). Global cycles: Capital flows, commodities, and sovereign defaults, 1815-2015. *American Economic Review, 106*(5), 574–580.

Reinhart, C. M., & Rogoff, K. S. (2009). *This time is different: Eight centuries of financial folly.* Princeton University Press.
Reinhart, C.M., & Reinhart, V. (2008). Capital flow bonanzas. CEPR discussion paper, no. 6996. London: Centre for Economic Policy Research.
Rey, H. (2013). Dilemma not trilemma: The global financial cycle and monetary policy Independence. Paper presented at the global dimensions of unconventional monetary policy. Jackson Hole, WY: Federal Reserve Bank of Kansas City Symposium.
Rey, H. (2016). International channels of transmission of monetary policy and the Mundellian Trilemma. *IMF Economic Review, 64*(1), 6–35.
Smyth, S. J. (2011). How the ship of fools was ship-wrecked: The Irish crisis and response. *Journal of Finance and Management in Public Services, 10*(1), 1–13.
Stiglitz, J. E. (2017). The fundamental flaws in the Eurozone framework. In N. da Costa Gabral, J. R. Conçalves, & N. C. Rodrigues (Eds.), *The euro and the crisis: Perspectives for the Eurozone as a Monetary and Budgetary Union* (pp. 11–16). Springer.
Stock, J.H., & Watson, M.W. (2002). Has the business cycle changed? NBER Macroeconomics Annual, vol. 17, pp. 159–218, National Bureau of Economic Research, .
Van den Noord, P., & Cournède, B. (2006). Short-term pain for long-term gain: The impact of structural reform on fiscal of outcomes in EMU. OECD Economics Department Working Papers, No. 522.
Viner, J. (1950). *The customs union issue.* Carnegie Endowment for International Peace.
Werner, P. (1970). *Report* to the Council and the Commission on the realisation by stages of economic and monetary union in the Community. Supplement to the Bulletin 11 – 1970 of the European Communities, Office for Official Publications of the European Communities.
Whelan, K. (2014). The ECB's collateral policy and its future as lender of last resort. Briefing paper for European Parliament Committee on Economic and Monetary Affairs, European Parliament.
Whelan, K. (2015). The ECB and financial assistance programmes: Has ECB acted beyond its mandate? Briefing paper for European Parliament Committee on Economic and Monetary Affairs, European Parliament.
Whelan, K. (2016). Banking union and the ECB as lender of last resort. In F. Allen, E. Carletti, J. Gray, & M. Gulati (Eds.), *Filling the gaps in governance: The case of Europe* (pp. 187–202). Robert Schuman Centre for Advanced Studies, European University Institute.
Whelan, K. (2019). The euro at 20: Successes, problems, progress and threats. Monetary dialogue, January. In-depth analysis PE 631.039 requested by the ECON Committee, Policy Department for Economic, Scientific and Quality of Life Policies Directorate-General for Internal Policies, European Parliament, January.
Wyplosz, C. (2015). Grexit: The staggering cost of central bank dependence. VoxEU, 29 June.

Chapter 6
A Critical Assessment of the Euro Project in Retrospect

> . . .I think the EU is one of the greatest events in history. But what is important about the EU is not a Parliament in Strasbourg, or a new central bank in some geographical place. It is the freer trade within this vast, important area of the world and the freer mobility of resource movements. That's what you must not lose, even if EMU starts and after a few years a number of countries like the UK find themselves falling out of that bed again. The UK poet Lord Tennyson put it well: It can be better to have loved and lost than never to have loved at all. So it is with the new EMU: better to be in it, even if in the end you can't stay in it, or may not want to pay the price to stay in it. Nothing is for ever these days. . . . *[emphasis added]*
> —*Paul, A. Samuelson (1997), op. cit., p. 16*

6.1 Introduction

In 1999, a momentous undertaking commenced as 11 European countries embarked on a monumental project in monetary history, the decision to relinquish their national currencies, along with the sovereignty in monetary policy that came with it. This sacrifice was made in exchange for the benefits of price stability, elimination of currency transaction costs in trade, access to international finance, and pursuit of a common political objective. The belief was that only through a monetary union could true integration of markets within the European Union be achieved, thereby laying the groundwork for the single market.

As almost more than two decades have passed, the landscape in terms of monetary, economic, financial, and political conditions has evolved significantly from those early days. *First*, the monetary union has undergone several expansions on its member states, with the possibility of additional countries joining in the near future. Additionally, there are six other states that utilize the currency despite not being official members of the union (namely, Montenegro, Kosovo, Andorra, Monaco, San Marino, and the Vatican City). *Second*, European economies have faced significant economic difficulties since the onset of the global financial crisis. Even though the crisis originated in the United States and impacted financial and real

I. T. Kokores, *Monetary Policy in Interdependent Economies*, Financial and Monetary Policy Studies 55, https://doi.org/10.1007/978-3-031-41958-4_6

estate markets globally, as it escalated, it led to numerous bank bailouts and a deteriorating financial performance. It, thus, transformed from a financial crisis into an economic one. The repercussions affected the real economy in the euro area (let alone globally), leading to a decline in intra-euro area trade due to reduced incomes. Subsequently, the crisis evolved into a complex combination of fiscal and financial challenges, which the European Union continued to grapple with in its recovery efforts for several subsequent years to date. *Third*, the series of shocks and underwhelming economic performance has compelled the European Central Bank to venture into unfamiliar territory. The ECB has resorted to a range of unconventional policy measures, surpassing its traditional scope and delving into unprecedented dimensions. Termed as *unconventional monetary policy*, its uniqueness within the euro area lies in its magnitude, structure, formulation, and extent, encroaching upon national fiscal policies and even political autonomy. *Fourth*, the subsequent crises prompted a recognition that the original monetary union was deficient, necessitating additional measures to enhance its resilience and ability to withstand shocks. To achieve this, there was a realization that the *monetary union* must be accompanied by a *banking and financial market union*. In recent years, significant efforts have been devoted to integrating the banking market, fostering cross-border banking activities, establishing a unified supervisory mechanism, and implementing coordinated macroprudential measures through the joint endeavors of the European Systemic Risk Board (ESRB) and the European Central Bank. *Fifth*, as a consequence of these turbulent circumstances, there has been a notable shift in the political environment. Anti-euro sentiment has gained momentum, particularly in countries subjected to sovereign bailout programs. However, due to fiscal pressures and challenges related to migration, this sentiment has spread to other member states that were not directly affected by such rescue programs. Furthermore, the disparities in economic performance among various regions within the Economic and Monetary Union have exacerbated divisions and led to increased segregation between member states, as well as within political parties at the national level (Gerba, 2019, p. 8). Consequently, the political landscape has become fraught and complex for both EMU members and those outside of it but still within the EU.

Therefore, the time has come to reflect on the euro project, assess its achievements and failures, as well as speculate on the challenges and prospects ahead. The rest of this section thus focuses on the economic problems that have affected the euro area and on the progress potentially made since the Eurozone sovereign debt crisis during the years 2010–2012. It finally considers the resilience of the euro project and the future challenges it is likely to face.

6.2 The Euro Crisis Management, Sovereign Default, and Steps Toward Crisis Prevention

The aspiration to establish a unified European currency was generated during the 1970s and gained significant traction following the reunification of Germany in the late 1980s. This initiative was a response to the dominant influence of the Bundesbank, whose monetary policies not only shaped the economic conditions within the bloc of smaller countries using the Deutsche Mark (such as Austria, Benelux, Denmark, and Finland) but also heavily influenced larger countries participating in the European Monetary System. While the Bundesbank's commitment to a strong currency regime had garnered global recognition, the concentration of monetary decision-making in a single country had perpetually frustrated other EMS members.

The signatories of the Maastricht Treaty sought to replicate the Bundesbank's position at the European level. This involved establishing the independence of the European Central Bank and the national central banks within the Eurosystem. The primary mandate of the ECB stated to ensure price stability, while a prohibition on monetizing public debt and a no bailout clause for sovereigns by other member states or the union as a whole were also integral to the agreement. The ECB's supranational role, without a corresponding fiscal authority at the EU or EMU level, was seen as an advantage in terms of bolstering the independence of the monetary authority even further, akin to a "gold standard without gold," and reducing the likelihood of government financing through money printing (Gern et al., 2019, p. 14).

To enforce fiscal discipline, all EU member states agreed to abide by the Stability and Growth Pact, which maintained the two fiscal criteria for joining the Eurozone (a deficit-to-GDP ratio of 3% and a public debt-to-GDP ratio of 60%), even after the introduction of the common currency. However, these rules may have inadvertently undermined the credibility of the no bailout clause and weakened the fiscal discipline expected from investors. Furthermore, the admission of countries like Italy, Belgium, and later Greece, despite having debt-to-GDP ratios exceeding 100%, based on assessments of sufficient convergence toward the Maastricht criteria, may have raised doubts about the strictness of the fiscal regime even before the Eurozone began its operations. In the period leading up to the official launch of the euro in 1999, interest rates in countries expected to adopt the common currency began to converge toward lower levels similar to those in Germany. This indicated a significant reduction in risk premia among Eurozone member states. In addition, inflation expectations reflected confidence in the newly established Eurosystem commitment to maintaining price stability. The choice of monetary strategy, which aimed for an *inflation rate below 2% in the medium term* and included *a reference level for the growth rate of M3*, was successfully built upon the reputation of the previous monetary traditions. The European Central Bank adopted a two-pillar approach, combining both monetary and economic analyses, although it differed from *the former approach of the Bundesbank, which emphasized a money supply target at the center of its communicated strategy.*

In 2003, this strategy underwent further adjustments, moving toward inflation targeting. *Price stability was redefined as maintaining inflation "below but close to 2%" in the medium term, and the importance of monitoring monetary aggregates, although still relevant, diminished compared to the previous approach.* This new policy framework carried significant implications. Previously, monetary policy was viewed as not excessively expansionary as long as consumer prices did not rise by more than 2% in the medium term. However, *under the new framework, monetary policy was considered insufficiently expansionary if consumer price inflation fell notably below the 2% target in the medium term. Therefore, when the euro was introduced, investors placed their trust in the currency's commitment to stability.*

The introduction of the euro in countries with previously weaker currencies had a positive impact on economic policies; it resulted in a *stability dividend* (Gern et al., 2019), which manifested as significantly reduced risk premia. The core countries of the Eurozone, particularly those previously using the Deutsche Mark, transferred their favorable reputation to the periphery countries. As a result, countries like Portugal, Spain, and Greece experienced lower borrowing costs, and lenders perceived reduced risks, especially with the elimination of exchange rate risks. Consequently, capital flowed into these countries, and credit creation within the Eurozone increased, with Ireland exhibiting the strongest momentum.

The influx of capital and the expansion of credit stimulated economic activity in the periphery countries, leading to above-average inflation and increases in unit labor costs, effectively resulting in real appreciation. Initially, these developments were regarded as a reflection of sound underlying factors related to the economic catch-up process in these economies. Despite stronger-than-expected money and credit growth, the Eurozone inflation rate remained on target, complicating the assessment of overheating and imbalanced growth within the Eurozone. Methodological issues in estimating output gaps further complicated the diagnosis of real-time booms, potentially providing incorrect signals. As a result, policymakers and supervisors insufficiently recognized the boom in the Eurozone periphery that was triggered by the reduction in financing costs and the robust credit expansion.

In fact according to Reinhart and Rogoff (2009), sovereign debt sustainability problems pose a challenge dating centuries in the past as old as sovereign debt issue itself and have tended to be solved through combination of high inflation, financial repression, and default. The first two are difficult to achieve in the euro area due to the ECB's price stability mandate and the EU's requirements for free movement of capital; it could have been argued that it was always likely that a euro area member state that got into severe fiscal trouble would have to default (see Whelan, 2019, p. 16). Indeed, a number of eminent economists during the 1990s expressed solid predictions of a likely number of sovereign defaults among euro area member states, due to the absence of alternative tools for resolving debt unsustainability (for a review, see Whelan, 2013).

Following the financial and sovereign debt crises, a renewed emphasis on banking sector and capital market regulation emerged, both globally and within the European Union. Several prudential regulatory changes were implemented, including stricter requirements for bank capital and liquidity.[1] However, in order to break the connection between banks and sovereign debt, it is necessary to address the special treatment that sovereigns still receive as debtors. Essentially, government debt should, thus, no longer be regarded as a risk-free asset. The direct result remains, therefore, that banks should be required to increase their capital reserves when holding public debt on their balance sheets. Additionally, there should be limitations on the scale of credit provided to governments in order to reduce concentration risk. By reducing the threat of substantial losses from sovereign debt restructuring, the banking sector would become more resilient, allowing monetary policy to focus solely on maintaining price stability with full independence.

In its efforts to assist with fiscal and structural reforms, the Eurosystem has found itself in a challenging situation, leading to unintended consequences. Starting from 2010, the Eurosystem has been functioning in a crisis-oriented mode. Initially, in response to the global financial crisis and the subsequent Great Recession, the Eurosystem reduced interest rates from 4.25% to 1% in 2008–2009. However, as the European debt crisis unfolded, the Eurosystem increasingly adopted expansionary monetary policies to mitigate its impact.[2] By 2010, it became evident that Greece and other Eurozone countries were facing significant public debt issues, which could necessitate debt restructuring or even result in their departure from the Eurozone. As a consequence, substantial disparities in sovereign yields among euro area member states resurfaced. The concerns regarding potential sovereign defaults were substantiated, leading to an agreement in 2011 that Greece would undergo debt restructuring in 2012. Although sovereign yields have once again converged as the Eurozone debt crisis eased and economic growth resumed, they are not completely aligned anymore. Financial markets have become highly sensitive to pricing risks associated with potential defaults or the possibility of countries exiting the Eurozone. The

[1] The Single Supervisory Mechanism (SSM) was implemented in an effort to avoid fragmentation among the euro area member states. Under the SSM, the ECB assumes direct supervision of the larger banks, while national authorities collaborate with the ECB to oversee the smaller banks. Additionally, channelling funds from the European Stability Mechanism (ESM) solely as a safeguard for the Single Resolution Mechanism (SRM) would shift the emphasis toward stabilizing banks rather than stabilizing the governments they are indebted to (Gern et al., 2019, p. 18).

[2] This involved implementing additional interest rate reductions (initiated in 2012, ultimately reaching 0% interest rates in 2016) and an unprecedented provision of liquidity, particularly through large-scale asset purchases commencing in 2015. As a result, the monetary base has expanded by 250%, and Target2 imbalances have reached unprecedented levels. The substantial acquisition of government debt has raised concerns regarding whether the Eurosystem is exceeding its mandate by effectively engaging in monetary financing of sovereigns. It has also prompted questions about the potential adverse effects of accommodating financing conditions for governments on the necessary reforms. While the ECB has stated that its highly accommodative monetary policy aims primarily to bring inflation rates closer to the target, it has consistently emphasized that monetary policy cannot substitute for structural reforms and fiscal consolidation, but rather offers a temporary respite to facilitate these processes. Nevertheless, the availability of low-cost financing for governments not only eased the implementation of reform programs but also tended to reduce the immediate cost of delaying reforms. Consequently, as Whelan (2019) remarks, there is a risk that efforts toward fiscal consolidation and structural reforms may weaken (Whelan, 2019, p. 19).

uncertainty surrounding sovereign default was not just a matter of unfortunate circumstances for EU policymakers and the ECB. Both the ECB and economic officials of European governments should have been more transparent in communicating the potential for default in countries with excessive public debt, and they should have made better preparations in the anticipation of these issues arising during an economic downturn. However, the EU failed to discourage financial markets from treating all euro area sovereign debt equally, and when the Greek crisis emerged, many prominent European politicians chose to deny the reality of the situation (Whelan, 2019, p. 16). During the early stages of the Greek crisis, senior European politicians, as, for example, the European Commissioner for Economic and Financial Affairs, Joaquin Almunia in early 2010 responded with comments like "No, Greece will not default. Please. In the euro area, default does not exist" (Monaghan, 2010). This policy stand was prevalent among leaders in the euro area at that time and contributed to an inadequate policy response to the Greek situation, as documented in Whelan (2013).

The ECB's handling of questions regarding sovereign default was also inadequate. Throughout the Greek crisis, the ECB played a significant role in presenting a potential Greek default as a catastrophic event for the euro area and in delaying the decision to allow such a default. Members of the ECB Executive Board, including Lorenzo Bini Smaghi, frequently delivered speeches portraying a Greek default as something that would trigger an "economic meltdown." Bini Smaghi (2011) argued against a default, stating that it would harm investors who believed in the sustainability of the adjustment program, discourage future investments in euro area member states, and emphasized the enforcement of debt payments, even via sanctions if necessary. ECB officials consistently threatened to cut off credit to the Greek banking system if a default were to occur, maintaining a firm stance until the decision to restructure Greek debt. Even as late as July 11, 2011, ECB President Jean-Claude Trichet insisted on this position stating "no credit event, no selective default, no default. That is the message of the Governing Council" (Trichet, 2011). Ultimately, the Greek debt restructuring occurred without significant adverse effects on financial stability across the euro area. It is now widely acknowledged that a sovereign default can occur within the euro area without causing a widespread crisis or necessitating the departure of the defaulting country from the euro.

Nevertheless, during the initial stages of the Eurozone sovereign debt crisis, it became evident that the International Monetary Fund (IMF) was unprepared to handle the extensive financial commitments necessary for implementing substantial and prolonged financial adjustment programs in euro area countries experiencing significant macroeconomic challenges. However, the establishment of the European Stability Mechanism addressed this deficiency, as it gained expertise in managing financial adjustment programs and the accompanying conditions in countries like Ireland, Greece, and Portugal. As a result, in future crises, less time has been expected to be wasted on determining which institutions should provide financial assistance and how these programs should be implemented (as evidenced by the policymakers' prompt response in the emergence of the COVID-19 pandemic crisis). The banking sector faced significant challenges during the crisis period from 2008 to 2012, and the burden of nonperforming loans kept affecting the banking sectors of several euro area countries. Substantial institutional reforms have been implemented in this domain over the past decade.

It is crucial to emphasize that in response to the European debt crisis, *policymakers made significant changes to the fiscal architecture of the Eurozone*. The suspension of the Maastricht no bailout principle occurred with the onset of the Greek sovereign debt crisis. While initially designed as a temporary measure, the European Financial Stability Facility (EFSF) was launched in 2010 with a volume of €440 billion and later expanded to €780 billion in 2011.[3] In fact, its successor, the European Stability Mechanism (ESM), was established in 2012 as a permanent intergovernmental institution comprising Eurozone member states, with a volume of €700 billion. The primary objective of these rescue packages was to prevent distressed countries from potentially exiting the Eurozone, which could have led to implicit exchange rate risks among member states and further increased risk premia. Recipients of the rescue funds were required to commit to structural reforms and fiscal consolidation programs, following the principle of conditionality.[4]

The restructuring of Greek debt marked a significant moment as it demonstrated that sovereign debt within the euro area could be reorganized without causing a widespread financial crisis. Nonetheless, as noted by Zettelmeyer et al. (2013), the terms of the Greek restructuring were quite lenient toward "holdout" investors, potentially setting an unfavorable precedent for future restructuring cases, even when conventional access clauses (CACs) were in place. Additionally, there is a concern that ESM funds could be used to provide financial assistance to a member state, enabling it to repay private creditors and subsequently seek debt restructuring from the ESM, similar to the Greek situation (Gern et al., 2019, pp. 17, 23). Nevertheless, it is important to acknowledge that the ESM recognizes the possibility of sovereign debt restructuring. The underlying treaty of the ESM states that "in accordance with IMF practice, in exceptional cases an adequate and proportionate form of private sector involvement shall be considered in cases where stability support is provided accompanied by conditionality in the form of a macro-economic adjustment programme" (quoted in Gern et al., 2019, p. 23). In this sense, the need for sovereign restructuring in some circumstances is now part of official euro area policy.

[3] In addition to the EFSF, the European Financial Stabilization Mechanism (EFSM) was also introduced in 2010, with a volume of €60 billion. The EFSM served as an emergency funding program managed by the European Commission, utilizing funds from the EU budget. Although smaller in scale compared to the EFSF, it played a role in providing financial support during the crisis.

[4] In order to decrease the likelihood of fiscal crises, the Stability and Growth Pact underwent reforms in 2012, resulting in the creation of the Treaty on Stability, Coordination, and Governance in the Economic and Monetary Union. This treaty combines enhanced supervision and coordination of economic policies, as well as stricter deficit regulations (Fiscal Compact), applicable to all Eurozone member states. It is worth noting that Bulgaria, Denmark, and Romania have also chosen to participate in these measures.

Despite all of the negative events of the decade following the advent of the GFC, the euro has remained intact as a common currency area. The popularity of the euro among the public plays an important role in restricting political movements to take countries out of the euro.[5] Two categories of factors can be identified as the basis for public support of euro membership. On one hand, there are positive factors that stem from the accomplishments and benefits associated with the euro. On the other hand, there are negative factors that arise from concerns about the consequences a country might face if it were to exit the euro. The *positive factors* contributing to public support for euro membership include the ECB's successful track record in maintaining favorable long-term inflation rates, as well as the convenience and cost savings for consumers and businesses resulting from the elimination of currency exchange expenses when engaging in transactions with other European countries. Many citizens may harbor doubts about their own country's politicians' ability to establish central bank institutions capable of achieving and sustaining the low inflation rates achieved within the euro area.

The *negative factors*, triggered by fear, hold significant importance. Apart from concerns about the long-term economic performance of a country exiting the euro, the process itself is expected to cause a significant short-term crisis. For a country to leave, it would require a democratic process involving a referendum or parliamentary vote to authorize such a decision. Organizing and conducting these votes take time, during which there would be substantial capital outflows as investors anticipate the potential redenomination of their investments into a new currency with a lower value than the euro. As a result, the imposition of capital controls is likely until the exit decision is executed.[6] Many of these negative factors exist regardless of the initial decision to join the euro. As Gern et al. (2019) remark, they demonstrate an asymmetry of the type "Even if joining the euro may not have been a wise choice, leaving now could prove to be highly unfavourable".[7] However, despite the current

---

[5]The popularity of the euro among citizens is the primary factor that has contributed to its continued existence. Surprisingly, despite experiencing multiple crises over the past decade, support for the euro has steadily increased among individuals residing in the Eurozone, currently reaching 75%. This demonstrates that the euro project has proven to be far more resilient than initially anticipated. In fact, the common currency has weathered numerous challenges that would have been expected to lead to the departure of one or more countries. These challenges include prolonged economic downturns in certain member states, EU-IMF financial programs with strict conditions, the implementation of capital controls in Greece and Cyprus, and the loss of depositor funds in Cypriot banks. In each of these instances, exiting the euro was a viable option, yet governments made the difficult decision to endure these hardships, emphasizing the significance they place on maintaining their membership in the eurozone (Gern et al., 2019, p. 26).

[6]Subsequently, the newly introduced currency, whether linked to the euro or left to fluctuate freely, would likely experience a significant devaluation compared to the euro. This considerable decrease in value could potentially result in a rise in inflation, which might be addressed through stringent monetary measures implemented by the country's central bank. Consequently, this could lead to an economic downturn or recession within the departing economy.

[7]After a country's departure from the euro, significant legal complications would arise concerning contracts that involve payment obligations in euros. The government of the departing country might attempt to pass legislation stating that domestic contracts referencing euros should now be

strong public support for the euro and the significant challenges associated with leaving the currency, it would be unwise to assume that all existential threats have been eliminated.[8]

One reason for this caution is the difficulty of extrapolating future outcomes based solely on the experiences of the past decade. Historical events may not always serve as reliable indicators of how countries will react in specific circumstances. While some countries have managed to navigate externally imposed financial adjustment programs in exchange for official assistance, others may find such measures less tolerable in the future. Moreover, citizens in different countries may come to the conclusion that leaving the euro is a preferable alternative to accepting capital controls or facing depositor haircuts, similar to those witnessed in Greece and Cyprus. The increase in support for populist and nationalistic parties across Europe further complicates the certainty regarding future events, as these developments create an environment where campaigns to exit the euro could potentially gain traction. If one country were to exit the euro, it would likely fuel speculation about the possibility of other countries doing the same. Consequently, it is not out of the realm of possibility that the departure of a single country, especially a larger member state of the euro area, could initiate a chain of events leading to the eventual dissolution of the entire euro area.

A decade after the crisis and antecedent to the burst of the COVID-19 pandemic crisis, the distressed member states still had high levels of public debt, much of which was held by domestic banks, despite the favorable financing conditions for governments in recent years. Additionally, significant structural reforms had not been in the agenda. Although nonperforming loans had been declining, they remained at elevated levels in countries such as Greece, Portugal, and Italy. Moreover, the prolonged period of low interest rates at the time increased the risk of zombie bank operation, namely, insolvent banks that remain in operation be it for explicit or implicit support from the government. The monetary experiment, therefore, remains still ongoing, and concerns have been raised whether the Eurosystem will be able to execute an exit strategy to restore normal monetary conditions. Gern

understood as referring to the new currency. However, such actions would likely face legal challenges in international courts. Prolonged and disruptive legal disputes would ensue, potentially lasting for years after the exit from the euro, resulting in ongoing harm to the economy. Additionally, the departing country's position within the European Union could be called into question, adding further uncertainties and complications (Gern et al., 2019, p. 27).

[8]For example, the fact that citizens of a country accepted a prolonged economic downturn in the past without considering leaving the euro does not guarantee that the euro will maintain its popularity if another extended period of economic hardship were to occur. This is especially true in countries where the constraints of euro membership could lead to the imposition of further austerity measures during the next recession. Each country may react differently to the possibility of sovereign default, particularly those with significant domestic holdings of sovereign debt. Additionally, while some argue that the ECB's Outright Monetary Transactions (OMT) program could prevent a crisis in the euro area, the political dynamics and feasibility of implementing an OMT program in Italy, combined with a formal adjustment program from the ESM, remain uncertain (Gern et al., 2019, p. 27).

et al. (2019) forecasted that "the real test for monetary policy will arise if inflation rates rise while the fiscal and financial sectors remain fragile and reliant on monetary support. In such a situation, the Eurosystem would face a challenging trade-off between maintaining price stability and ensuring financial stability" (p. 27).

6.3 An Evaluation of the Euro Project and the Crisis Management

Apart from the advantages of low inflation, the introduction of the common currency has eliminated exchange rate fluctuations among member states, which has been beneficial for businesses and consumers in the euro area. The transition to euro notes and coins in 2002 was successful, and the common currency has simplified transactions for consumers, eliminating the need to exchange currencies when traveling or making purchases across European countries. However, it seems that the previous assertions that the euro would greatly enhance intra-European trade have not been validated (Glick & Rose, 2016).

Monetary union effectively eliminated the perceived risk of currency devaluation for investors in countries that were known for devaluing their currencies in the past, such as Germany, when investing in euro area countries. This had a significant impact on cross-border capital flows, as investors became more willing to invest in financial assets in peripheral euro area countries, and banks showed interest in expanding their operations in other member states. The European Central Bank's indicators of financial integration reflected these changes, showing substantial increases. However, starting from 2008, concerns about default risk in peripheral economies and the possibility of these countries exiting the euro and reintroducing their weaker currencies led to a reversal in the trend of financial integration. As the euro crisis has gradually subsided in recent years, financial integration has started to recover, but it has not yet reached the levels observed just before the global financial crisis. The second decade of the euro has highlighted several significant challenges in implementing a common monetary and exchange rate policy among a diverse group of countries. While some of these challenges were foreseen by critics of EMU prior to its establishment in 1999, others emerged unexpectedly.

As reported in Jonung and Drea (2010), the discussions surrounding EMU in the 1990s often led to a division between European economists, who generally supported the EMU project, and skeptical US economists. Critics from the United States effectively argued that the Eurozone did not meet the criteria for being an optimal currency area. In particular, skeptics, including Feldstein (1992), highlighted the absence of a substantial federal budget within the euro area, which would have allowed for centralized transfers and taxes to mitigate the impact of asymmetric shocks. Sims (1999) among others expressed concerns about the "precarious fiscal foundations of EMU," suggesting that the accumulation of excessive debts by member states could jeopardize price stability. Regarding the latter, the architects of EMU also expressed concerns about the impact of fiscal debt on the stability of the euro. The Maastricht Treaty included several provisions aimed at mitigating the effects of fiscal problems on price stability. One notable provision, known as the "no bailout" clause, was widely believed to prohibit member states from assisting other states facing sovereign debt issues, and the ECB was prohibited from engaging in "monetary financing" through direct purchases of sovereign bonds. However, in practice, it was observed that the no bailout clause did not prevent bailouts, and the monetary financing clause did not prevent the ECB from buying sovereign bonds, thus raising doubts about the effectiveness of these provisions (Whelan, 2019). Euro's founders accepted that the sole instrument to control fiscal debt was the Stability and Growth Pact.[9]

Despite recent revisions, the fiscal rules have become more complex without clear evidence of significant improvement in their effectiveness. It is likely that these rules are not received with much higher regard today by economists or politicians compared to 2002 when the former European Commission President, Romano Prodi, criticized them as "stupid" and "rigid".[10] Even if the Stability and Growth Pact had been successful in its initial decade by controlling deficits and reducing debt-to-GDP ratios before the global financial crisis, it is doubtful that such rules alone would have addressed the fundamental issue that euro area countries lack sufficient macroeconomic tools to effectively respond to significant negative shocks that disproportionately affect their economies. The expectation was that countries in the EMU would manage their national budgets prudently during economic expansions, allowing them to have sufficient fiscal space to implement countercyclical fiscal policies in the absence of national interest rate instruments or adjustable exchange rates. However, in practice, even countries like Ireland and Spain, which had strong public finances before the GFC, were unable to effectively use fiscal policies to mitigate the impact of significant shocks specific to their economies. In fact, countries such as Greece, Portugal, and others experienced procyclical fiscal policies throughout the decade that followed the advent of the GFC. Despite the relatively small fiscal multipliers in most smaller euro area countries, even if they had been able to pursue independent expansionary fiscal policies during the crises, the impact might have been limited compared to a coordinated fiscal expansion across the entire euro area, which could have stimulated demand on a broader scale.

[9]Regrettably, the initial period of the common currency demonstrated that the SGP was unlikely to be effective. In 2003, the European Commission determined that both Germany and France had breached the SGP and proposed that the ECOFIN imposes corrective measures on these countries through the excessive deficit procedure. However, the politicians serving on the ECOFIN committee chose not to adhere to the Commission's recommendations. As a result, with the leading economies of the euro area unwilling to comply with the SGP's terms, the Pact was violated almost as frequently as it was adhered to by member states in the subsequent years (Whelan, 2019).

[10]In an interview at the French *Le Monde*, Prodi stated, "I know very well that the stability pact is stupid, like all decisions which are rigid. The pact is imperfect. We need a more intelligent tool and more flexibility" (see also Osborn, 2002).

Given the absence of an independent exchange rate and the limited scope of macroeconomic policy tools, such as national monetary policy, the euro area economies have experienced significantly sluggish adjustments in response to the substantial shocks of 2008–2010. This stands in contrast to other countries that possess a broader range of macroeconomic policy instruments, including the ability to devalue their exchange rates, and have witnessed more prompt recoveries from similar crises. An examination of current account balances offers insights into the slow adjustment process. Following the global recession and shifts in financial market conditions in 2008, peripheral euro area countries found themselves in precarious positions, necessitating improvements in both public and private sector balances. Typically, fiscal adjustment is employed to address public sector imbalances, while devaluation of the exchange rate can improve private sector balances. In the late 1990s East Asian crises, for instance, current account balances swiftly shifted from deficits to surpluses, accompanied by significant devaluations. However, in Greece, Italy, Spain, and Portugal, the gradual return of current account balances to equilibrium took approximately a decade (see Whelan, 2019, Fig. 4, p. 17). Throughout this period, these countries experienced fiscal austerity measures and pressure on domestic costs, which exerted constraints on their domestic economies. The sluggish process of recovery from the crisis and the significant long-term consequences it has had on people can also be exemplified by looking at unemployment rates in euro area countries affected by debt crises. It has taken 10 years for Portugal and Ireland to bring their unemployment rates back to levels similar to those observed before the crisis. However, Spain and Greece still have unemployment rates that far exceed the pre-2008 levels. This indicates the enduring challenges and persistent job market difficulties these countries have faced in achieving a full recovery.

The slow adjustment process observed in response to significant shocks can be attributed to two key factors: Firstly, the absence of an independent exchange rate, which would have likely been devalued, had these countries not been part of the euro area. Secondly, the ECB's provision of funding to banks in these countries when private investors were withdrawing funds. Without the ECB's policy of full allotment on credit provision, these countries would have likely faced more intense but shorter crises triggered by the sudden stop in capital flows. This would have resulted in a more rapid decline in current account deficits and a more immediate increase in unemployment. However, it is also plausible that a swifter recovery would have followed such a scenario. The effectiveness of these options can be subject to debate, but the willingness of the countries most affected by the euro crisis to endure another extended period of economic stagnation, commonly referred to as a "lost decade," in the event of another significant recession in the coming years has been doubtful.

The pre-EMU discussion primarily revolved around the concept of whether the euro area was an "optimum currency area" (as in Mundell, 1961). Critics emphasized the significant differences in economic structures across the region, suggesting the likelihood of significant "asymmetric shocks" that would affect some areas more than others. However, proponents of EMU argued that the currency union would enhance trade links among member states, leading to more correlated business cycles (Frankel & Rose, 1997) in countries with close trade ties. Ironically, the near harmonization of private borrowing rates proved to be a far more significant asymmetric shock than anticipated in this debate (Whelan, 2019, p. 18). While interest rates in Germany and other "core" euro members remained at pre-EMU levels, borrowing rates for businesses and households in many other euro area countries decreased significantly, having a profound impact on these nations. As the removal of devaluation risk within the EMU had a significant impact on financial flows within the euro area and the reduction in borrowing costs and the availability of cheap credit attracted a multitude of lenders, a surge in private debt levels in the "peripheral" member states emerged. With the benefit of hindsight, it becomes evident that the rapid growth of private debt posed a significant risk to the sovereign debt of these nations. Although Spain and Ireland had relatively low and declining public debt ratios prior to the crisis, the substantial increase in private debt fuelled housing bubbles that concealed underlying issues with their public finances (Portes, 2014, p. 425; Whelan 2019, p. 18).

The profound effect on EU economy posed by the GFC is evidenced not only in the widespread recession that emerged but also to the significant damage to budgetary positions. Additionally, due to the global reevaluation of risk, the viability of banking models that relied on high-leverage and risky investments was put into question. As a result, creditors who were previously willing to provide loans to banks in peripheral euro area countries became cautious about extending further credit to economies grappling with high debt levels and deep economic downturns. The escalated debt burdens faced by households and businesses, which seemed manageable during periods of economic expansion, now raised concerns about the solvency of banks due to the surge in nonperforming loans. These banking problems in the euro area's peripheral members exacerbated the already sharp global recession in these countries.

European policymakers were forced to recognize the "doom loop" between sovereigns and banks (Portes, 2014, p. 427). In fact, over the last decade, the European Central Bank and euro area governments have encountered numerous difficulties. As a result, there have been several adjustments made to the structure of the EMU. Despite facing criticism for its relatively delayed response to macroeconomic downturns, the ECB has actually been at the forefront of developing novel and advanced monetary policy instruments, surpassing other major global central banks in this regard[11] (Whelan, 2019, p. 21). Additionally, European citizens have

[11] Apart from the asset purchase programs implemented by the US Federal Reserve and the Bank of England, the ECB has also employed a negative deposit rate on reserves (for an extensive discussion, see Kokores, 2022, pp. 339–352). This rate, in combination with the significant increase in bank reserves resulting from the Eurosystem's asset purchases, has likely played a significant role in reducing bond yields in the euro area in recent years. To examine how individual banks in the euro area are adjusting their balance sheets in response to negative rates and increased reserves, see, for example, Ryan and Whelan (2021). Additionally, the ECB has introduced a new tool called Outright Monetary Transactions (OMT) in 2012, following Mario Draghi's statement to do "whatever it takes" to safeguard the euro. The announcement of the OMT instrument had a notable impact in countering negative market sentiment regarding peripheral sovereign bond yields during the peak of the euro crisis in 2012. However, the OMT instrument has not been utilized thus far, and

experienced significant benefits as a result of economic and monetary union, and the euro has gained popularity among the public. Despite enduring challenges such as sovereign defaults, capital controls, depositor haircuts, and a lengthy recovery from a prolonged slump, the euro project has demonstrated resilience. However, it would be overly optimistic to assume that the worst is behind and that the success of the euro is guaranteed. This cautious outlook is supported, for example, by Whelan (2019, p. 29). While the euro is officially described as "fixed and immutable," the continuous discussions among European finance ministers about the possibility of Greece exiting the euro have demonstrated that this may not hold true. In a broader sense, relying solely on economic arguments against leaving the euro is insufficient to deter political movements that could potentially lead to a country's withdrawal from the euro.

In a similar vein, the Brexit process offers valuable lessons for the rest of Europe. It highlights that the economic advantages of EU membership are often greater than those derived from being part of the Eurozone. Consequently, some EU member states have opted to remain outside the single currency. In the case of the United Kingdom, numerous expert analyses warned of significant losses under various exit scenarios.[12] In order to maintain the unity of the Eurozone, European politicians must strive to reduce the likelihood of crises within the Eurozone and make it a more accommodating environment during the expected economic downturns that will occur in the future (Whelan, 2019). Although European leaders have often been criticized for their reluctance to embrace change, they have actually made significant advancements in improving the economic and financial structure of the Eurozone,

there are still many uncertainties surrounding its practical implementation; as Demertzis (2020) eloquently remarks, "OMT was always meant to be the nuclear option; the kind of thing you put in place so that you do not have to use it" (para. 3). It had been predicted *antecedent* to the emergence of the COVID-19 pandemic (see, for example, Whelan (2019) that asserts that "given the low policy rates of recent years and the likelihood of another recession in the coming years, it is likely that the ECB will need to use all of its newly-developed tools (and perhaps some new ones) to fight any future severe recession but with these tools in place, it is possible the policy response to the next crisis will be quicker" (p. 21)).

[12]Despite the clear negative economic consequences in the short and long term, the rhetoric surrounding "reclaiming sovereignty over our currency and budgets" could potentially gain traction among nationalist parties. These parties may draw inspiration from the strategies employed by proponents of Brexit, who effectively dismissed counterarguments as fear-based tactics employed by an elitist establishment (Offe, 2017). While opinion polls can provide insights into public sentiment at a specific moment, the Brexit process demonstrated that public opinions on economic matters can quickly become radicalized under certain circumstances. For example, recent surveys indicate surprisingly high levels of backing in the United Kingdom for an extremely rigid form of Brexit, aimed at enabling the country to pursue new trade agreements with non-EU nations. Prior to the Brexit referendum, there was limited evidence of support for such an approach, and from an economic perspective, it lacks a sound basis. However, within a relatively short timeframe, this viewpoint transitioned from being held by a small group of radical think tanks to becoming an official policy of the UK government. Similar arguments could be applied to UK migration policy, where concerns voiced by a minority of the electorate ultimately led to a significant shift and the adoption of government policies that have had adverse economic consequences (see, for example, Office for Budget Responsibility, 2021).

demonstrating a greater willingness to share sovereignty than previously anticipated. However, there are still notable deficiencies in terms of fiscal capacity and financial stability that need to be addressed.

For instance, recent surveys indicate surprisingly high levels of backing in the United Kingdom for an extremely rigid form of Brexit, aimed at enabling the country to pursue new trade agreements with non-EU nations. Prior to the Brexit referendum, there was limited evidence of support for such an approach, and from an economic perspective, it lacks a sound basis. However, within a relatively short timeframe, this viewpoint transitioned from being held by a small group of radical think tanks to becoming an official policy of the UK government. Similar arguments could be applied to UK migration policy, where concerns voiced by a minority of the electorate ultimately led to a significant shift and the adoption of government policies that have had adverse economic consequences (Pickup et al., 2021; see also Schwartz et al., 2021). The field of economics has put forth numerous proposals for comprehensive institutional enhancements aimed at strengthening the euro area, including the notable Franco-German plan devised by 14 esteemed economists (Weder di Mauro et al., 2018). The responsibility now lies with Europe's politicians across all branches of governance, namely, the Council, the Commission, and the Parliament, to diligently transform these and other recommendations into tangible measures in the next decade. By persistently addressing its weaknesses, policymakers can minimize the likelihood of a significant future existential crisis within the economic and monetary union.

6.4 Conclusions

In November 2008, in the midst of the global financial crisis, the ECB organized a conference titled "The Euro@Ten," which primarily revolved around self-congratulation from ECB officials and esteemed European economists regarding the success of the euro. However, the commemorations marking the Euro's 20th anniversary have been comparatively more subdued, reflecting the challenges faced by the common currency in its second decade. Over the past 10 years, numerous structural vulnerabilities that were initially raised by critics of the euro prior to EMU have been exposed, alongside additional significant weaknesses that were largely disregarded (Whelan, 2019). It is considered vital to address the significance of cross-border policy interactions and cooperation. A fundamental starting point can be traced back to Keynes' concerns regarding the "adjustment problem" within an international monetary system, such as the Bretton Woods system, where the responsibility of correcting cross-border imbalances falls primarily on deficit countries, while surplus countries are free to focus on domestic goals. According to Keynes, this imbalance creates a systematic bias toward a policy approach that is globally contractionary (Bartsch et al., 2020, p. 21). Surplus countries only require enough policy stimulus to maintain full employment, while deficit countries must restrain domestic demand, reduce imports, and potentially stimulate exports through real depreciation. Consequently, the collective global stimulus, which is the sum of "just enough" in surplus countries and contraction in deficit countries, is insufficient to sustain full employment at a global level. In theory, cross-border cooperation has the potential to alleviate the contractionary bias by establishing a commitment among all countries to share the burden. However, the track record in this regard is discouraging (Bartsch et al., 2020, p. 30). Cooperation has rarely been effective in persuading surplus countries to implement expansionary policies aimed at reducing the adjustment costs faced by deficit countries.

The issue lies at the heart of the euro area's functioning. Unlike a fixed exchange rate system, having a common central bank provides a certain level of risk and cost-sharing. However, the mandate of the European Central Bank is to target inflation and economic activity across the entire union, while fiscal policy is responsible for providing residual stabilization at the national level in the event of asymmetric shocks or divergent impacts of common shocks. In the euro area, individual countries have the autonomy to set their fiscal policies, guided by both union-wide rules (such as the Stability and Growth Pact) and national regulations aimed at ensuring fiscal sustainability in the medium and long term. The challenge for the euro area, as an incomplete monetary union, is to establish an effective institutional framework and political equilibrium that can simultaneously facilitate efficient stabilization at the national level and maintain an appropriate monetary stance at the EU level.

The implications for the policy mix within the euro area are evident. The persistent failure of fiscal coordination in attaining a desirable union-wide fiscal stance increases the burden on monetary policy. This may not pose a significant issue at the union level during normal times, with the important caveat that a common monetary policy cannot effectively address country-specific disturbances. However, it can have substantial consequences when policy rates reach the effective lower bound, as larger cross-border fiscal spillovers can be expected without internalized coordination. Given the challenges of achieving horizontal coordination, the future resilience of the euro area will rely on its ability to progress toward coordination through vertical means or the establishment of a central fiscal capacity, particularly in circumstances where this becomes highly valuable. An exemplary instance of such vertical coordination is the Recovery and Resilience Facility, which was agreed upon in 2020 to ensure a prompt and sustainable recovery following the COVID-19 pandemic (on this issue, see Bartsch et al., 2020, Chap. 4).

Indeed, in the initial stages of the monetary union, the foundation for future crises and conflicts was laid as macroeconomic imbalances quietly accumulated beneath the surface of seemingly prosperous economies and the overall promising performance of the Eurozone. The European debt crisis exposed the vulnerability of the Eurozone to the fiscal failures of individual member states. This fiscal fragility had a direct impact on the financial stability of the Eurozone's banking sector, consequently disrupting the transmission mechanisms of monetary policy. A decade after the GFC began and prior to the emergence of the COVID-19 pandemic crisis, opinions regarding the current state of the monetary union remained divided, with significant disagreement on the appropriate course of action. In his optimistic view, Draghi (2019), a prominent advocate for the single currency, asserts that the

Eurozone has successfully overcome a severe crisis that threatened its very existence. He highlights the policy response and significant structural changes made to the EMU as contributing factors to its recovery, resulting in a stronger monetary union today compared to 2008. However, he acknowledges that further efforts are required to enhance the resilience of the EMU in preparation for future crises. On the other hand, Eichengreen (2019), who believes that a well-functioning monetary union necessitates substantial progress toward fiscal and political integration, holds a more pessimistic stance. He predicts that the euro will continue to stumble forward, with dissatisfaction regarding its operation persisting. Nevertheless, he expects that no member country will choose to exit the monetary union and any progress achieved will be minimal.

The ECB has effectively fulfilled its main objective of maintaining price stability, and the introduction of the common currency has brought several advantages, including cost savings in currency exchanges, enhanced payment systems, and increased integration of financial markets within the euro area. Notably, the common currency enjoys popularity among the citizens of the euro area. Despite these accomplishments, the euro area is an ongoing project and may encounter significant challenges that could potentially jeopardize its existence in the future. While the euro may have contributed to some efficiency gains,[13] it seems to have done little to facilitate intra-euro area trade (see Glick & Rose, 2016), and the process of greater financial integration has had a destabilizing effect on the euro area, rather than serving as a catalyst for sustainable economic growth.

Overall, the GFC and the consequent Eurozone sovereign debt crisis have had significant structural impacts. According to the Commission Economic Autumn forecast of 2016, the potential growth in the euro area declined from 1.9% in the period of 2000–2008 to 0.5% in 2009–2014. Additionally, the report highlights a decrease of approximately 20% in total investment in the EU between 2008 and 2013. Despite the subsequent recovery and the implementation of a new EU investment plan, investment as a percentage of GDP has not yet reached precrisis levels. Moreover, the overall public debt level of the EU, which was already relatively high prior to the crisis (ranging between 60% and 70% of GDP), remained above 80% throughout the decade following the crisis (European Court of Auditors, 2020, p. 7). The euro area's growth performance has been underwhelming, with an average annual growth rate of 1.37% between 1999 and 2017. This figure represents a decline compared to the decade antecedent to the GFC, during which the same group of countries experienced an average annual growth rate of 2.17% (ECB's area-wide model-based calculations).

The ECB can be partially held responsible for the relatively poor economic performance in the euro area. While the ECB has played a role in maintaining

[13]During the introduction of the euro, there was a sense of optimism among certain parties who believed that the efficiencies associated with the EMU would lead to an increase in economic growth. It was anticipated that the reduction of trade barriers would enhance intra-European trade and efficiency and the less affluent members of the euro area would benefit from external investments facilitated by deeper financial integration (Whelan, 2019, p. 19).

macroeconomic stability by keeping inflation in check, it can be argued that its response to the prolonged economic weakness in the region since 2008 was too sluggish. The ECB was slow in reducing policy rates to zero and introducing unconventional measures like asset purchase programs (see Whelan, 2014, for a summary at a primary stage). This delayed response likely resulted in lower economic growth in recent years compared to what could have been achieved (Portes, 2014, p. 423; Whelan, 2019, p. 19).

Nevertheless, the main causes of sluggish growth in the euro area are primarily attributed to factors beyond the control of the ECB. These include the gradual decline in the working-age population and the limited growth in total factor productivity (Whelan, 2018). It is important to acknowledge that these factors are not within the ECB's purview, and there are limited actions the ECB can take to directly address them. Indeed, however, the ECB has demonstrated its commitment to fulfilling its mandate of maintaining price stability through the implementation of asset purchase programs and long-term refinancing operations. These measures have been effective in mitigating risk polarization (Bartsch et al., 2020, p. 63). Additionally, in response to the COVID-19 crisis, the ECB introduced the Pandemic Emergency Purchase Programme (PEPP), which has provided temporary flexibility and enhanced monetary firepower. However, concerns persisted regarding future actions as the pandemic unfolded, particularly in light of the perplexing arguments raised by the German constitutional court, which questioned the legitimacy of ECB measures that were clearly aligned with international best practices and proportionate to the challenges at hand (see Orphanides, 2018; Bofinger et al., 2020).

References

Bartsch, E., Benassy-Queré, A., Corsetti, G., & Debrun, X. (2020). It's all in the mix: How can monetary and fiscal policies work or fail together. *Geneva reports on the world economy* 23, International Centre of Monetary and Banking Studies, Geneva, Switzerland, and Centre for Economic Policy Research, London, UK.

Bini Smaghi, L. B. (2011). Greek debt restructuring. Business Insider, May. Available online: http://www.businessinsider.com/smaghi-greek-debt-restructuring-2011-5.

Bofinger, P., Hellwig, M., Huther, M., Schnitzer, M., & Schularick, M. (2020). The independence of the central bank at risk. VoxEU.org, 8 June.

Demertzis, M. (2020). Why OMT is not the solution for Italy right now. Bruegel blogpost, Brussels, 16 March.

Draghi, M. (2019). Stabilisation policies in a monetary union. *Speech* of the President of the European Central Bank -ECB at the Academy of Athens, Athens, Greece, October 1st.

Eichengreen, B. (2019). The euro at 20: An enduring success but a fundamental failure. January 4th. Available online at: http://theconversation.com/the-euro-at-20-an-enduring-success-but-a-fundamental-failure-108149

European Court of Auditors (2020). How the EU took account of lessons learned from the 2008–2012 financial and sovereign debt crises. *Review* No 5, European Court of Auditors, European Union, Luxembourg.

Feldstein, M. (1992). Europe's monetary union: The case against EMU. *The Economist.*

Frankel, J. A., & Rose, A. (1997). Is EMU more justifiable ex post than ex ante? *European Economic Review, 41*, 753–760.

Gerba, E. (2019). Euro project, 20 years on: A critical assessment and the road ahead. *Report* European Parliament's Committee on Economic and Monetary Affairs. Available online: http://www.europarl.europa.eu/committees/en/econ/monetary-dialogue.html

Gern, K. J., Kooths, S., & Stolzenburg, U. (2019). Euro at 20: The monetary union from a bird's-eye view. In *Depth analysis*, PE 631.038, European Parliament, January.

Glick, R., & Rose, A. K. (2016). Currency unions and trade: A post-EMU reassessment. *European Economic Review, 87C*, 78–91.

Jonung, L., & Drea, E. (2010). It Can't happen, It's a bad idea, it Won't last: U.S. economists on the EMU and the euro, 1989-2002. *Econ Journal Watch, 7*, 4–52.

Kokores, I. T. (2022). *Monetary policy and financial stability: Challenges before and after the global financial crisis*. Cambridge Scholars Publishing.

Monaghan, A. (2010). Joaquin Almunia: We don't need a Greek bail-out because the country won't default. *The Telegraph*.

Mundell, R. (1961). A theory of optimum currency areas. *American Economic Review, 51*(4), 657–665.

OBR – Office for Budget Responsibility (2021). *The Initial Impact of Brexit on UK Trade with the EU*. Office for Budget Responsibility, London, UK.

Offe, C. (2017). Referendum vs. institutionalized deliberation: What democratic theorists can learn from the 2016 Brexit decision. *Daedalus, 146*, 14–27.

Orphanides, A. (2018). The boundaries of Central Bank independence: Lessons from unconventional times. *Bank of Japan Monetary and Economic Studies*, 35–56.

Osborn, A. (2002). Prodi disowns 'stupid' stability pact. *The Guardian*.

Pickup, M., de Rooij, E. A., van der Linden, C., & Goodwin, M. J. (2021). Brexit, COVID-19, and attitudes toward immigration in Britain. *Social Science Quarterly, 102*(5), 2184–2193.

Portes, R. (2014). The Eurozone crisis. In D. D. Evanoff, C. Holthausen, G. G. Kaufman, & M. Kremer (Eds.), *The role of central banks in financial stability: How has it changed?* (30th world scientific studies in international economics) (pp. 423–432). World Scientific Publishing Co. Pte. Ltd.

Ryan, E., & Whelan, K. (2021). Quantitative easing and the hot potato effect: Evidence from euro area banks. *Journal of International Money and Finance, 115*, 102354.

Reinhart, C. M., & Rogoff, K. S. (2009). *This time is different: Eight centuries of financial folly*. Princeton University Press.

Samuelson, P. A. (1997). Wherein do the European and American models differ? *Banca d'Italia Temi di Discussione, 320*, Banca d' Italia.

Schwartz, C., Simon, M., Hudson, D., & van-Heerde-Hudson, J. (2021). A populist paradox? How Brexit softened anti-immigrant attitudes. *British Journal of Political Science, 51*(3), 1160–1180.

Sims, C. A. (1999). The precarious fiscal foundations of EMU. *De Economist, 147*(4), 415–436.

Trichet, J. C. (2011). *President of the ECB Press conference* (p. 7). European Central Bank.

Weder di Mauro, B., Zettelmeyer, J., Rey, H., Véron, N., Martin, P., Pisani, F., Fuest, C., Gourinchas, P.-O., Fratzscher, M., Farhi, E., Enderlein, H., Brunnermeier, M. K., & Bénassy-Quéré, A. (2018). *Reconciling risk sharing with market discipline: A constructive approach to euro area reform, CEPR policy insight 91*. Centre for Economic Policy Research.

Whelan, K. (2013). Sovereign default and the euro. *Oxford Review of Economic Policy, 29*, 478–501.

Whelan, K. (2014). The ECB and non-standard policies: Too little too late? Briefing paper for European Parliament Committee on Economic and Monetary Affairs, European Parliament.

Whelan, K. (2018). Monetary Policy in an Era of Low Average Growth Rates. Monetary Dialogue, November. In-Depth Analysis PE 626.094 Requested by the ECON Committee, Policy Department for Economic, Scientific and Quality of Life Policies Directorate-General for Internal Policies, European Parliament, November.

Whelan, K. (2019). The euro at 20: Successes, problems, progress and threats. Monetary dialogue, January. In-depth analysis PE 631.039 requested by the ECON Committee, Policy Department for Economic, Scientific and Quality of Life Policies Directorate-General for Internal Policies, European Parliament, January.

Zettelmeyer, J., Trebesch, C., & Gulati, M. (2013). The Greek debt exchange: An autopsy. *Economic Policy*, 513–563.

Part III
The Task Ahead: Monetary Policy in Uncharted Waters

Chapter 7
Monetary Theory and Policy: The Implications of Radical Uncertainty

> A major function of economic history, as I see it, is to be a forum where economists and political scientists, lawyers, sociologists, and historians -historians of events and of ideas and of technologies- can meet and talk to one another. . . . We shall look over our shoulders at the historical record, so as to see that we do not put our logical process into a form which clashes with the largest and most obvious fact. (This is only the first stage of fitting, but it is as far as we shall go.) . . . But we shall not be able (as a deterministic theorist might think he was able) to extrapolate into the future; all we shall be able to do, all the economist is ever able to do, is to speculate about things which, more or less probably, may happen. *[emphasis added]*
>
> —*John R. Hicks (1969), p. 2, 8*

7.1 Introduction: The Consensus to Date

The main goal of macroeconomic policy is welfare maximization, usually measured by income per person. When striving to achieve this objective, the initial consideration is whether policymakers should focus on maintaining a stable economy in line with its long-term growth path. If stabilizing the economy does not significantly impact real growth, it becomes less important, although fluctuations in the economy can have implications for income distribution. Nonetheless, the direct effects of monetary policy on distribution should also be taken into account, as interest rate policies can influence income distribution as well.[1]

The consensus to date, reflected in various New Keynesian models, is that high volatility can diminish the overall level of long-term economic growth. Consequently, reducing fluctuations in the economy has significant effects on overall

[1]This raises the question of whether we would be concerned about economic fluctuations if the impact of those fluctuations were evenly distributed among the entire population. In other words, if a 2% decline in GDP resulted in a 2% decrease in everyone's income, the question remains open whether we would still consider business cycles as significant (Cecchetti et al., 2009a, 2009b, p. 2).

I. T. Kokores, *Monetary Policy in Interdependent Economies*, Financial and Monetary Policy Studies 55, https://doi.org/10.1007/978-3-031-41958-4_7

welfare. While there are dissenting viewpoints, such as those expressed by Lucas and Sargent (1979) and Lucas (2003), the idea that smoothing out output fluctuations is beneficial is widely accepted among policymakers. This is evident in the explicit or implicit emphasis on output stability in the objectives of many central banks. These widely used New Keynesian models also suggest that a combination of monetary and fiscal policy can potentially stabilize economic growth and prices, at least in theory. However, the prevailing viewpoint is that fiscal policy has significant limitations as a tool for countercyclical measures. While it does serve as an automatic stabilizer, there are practical and political challenges that make it extremely difficult to implement discretionary fiscal policy effectively in order to smooth out real economic fluctuations. Instead, fiscal policy primarily serves as the main mechanism through which society determines the allocation of output among various final uses (such as consumption, investment, government size, and net exports) and lays the groundwork for long-term economic growth.

According to this view, monetary policy is regarded as the primary instrument for actively implementing stabilization policies. It is characterized as quick, agile, and capable of producing rapid effects. By utilizing interest rates, along with a flexible exchange rate and capital mobility, policymakers can strive for price stability while also having the ability to smooth short-run fluctuations in output.[2] In fact, certain versions of the standard economic model suggest that strictly targeting inflation is optimal, with output fluctuations being smoothed only to the extent that they impact inflation forecasts (for further discussion, see Blanchard & Galí, 2007; Blanchard, 2008). It is not surprising that this theoretical consensus is reflected in the actual monetary policy frameworks implemented in advanced economies over the past two decades, including prior to the recent GFC (Cecchetti et al., 2009a, 2009b).

Upon reflecting on the global financial crisis, Cecchetti et al. (2009a, 2009b) questioned the relevance of the existing macroeconomic models, even though the crisis had not yet concluded at that time. Despite their elegance, intricate microeconomic foundations, and complex endogenous dynamics, these models formed the basis for monetary policy that had fostered a period of stability lasting for almost three decades. This era, known as the Great Moderation, was characterized by low inflation, robust economic growth, and overall stability. However, in hindsight, there was a sense of complacency. Academic literature was replete with articles attributing this stability to sound policy, and policymakers heeded these claims. It was believed that the economy possessed inherent stability and robust self-correcting mechanisms.

The recurrent financial crashes that plagued the pre-mid-twentieth-century period were believed to have been eradicated due to our deep and profound understanding, translated into mathematical models. However, these models did not prevent the

[2] The discussion presented overlooks the significant importance of exchange rate stabilization in the monetary policy of numerous small open economies and emerging markets. Despite some inherent challenges, the consensus has incorporated these frameworks, albeit with some difficulties (Cecchetti et al., 2009a, 2009b, p. 3).

occurrence of the crisis, nor did they offer guidance on implementing policies to mitigate its impact. They proved to be wholly inadequate in guiding the development of an institutional framework capable of averting systemic financial collapse. While there were indeed warnings[3] and certain models hinted at the underlying issues economies worldwide faced after the advent of the GFC and the subsequent crises, ultimately, the risks were disregarded by both policymakers and most academic researchers. Although economic reasoning can provide us with a perspective to begin comprehending the events and their causes, these warnings have been overlooked.

Reviewing the pre-GFC consensus that provided the basis for stabilization policy as it has been conducted since around 1980, it is evident that a crucial step forward is necessary. The key conclusion is straightforward: we must construct economic models that effectively incorporate the financial sector, giving due consideration to the role played by financial intermediaries and their interconnectedness, both within the financial system and with the real economy. Importantly, these models should have the ability to internally generate financial strain that can accumulate over time until it reaches a crisis point. In other words, we need models that acknowledge and account for the normal occurrence of economic booms and busts.

7.2 Discussion on the Limited Help of the Traditional Structural Model

Indeed, based on the prevailing models employed by central banks and international financial institutions, the occurrence of the GFC was not anticipated, nor deemed possible. These modern macroeconomic models, including the New Classical, New Keynesian, and dynamic stochastic general equilibrium (DSGE) models, inherently exclude the existence of prolonged economic imbalances through their underlying assumptions.

Macro-policy models developed after Keynes were primarily focused on static equilibria. In these models, consumption was determined solely by current income, rather than considering the impact of expected wealth over time as in classical economic theories (Fisher, 1930, Chaps. 5 and 10). Investment decisions aimed to equalize the marginal productivities of capital goods with the fixed cost of capital. High interest rates discouraged the purchase of capital goods, while low interest rates encouraged such purchases. These Keynesian models, including popular versions like the IS-LM models by Hicks (1937), Hansen (1949, Chap. 5), and Ackley (1961, Chap. 14), had countercyclical implications. For example, they suggested raising interest rates to moderate demand during boom times and reducing rates when demand was weak. However, most of these models assumed fixed prices, neglecting one of the US Federal Reserve's primary concerns and disregarding the reality of one

[3] See Wood (2015, p. 149) Table 6.1 and BIS (2009) for a discussion of the warnings.

of the most significant peacetime inflations in history. The purpose of their monetary policy was to accommodate fiscal deficits, with inflation being attributed to wage and price-setting practices of unions and corporations. The focus on money and its relationship to prices did not regain prominence in economic theory and policy until Friedman and Schwartz's (1963) *A Monetary History of the United States* and the realization that Congress was too cumbersome and not fully committed to implementing effective countercyclical fiscal policy (Wood, 2009, Chap. 4).

The static equilibrium nature of economists' models also resulted in abstraction from the crucial issue of credibility. For instance, a cut in interest rates might or might not stimulate demand, depending on expectations about future changes. If a rate reduction was seen as a step toward even lower rates, it could depress demand (Wood, 2015, p. 108). More traditional structural models inadvertently neglect prolonged economic imbalances by not adequately considering the factors that are now widely believed to have both triggered and prolonged the GFC. These factors include credit, leverage, stock (especially debt), and the gradual accumulation (and eventual unwinding) of "imbalances" in the real economy. The term "imbalances" refers to asset prices that reached increasingly difficult-to-explain levels based on fundamental factors, as well as financial institutions that became exposed to various risks jeopardizing their solvency. The dangers arising from these financial imbalances have eventually been addressed in the broader context of the pursuit of financial stability.

However, other imbalances also emerged, affecting the real side of the global economy. Household savings rates in English-speaking countries among others declined to zero or even lower. Additionally, fixed investment ratios in China surpassed 50% of GDP, a level unprecedented in market-based economies. These domestic imbalances led to a surge in global trade imbalances to unprecedented levels. Furthermore, as supply responded to demand-side pressures, certain industries expanded beyond sustainable levels, such as construction, financial services, and global distribution networks, necessitating subsequent downsizing.

Regrettably, these real-side imbalances did not receive the timely attention they warranted (White, 2011, p. 124). Trichet (2011) admits that "As a policymaker during the crisis, I found the available models of limited help. In fact, I would go further: in the face of the crisis, we felt abandoned by conventional tools. In the absence of clear guidance from existing analytical frameworks, policymakers had to place particular reliance on our experience. Judgement and experience inevitably played a key role. In exercising judgement, we were helped by one area of the economic literature: historical analysis" (p. 18).

Examinations of past crisis episodes through historical studies shed light on anticipated issues (Reinhart & Rogoff, 2010) and offered potential remedies (Jonung, 2009). Crucially, the historical record revealed the pitfalls to be avoided (Bernanke, 2000, gives an account of the guidance offered by economic history). However, relying solely on subjective judgment inherently carries risks. It is essential to have macroeconomic and financial models that provide a framework for guiding and organizing judgment-based analysis, thereby adding discipline and structure to the decision-making process.

The primary lesson derived from the experience of central bankers is the risk associated with relying solely on a single tool, methodology, or paradigm. Policymakers should seek input from various theoretical perspectives and utilize a range of empirical approaches. *It is crucial to reconsider the characterization of the homo economicus, the economic agent at the core of any model* (Mishkin, 2011, p. 124). The existing models, which feature atomistic, optimizing agents, fail to capture behavior accurately during times of crisis. A better understanding of heterogeneity among agents and their interactions is necessary. Trichet (2011) highlights the importance of considering alternative motivations for economic choices. Behavioral economics, drawing from psychology, provides explanations for decision-making in crisis situations (Diamond & Vartiainen, 2007). Agent-based modeling, which moves away from the optimization assumption, enables the modeling of more complex interactions among agents (LeBaron, 2000). Trichet suggests that these approaches deserve attention, particularly in terms of developing a richer characterization of expectation formation. He acknowledges the significant progress made by rational expectations theory in macroeconomic analysis over the past four decades but emphasizes the need to re-examine this assumption. Ongoing research on concepts like learning (Evans & Honkapohja, 2001; Evans et al., 2022) and rational inattention (Sims, 2003); Maćkowiak and Wiederholt, 2009) shows promise. However, Mishkin (2011) cautions against a complete dismissal of expectations in response to the current backlash against economic theory. Some economists mistakenly believe that fiscal stimulus will always have the same impact, regardless of a country's fiscal position. The international dimension is crucial, as policies implemented in one country have effects on others (Mishkin, 2011, p. 134).

In researchers' crucial effort to improve the integration of the financial system within our macroeconomic models, one approach involves adding a financial sector to the existing framework (Christiano et al., 2003), although more extensive modifications may be necessary. It is particularly important to address the nonlinear behavior of the financial system, considering the procyclical accumulation of leverage and vulnerabilities (Geanakoplos, 2010). These areas present significant opportunities for exploring alternative approaches to economic analysis. Trichet (2011) emphasizes the need to draw inspiration from other disciplines such as physics, engineering, psychology, and biology. Bringing together experts from these fields, along with economists and central bankers, has the potential to foster creativity and provide valuable insights (New York Federal Reserve, 2007).[4] However, these

[4]Scientists have developed advanced tools for analyzing complex dynamic systems in a rigorous manner. These techniques rely on models that are based on principles such as the law of large numbers, which is exemplified by the statistical physics underlying modern thermodynamics. They also utilize advancements in mathematical analysis, as seen in hydrodynamics and turbulence theory. The common thread among these approaches is that they explain complex macro-level phenomena by postulating simple behaviors of micro-level elements (such as atoms, particles, or molecules) that form the basis of the studied process. These postulates are then empirically evaluated using statistical and simulation methods. These models have proven valuable in understanding various complex phenomena, including epidemics, weather patterns, crowd psychology,

methods emphasize an empirical approach that gives significant importance to inductive reasoning based on data rather than relying on deductive reasoning rooted in abstract assumptions or premises. The core of these methods is to prioritize an empirical approach. Simulations will be valuable in implementing these insights (Bouchaud, 2009) and can aid in deepening our comprehension of market dynamics and economic behavior. By employing such approaches, we can enhance our understanding of how the economy operates and how market dynamics unfold (Trichet, 2011, pp. 19–20).

7.3 Lessons from the Crisis for the Theory and Practice of Monetary Policy

The global financial crisis has caused a reconsideration of one of the central arguments supporting the Greenspan doctrine, which claimed that the aftermath of an asset price bubble bursting would have minimal costs. Contrary to this belief, it is now widely recognized that the costs of addressing the consequences of a bursting of a bubble, especially when accompanied by a financial crisis, can be exceedingly high. In addition to the evident impact of a significant decline in overall economic output due to the global recession, the global financial crisis has revealed the presence of additional costs that significantly elevate the overall expenses. Firstly, financial crises often result in prolonged periods of sluggish economic growth, and secondly, governments experience a sharp deterioration in their budgetary positions.

During severe economic downturns, it is commonly observed that economies subsequently experience robust recoveries, often referred to as V-shaped recoveries. However, Reinhart and Reinhart (2010) have shown that this typical V-shaped pattern does not hold true for recessions that follow financial crises. The process of deleveraging, which involves reducing debt levels, is a lengthy one, leading to significant obstacles for economic growth. It is now widely acknowledged that the cumulative output losses resulting from financial crises are substantial and the present crisis is no exception. As highlighted by Reinhart and Rogoff (2009), one consistent outcome of financial crises is a sharp increase in government debt. As Mishkin (2014) remarks, we have witnessed this very outcome in the aftermath of the current crisis (Mishkin, 2014, p. 412).

---

and magnetic fields. Market practitioners have also applied these tools to make portfolio management decisions, occasionally with some success. Trichet (2011, p. 19) expresses optimism that central banks can likewise benefit from these insights when developing tools to analyze financial markets and monetary policy transmission. Researchers from other fields bring an important perspective to economics, focusing on identifying the features that explain observed economic systems. Many aspects of the behavior observed in financial markets do not align well with the "efficient markets" hypothesis (Fama, 1970), which is central to most conventional models (Farmer & Geanakoplos, 2008). However, determining the key features that explain these phenomena remains a challenging and unresolved problem (Bouchaud, 2010).

The extensive financial institution bailouts, implementation of fiscal stimulus measures, and significant economic contractions worldwide have had adverse effects on the fiscal positions of many countries. Advanced nations, such as the United States, have witnessed budget deficits exceeding 10% of their GDP, becoming a common occurrence. Moreover, this surge in indebtedness has raised concerns about the potential for sovereign debt defaults, particularly in Europe. The necessary fiscal adjustments to restore fiscal balances to sustainable levels both are likely to be contractionary and result in increased societal strain. In fact, there is even a possibility that the fiscal challenges stemming from the crisis could pose a threat to the survival of the euro.

Furthermore, eventually, the significant expenses incurred in the aftermath of the asset price bubble burst have prompted a substantial reconsideration of the *"lean versus clean" debate*. Initially, this debate primarily revolved around whether monetary policy should respond to potential asset price bubbles. However, in light of the interplay between the housing price bubble and credit markets leading up to the global financial crisis, it is now acknowledged that we must differentiate between two distinct types of asset price bubbles (see, for example, Detken et al., 2010).

The role of asset prices in shaping monetary policy has been the subject of a significant and ongoing debate in recent years. The volatility of asset prices has raised concerns about the stability of the financial system and its potential impact on macroeconomic and price stability. One perspective in this debate argues for a wait-and-see approach, suggesting that it is preferable to allow asset bubbles to deflate naturally before implementing aggressive monetary policy measures to support the banking system and the overall economy. From this viewpoint, a decisive easing of monetary policy following the bursting of a bubble can contribute to both price stability and financial stability. However, there is a potential downside to this approach, as it may create moral hazard and encourage excessive risk-taking in future periods of economic expansion, with market participants factoring in the expectation of public interventions to rescue them. There has been ongoing discussion within academic and policy circles regarding an alternative approach to monetary policy known as "leaning against the wind." This approach involves the central bank adjusting the policy rate in response to financial imbalances with the aim of ensuring price stability in the medium to long term, even if it means accepting potentially higher volatility in consumer prices in the short to medium term. The rationale behind this approach is to proactively address the risk of an asset price bubble and prevent the potential negative consequences for price stability and the overall economy that could arise from a future collapse in asset prices.

Regarding the suitable policy response to the accumulation of financial imbalances, economists generally agree that monetary policy is not the most effective initial defense against systemic asset price cycles. Instead, regulatory and supervisory policies are considered more appropriate in addressing such challenges. However, this does not diminish the significance of the issue for monetary policymakers. There will likely be instances in the future where the central bank will need to consider whether monetary policy should complement existing policies by "leaning against the wind." Looking at historical patterns, there may be a need for monetary policy to support regulatory and supervisory measures due to potential delays in adapting to innovative financial market developments or cautious and slow implementation of such policies.

Given this context, it is important to highlight that, for example, the ECB's monetary policy strategy, which emphasizes the significance of money and credit, enables the assessment of asset price developments and their potential impact on price stability over the long term.[5] Quantitative indicators, such as measures of "excess liquidity" and "excess credit," offer valuable evidence to the central bank. These indicators can provide insights that deviate from the monetary policy stance inferred from economic analysis and inflation projections alone, potentially indicating a more accommodative policy stance.[6]

As Hetzel (2007) eloquently remarks, "consensus in marcoeconomics coalesces around common interpretations of major historical events" (p. 1). The aftermath of the recent financial crisis has revealed the substantial costs associated with financial instability and systemic financial crises, to the extent that the notion of simply "cleaning up" has become outdated. Remarkably, Bernanke (2009) asserts (during the economic turmoil) that "due to the problems credit markets in most economies experience, conventional monetary policy alone seems inadequate to bolster the economy now that is most necessary" (p. 2).

The global financial crisis has provided evidence of how shifts in credit supply may have a significant impact on macroeconomic fluctuations, underscoring the importance of financial factors in the implementation of monetary policy. According to Cecchetti et al. (2006) and Dynan et al. (2006), changes in the financial system have played a crucial role in stabilizing the economy in recent decades. Cecchetti (2008), for instance, raises the question of the relationship between financial system development and both the level and stability of real economic growth. He argues that this inquiry naturally leads to considering whether the effects of asset price bubbles on measures such as GDP at risk or price level at risk are influenced by the structure of the financial system (Cecchetti, 2008, p. 28).

However, precrisis models discussing the conventional debate between "lean" and "clean" approaches failed to consider the effects of credit supply resulting from the behavior of financial intermediaries. Specifically, the widely used New Keynesian DSGE models, employed by central banks in many developed countries, did not

[5]The ECB's monetary analysis framework focuses on examining the levels of excess liquidity and credit creation, among other factors relevant to monetary policy. This analysis helps identify potential unsustainable trends in asset valuations and informs the central bank's assessment of the appropriate policy stance. By understanding the relationship between these factors, the ECB can determine whether observed movements in asset prices indicate the formation of an unsustainable bubble.

[6]In conjunction with the conventional indicators of asset price overvaluation, incorporating these additional measures would serve to confirm concerns about the potential formation of a bubble. Moreover, the cross-validation between economic analysis and monetary analysis, as exemplified in the ECB's strategy, extends the timeframe within which the ECB assesses future trends in consumer prices (Detken et al., 2010, p. 323).

include components related to frictions in the functioning of the financial sector and its interaction with the real economy. Kokores (2015) examines the transformation in the literature on monetary policy following the global financial crisis and demonstrates a shift in favor of the "lean-against-the-wind" perspective within the context of the "lean versus clean" debate. She argues that the conventional view before the crisis actually incorporated elements of the "lean-against-the-wind" view by eventually addressing financial frictions in the economic models used for monetary policy. Furthermore, the "lean-against-the-wind" view itself has evolved in the postcrisis period, acknowledging the complex interactions between monetary and macroprudential policies and recognizing the potential for significant spillover effects between them. Consequently, it emphasizes the importance of enhanced cooperation between monetary and macroprudential policies.

The crises experience in the past two decades has taught us an important lesson regarding the limitations of financial regulators in accurately predicting the severity and scope of financial instability and crises. As Mishkin (2009) emphasizes, to focus solely on individual institutions can cause regulators to overlook significant changes in the overall financial system. For instance, the rapid growth of securitized assets and the emergence of lightly regulated financial institutions in the years that led to the GFC were not adequately addressed by existing regulatory structures (Mishkin, 2009, p. 1).[7]

While academic economists and central bankers recognize the importance of macroprudential policy in maintaining financial stability, they acknowledge that its effectiveness and design are still evolving and have not been proven to prevent systemic crises. Additionally, certain unconventional monetary policy instruments employed during the recent crisis, such as collateral rules, reserve requirements, and asset purchases, blur the distinction between monetary policy and macroprudential policy tools. These instruments not only aim to address financial market dysfunction but also impact the transmission channels of macroprudential policy (Kokores, 2015).

Hence, recent evidence has revealed that the traditional approach to conducting monetary policy is closely intertwined with significant drivers of financial imbalances such as liquidity, credit, and risk-taking. The global financial crisis exposed the limitations of modern macroeconomic analysis in adequately capturing and modeling the role of financial intermediaries as crucial elements in the functioning of the monetary transmission mechanism. The *effectiveness* and *efficiency* of monetary policy and its impact on the real economy are increasingly being explored through alternative models that emphasize the influence of financial frictions arising from various aspects of the behavior of *participants* in the financial system, including borrowers, lenders, regulators, and lender-of-last-resort policymakers. However,

[7]According to Greenspan (2009), regulation often proves to be expensive and ineffective, and it tends to fall short in enhancing financial institutions' capability to allocate a country's savings toward the most beneficial and productive capital investments (Greenspan, 2009, p. 2).

achieving a consensus model that effectively addresses these complexities remains a challenge for future research.

As numerous deficiencies in the prevailing consensus regarding macroeconomic theory and policy emerged since the advent of the financial crisis that initiated in 2007, several questions have emerged. The primary lesson learned is that conventional stabilization policies can prove highly ineffective. One of the fundamental responsibilities of monetary policy is to shield the real economy from shocks originating in the financial sector, but it failed to do so. Global economic growth has likely reached its lowest level in over 50 years, and several advanced economies have experienced the most significant contractions since the 1930s. In light of these developments, for example, Cecchetti et al. (2009a, 2009b) raise doubts about various aspects of the existing consensus in the following areas:

1. *Does financial instability have important real effects?* The lessons derived from the financial crisis regarding long-term stabilization policies are clear: financial instability can significantly impact both macroeconomic stability and potentially long-term growth. To achieve economic stability, it is essential to give careful consideration to ensuring financial stability (see Shirakawa, 2009, for a discussion by policymakers).
2. *Does fiscal policy have a role?* Since September 2008, there has been a widespread implementation of extensive fiscal stimulus measures on a global scale. This resurgence has reignited a debate that many believed had been resolved: under what circumstances, if any, is fiscal policy beneficial?[8]
3. *Are interest rates enough?* The urgent necessity for additional tools to stabilize the economy, both from within and beyond the central bank, has become abundantly clear. Conventional monetary policy has quickly reached its limits, such as the zero lower bound for interest rates, and the functioning of credit markets by intermediaries has been compromised, thereby hindering the traditional channels through which monetary policy is transmitted. This raises the question of what alternative tools can be employed by central banks and whether new ones need to be developed. Additionally, if we aim to mitigate the impact of economic booms and busts, it may be necessary to adopt a complementary set of regulatory macroprudential instruments. Overall, the existing framework for understanding monetary policy requires reevaluation and revision.

   The second significant lesson learned is that both the overall amounts and the net positions of financial assets and liabilities have a significant impact on real economic activity. This realization represents a departure from conventional

[8]Even among proponents of utilizing fiscal policy for economic stabilization, there is a lack of scholarly consensus on the most effective form that fiscal stimulus should take. This is exemplified by the uncertainty surrounding the magnitude of fiscal multipliers associated with various fiscal measures.

wisdom, as modern mainstream macroeconomic models have not incorporated such considerations.[9]

4. *What place should gross financial quantities have in macroeconomic models?* In the realm of financial instruments, the quantity of outstanding instruments and the capital and collateral supporting them play a crucial role. In financial markets, the volume of trading and the specific platform where trading takes place are important factors. Financial institutions' size and the size of their counterparties have implications. Similarly, for central banks, the size and composition of assets and liabilities on their balance sheet carry significance.

The final lesson is about history: we need to study the past with a much more critical eye. Economics is fundamentally about history (Hicks, 1969, p. 2). The relationship between modeling and data is crucial, but there is a fundamental aspect that has been overlooked: the frequency of financial crises. As evidenced by studies such as Bordo and Landon-Lane (2010), Reinhart and Rogoff (2008), banking crises have occurred at an average rate of three or four per year over the past 25 years. Instead of considering financial crises as rare and isolated incidents, we require models that account for the regular occurrence of such events.

This leads us to the central task macroeconomists face, namely, the *need to build macroeconomic models that create severe financial stress endogenously*. To achieve this, there must be a shift in research focus on two key fronts: Firstly, as mentioned earlier, there must be a substantive connection between financial factors and the real economy. This entails explicitly incorporating the role of financial intermediaries and institutions, including *interbank markets* with their *network effects* that we have learned from the initial crisis years. Secondly, it is necessary to introduce endogenous mechanisms for propagating shocks that mirror the self-reinforcing feedback loops that underlie boom-bust cycles. This requires a deeper understanding of the incentives that drive the behavior of agents in financial markets, as well as the dynamics of asset prices, credit expansion, leverage, various risk premiums, and the interconnections that bind them together. Constructing models that enable us to comprehend the origins of systemic collapse requires a reevaluation of several foundational assumptions inherent in modern macroeconomic models[10] (Cecchetti et al., 2009a, 2009b p. 5).

If financial crises are perceived as mere random occurrences, resulting from external shocks independent of the financial system framework or policy measures implemented, then there would be limited scope for intervention. However, if, as

[9] "While it is new for modern macroeconomic models, it may be more accurate to characterise it as having been forgotten. Financial quantities did play a prominent role in the older monetarist literature such as Brunner and Meltzer (1963), as well as in Tobin (1969)" (quoted from Cecchetti et al., 2009a, 2009b).

[10] To enhance clarity of exposition, Cecchetti et al. (2009a, 2009b) discuss these in two related steps: First, they examine mechanisms that admit the linkage between the financial sector and the real economy. And second, they suggest the sorts of refinements that might lead to endogenous financial booms and busts (Cecchetti et al., 2009a, 2009b, p. 5).

strongly indicated by Cecchetti et al. (2009a, 2009b), financial crises are inherent to the economy and occur naturally, then it becomes imperative to develop a new generation of macroeconomic models that consider the interconnections between the financial system, the real economy, and the potential actions of policymakers. According to Cecchetti et al. (2009a, 2009b), there is already some foundation to build upon in incorporating financial instability into macroeconomic models. The influential research on the financial accelerator by Bernanke et al. (1999) and the study of endogenous credit cycles by Kiyotaki and Moore (1997) provide a strong starting point. However, further developments are necessary. In Cecchetti et al. (2009a, 2009b) work, they discuss the specific components of conventional macroeconomic models that require scrutiny and examination for a meaningful integration of financial instability.

The financial crisis has taught macroeconomists a crucial lesson: the need to assign a more significant role to finance in their models. The frequency and costliness of financial stress episodes indicate that they cannot be dismissed as mere instances of "bad luck" with minimal implications for proactive stabilization policy, as Lucas (2009) suggests. Instead, it becomes essential to explore whether policy can and should intervene to reduce the likelihood and mitigate the harmful effects of inevitable financial stress. Although the New Keynesian models, which emphasize the role of stabilization policies, provide a starting point, they fall short in addressing the broader issue of economic stability by neglecting the importance of financial instability. To truly understand how to achieve economic stability, it is crucial to also comprehend how to prevent financial instability. In order to model and understand financial booms and busts, it is necessary to develop a framework that recognizes the impact of financial imbalances on the real economy. As Cecchetti et al. (2009a, 2009b) suggest, this entails critically examining fundamental assumptions in current macroeconomic models, such as the functioning of capital markets, the rationality of individuals, the validity of the representative agent assumption, and the efficiency of market clearing mechanisms.

Although the task may appear daunting, there are encouraging signs of progress in addressing these challenges. There is a growing recognition of the magnitude of the task at hand, as highlighted by Bean (2009). Moreover, efforts are already underway to advance the field: researchers are actively working on solving models that incorporate heterogeneous agents, exploring the implications of bounded rationality and learning, simulating agent-based models, and introducing incomplete financial markets and significant financial frictions into their analyses. These developments demonstrate a commitment to enhancing our understanding of the complex dynamics between the financial system and the real economy. The successful integration of financial imbalances into models of economic fluctuations holds the promise of providing policymakers with a valuable toolkit. This integration will not only assist in the development of new tools for stabilization purposes but also enhance the effectiveness of existing ones. Additionally, it will enable us to effectively monitor and measure financial stress in real time, ensuring *transparency* and *accountability* in policymaking, similar to the crucial role of price measurement in holding inflation targeting central banks accountable. While the journey ahead may not be without challenges, it is worth noting that *conventional monetary policymaking faced similar daunting prospects half a century ago.* Hopefully, this time, the process of finding solutions and making progress will be expedited.

7.4 Further Discussion on the Serious Limitations of the Existing Macro-Models

The onset of the GFC exposed the significant shortcomings of prevailing economic and financial models. In numerous market sectors, the breakdown of arbitrage occurred as panic gripped market participants and caused market freeze. The crisis unfolded in a manner that existing macroeconomic models failed to predict, leaving them unable to provide a compelling explanation for the unfolding economic events (Caballero, 2010).

Within the prevailing models that currently shape central bank perspectives, inflation is effectively controlled by a central bank "reaction function," which ensures that interest rates or quantitative easing measures are adjusted to steer inflation back to its target level. However, in a world characterized by radical uncertainty, where the true dynamics of the economy remain unknown, there is no guarantee that central banks will consistently act in a manner that aligns with achieving the inflation target. In this context, expectations become fragile and insufficient to firmly anchor inflation. The traditional notion that inflation results from "too much money chasing too few goods" holds more relevance than the idea that it is solely driven by expectations. However, it is concerning that the concept of money has been largely disregarded in modern models of inflation. While it is not necessary to believe in a direct and stable relationship between a specific measure of money and inflation, it is regrettable that this aspect has been neglected. Expectations certainly play a role, but they provide an incomplete understanding of how changes in interest rates and the money supply influence prices. Moreover, when public trust in the central bank diminishes, people tend to scrutinize monetary indicators, particularly broad money supply, to assess the inflation outlook (King, 2022, p. 3). Therefore, *a critical question arises of whether monetary policy has lost its conceptual foundation.*

The insightful seminal analyses of a monetary economy developed by Keynes, Patinkin, Tobin, Brunner, and Meltzer, among others, have been replaced by models that essentially assume complete markets.[11] It is remarkable that these models, devoid of any consideration of money, can still be used to explain a decline in the value of money. Another implication of these models is the assumption of a static economic structure over long periods of time, commonly referred to as stationarity. This assumption is crucial for using econometric models to identify stable

[11] King (2022, p. 4) accepts that the quirk of the increasing mathematization of economic models was foreshadowed by Samuelson (1968).

relationships over time. However, conventional models failed to predict or provide an explanation for the global financial crisis precisely because the world is characterized by non-stationarity (Hendry & Mizon, 2014). The forecasting models employed by central banks perform reasonably well when there are no significant disruptions, but they prove highly inadequate when faced with major events (King, 2022, p. 4), precisely when we would expect them to offer more than mere extrapolation of past trends. Radical uncertainty and non-stationarity are closely intertwined.

7.4.1 *Illusions in Recent Years of the Theory and Practice of Monetary Policy*

The focus in this subsection is shed on the *three illusions that have influenced both the theory and the practice of monetary policy in recent years*. These illusions pertain to the belief in models as accurate descriptions of the world and reliable predictors of future outcomes, the misinterpretation of economic developments resulting from overreliance on a narrow model, and the reliance on forward guidance. *First*, it is important to recognize that models are not inherently right or wrong; their usefulness varies. They do not provide a comprehensive representation of the real world, which explains why economic forecasts often fall short. While models can offer valuable insights, they cannot replace the necessity of understanding the larger context and dynamics of the world. Kay and King (2020) advocate for consistently questioning "what is going on here?", a seemingly simple question, which proves immensely beneficial in interpreting economic data.

A compelling illustration of the significance of asking the above question can be seen in the case of the Bank of England's early recognition (King, 2022), of the significant influx of migrant workers into the United Kingdom from Eastern European accession countries after 2004, despite official statistics indicating otherwise. This realization challenged the relevance of the output gap, which measures the disparity between aggregate demand and potential supply, in guiding monetary policy. The reason is that demand was generating its own supply of labor, rendering the Phillips curve flatter, and diminishing the significance of the output gap. However, the narrative has shifted once again following Brexit, with the elastic supply of labor largely dissipating and the output gap becoming relevant once more in assessing the appropriate stance for monetary policy.

The Phillips curve is a vital concept in understanding how central bankers approach inflation. It represents a statistical relationship that captures the intuitive notion that higher levels of unemployment and economic slack correspond to lower inflation rates, assuming other factors remain constant. When the Phillips curve is steep, as it was in many countries during the high inflation period of the 1970s, even small fluctuations in slack can result in significant changes in inflation. Conversely, a flatter Phillips curve implies that inflation remains relatively stable even as unemployment levels vary widely. It is widely recognized among economists that, at least in advanced economies, Phillips curves became flatter from the 1970s to the 1990s and continued to exhibit this characteristic (Blanchard et al., 2015), until the emergence of the COVID-19 pandemic (Obstfeld, 2022).

This development brought both positive and negative implications for monetary policy. On the positive side, when inflation expectations remain stable, significant temporary fluctuations in economic slack do not necessarily pose a threat to price stability. However, on the negative side, if inflation expectations deviate from the targets set by central banks, it would require substantial changes in economic activity and employment to bring inflation back to the desired level. As highlighted in Schnabel (2022), *a flat Phillips curve in today's context implies that reducing inflation, once it has become firmly established, could potentially necessitate a significant economic contraction.* The confidence in a stable and flat Phillips curve, coupled with the belief in the central banks' own credibility to effectively manage inflation, can elucidate why monetary policymakers did not foresee the current surge in inflation. Central bankers have been caught unawares by rising prices that have exposed their *"King Canute" theory of inflation*, as labeled by former Governor of the Bank of England Mervyn King (see Elliot, 2021, November 23). This explanation holds true *even when excluding unpredictable events such as the war in Ukraine.*[12] Furthermore, it can clarify why policymakers might be overestimating the extent of monetary tightening required to curb the rise in prices.

In reality, it is possible that the Phillips curve has steepened as economies reopened following the COVID-19 pandemic (Obstfeld, 2022). The combination of high demand- and supply-side pressures led to an increase in prices, while some central banks delayed taking decisive action and maintained that price pressures would be temporary. However, if inflation permeates expectations unchallenged, it can become self-fulfilling and alter the shape and position of the Phillips curve. Price inflation is influenced by the decisions of numerous businesses that set prices based on anticipated production costs in the coming quarters. If businesses anticipate sustained cost pressures without significant resistance from central banks, then instances of excess demand over supply, like those observed by mid-2021, can prompt them to raise prices more rapidly, resulting in a steepening of the Phillips

[12] For a May 2021 argument that a flat Phillips curve could keep US inflation low during a relatively transitory period of low slack, see Spilimbergo et al. (2021).

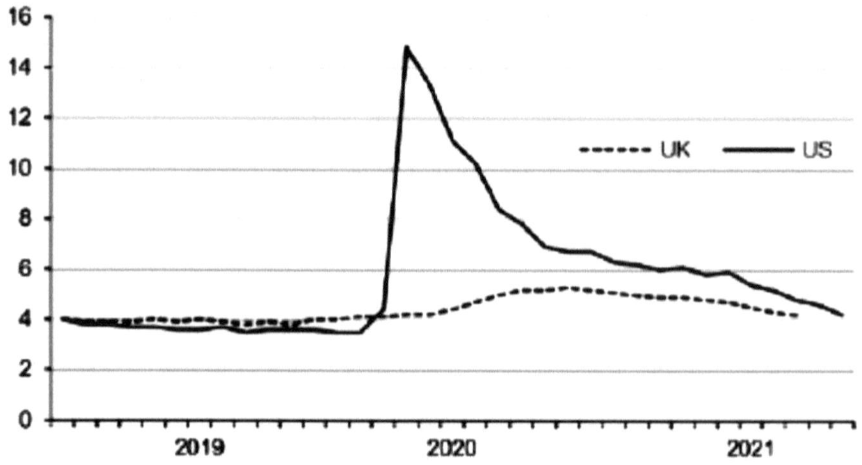

Fig. 7.1 Unemployment rate (%) in the United States and the United Kingdom, 2019–2021. *Source*: King (2022), p. 6; United States, Federal Reserve Economic Data; United Kingdom, Office for National Statistics

curve.[13] It is uncertain whether the Phillips curve will quickly flatten out again as central banks demonstrate greater determination to combat inflation.[14]

Second, there was a misinterpretation of economic developments, particularly in response to the COVID-19 pandemic. Initially, the need for significant monetary expansion in March 2020 was justified as a response to dysfunctional markets. However, even after financial markets returned to normal functioning, the monetary injection was not withdrawn. Instead, the justification for the stimulus shifted to "supporting the economy" (King, 2022, pp. 5–6). Indeed, the government played a crucial role in supporting the economy during the pandemic. In Europe, furlough schemes were implemented, while the United States provided more generous unemployment compensation. The effectiveness of these measures can be observed in Fig. 7.1, which shows that unemployment rates in both countries initially rose significantly in 2020 but have since returned to pre-COVID levels. It is worth noting

[13]Gopinath (2022) reports a steeper post-COVID inflation-versus-slack relationship across industrial economies. Blanchard (2021) similarly anticipated for the United States. With hindsight, these developments could have been anticipated. The correlation observed in the Phillips curve is not a true structural relationship, and its shape is influenced by various factors, including the monetary policy regime (McLeay & Tenreyro, 2020). Their argument builds upon the well-known Lucas critique from the 1970s. Even before the COVID-19 pandemic, Gagnon and Collins (2019) suggested that the US Phillips curve exhibits a kink, becoming steeper when unemployment rates are extremely low. Consequently, this implies that inflation rises at a faster pace as unemployment decreases further, particularly when it is already at a low level.

[14]Schnabel (2022) argued that even if the Phillips curve is steeper for now, vanquishing inflation will still likely require harsh recessions because "the fact that it is often *global* rather than domestic slack that matters for price-setting reduces the sensitivity of the economy to interest rate changes on a much broader level."

that the furlough scheme in the United Kingdom resulted in minimal increases in unemployment throughout the entire pandemic period. The purpose of the furlough scheme was to enable businesses to maintain employment levels despite sharp declines in revenue, rather than to stimulate aggregate demand. Essentially, it involved transferring funds from future taxpayers to businesses to support them during the challenging period.

Monetary stimulus is deemed suitable when the overall demand in the economy falls below the level of aggregate supply. During a typical business cycle, demand decreases during a recession while potential supply remains relatively stable; this creates an output gap, and monetary policy can be employed to mitigate this situation. This approach seems reasonable thus far. However, the COVID-19 pandemic triggered a downturn that deviated from the characteristics of a typical business cycle, thus calling for unconventional monetary policy measures like quantitative easing (QE). QE involves expanding the money supply, although central banks often avoid explicitly characterizing it as such. This has resulted in challenges when it comes to calibrating changes to QE, making them appear arbitrary. Unlike its previous use following the banking crisis, where the aim was to prevent a decline in broad money, QE as a response to the economic effects of the pandemic has led to a significant surplus of money in circulation. In the United States, M3, a measure of broad money, experienced an annual growth rate of 24% in late 2020, which has since decreased to around 13% in the latest data. Similarly, in the United Kingdom, M3 had a yearly growth rate of 13% in the spring but has now subsided to approximately 7%. While it is possible to debate the exact transmission mechanism between an increase in broad money and its impact on inflation, the undeniable fact remains that we have witnessed a substantial, albeit temporary, increase in the growth rate of broad money (King, 2022). Consequently, we are now observing a noticeable, albeit potentially temporary, rise in inflation.

According to the Economic Affairs Committee—House of Lords (2021)—with reference to the United Kingdom, QE has become the go-to measure for central banks in response to various negative developments. However, the problem arises when central banks fail to retract QE even in the presence of positive news or the absence of negative news, resulting in a continuous expansion of central bank balance sheets. This situation is not sustainable. Furthermore, it is evident that reducing the *size* of these balance sheets becomes challenging, especially when accompanied by significant budget deficits.

Third, the use of forward guidance as a monetary policy tool presents its own challenges. Given the inherent uncertainty of the future, it is unwise for a central bank to speculate on its own future decisions. The US Federal Reserve, for instance, cannot accurately predict the short-term policy rate it will set in the coming months, let alone in the years ahead. The risk currently is that while financial markets may have lost confidence in the forward guidance executed by central banks, the central banks themselves continue to believe in it and maintain a narrative about the future trajectory of interest rates that lacks credibility, which poses problems for effectively communicating policy decisions (King, 2022). Market participants assess the future path of interest rates based on their own perception of how the economy will evolve, which may differ from the central bank's view. Challenging these narratives is essential for a healthy market environment. Forward guidance, which blends the central bank's reaction function with its narrative, is risky as it diminishes the impact of economic debates and shifts market attention to the quasi-commitments made by central banks regarding future interest rate paths. This approach offers little benefit while potentially eroding the central bank's credibility.

Equally ill-advised are the close substitutes for forward guidance, such as the *yield curve control* implemented in Japan and Australia, the *flexible average inflation targeting* announced by the US Federal Reserve in 2020, and the notion of intentionally aiming for higher inflation to reduce the perceived real interest rate. The Federal Reserve's introduction of flexible average inflation targeting appears to have come at the worst possible time, since no one argued that inflation exceeding 6% was desirable in order to offset previous target shortfalls. It was always a fallacy to believe that inflation could be precisely controlled to the extent of intentionally surpassing the target by a small margin for a brief period to compensate for prior shortfalls (King, 2022).

Forward guidance can quickly be perceived as a sign of complacency. It is perfectly acceptable for a central bank to admit that it cannot predict the future path of interest rates because it cannot accurately forecast the trajectory of the economy in the coming months and years. Regardless of the various economic models employed prior to January 1, 2020, none of them accounted for the potential scenario of widespread economic shutdowns in response to the COVID-19 pandemic. A central bank possesses clear knowledge merely of its own reaction function, which involves the objective of returning inflation to its target within a timeframe that aligns with the nature of the economic shocks (King, 2022). The central bank's primary responsibility is to concentrate on the current determination of policy instruments such as interest rates and QE, rather than attempting to predict their state 3 years into the future (Goodfriend & King, 2015). Effective communication from the central bank should revolve around explaining its reaction function and constructing a narrative about the evolving economic conditions, which can change gradually with each meeting and report. The essential forward guidance required by markets and economic participants is a steadfast commitment to maintaining price stability. According to Alan Blinder, a Princeton Economist and former Vice Chairman of the US Federal Reserve, *price stability* is achieved *when ordinary people stop talking and worrying about inflation* (quoted in Griffiths, 2020, *The Article*, August 5). However, after the Great Moderation, inflation has once again become a topic of concern. In this context, the primary responsibility of a central bank is to advocate for price stability. To safeguard their valuable and hard-earned independence, central banks should embrace and emphasize the fact that their mandate is focused and limited in scope.

Inflation will remain a major challenge in the years ahead as we embark on *a significant reallocation of resources in our economies*—resulting from the greater focus on resilience as we emerge from the pandemic, the political pressures to raise public spending, and the restructuring required to meet climate change targets. *This reallocation of resources will imply big changes in relative prices and wages.*

Whether this can easily be achieved while keeping overall inflation close to 2% remains to be seen. *The consequences of a shift in resources within the economy from low to more profitable sectors are not something that appear in the current models of monetary policy* (King, 2022, p. 10). Placing unwavering faith in these models as an accurate depiction of the world has harmed the credibility of central banks, as evidenced by communication challenges faced by several central banks in recent years. Unless a fundamental change in mindset occurs, this issue will persist and continue to undermine their credibility.

After enduring a prolonged period of slow economic growth, despite implementing unprecedented levels of monetary stimulus, it is crucial to acknowledge that numerous economic challenges cannot be effectively resolved through monetary policy alone. As we enter the next decade, economies worldwide will undergo significant restructuring. It will become increasingly necessary to question and understand the underlying dynamics of these transformations by asking. Central banks will have to cope with the challenge of setting monetary policy, not in a small model but in the large world of *radical uncertainty. The current scale of monetary expansion cannot persist for long without inflationary consequences* (Cecchetti & Schoenholtz, 2021). Now is the time for central banks to take a gentle step back from being in thrall to the latest theoretical advance and avoid becoming the slaves of living economists (King, 2022). When US President Clinton nominated Alan Greenspan for his fourth term in office as chairman of the US Federal Reserve in 2000, he hailed a "rare combination of technical expertise, sophisticated analysis and old-fashioned common sense" (Politi & Smith, 2021). *Common sense suggests that when too much money is chasing too few goods the result is inflation.* An overreliance on expectations and central bank communication has proved a dragging anchor for monetary policy in the industrialized world. It is time to change policy and to secure a more reliable intellectual anchor (King, 2022, p. 10).

7.5 Eliminating Policy Surprises

The concept of a policy surprise holds significance because policies primarily impact real economic activity through unexpected measures. To illustrate this point, we consider a simplified example that disregards some complexities of the actual world. It is important to note that adding complexity or aligning it more closely with reality would not alter the underlying conclusions. In a scenario where prevailing wages and their growth rate are determined in contractual negotiations between companies and workers, these negotiations assume that the inflation rate will remain steady due to the monetary authority's commitment to maintaining stable money growth. Disregarding uncertainties stemming from factors other than the government, labor contracts would allow wages to increase at a rate equivalent to the growth rate of productivity plus the anticipated inflation rate.

In a scenario where the monetary authority perceives the inflation rate as too high and unexpectedly opts to reduce the growth rate of money, this reduction leads to a

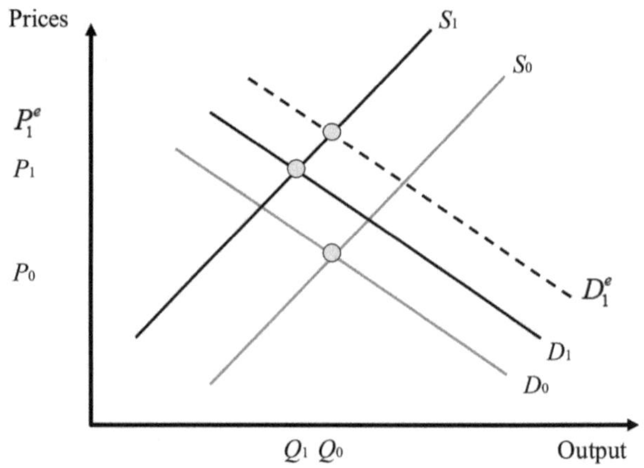

Fig. 7.2 Adjustment to a policy surprise. Source: FRB of Minneapolis (1978), pp. 1–2

decrease in the overall growth rate of aggregate demand. As a consequence, businesses find it necessary to adjust their pricing strategies and increase prices at a slower pace than initially anticipated. Consequently, these businesses realize that it is in their best interest to lay off some workers. Although each worker continues to produce the expected amount of goods, the market value of these goods is lower than expected, resulting in less revenue compared to the projections made when wage rates were established. Essentially, workers at the margins become unable to sustain their employment due to these unexpected policy changes. As a result of this surprising shift in policy, the economy achieves a lower inflation rate. However, it also experiences reduced levels of production, employment, personal income, and profits.

7.5.1 Policy Surprises Affect Output and Prices

Adjustment to a policy surprise is illustrated in Fig. 7.2. The D_0 curve, which represents the aggregate demand, shows the amount of output that consumers, investors, and the government desire at different price levels prior to the unexpected policy change. Similarly, the S_0 curve, representing the aggregate supply, illustrates the quantity of output supplied by all producers at different price levels before the surprise policy shift. The price level at this point is denoted as P_0 and the corresponding output is Q_0. Prior to the unexpected policy change, private decision-makers anticipated an increase in aggregate demand, represented byD_1^e. Wage contracts were made that included wage hikes designed to preserve the purchasing power of individuals, thereby pushing the aggregate supply curve (or the economy's cost curve) to S_1. In the absence of the surprise policy change, prices would have risen toP_1^e, while the output would have remained at Q_0.

However, with the implementation of the surprise policy change and the subsequent slower increase in the money supply, the rise in aggregate demand is not as significant as initially anticipated, resulting in a lower level of prices. Consequently, the increase in prices is slower than expected, reaching P_1 instead of P_1^e. This slower pace of price growth, however, leads to a decrease in the value of workers' output. In fact, the value of output for all workers is lower than what was expected during the settlement of wage contracts. For many workers operating on the margins, this reduced value falls below their wage costs. As a consequence, some workers are laid off, resulting in a decline in output to Q_1.

After the policy change is acknowledged, an adjustment process is set in motion. With a portion of the workforce unemployed and the inflation rate lower than previously projected, new labor agreements are reached that stipulate slower wage growth. Consequently, marginal workers who were previously laid off can reenter the workforce, as their wages no longer exceed the value of their output. This leads to a restoration of aggregate output to its initial level. In essence, once the policy change is acknowledged, the system adapts, returning to its original level of economic activity and real income. However, the subsequent price and wage increases become less significant. If both firms and laborers were able to anticipate the monetary authority's decision to decrease the rate of money growth, it would be possible to slow down inflation without experiencing higher unemployment or reduced output. The temporary increase in unemployment and output shortfall could be avoided if the monetary authority provided advance notice of the impending reduction in money growth and if this announcement was believed by the public.

In such a scenario, firms and workers could engage in negotiations to establish appropriate wage contracts. They could include clauses that allow for adjustments to money wages in order to maintain constant real wages. Alternatively, they could negotiate the growth rate of their money wages, taking into consideration the new and lower money supply growth and the revised inflation rate. Acting in their own best interests, firms and workers would recognize the importance of these adjustments to avoid making labor costs excessive and potentially leading to layoffs.

Virtually, all economists would agree that tighter macroeconomic policies can lower inflation. However, due to previous occurrences, there is a prevalent belief that even a small reduction in the government budget deficit or money growth would result in significant unemployment or prolonged periods of sluggish economic growth and high unemployment. These beliefs stem from a misunderstanding. Since labor markets often do not immediately adapt to unexpected policy actions, some individuals assume that any policy measure aimed at reducing money growth and the federal budget deficit will inevitably lead to high unemployment, regardless of how it is implemented. They appear to assume that labor markets adjust at a sluggish pace, or perhaps not at all, in response to policy changes.

If restrictive policies were implemented and managed to remain as surprises, it would take an extended period of high unemployment to bring the inflation rate down to zero. However, this scenario is highly unlikely. Sustaining a new permanent policy as a surprise year after year would require people to be deceived for prolonged periods of time, and their expectations of future inflation would need to be solely based on past policies and economic conditions.[15] In reality, when policy changes, individuals' expectations also change. Their expectations are shaped by all available information, including details about new policies or anti-inflation programs. If people indeed act in their own best interests, as economists have argued for the past two centuries, they will not disregard changes in money growth or inflation rates when negotiating wage contracts. Ignoring a new economic policy could result in financial losses for a firm, as the policy affects the wages it must pay its employees and the prices it can charge for its products. Workers, on the other hand, could risk unemployment if they assume that inflation will be higher than it actually turns out to be and demand high wage settlements. Conversely, if workers anticipate lower inflation than what occurs and agree to low-wage settlements, they might experience a decline in their incomes when adjusted for inflation.

7.6 The (Changing) Role of Central Banks in Financial Stability Policies

Pertinent research and policy analysis calls for vast changes in central banks' institutional setup and their monetary policy strategies aiming to prioritize both price stability and financial stability equally. As Praet (2014, pp. 6–9) suggests, by contrast, major changes in the institutional and strategic framework of monetary policy are not necessary, but "business as usual" in central banking will not do it, either. Continuing with the usual approach would involve following the principles of the "Jackson Hole consensus." This precrisis agreement suggests that central banks should only address asset prices and financial imbalances if they have an impact on short-term inflation forecasts (Bernanke & Gertler, 1999). In the event that financial imbalances do arise, central banks should adopt a "cleanup" strategy after the bubble has burst. The primary focus should be on maintaining price stability, as it is considered the most effective contribution central banks can make to financial stability.

This perspective entails a clear distinction between monetary policy and financial stability policy. Central banks recognized the significance of financial stability in facilitating the execution of monetary policy and understood their diverse responsibilities in ensuring financial stability. However, they underestimated the potential implications of financial imbalances and failed to systematically incorporate them into the analytical framework that supported monetary policy decisions. This flaw in

[15] Early accounts include, for example, Anderson (1978) that report results to an experiment using a prominent econometric model of the time to examine the consequences of a permanent doubling of the money growth rate. He instructed the model to compare the price expectations embedded within it over a 3-year period with the actual price movements observed during the same timeframe. The findings of the model revealed a significant disparity in expectations. According to the model's results, people's estimations of inflation would deviate increasingly from the actual price performance over the 3-year period and would only begin to converge with reality in the fourth year.

the underlying theoretical foundation led central banks to downplay their role in maintaining financial stability and reinforced the notion that monetary policy and microprudential policy could be pursued separately. In this approach, monetary policy instruments were designed to achieve macroeconomic stability, while financial regulation and supervision were aimed at preserving financial stability, following the principles of Tinbergen (1952) policy assignment rule (see Mishkin, 2011).

Nevertheless, it is evident at this point that the notion of a rigid separation between monetary policy and financial stability policy is fundamentally flawed, as these two aspects are inherently interconnected due to the significant interplay between financial and economic conditions. The GFC and the event that followed served as a compelling illustration of the inadequacy of the previous approach, which primarily focused on microprudential measures in financial regulation and supervision. It failed to effectively address the propensity of the increasingly intricate and nontransparent financial system to generate excessive levels of systemic risk. The unwinding of these related financial imbalances resulted in the largest financial and economic crisis since World War II, which in turn had a profound impact on the implementation of monetary policy. With the disruption of the usual monetary policy transmission channels, central banks were compelled to adopt "unconventional" measures.

The crisis also provided us with valuable lessons, showing that disregarding the costs of addressing financial imbalances ex ante through a "leaning" approach can be highly detrimental. Furthermore, we realized the significance of the moral hazard inherent in the previous consensus view of monetary policy, where the asymmetry was underestimated. In light of the evident failure of the Jackson Hole consensus, there is a growing support for the idea that central banks should proactively "lean" against the emergence of financial imbalances in certain situations. This approach aims to mitigate systemic risk and address the potential long-term risks to price stability and economic well-being (Borio, 2011).

Gaining a deeper comprehension of the interconnections between financial and real sectors is crucial. Although progress has been made in examining alternative channels of transmission, such as the risk-taking channel, there are still unresolved matters that require further research, as, for example, understanding the impact of interest rates on risk tolerance and exploring the relationship between funding and market liquidity (Praet, 2014). Understanding the factors that drive the leverage cycle and the influence of financial innovation on it is also essential. Considering the intricacy of these matters, it is necessary to acknowledge that establishing a practical framework that connects monetary policy with different types of systemic risk is highly complex and presents significant intellectual hurdles (Kokores & Kanas, 2021). Financial stability risks may also arise from excessive monetary policy activism geared toward buying insurance against adverse macroeconomic and/or financial stability conditions (Praet, 2014, p. 8). For instance, central banks might threaten future economic and financial stability if they keep policy rates too low for too long in the aftermath of a crisis (Maddaloni & Peydró, 2011).

In the context of the GFC and Eurozone crises, the risk of missing the right time to exit from unconventional monetary policy measures offers a case in point. In the light of these insights, it should be clear that monetary policy cannot do it alone. Financial stability should mainly be pursued by microprudential and macroprudential policies.[16] Excessive monetary policy activism aimed at mitigating macroeconomic or financial stability risks can itself pose a threat to financial stability. For example, if central banks maintain low policy rates for an extended period after a crisis, it may jeopardize future economic and financial stability. The recent crises highlight the risk of misjudging the appropriate timing to withdraw unconventional monetary policy measures. These observations underscore the fact that monetary policy alone is insufficient. The primary responsibility for promoting financial stability lies with microprudential and macroprudential policies. Therefore, in order to attain both price stability and financial stability, it is crucial to implement suitable policies in collaboration with all relevant authorities. One approach could involve assigning a specific agent the responsibility of evaluating the financial stability implications of regulatory and tax changes, whenever applicable. Nevertheless, achieving policy coordination is typically challenging (for an extensive discussion and analysis, see Kokores, 1989).

Coordination efforts may be hindered by issues of time inconsistency, where the objectives of the involved authorities may diverge. For example, governments may yield to the temptation of responding to electoral pressures or lobbying efforts from the financial sector. Granting excessive discretion in instrument setting to a macroprudential authority can lead to potential policy failures. Hence, it may be advantageous to adopt a more rule-based approach in the implementation of macroprudential policy. Policy coordination poses additional difficulties within a currency union, especially when credit cycles, such as real estate cycles, are not synchronized across member countries. Furthermore, the process of monetary integration within the European Monetary Union has progressed at a much faster rate compared to the integration of financial stability and fiscal policies.

In conclusion, *the challenges faced in ensuring financial stability are substantial, encompassing both technical and governance aspects*. The primary objective is to strengthen mechanisms that promote discipline in both private and public debt markets. Action is required in various domains, and central banks are well-positioned to assume the roles of coordinator, facilitator, and initiator. It is essential for central banks to undertake these responsibilities to prevent an excessive burden on monetary policy. The deLarosière Group (2009, p. 6) expressed the belief that global monetary authorities, regulatory bodies, and financial supervisory authorities have the potential to significantly improve their efforts in reducing the likelihood of similar events occurring in the future. It is acknowledged that it may not be possible to prevent all future crises, as they are difficult to predict and resolve. However, the

[16]Indeed, recent research conducted within the Macroprudential Research (MaRS) network of the European System of Central Banks provides backing for such a division of responsibilities. In the majority of cases, it has been found that macroprudential policy measures, such as implementing countercyclical loan-to-value ratios, are more effective in addressing financial imbalances compared to using monetary policy to "lean against the wind" (Praet, 2014; Beau et al., 2012; Lambertini et al., 2011).

focus should be on preventing the specific systemic and interconnected vulnerabilities that have had such widespread and contagious effects. To prevent the recurrence of such crises, several critical policy changes are necessary, both within the European Union, national economies, and the global financial system as a whole.

7.7 Concluding Remarks: Eliminating Policy Surprises to Beat Uncertainty and Inflation

The effective implementation of monetary policy relies heavily on inflation expectations. When a central bank can anchor long-term inflation expectations close to its inflation target, it increases the likelihood of achieving low and stable inflation. Inflation expectations play a crucial role in transmitting monetary policy as they influence current inflation by shaping wage and price decisions (Bernanke et al., 2001). Understanding how inflation expectations are influenced by both domestic and global shocks is vital for central banks. Extensive theoretical and empirical research exists on inflation expectations. Theoretical studies have explored how economic agents utilize public and private information to form their inflation expectations. Empirical investigations have examined the accuracy of these theoretical models and assessed the degree to which inflation expectations remain anchored by measuring their responsiveness to different shocks, such as macroeconomic news or price fluctuations like oil prices (Bernanke et al., 2001).[17]

Furthermore, in view of recent events although there is considerable uncertainty in measuring output gaps (especially during the pandemic), there is still a notable connection between economic slack and inflation. Long-term inflation expectations have remained relatively stable thus far, indicating that recent extraordinary policy measures have not significantly disrupted those expectations (see IMF, 2021, p. 45). Since the start of 2021, advanced and emerging market economies have witnessed an increase in headline consumer price index inflation. This surge can be attributed to strengthening demand, shortages of inputs, and the rapid escalation of commodity prices.

Given the unprecedented nature of the economic recovery, there remains a substantial amount of uncertainty, especially when it comes to assessing the extent of economic slack. Prolonged disruptions in the supply chain, unexpected shocks to commodity and housing prices, long-term commitments in expenditures, and a potential shift in inflation expectations could result in higher inflation levels than what is projected in the baseline scenario. However, by adopting transparent communication practices and implementing appropriate monetary and fiscal policies

[17] The literature, however, has mainly focused on advanced economies. For background on market- and survey-based measures of inflation expectations, see Coibon et al. (2018, 2018) and Grothe and Meyler (2018) for the United States and the euro area and Sousa and Yerman (2016) for emerging market and developing economies.

tailored to the specific circumstances of each country, policymakers can prevent widespread concerns about inflation that could unsettle inflation expectations. To effectively combat inflation, policymakers must strive to minimize surprises in their monetary and fiscal actions, creating a set of policies that the public trusts and considers when forming expectations about future inflation and spending.

In summary, the primary responsibility of a central bank is to advocate for price stability. In order to protect their valuable and hard-earned independence, central banks should embrace and emphasize the importance of their narrow mandate. In the coming years, inflation will continue to present a significant challenge as we navigate a substantial reallocation of resources in our economies (King, 2022, p. 10). This reallocation is driven by the increased emphasis on resilience following the pandemic, the political pressures to increase public spending, and the necessary restructuring to meet climate change goals. Consequently, there will be substantial shifts in relative prices and wages.

References

Ackley, H. G. (1961). *Macroeconomic theory*. Macmillan.

Anderson, P. A. (1978). Rational expectations: How important for econometric policy analysis? *Federal Reserve Bank of Minneapolis Quarterly Review, 2*(Fall), 4–9.

Bean, C. (2009). The great moderation, the great panic and the great contraction. Schumpeter lecture, annual congress of the European Economic Association, August.

Beau, D., Clerc, L., & Mojon, B. (2012). Macro-prudential policy and the conduct of monetary policy. *Banque de France working paper* 390, Banque de France, Paris, France.

Bernanke, B. S. (2000). *Essays on the great depression*. Princeton University Press.

Bernanke, B. S. (2009). Four questions about the financial crisis. Speech at the Morehouse College, Atlanta, Georgia, April 14.

Bernanke, B.S., & Gertler, M. (1999). Monetary policy and asset price volatility. *Economic review of the Federal Reserve Bank of Kansas City*, 4th Quarter, also published at (2000) *NBER Working Papers* 7559 [the response by Cecchetti, S. G., *et al.*, 2000, "Asset prices and central bank policy," Geneva Reports on the World Economy No. 2, London: Centre for Economic Policy Research, July].

Bernanke, B. S., Gertler, M., & Gilchrist, S. (1999). The financial accelerator in a quantitative business cycle framework. In J. B. Taylor & M. Woodford (Eds.), *Handbook of macroeconomics* (Vol. 1, part 3, pp. 1341–1393). North-Holland.

Bernanke, B. S., Laubach, T., Mishkin, F. S., & Posen, A. S. (2001). *Inflation targeting: Lessons from the international experience*. Princeton University Press.

BIS—Bank for International Settlements. (2009). 79th annual report, Basel, Switzerland.

Blanchard, O. (2021). In defence of concerns over the $1.9 trillion relief plan. *PIIE realtime economics blogpost*. Peterson Institute for International Economics. Washington, DC, February 18.

Blanchard, O., & Galí, J. (2007). Real wage rigidities and the new Keynesian model. *Journal of Money, Credit and Banking, 39*(02, s1), 35–65.

Blanchard, O. (2008). The state of macro. NBER Working Papers, no 14259.

Blanchard, O., Cerrutti E., & Summers, L. (2015). Inflation and activity: Two explorations, and their monetary policy implications. *Conference proceedings*, inflation and unemployment in Europe, European Central Bank, Sintra, Portugal, 21–23 May.

Bordo, M. D., & Landon-Lane, J. S. (2010). The global financial crisis: Is it unprecedented? *Proceedings* EWC/KDI on 'Global Economic Crisis: Impacts, Transmission, and Recovery', Hawaii, 19–20 August.

Borio, C. (2011). Central banking post-crisis: What compass for unchartered waters?. *BIS, Working Paper* 353, September, Bank for International Settlements, Basel, Switzerland.

Bouchaud, J. -P. (2009). The (unfortunate) complexity of the economy. *Physics World* (April), pp 28–32.

Bouchaud, J. -P. (2010). The endogenous dynamics of markets: Price impact and feedback loops. *arXiv*:1009.2928v1 (15 September 2010).

Brunner, K., & Meltzer, A. H. (1963). The place of financial intermediaries in the transmission of monetary policy. *American Economic Review, 53*(3), 372–382.

Caballero, R. J. (2010). Macroeconomics after the crisis: Time to deal with the pretense-of-knowledge syndrome. *NBER Working Paper* No 16429, National Bureau of Economic Research, Cambridge, MA, USA.

Cecchetti S.G., Disyatat, P., & Kohler, M. (2009a). Integrating financial stability: New models for a new challenge. Proceedings joint BIS-ECB workshop on "Monetary Policy and Financial Stability", Basel, Switzerland, 10–11 September.

Cecchetti, S. G. (2008). Measuring the macroeconomic risks posed by asset price booms. In J. Y. Campbell (Ed.), *Asset prices and monetary policy, NBER conference report* (pp. 9–43). University of Chicago Press.

Cecchetti, S. G., & Schoenholtz, K. (2021). Inflation policy. Money and banking, 18 November. https://www.moneyandbanking.com/commentary/2021/11/18/inflation-policy. Accessed 22 Dec 2021.

Cecchetti, S. G., Disyatat, P., & Kohler, M. (2009b). Integrating financial stability: New models for a new challenge. Proceedings of the joint BIS-ECB workshop on '*Monetary policy and financial stability*', Basel, Switzerland, 10–11 September.

Cecchetti, S. G., Flores-Lagunes, A., & Krause, S. (2006). Assessing the sources of changes in the volatility of real growth. In C. Kent & D. Norman (Eds.), *The changing nature of the business cycle, proceedings of the research conference of the Reserve Bank of Australia, Nov. 2005* (pp. 115–138). Reserve Bank of Australia.

Christiano, L. J., Motto, R., & Rostagno, M. (2003). The great depression and the Friedman-Schwartz hypothesis. *Journal of Money, Credit and Banking, 35*(6), 1119–1198.

Coibon, O., Gorodnichenko, Y., & Kumar, S. (2018). How do firms form their expectations? New survey evidence. *American Economic Review, 108*(9), 2671–2713.

Coibon, O., Gorodnichenko, Y., & Kamdar, R. (2018). The formation of expectations, inflation, and the Phillips curve. *Journal of Economic Literature, 56*(4), 1447–1491.

Detken, C., Gerdesmeier, D., & Roffia, B. (2010). Interlinkages between money, credit and asset prices and their implications for consumer price inflation: Recent empirical work. In L. Papademos & Stark (Eds.), *Enhancing monetary analysis* (pp. 307–327). ECB.

Diamond, P., & Vartiainen, H. (Eds.). (2007). *Behavioural economics and its applications*. Princeton University Press.

Dynan, K. E., Elmendorf, D. W., & Sichel, D. E. (2006). Can financial innovation explain the reduced volatility of economic activity? *Journal of Monetary Economics, 53*(1), 123–150.

Elliot, L. (2021). Central Banks have 'King Canute' theory of inflation, say former governor. *The Guardian*, U.K., November 23rd.

Evans, G. W., & Honkapohja, S. (2001). *Learning and expectations in macroeconomics*. Princeton University Press.

Evans, G. W., Honkapohja, S., & Mitra, K. (2022). Expectations, stagnation, and fiscal policy: A nonlinear analysis. *International Economic Review, 63*, 1397–1425.

Fama, E. F. (1970). Efficient capital markets: A review of theory and empirical work. *Journal of Finance, 25*(2), 383–417.

Farmer, J., & Geanakoplos, J. (2008). The virtues and vices of equilibrium and the future of financial economics. Cowles foundation discussion paper no 1647.

Fisher, I. (1930). *The theory of interest.* Macmillan.
Friedman, M., & Schwartz, A. J. (1963). *A monetary history of the United States, 1867–1960.* Princeton University Press.
Gagnon, J. E., & Collins, C. G. (2019). Low inflation bends the curve. *PIIE Working Paper* 19-6. Peterson Institute for International Economics. Washington, DC.
Geanakoplos, J. (2010). The leverage cycle. *NBER Macroeconomics Annual, 24*, 1–65.
Goodfriend, M., & King. M. (2015). *Review of the Riksbank's Monetary Policy* 2010–2015. Riksdagstryckeriet.
Gopinath, G. (2022). How will the pandemic and war shape future monetary policy. Remarks in Federal Reserve Bank of Kansas City, Jackson hole economic policy symposium. Kansas City, MO, Kansas City Fed. August 29.
Greenspan, A. (2009). We need a better cushion against risk. *The Financial Times.*
Griffiths, B. (2020). The spectre of inflation. The Article, August 5.
Grothe, M., & Meyler, A. (2018). Inflation forecasts: Are market-based and survey-based measures informative? *International Journal of Financial Research, 9*(1), 171–188.
Hansen, A. H. (1949). *Monetary theory and fiscal policy.* McGraw- Hill.
Hendry, D., & Mizon, G. (2014). Why DSGEs crash during crises. VoxEU.org, CEPR, 18 June. https://voxeu.org/article/why-standard-macro-models-fail-crises. Accessed 22 December 2021.
Hetzel, R. (2007). Rules vs. Discretion: Lessons from the Volcker-Greenspan Era. Federal Reserve Bank of Richmond.
Hicks, J. R. (1937). Mr. Keynes and the 'Classics'. *Econometrica.*
Hicks, J. R. (1969). *A theory of economic history.* Oxford Clarendon Press.
IMF—International Monetary Fund. (2021). *World economic outlook: Recovery during a pandemic—health concerns, supply disruptions.* Price Pressures.
Jonung, L. (2009). The Swedish model for resolving the banking crisis of 1991-93: Seven reasons why it was successful. *Economic papers* no 360, European Commission—Economic and Financial Affairs Directorate General.
Kay, J., & King, M. (2020). *Radical uncertainty: Decision-making for an unknowable future.* Bridge Street Press.
King, M. (2022). Monetary policy in a world of radical uncertainty. *Conference Paper* 1, Institute of International Monetary Research, University of Buckingham, UK, January.
Kiyotaki, N., & Moore, J. (1997). Credit cycles. *Journal of Political Economy, 105*, 211–248.
Kokores, I. T. (2015). Lean-against-the-wind monetary policy: The post crisis shift in the literature. *SPOUDAI Journal of Economics and Business, 65*(3–4), 66–99.
Kokores, I. T., & Kanas, A. (2021). Monetary policy and systemic risk: U.S. evidence. In I. T. Kokores, P. Pantelidis, T. Pelagidis, & D. Yannelis (Eds.), *Money, trade and finance: Recent trends and methodological issues* (pp. 131–140). Palgrave Macmillan.
Kokores, T. (1989). *Euro-banking innovations and EEC monetary coordination (studies 4).* Institute of European Civilization. Papazisis.
Lambertini, C., Mendicino, M., & Punzi, T. (2011). Leaning against boom-bust cycles in credit and housing prices. Banco de Portugal Working Paper 8.
LeBaron, B. (2000). Agent-based computational finance: Suggested readings and early research. *Journal of Economic Dynamics and Control, 24*, 679–702.
Lucas, R. (2003). Macroeconomic priorities. *American Economic Review, 93*(1), 1–14.
Lucas, R. (2009). In defence of the dismal science. *The Economist.*
Lucas, R., & Sargent, T. (1979). After Keynesian macroeconomics. Quarterly Review, Federal Reserve Bank of Minneapolis, Spring.
Maćkowiak, B., & Wiederholt, M. (2009). Optimal sticky prices under rational inattention. *American Economic Review, 99*(3), 769–803.
Maddaloni, A., & Peydró, J.-L. (2011). Bank risk-taking, securitization, supervision, and low interest rates: Evidence from the euro-area and the U.S. lending standards. *The Review of Financial Studies, 24*(6), 2121–2165.

McLeay, M., & Tenreyro, S. (2020). Optimal inflation and the identification of the Phillips curve. In M. S. Eichenbaum, E. Hurst, & J. A. Parker (Eds.), *NBER macroeconomics annual 2019* (Vol. 34, pp. 199–255). National Bureau of Economic Research, University of Chicago Press.

Mishkin, F. S. (2009). Why all regulatory roads lead to the fed. *Financial Times*.

Mishkin, F. S. (2011). Monetary policy strategy: Lessons from the crisis. In M. Jarociñki, F. Smets, & C. Thimann (Eds.), *Approaches to monetary policy revisited—lessons from the crisis, sixth ECB central banking conference proceedings* (pp. 67–118).

Mishkin, F. S. (2014). Macrorpudential and monetary policies. In D. D. Evanoff, C. Holthausen, G. G. Kaufman, & M. Kremer (Eds.), *The role of central banks in financial stability: How has it changed?. 30th world scientific studies in international economics* (pp. 409–422). World Scientific Publishing.

New York Federal Reserve (2007). *New Directions for Understanding Systemic Risk. Proceedings* of the conference organized by the Federal Reserve Bank of New York and the US National Academy of Sciences in May 2006. New York Federal Reserve. Available online at: http://www.newyorkfed.org/research/epr/2007n1.html

Obstfeld, M. (2022). Uncoordinated monetary policies risk a historic global slowdown. *Realtime Economics Blogpost*. Peterson Institute for International Economics. 12 Sept.

Politi, J., & Smith, C. (2021). A dangerous man: The messy politics of fed chair nominations. *Financial Times*.

Praet, P. (2014). The (changing) role of Central Banks in financial stability policies. In D. D. Evanoff, C. Holthausen, G. G. Kaufman, & M. Kremer (Eds.), *The role of central banks in financial stability: How has it changed? 30th world scientific studies in international economics* (pp. 3–10). World Scientific Publishing Co. Pte. Ltd.

Reinhart, C. M., & Rogoff, K. S. (2009). *This time is different: Eight centuries of financial folly*. Princeton University Press.

Reinhart, C. M., & Reinhart, V. R. (2010). After the fall. In *Macroeconomic challenges: The decade ahead, proceedings—economic policy symposium—Jackson Hole* (pp. 17–60). Federal Reserve Bank of Kansas City Symposium.

Reinhart, C. M., & Rogoff, K. S. (2008). Is the 2007 sub-prime financial crisis so different? An international historical comparison. *NBER working paper*, no. 13761, January, Cambridge, MA: National Bureau of Economic Research.

Reinhart, C. M., & Rogoff, K. S. (2010). From financial crash to debt crisis. NBER Working Paper No 15795 Cambridge, MA: National Bureau of Economic Research.

Samuelson, P. A. (1968). What classical and neoclassical monetary theory was. *Canadian Journal of Economics, 1*(1), 1–15.

Schnabel, I. (2022). Monetary policy and the great volatility. Speech Jackson Hole Economic Policy Symposium, Federal Reserve of Kansas City, Jackson Hole, Wyoming, August 27.

Shirakawa, M. (2009). *International policy response to financial crises. Remarks by Masaaki Shirakawa, governor of the Bank of Japan, at a symposium sponsored by the Federal Reserve Bank of Kansas City*. Jackson Hole.

Sims, C. A. (2003). Implications of rational inattention. *Journal of monetary economics, 50*(3), 665–690.

Sousa, R., & Yetman, J. (2016). Inflation expectations and monetary policy. *BIS Paper* 89d, Bank of International Settlements, Basel, Switzerland.

Spilimbergo, A., Mishra, P., Gopinath, G., Leigh, D., & Ball, L. (2021). US inflation: Set for take-off? *VoxEU*. CEPR, UK. May 7.

Tinbergen, J. (1952). *On the theory of economic policy*. North Holland.

Tobin, J. (1969). A general equilibrium view of monetary theory. *Journal of Money, Credit and Banking, 1*(1), 15–29.

Trichet, J. C. (2011). Reflections on the nature of monetary policy non-standard measures and finance theory. In M. Jarociński, F. Smets, & C. Thimann (Eds.), *Approaches to monetary policy revisited: Lessons from the crisis* (pp. 12–22). European Central Bank.

White, W. R. (2011). Comment on Mishkin, Frederic S. (2011). Monetary policy strategy: Lessons from the crisis. In M. Jarociński, F. Smets, & C. Thimann (Eds.), *Approaches to monetary policy revisited—lessons from the crisis, sixth ECB central banking conference proceedings* (pp. 124–132).

Wood, J. H. (2009). *A history of macroeconomic policy in the United States. Routledge explorations in economic history*. Routledge.

Wood, J. H. (2015). *Central banking in a democracy: The Federal Reserve and its alternatives* (Routledge explorations in economic history). Routledge.

Chapter 8
Monetary Policy in Interdependent Economies: The Task Ahead

> The central bank must keep public opinion on its side, because the public is the ultimate source of its power and independence.
> —*Markus K. Brunnermeier (2023), p. 7*

8.1 Introduction: Unconventional Times and Challenges of Central Bank Independence

Since the onset of the global financial crisis, central banks have increasingly expanded their conventional methods of operation and started utilizing their balance sheets (including its size and composition) more extensively as a policy instrument. In numerous jurisdictions, the use of the central bank balance sheet has evolved from reactive and limited provision of liquidity, which had little influence on overall financial conditions, to active and controlled utilization aimed at impacting broader financial conditions. As a result, apart from the traditional role of providing funding support during times of financial strain, central banks have also employed their balance sheets to tackle obstacles in the transmission of monetary policy and to provide policy accommodation when nominal interest rates were constrained at low levels (ECB, 2015, p. 77). In summary, the central bank balance sheet has proven to be a versatile tool that can address various policy requirements.

Unconventional monetary policy presents several significant challenges. The extensive purchase of assets required to counter the limitations imposed by the recent regime of lowest possible nominal interest rates led to undesirable fiscal and distributional outcomes and placed central banks at higher risks with their balance sheets. The absence of a clear definition for price stability, combined with apprehensions regarding the credibility of significant expansions in the balance sheet, hampers policymaking. This situation prompted central banks to avoid implementing the necessary and effective quantitative easing measures to stimulate economic growth and instead opt for accommodating persistently low inflation levels (Orphanides, 2018, p. 35), while, additionally, it was the exceptional nature of these policies that suggested that their effectiveness cannot be fully comprehended using conventional frameworks and models (Fahr et al., 2011,

I. T. Kokores, *Monetary Policy in Interdependent Economies*, Financial and Monetary Policy Studies 55, https://doi.org/10.1007/978-3-031-41958-4_8

p. 49). Therefore, it becomes necessary to establish new standards for determining conventional policy and develop new tools for interpretation before alternative policy approaches can be examined. This can be done with the advantage of hindsight, which provides valuable insights and understanding.

The practice of monetary policy in various countries has been significantly influenced by the advent of the global financial crisis and the crises that succeeded it. The rapid and forceful developments in financial markets and the overall economy necessitated innovative approaches. The primary concern now is whether these changes are temporary adjustments or if they represent permanent shifts in the way monetary policy is conducted. Blinder et al. (2017) address this inquiry by conducting two nearly identical surveys—one targeting central bank governors and the other targeting academic specialists. They also consider the existing academic literature alongside the survey data to provide insights on this matter. According to their findings, *necessity* has played a significant role in driving the adoption of new policies by central banks. In GFC-affected countries, central banks were more inclined to implement innovative measures, engage in discussions about their mandates, enhance communication, and face criticism. However, there has been a broader shift in thinking across central banks, including those in noncrisis countries. These central banks have also reevaluated their mandates and implemented macroprudential measures.

Based on these observations, Blinder et al. (2017, p. 2) anticipate that central banks in the future will have broader mandates, employ macroprudential tools more extensively, and emphasize communication compared to the precrisis era. While there is still no consensus on the future utilization of unconventional monetary policy tools, it is expected that most of these tools will remain in central banks' toolkits. This is particularly because central bank governors who gain experience with a specific tool are more likely to evaluate it positively. Lastly, the relationship between central banks and governments may have undergone changes, with central banks more frequently crossing boundaries compared to the past. However, only time will reveal the new status quo in this particular aspect.

Furthermore, as Blinder et al. (2017) report, notable disparities exist between the viewpoints of academics and central banking practitioners. Firstly, while many scholars tend to support retaining most unconventional policies within central banks' toolkits, central bank governors are significantly more skeptical and often express that it is premature to make judgments. Central bank governors who have hands-on experience with unconventional tools tend to hold more positive assessments of these tools. However, the cautious stance of many central bank governors regarding the future use of unconventional tools suggests lingering uncertainty regarding their costs and benefits. Secondly, although both governors and academics agree that central bank communication has become more frequent since the crisis and that these changes are likely to continue or even expand further, there are differences in the perceived usefulness of forward guidance as both a policy and a communication tool. Academics show a strong preference for data-driven forward guidance, whereas qualitative forward guidance is the more popular form among central bank governors. Thirdly, regarding the issue of crossing into the political realm, central bank governors generally feel that they faced minimal criticism for engaging in politically influenced actions or crossing political boundaries during the crisis. In contrast, the majority of academic respondents believe that central banks were indeed criticized for overstepping into politics.

8.2 Central Bank Independence in Democratic Societies

Similar to other aspects of effective economic governance within democratic societies, the argument in favor of central bank independence remains under a minor debate, as the precise limits and boundaries of independence are not consistently well-defined (see Kokores, 2022, Chaps. 9.12 and 9.13, for a discussion). As US Federal Reserve Chairman since February 2018, Jerome Powell (2023) suggests, in a well-functioning democracy, the responsibility of making significant public policy decisions generally lies with the elected branches of government.[1] With independence, the central bank assumes the obligation to ensure transparency, allowing for effective oversight by Congress, which in turn upholds the democratic legitimacy of the central bank. The central bank's primary focus remains on fulfilling its legal mandate and providing transparent information that is relevant and appropriate. It is crucial that monetary policymakers adhere to the central bank's statutory objectives and authorities, resisting the temptation to expand their scope to address other pressing social issues of the time.

Powell (2023, p. 2) recognizes that while the US Federal Reserve has enjoyed independence since its establishment in 1914, the dual mandate—targeting both employment and inflation—was only incorporated into the law in 1977 (Bernanke, 2010). The existence of this dual mandate recognizes that the Federal Reserve's independence in monetary policy corresponds to *operational* or *instrumental independence* rather than *independence in determining goals*; Debelle and Fischer (1994) provide an analysis of the distinction between different types of independence. Nevertheless, to assume new objectives, irrespective of how worthwhile they may be, without a clear statutory mandate would undermine the rationale for the central bank's independence.

Furthermore, balancing economic efficiency through delegated discretionary power and upholding democratic legitimacy presents a complex institutional design challenge (Orphanides, 2018, p. 38). Simply increasing independence does not guarantee superior macroeconomic performance in the long run compared to having less independence. It is crucial to comprehend the practical issues and challenges involved to determine the appropriate limits of central bank independence and to foster policies that effectively contribute to the overall welfare of society. As

[1]Granting of independence to agencies should be exceptionally uncommon, clearly specified, carefully defined, and restricted to matters that unquestionably require safeguarding from immediate political influences (Powell, 2023, p. 2).

monetary policy holds significant influence over a nation's economy, when placed in the hands of political authorities who tend to prioritize short-term gains, the potential for misuse arises. The allure of implementing expansionary monetary policy to enjoy immediate benefits often outweighs concerns about the long-term consequences of higher inflation. This inclination toward short-term gains commonly results in an inflationary bias when political authorities retain control over monetary policy. As a result, the pursuit of price stability becomes compromised, leading to a decline in economic welfare without any noticeable economic advantages.

Central bank independence emerges as a solution to this inherent problem of dynamic consistency. By delegating monetary policy to an independent central bank with a mandate for ensuring price stability, the risks of inflationary bias can be mitigated. Another alternative solution is the adoption of a monetary rule that aims to maintain price stability over time while providing systematic countercyclical support to the economy. These approaches help address the challenges of maintaining economic welfare while minimizing the negative impacts of shortsighted decision-making in monetary policy.

The concept of central bank independence and systematic monetary policy gained prominence as a formal theory in response to the widespread experience of stagflation during the 1970s, which affected numerous advanced economies.[2] Nevertheless, the core arguments supporting these ideas had already been presented earlier. In an important article written in 1962, Milton Friedman described the essence of why central bank independence may be desirable as follows: "The device of an independent central bank embodies the very appealing idea that it is essential to prevent monetary policy from being a day-to-day plaything at the mercy of every whim of the current political authorities" (Friedman (1968, pp. 177–178)). While acknowledging the attractiveness of central bank independence, Friedman expressed a set of reservations that ultimately led him to conclude that, in practical terms, adopting a monetary policy rule would be more preferable than delegating discretionary power to an independent central bank. In Friedman's analysis, the reference point for central bank independence was the US Federal Reserve, which possessed broad discretionary authority and a mandate that lacked a clear operational interpretation.[3] In this context, an independent central bank could be influenced by personal characteristics and potential biases, potentially resulting in policy that is overly responsive to individual preferences. Unless policy remains systematic and adheres

[2]See, in particular, the theoretical contributions by Kydland and Prescott (1977), Barro and Gordon (1983a, 1983b), and Rogoff (1985) and Cukierman (1992) who connected the theory with empirical evidence.

[3]The US Federal Reserve Act of 1913 mandated the Federal Reserve to establish policies that accommodate commerce and business. However, a revision to the Act in 1977 introduced the current formulation, directing the Federal Reserve to effectively promote the objectives of maximum employment, stable prices, and moderate long-term interest rates. The specific definition of price stability as a 2% inflation goal was adopted in 2012. For further insights into the evolving interpretation of the Fed's mandate, refer to Orphanides (2014) and Wood (2015).

to a well-designed rule, discretionary actions by an independent central bank could lead to significant policy mistakes (Orphanides, 2018, p. 38).

Friedman raised a specific concern regarding the "technical defect" of dividing macroeconomic policy among multiple decision-makers without clear accountability for the ultimate outcome of macroeconomic stability and economic welfare. According to Friedman, an independent central bank operating with discretionary power could result in a dispersion of responsibility, leading to a tendency to shirk responsibility during uncertain and challenging times. Friedman drew on historical examples from the US Federal Reserve to support his argument in favor of monetary rules. He attributed some policy errors to individual personalities and highlighted the drawback of excessive reliance on personalities when conducting discretionary monetary policy through an independent central bank. In essence, Friedman believed that central bank independence with broad discretionary powers not only fell short of promoting favorable policy outcomes but could even be counterproductive during periods of uncertainty and difficulty (Friedman, 1968, pp. 177–78, 186–87; Orphanides, 2018). Challenging episodes such as the Great Depression, the Great Recession, bubble collapses, or major financial crises, which require close coordination of monetary, fiscal, and other policies, could potentially lead to problems stemming from the undesirable dispersion of responsibility if central bank independence with broad discretionary authority is maintained.

Consequently, Tucker (2018a) questions whether the world's major central banks have become excessively powerful in the aftermath of the financial crisis: whether this expansion of power aligns with modern societies' democratic principles. He admits that the increasing accumulation of power by central banks since the GFC raises important questions and contends that if we aim to maintain central bank independence and uphold confidence in our system of government, the delegation of power by legislatures must be conducted carefully and thoughtfully. Furthermore, the major central banks have been granted significant regulatory powers, encompassing both microprudential and macroprudential aspects. In certain jurisdictions, particularly the United States, they have become the primary authority to whom everyone turns in times of turmoil. In other places, as, for example, the United Kingdom, the central bank is formally recognized as the authoritative figure responsible for stability policy. Across the board, central banks have unmistakably become integral components of the regulatory state and the fiscal state. Tucker (2018a) further remarks that alongside activist judges, central bankers have, indeed, become the prominent figures of *unelected power*. It is hardly surprising, then, that more people have been asking whether the insulation of the monetary authorities from day-to-day political influence can still be justified.

This issue reflects more extensive and increasing concern regarding our system of government and the challenge of avoiding an unfortunate dichotomy between technocracy and populism. Independent central banks and regulatory agencies can, at times, achieve more favorable outcomes by avoiding the fluctuations in public policy linked to electoral politics. However, excessive delegation coupled with political insulation could potentially lead us toward a form of undemocratic liberalism. In such a scenario, crucial decisions that significantly impact our lives would be made by unelected technocrats, subject only to judicial oversight. It has been contented that the discipline imposed by a globalized market economy is pushing us in this direction[4] (Tucker, 2018a, 2018b). If we genuinely prioritize our democratic values and traditions, it is insufficient for decisions regarding delegation to be made solely by duly elected legislatures. This is especially true if these decisions result in vague or multiple objectives, effectively handing over the responsibility of shaping significant policies to unelected technocrats.

Merely relying on judges to oversee the exercise of delegated powers, ensuring adherence to procedural standards and occasionally substituting their own policy perspectives after evaluating the substantive merits of agencies' decisions and actions, is insufficient. In this somewhat realistic representation of the world, there are virtually no constraints on what can be delegated, with the courts only requiring assurance that power has not been misused. This diluted form of legal liberalism fails to fully uphold our democratic values (Tucker, 2018b) and is consequently prone, albeit gradually, to undermining the backing for our democratic system of governance.[5]

In fact, *the missions of preserving banking stability and price stability are intertwined—not only for society but also for the central banks themselves in their most elemental function, namely, of creating money.* The criticisms directed at major advanced economies' monetary authorities may at times appear impractical to central bankers, but they should nonetheless take seriously the contention that the limitations on their powers and actions lack principled foundations. In order to maintain the health and resilience of our democracies, it is crucial to establish norms that determine when and how to delegate authority to independent agencies. These principles should align with the fundamental political values associated with democracy, the rule of law, and constitutionalism. Tucker (2018a) puts forth a set of

[4]In an attempt to comprehend these concerns, Tucker (2018a) puts forth principles that, if widely recognized as political norms, could validate the exceptional authority held by central banks (and other independent regulatory bodies), thus safeguarding the democratic nature of our societies. While this oversimplifies the main argument of the book, one of its fundamental ideas is that a specific form of liberalism, which revolves around legal formalism and judicial supervision, is inadequate to bestow legitimacy upon our unelected policymakers.

[5]These issues are not abstract matters that only interest those who are passionate about economic policy or government structure. The potential consequences of uncontrolled unelected power can be significant. Consider an independent agency with extensive authority but lacking clear purposes and objectives. How would anyone determine whether it has successfully fulfilled its mission if it sets its own standards? Just as "no taxation without representation" was a rallying cry in the past, Tucker (2018a) questions the legitimacy of a demand at present of "no regulation without representation," as in insisting that elected legislators establish the high-level policies and key parameters when they delegate powers to independent agencies. It should be noted that unelected power (Tucker, 2018b) primarily focuses on agencies that are insulated from both elected branches of government. In the United States, these agencies, among other things, are not subject to annual budget approvals from Congress, yet US legal scholars often use the term "independent agency" more narrowly to refer to insulation from the president (see Tucker, 2018a, p. 52).

Principles for Delegation[6] that propose and defend such norms. Each of the functions currently performed by central banks, including monetary policy, stability policy, supervision of individual banks, and emergency liquidity provision, should be guided and constrained by similar principles. Very few areas would remain untouched. For instance, in Europe, the decision-making body of the ECB is deemed too large (with 25 voting members) to facilitate effective deliberation, similar to the case of the US Federal Reserve's Open Market Committee (comprised of 12 voting members and 7 regional presidents who have a speaking role but no vote). Moreover, the US Federal Reserve has independently specified its inflation objective without much public debate.

8.2.1 Monetary Policy Independence

Nevertheless, to varying extents, monetary policy frameworks in major democracies largely adhere to the general principles mentioned above. Transparency has significantly improved everywhere, particularly with the adoption of inflation targeting regimes in the 1990s. This approach made the policy tools (such as short-term interest rates) and their outcomes (such as inflation) much more transparent and understandable to the public and legislators. Even in the United States, the Federal Reserve eventually took the initiative, led by Chairman Ben Bernanke, to publish its interpretation of "stable prices" and "maximum employment" (Bernanke, 2003), which are the two elements of its statutory mandate.[7] The ECB progressed in the aftermath of the three crises over the last two decades to publish a new definition of price stability, which is symmetric and allows for temporary overshooting, as needed, while also remaining vague regarding the margin of tolerance and the time allowed for overshoots (see Wyplosz, 2021).

Given the role of central banks as the ultimate providers of financial support during crises, it is necessary for them to have the ability to shape and influence

[6]According to Tucker (2018a, p. 53), several key principles should be considered: First, power should be delegated to politically insulated agencies only when the public's objectives are widely agreed upon, the credibility can be enhanced, and the technocrats do not have to make significant decisions on values and distribution. Second, elected politicians should provide these agencies with clear and easily monitored objectives, and oversight should be led by the legislative body itself when deciding whether to maintain the delegation. Third, the agency's exercise of discretion should be systematic and guided by publicly available operating principles. Fourth, decisions should be made by committees using a one-person, one-vote approach after thoughtful deliberation. Fifth, if an independent agency, like postcrisis central banks, has multiple missions, each mission should be the responsibility of a separate policy body within the agency, with committee members predominantly focused on their respective bodies.

[7]According to Blinder (1996), the US Federal Reserve has a third legislated goal of "moderate long-term interest rates." However, since achieving price stability will almost surely produce low long-term rates, the Fed is viewed as having a dual mandate of pursuing full employment and stable prices (Thorbecke, 2002); see also Board of Governors of the Federal Reserve System (2023).

regulatory and supervisory frameworks. Due to a combination of factors, including perceived effectiveness and prevailing trends, the granting of independence to central banks gained significant popularity in the 1990s. This trend was further reinforced through support and conditions imposed by the International Monetary Fund. However, after two decades, the concept of central bank independence is now being reevaluated and questioned.

8.2.2 Is Monetary Independence Outdated?

The most prominent criticism voiced by economists is that the issue of inflation experienced in the 1970s was an exceptional and significant one, which has now been effectively addressed. According to this critique, the current challenges of low productivity growth and excessive debt could be better tackled by consolidating all macroeconomic policy tools under a single political authority, removing artificial barriers that separate monetary and fiscal strategies. In essence, the argument suggests that the conditions that justified the need for monetary independence are no longer relevant, and it is time to move away from strict adherence to the separation of monetary and fiscal spheres. These arguments, however, overlook a crucial aspect by assuming that the justification for central bank independence was solely based on addressing an inflation bias resulting from a time inconsistency problem, where policymakers are tempted to prioritize short-term growth and employment over long-term price stability. However, the challenges related to committing to a consistent monetary policy extend beyond this specific issue and have wider and deeper implications (Bernanke, 2017).

Regardless of the personal inclinations of central bankers, their legal obligation in the early stages of 2009 was evident: they were required to fulfill their statutory mandate, but not exceed it. The clear directive was to stimulate spending in order to prevent deflation and maintain price stability. It is difficult to imagine that elected policymakers in charge of monetary affairs would have been as prepared or capable of providing the exceptional stimulus measures that successfully averted an economic depression a decade ago.[8]

[8] Tucker (2018a, pp. 53–54) argues that elected policymakers might not have been prepared for the necessary measures due to potential unpopularity among certain segments of the electorate, particularly because these measures would have resulted in persistently low returns on savings. Even if they had been willing, they might have lacked the capability to implement the required but limited stimulus. Furthermore, there is doubt whether politicians with control over monetary policy would have been trusted to resist the temptation of resorting to excessive inflation as a means to alleviate government debt burdens. In essence, political control of monetary policy would have carried the risks of both inadequate response and excessive reaction to the economic crisis. These concerns extend beyond economics, as granting day-to-day political authority over monetary policy would violate the principle of separation of powers fundamental to the Western system of constitutional democracy. It is not often emphasized, but independent monetary authorities serve as a mechanism to mitigate the output and employment volatility associated with fixed standards like the

The entity responsible for issuing a country's currency possesses a unique power: the ability to create money at its discretion. When there are abrupt shifts in the demand for the currency, the monetary authority must accommodate these changes in order to prevent unintentional restrictions or stimulation of economic activity. Instances of bank runs, where individuals demand immediate withdrawal of their deposits in cash, represent an increase in the demand for the central bank's currency. If even financially sound banks do not possess enough central bank currency (or assets that can be converted into central bank currency through the market) to fulfill their customers' cash demands, they would face insolvency unless they can approach the central bank and exchange illiquid assets for cash. In such a scenario, the central bank serves two simultaneous purposes (Tucker, 2018a): Firstly, it stabilizes the banking system by acting as a lender of last resort, and secondly, it ensures that the shortage of liquidity does not hinder the implementation of monetary policy. This phenomenon has profound implications. At a fundamental level, our monetary and banking system is designed in a way that separates the allocation of credit from the state, aiming for efficiency and, to some extent, fairness. However, it does not restrict the authority to create money solely to the state; instead, it permits private firms to issue their own forms of currency. This system, known as fractional reserve banking, combines the payment system (money) with the credit system (loans) without fully merging them together.

Banks, including those entities referred to as "shadow banks," play a significant role in the monetary system. These entities possess the economic characteristics of traditional banks but may not adhere to the same legal framework. As a result, the objectives of maintaining stability in both the banking sector and price levels are closely interconnected. This interdependence applies not only to society as a whole but also to central banks themselves, particularly in their fundamental role of money creation. Elected officials should reiterate and reinforce the role of central banks as lenders of last resort in accordance with a well-defined statutory objective. This objective should aim to prevent or minimize the societal consequences that arise from the disruptive failure of solvent financial intermediaries or the restriction of credit and other essential services due to their self-interest in survival (Tucker, 2018a, p. 55). However, it is crucial to establish constraints, above all, in the same way that the "no monetary financing" clause of the government is essential to maintain an independent monetary policy, a fundamental principle for an independent lender of last resort should be, according to Tucker (2018a), a "no provision of loans to fundamentally insolvent businesses" clause. In fact, he contends that when a troubled company is fundamentally bankrupt, to provide liquidity assistance only allows short-term creditors to avoid losses while burdening long-term creditors,

---

nineteenth-century gold standard, which would be deemed unacceptable in a full-franchise democracy, all while upholding our constitutional values.

without preventing the eventual closure of the company, which lies against the intended purpose of central banking.[9]

Given that central banks serve as lenders of last resort, it becomes necessary for them to be involved in the regulation and supervision of banks. Their primary concern when providing loans is to ensure that the borrowed funds are repaid. Therefore, they need to assess which banks (and potentially similar financial institutions) should have access to liquidity and under what conditions. This is the foundation of their established authority over banking practices. Even critics of "broad central banking" generally acknowledge that as lenders of last resort, central banks cannot avoid inspecting banks that seek borrowing assistance. The events that unfolded in the United Kingdom during 2007, when Northern Rock encountered difficulties and the central bank lacked supervisory powers, demonstrated the risks associated with hastily assuming the role of lender of last resort. A central bank must have the ability to monitor the financial health of individual banks during stable times to effectively act as a source of liquidity support when needed. Furthermore, this capability is essential for making informed judgments about how their monetary decisions will impact the financial system and the broader economy.

The role of central banks in supervision and regulation should be defined through formal mechanisms, but it should also have clear limitations. This aspect is particularly significant because historically, financial regulation has encompassed a broad scope beyond the mere preservation of "stability." For instance, should central banks intervene in every instance of perceived credit or asset price bubbles? If they were to take on that responsibility, how could we effectively monitor whether they were exercising excessive or insufficient control? These questions highlight the challenge of striking the right balance and establishing appropriate boundaries for central banks' regulatory actions.

There exists a strategic conflict between central banks and elected fiscal policymakers, as the latter have considerable discretionary powers but are not bound by specific legal obligations. As a result, when immediate political considerations hinder politicians from taking action to address a crisis or stimulate economic recovery, they can choose to refrain from intervention, knowing that the central bank is obligated by its mandate to make efforts in such situations (Tucker, 2018a, p. 57). This presents the fundamental dilemma faced by central banks that to maintain democratic legitimacy and prevent accusations of exceeding their authority, *central*

[9] With the recent development of legal frameworks that enable the resolution of financially unstable companies without relying on taxpayer funds, present-day central bankers have no justification for being more lenient than their counterparts in the nineteenth century. Historically, these bankers famously refused to provide assistance to fundamentally bankrupt firms seeking access to financial support (Tucker, 2018a, for example, refers to the most famous case is the Bank of England saying "no" to *Overend, Gurney and Company* in 1866). Lender of last resort assistance is fundamentally different from and, in practical terms, can now genuinely avoid being perceived as a bailout or rescue of fundamentally unsound companies. The advancements in resolution technology have completely transformed the role of lender of last resort, allowing central banks to reject requests when it is appropriate to do so (Tucker, 2018a).

bankers require well-defined frameworks with clear objectives for all aspects of their responsibilities. However, the establishment of such frameworks runs the risk of intensifying the strategic interplay with fiscal authorities, leaving central banks as the sole viable option and potentially burdening them with excessive expectations and responsibilities. Currently, a readily available solution that can address all the complexities has not emerged. To establish a comprehensive and robust central bank regime requires the presence of a well-defined fiscal constitution. It is essential to consider the broader context beyond the boundaries of central banking authority. Resolving this issue is likely to be a long-term process that may span a generation (Tucker, 2018b). In the interim, central bankers must resist the temptation to overstep their role and encroach into fiscal domains. This challenge is expected to become more evident during the next economic downturn, which is inevitable. Ultimately, the main challenge lies to legislators inasmuch as to central bankers.

8.3 The Quest for New Horizons for Central Banks

The global financial crisis of 2008–2009 led to the most severe economic downturn in advanced economies since the 1930s. Initially, central banks responded by significantly lowering policy interest rates. However, as these rates approached zero, a new challenge emerged: the possibility of entering a liquidity trap, where traditional monetary expansion measures become ineffective. To provide additional stimulus, central banks ventured into unconventional policies, such as forward guidance on future policy, extensive purchases of assets (known as quantitative easing), and managing exchange rates. Negative interest rates were also introduced later as some central banks explored the limits of how low their policy rates could go while maintaining safety and effectiveness.

Unconventional expansionary monetary policies have proven effective in loosening financial conditions, resulting in a more substantial rebound in output and employment compared to what would have been achieved otherwise. However, the policy measures implemented since the crisis were not sufficiently robust or timely to prevent a lackluster macroeconomic performance (Ball et al., 2016). The recovery has been sluggish compared to previous recoveries following severe recessions, with many regions worldwide far from achieving full employment. The analytical argument in pertinent research (see, for example, Ball et al., 2016) revolves around two key inquiries: Firstly, whether central banks possess effective measures for stimulating the economy when nominal interest rates reach zero and, secondly, how central banks can minimize the probability of encountering the lower bound in the future. Main conclusions suggest that even when nominal interest rates have dropped to zero, central banks have additional tools at their disposal to encourage economic growth and inflation (Lilley & Rogoff, 2020).

Ball et al. (2016) propose that various policy options exist that could decrease the likelihood of reaching zero interest rates again in future circumstances. In the future, if zero is seen as the lowest possible level for nominal interest rates, this limitation on policy is expected to have an impact whenever the unemployment rate is only slightly higher than its long-term average, meaning it will affect both mild and severe economic downturns. This is due to the persistently low level of the neutral real interest rate and the low inflation targets set by central banks. As a result, nominal interest rates are likely to remain consistently low, and central banks will have limited room to lower rates significantly during economic downturns.

However, the limitation of the lower bound on interest rates does not leave central banks powerless, both in the present and going forward. Initially, one approach to overcoming the lower bound on interest rates is to implement negative nominal short-term policy rates, which allows for further monetary policy loosening through conventional means. Several central banks have already ventured into negative rate territory, and these negative rates have influenced domestic asset prices and exchange rates in a similar manner to when policy rates were positive. Additionally, the concerns regarding the potential negative impact of negative policy rates on the functioning of the banking system have not been substantiated in practice thus far. It appears plausible that rates can be pushed even lower than previous attempts, albeit to a limited extent, without significant adverse consequences.

Another avenue available to central banks is the utilization of quantitative easing as a means of implementing further monetary easing. QE initiatives have already demonstrated significant impacts in the countries where they have been implemented.[10] Another strategy employed by certain central banks involves providing subsidized and specifically directed loans to the banking system. QE measures could be expanded by broadening the scope of assets purchased by central banks to include higher-risk assets like corporate debt and equities. By incorporating these additional assets into QE programs, the impact on asset prices, funding costs, and ultimately economic activity could potentially be more pronounced compared to purchases limited to government bonds, even when the quantities of asset purchases are kept constant.[11]

Naturally, monetary policy alone cannot address all economic challenges, especially in terms of increasing an economy's potential growth rate. However, monetary policy has the ability to achieve a desired inflation rate over the medium term and contribute to stabilizing output around its potential level. Fiscal policy may play a

[10]The United States, for example, where it has been estimated that the macroeconomic impacts of quantitative easing measures, involving the purchase of long-term bonds from 2008 to 2015, were comparable to the effects of a continuous reduction of approximately 200 to 250 basis points in the policy interest rate. If a larger quantity of purchases had been made, the effects could have been even more substantial, scaling up proportionately (Ball et al., 2016, p. 2).

[11]The potential drawbacks of expansionary monetary policy have been emphasized. These concerns include the possibility of an inflationary surge caused by an overshoot, the risk of asset price bubbles, disruptions to the banking system such as disintermediation and hoarding of cash, challenges to the profitability of banks and/or the central bank, potential threats to monetary policy independence, and perceived distributional effects. However, there is currently limited evidence of significant adverse side effects. Generally, these risks are diminished during the depressed conditions that typically accompany a liquidity trap. If any adverse effects do arise, they can be mitigated or managed effectively (Ball et al., 2016, p. 2).

role in expediting recovery from a severe recession and lessening the reliance on monetary policy. The analysis primarily focuses on the capabilities of central banks; thus, we do not delve into fiscal policy extensively. Nonetheless, we briefly touch upon the concept of *helicopter money*, which refers to the combined use of fiscal and monetary policy.

8.3.1 Helicopter Money: A Bird's-Eye View

While QE operates by affecting the cost of finance like standard monetary policy, helicopter money policies aim to distribute liquid purchasing power directly to individuals or entities who are more inclined to spend it. This approach combines elements of QE with a significant fiscal component, which goes beyond the typical mandate of central banks. Helicopter money is regarded as a potent policy tool due to its coordinated fiscal and monetary nature, although it falls outside the scope of this analysis; for further insights, refer to Friedman (1969), Ball et al. (2016), and Cecchetti and Schoenholtz (2020). Helicopter money refers to a situation where the central bank directly funds government spending. In such cases, the fiscal authority, through its management of debt, has control over the central bank's balance sheet size. This arrangement involves monetary finance resulting from fiscal dominance, where the fiscal authority takes over the role of the independent central bank in determining the amount of base money (which includes currency and bank reserves held at the central bank) with the aim of increasing seigniorage (Cecchetti and Schoenholtz 2020).[12]

Following the global financial crisis (GFC), central banks found themselves with limited options to use traditional monetary policy tools, which primarily affect the short-term funding costs of financial intermediaries. As a result, they introduced new instruments that allowed for more direct and targeted actions, such as significant purchases of different types of assets, including government securities. These facilities have been re-established or expanded in response to the COVID-19 crisis. The European Central Bank has refrained from implementing direct measures primarily due to provisions outlined in European treaties, which emphasize the separation between monetary and fiscal responsibilities (Bartsch et al., 2020, p. 11). While the ECB has introduced targeted longer-term refinancing operations (TLTROs) since 2014, these operations primarily support the lending activities of financial institutions in general, rather than targeting specific borrower categories. The role of financial institutions as gatekeepers remains intact.

The ultimate example of a go-direct strategy would involve the implementation of helicopter money, in which the central bank openly assumes a fiscal role and directly

[12] Fiscal policy need not be "helicopter" money, while "helicopter" money is *always* fiscal policy. Indeed, as Cecchetti and Schoenholtz (2020) describe, helicopter money is *not* monetary policy. If the Fed were to drop $100 bills out of helicopters, it would be doing the Treasury's bidding.

provides liquidity to economic agents. This approach would effectively merge monetary and fiscal policies, leading to significant practical and conceptual challenges. Various studies and discussions by Reichlin et al. (2013), Buiter (2014), Bernanke (2016), Blanchard and Pisani-Ferry (2019), and Gali (2020) have explored the implications and complexities of helicopter money. Another noteworthy aspect of the go-direct approach is the expansion of the central banks' traditional role as the lender of last resort to include acting as "market makers of last resort," aiming to prevent the destabilization of specific financial market segments; for further analysis of these developments, see Bartsch et al. (2020), specifically Chap. 3. Cecchetti and Schoenholtz (2020) provides a concise overview of helicopter money. The process is relatively simple: initially, the fiscal authority issues a bond directly to the central bank instead of offering it to the general public. In return, the fiscal agent receives a credit to its deposit account. Subsequently, the funds are distributed either through the purchase of goods or services or by directly transferring the money to an individual or a company. The recipient then deposits the funds into their bank account, causing a transfer of liability on the central bank's balance sheet from the government's account to the reserve account of the commercial bank. Yet, helicopter money differs from the central bank's large-scale purchases of government bonds. In the case of QE, which has become well-known, the central bank expands its balance sheet by purchasing government bonds on the open market and crediting the reserve account of the seller's commercial bank.

At first glance, the effect on the central bank's balance sheet from a QE operation appears similar to that of a helicopter money distribution combined with a government transfer: both scenarios result in an equal increase in government bond assets and liabilities in the reserve accounts of commercial banks. However, there is a crucial distinction between these two policies. In the case of helicopter money, the central bank directly receives bonds from the government, as it is obligated to purchase them in the primary market at the request of the fiscal authority. Moreover, the scale of the helicopter money distribution is determined by the government, not the central bank. On the other hand, in the case of quantitative easing, the central bank independently determines the amount of assets to acquire and purchases them in the secondary market. This allows the central bank to maintain control over the size of its balance sheet. The latter approach aligns with the actions of an independent central bank, while the former does not.

Bernanke (2016) contended that despite the constraints posed by already low interest rates, the Federal Reserve has alternative policy instruments at its disposal. These include providing forward guidance on future rate policies, implementing further quantitative easing measures, and targeting longer-term rates. However, as long as individuals have the option to hold physical currency, there are inherent limits to the extent to which the Federal Reserve or any central bank can reduce interest rates.[13] Furthermore, the advantages of low rates may diminish over time,

[13]Rogoff (2015) has discussed the costs and benefits of eliminating paper currency, at least bills of large denominations.

while the associated costs are likely to escalate. As a result, there comes a point where the efficacy of monetary policy experiences diminishing returns.

When traditional monetary policy measures prove insufficient to stimulate economic recovery or prevent low inflation, fiscal policy emerges as a potent alternative, particularly when interest rates remain close to zero. However, in recent times, legislative bodies in advanced industrial economies have been hesitant to employ fiscal tools, primarily due to concerns regarding already high government debt levels. In this context, the concept of "helicopter money," as proposed by Milton Friedman, has garnered attention and support from influential figures such as Adair Turner, Willem Buiter, and Jordi Gali. Bernanke (2016) explores the viability of helicopter money as a potential last-resort strategy for policymakers. Bernanke (2016) makes two key points: Firstly, in theory, helicopter money could be a valuable instrument, particularly because it can be effective even when conventional monetary policies fail and government debt is already elevated. However, secondly, the practical implementation of helicopter money raises challenging issues. These include integrating this approach with existing monetary policy frameworks and ensuring the necessary coordination between fiscal and monetary policymakers without compromising central bank independence or long-term fiscal discipline. Bernanke (2016) puts forward some preliminary solutions to address these concerns.

As Bernanke accepts when he discussed the concept in 2002 (Bernanke, 2016), the concept of "helicopter money" can be unsettling for many individuals. However, employing unrealistic scenarios can sometimes serve as an effective means of grasping the core of an issue.[14] Although it is evident that no responsible government would actually distribute money from the sky, this should not deter us from examining the rationale behind Friedman's hypothetical experiment. Its purpose was to demonstrate, albeit in extreme terms, why governments should never be compelled to succumb to deflation. A "helicopter drop" of money refers to an expansionary fiscal policy, which involves a boost in public spending or a tax reduction, funded by a permanent increase in the money stock. Friedman's example corresponded specifically to a money-financed tax cut. To move away from the imaginative imagery, this policy may better be referred as a money-financed fiscal program. The theoretical advantage of a money-financed fiscal program is that it can impact the economy through various channels, making it highly probable to be effective, *even if government debt is already substantial or interest rates are at or below zero.* According to Bernanke (2016), these channels would include (1) the direct effects of the public works spending on GDP, jobs, and income; (2) the increase in household income from the rebate, which should induce greater consumer spending; (3) a temporary increase in expected inflation, the result of the increase in the money supply (In situations where nominal interest rates are close to

[14]When Albert Einstein was formulating the principles of special relativity, he employed the technique of thought experiments. These involved hypothetical scenarios such as trains and elevators moving at high speeds in empty space. Despite their unrealistic nature, these examples played a crucial role in developing Einstein's understanding and intuition, proving their value in contemplating the real world of physics (Bernanke, 2016).

zero, the upsurge in expected inflation leads to a reduction in real interest rates. This, in turn, encourages capital investments and other forms of expenditure.); and (4) the fact that, unlike debt-financed fiscal programs, a money-financed program does not increase future tax burdens. "Tax burdens" refer to the actual tax payments made to the government. While it is true that higher inflation effectively acts as a tax on money holdings, this tax only becomes significant if there is an actual increase in inflation. Such an increase in inflation would indicate that the program is successfully achieving its objective of stimulating spending (Bernanke, 2016).

Conventional fiscal programs, which are financed through debt issuance, also operate through the same channels mentioned above, namely, (1) and (2). However, in the standard case, where increased spending or tax cuts are funded by issuing debt, future costs of servicing the debt and subsequent tax burdens rise. This anticipation of future taxes or the general awareness of increased national debt may cause households to reduce their current spending, thereby offsetting some of the expansionary impact of the program.[15] On the other hand, a fiscal expansion funded through the creation of money does not raise government debt or result in higher future tax payments for households. As a result, it is expected to have a greater impact on household spending, assuming other factors remain constant—channel (iv). Additionally, the increase in the money supply resulting from the money-financed fiscal program should lead to higher anticipated inflation—channel (3)—which is seen as a favorable outcome in this context. This distinguishes it from debt-financed fiscal policies.

On whether it is possible for the central bank to implement a money-financed fiscal program independently, an alternative approach labeled "quantitative easing for people" has been proposed (Muellbauer, 2014; Coppola, 2019), where the central bank creates money and distributes it directly to the public. From a purely economic standpoint, "QE for people" would be equivalent to a money-financed tax cut, similar to Friedman's original concept of a helicopter drop, but potentially more targeted. In particular, with reference to the Eurozone, Muellbauer (2014) argues that QE in its standard form is bound to be less effective than in the United States because the housing collateral channel does not work in the core Eurozone and the down payment constraint for mortgages is far tighter than in the United States and households in the Eurozone hold far less in equities relative to income than do US households, so the undisputed uplift on consumer spending from higher stock market valuations is small compared to that in the United States. However, the

[15] In a "Ricardian economy," where households possess perfect foresight and have the ability to borrow and lend without restrictions, a temporary tax cut is expected to have no impact on consumer spending. In this theoretical economy, households understand that the tax cut does not improve their overall financial situation, as the additional funds received through the tax cut are offset by the present value of their future tax obligations. However, empirical evidence suggests that the adjustment of expected future taxes against current income is not completely offset. This means that tax cuts, even if financed through debt, still influence household spending to some extent. On the other hand, fiscal spending, such as investments in public infrastructure, has an impact on output and incomes even in a hypothetical Ricardian economy (Bernanke, 2016).

issue with this policy is not its economic rationale, but rather its political legitimacy (Bernanke, 2016). It would likely be deemed illegal in most jurisdictions as the distribution of funds, which effectively act as tax rebates, should be subject to legislative approval rather than unilaterally determined by the central bank.

8.3.2 Helicopter Money: How Does It Work?

Due to the cash or liquidity constraints faced by several households (and these include those that possess liquid assets only sufficient to meet their precautionary savings or buffer-stock motives), if they were to receive funds through a helicopter money distribution, they would likely spend a significant portion of it. Similar effects on spending can be observed with other types of government expenditures if accompanied by supportive monetary measures such as quantitative easing, which prevents an undesired increase in bond yields. Conversely, if market expectations suggest that monetary policy will be tightened in the future following a "helicopter money" measure, it could dampen the overall impact on aggregate demand. This is because no central bank can definitively commit to never reducing the base money created through helicopter money (Ball et al., 2016). In fact, under certain circumstances, the long-term effect of helicopter money on aggregate demand can be demonstrated to be equivalent to that of a deficit financed by government bonds.[16]

The appeal of "helicopter money" lies in its potential to provide a short-term stimulus to demand. It is primarily useful in situations where market imperfections have led to an imbalance in the macroeconomy, with aggregate demand being too low. By injecting liquidity into the hands of economically constrained agents who can immediately spend it, helicopter money has the potential to effectively boost spending in such circumstances. The overall impact on spending in these conditions is unlikely to be completely offset by long-term expectations of future interest rate increases and the corresponding tax burden, which may have different implications.

The purpose of helicopter money policies is not simply to increase the monetary base per se, but rather to stimulate spending by addressing existing constraints on spending. Similar to other easing measures, the effectiveness of helicopter money can be diminished if inadequate communication surrounding the policy announcement leads market participants to reassess risks in a negative manner. While it is conceivable for helicopter money to be implemented solely by the central bank as an independent action aligned with its mandate, this would extend beyond the typical role of central banking. The concern does not primarily lie in the distributional effects of allocating spending power to households or other economic agents, as this

[16] As an illustration, the eventual normalization of central bank policy may necessitate higher interest rates to address the surplus liquidity. This adjustment could have negative consequences for the combined income statements of both the central bank and the government, resulting in a similar net outcome as if the deficit had been financed through bonds, as discussed in Ball et al. (2016), Borio et al. (2016), and Buiter (2014).

is also true of conventional monetary policy. Rather, the concern arises from the direct and intentional distributional effects that impact specific recipients. Unlike open market purchases, for example, which affect all market participants, the chosen recipients of helicopter money are directly impacted. As, for example, Ball et al. (2016) argue, the question arises of what authority does the central bank have to determine how spending power is distributed.[17]

Therefore, recognizing the fiscal implications of distributing cash through helicopter money measures, a collaborative agreement between the central bank and the government could be considered. However, such a joint decision would significantly undermine the independence of the central bank, as it would involve determining monetary accommodation based on fiscal considerations, rather than solely focusing on monetary and macroeconomic stability. In fact, the establishment of central bank independence was primarily motivated by the desire to prevent the central bank's policies from being influenced by fiscal requirements. The central bank can maintain its independence by adjusting its monetary policy measures to fulfill its mandate, considering the fiscal policy actions as given. This approach allows the central bank to uphold monetary stability and prevent any prolonged delay in exiting the helicopter money policy.

However, in order to ensure a secure implementation of fiscal expansion, the fiscal authority needs to be aware of the anticipated response from the monetary authority to an increased deficit. Therefore, helicopter money would entail a coordinated effort between fiscal and monetary authorities, with each entity considering the actions of the other and sharing a mutual understanding of the current economic conditions and policy requirements. Therefore, helicopter money can be understood as a fusion of fiscal and monetary measures that stimulate spending among individuals who are currently limited by a lack of cash. Ideally, it is the result of independent actions taken by both fiscal and monetary authorities, with each entity considering and coordinating their efforts with the other. Nevertheless, while policymakers possess tools to stimulate the economy when interest rates are near zero, ensuring full employment would be more assured if policy frameworks were modified to minimize or eliminate the possibility of nominal rates reaching zero.[18]

[17] Should the same amount of cash be distributed to every citizen, resident, adult, or household? Should the amount be based on household income or income tax liability? These questions pertain to fiscal policy and are within the purview of the government, rather than the central bank. In the context of the Eurozone, should the amount be uniform across member states despite significant differences in average income levels? These considerations are important as the potential impact is substantial. For instance, if the monthly volume of quantitative easing currently implemented by the ECB were instead evenly distributed among the population of the Eurozone, it would result in a significant increase of over 25% in annual personal income, particularly in lower-income countries like Latvia, Lithuania, and Slovakia (Ball et al., 2016, p. 45).

[18] One possible adjustment that could mitigate the lower bound on nominal interest rates is a moderate increase in the inflation targets set by central banks (see Kokores, 2022, pp. 353–363). The recent low levels of nominal interest rates stem from both lower real interest rates and the relatively low inflation targets typically maintained by central banks in advanced economies, often at 2% or below. By raising the inflation target to, for instance, 3% or 4%, the frequency at which the

8.3.3 The Trend Toward a Cashless Society

Ball et al. (2016) examined the potential solution for eliminating the lower bound on nominal interest rates, namely, the ongoing shift toward a society without physical cash. The presence of cash, represented by currency notes, which is an asset provided by the central bank with a fixed nominal return of zero, is the fundamental cause of the lower bound. Without the existence of cash, there would be no lower limit, allowing policymakers to implement negative interest rates as required to stimulate a robust and swift economic rebound during periods of downturn. In particular, they remark:

> Cash is steadily being replaced by new electronic means of payments in retail transactions. This trend is likely to gain pace, driven by market forces, and eventually cash will become redundant in most countries. Some countries are already well on the way. An abrupt abolition of cash in order to facilitate an immediate move to deeply negative interest rates is clearly both politically and practically unrealistic. Yet, someday, the existence of cash may be remembered in the same way as the gold standard—an obsolete payments technology whose persistence hampered economic performance. (p. 3)

The prospect of cashless economies presents a potential solution to completely eliminate the lower bound on interest rates. Without the existence of cash as a riskless asset with zero nominal return, central banks would have the flexibility to set negative nominal interest rates as necessary to stimulate economic recoveries during recessions. The advancement of payment technologies has already led some countries to make significant progress in reducing cash usage, and the COVID-19 pandemic has further accelerated this trend. While an immediate and abrupt transition to cashless economies with deeply negative interest rates is not currently feasible due to practical and political constraints, there is a possibility that future generations may inhabit such economies where the challenges posed by the lower bound on interest rates are no longer prominent.

8.4 Monetary Policy in a Post-Cash Economy

The adoption of electronic payment systems is currently driven by market forces, and the COVID-19 pandemic has further accelerated this trend. Cash usage is diminishing in most countries and is expected to continue declining in the future. The increasing popularity of card payments as an alternative to cash has been

economy reaches the zero bound and the associated risk of persistent underemployment could be significantly reduced. The decline of the equilibrium real interest rate and the severity of the Great Recession have shifted the cost-benefit analysis in favor of a higher inflation target. While transitioning to a higher inflation target may involve tactical challenges, concerns about destabilizing inflation expectations or undermining central bank credibility are exaggerated. In fact, central banks are likely to enhance their credibility by demonstrating their capacity to adapt to changing circumstances in a deliberate and measured manner (Ball et al., 2016, pp. 2–3).

observed for several years, and recently, there has been a rapid growth in the utilization of mobile contactless payment systems in certain countries (e.g., China or Kenya). The COVID-19 pandemic has significantly expedited this shift toward cashless payments. In a full electronic payment system where physical currency is eliminated, there is no physical asset that maintains a fixed nominal value, which means that market participants cannot avoid nominal negative interest rates. In such a scenario, the conventional monetary policy tool, the short-term policy rate, can theoretically be reduced below zero to any level considered appropriate by the central bank in order to fulfill its objectives.[19]

In cashless economies where monetary policy is not limited by a lower bound, there may be scope for lower optimal inflation targets compared to current levels. While the immediate phasing out of cash is not a viable policy option, considering the concerns surrounding the rapid spread of COVID-19, we anticipate that market-driven advancements in payment systems will lead to the inevitability of cashless societies in many countries in the near future. This transformation in payment systems is not unprecedented in history, as evidenced by past developments such as the nationalization of money in the seventeenth century, the transition from gold to fiat currency in the twentieth century (see James, 2015), and the elimination of national currencies in European countries in 1999, which were all significant changes. However, the transition to cashless economies may not be without challenges, as payment habits and public perceptions regarding the role of cash and negative interest rates may persistently influence the process. According to Ball et al. (2016), certain countries have made significant progress in embracing electronic payment systems, positioning them at the forefront of the potential phaseout of cash in a manner that is socially responsible. This development offers a potential solution to the challenge posed by the lower bound on interest rates. The authors go on to explore the implications of monetary policy in cashless economies and also address various policy considerations associated with the current usage of cash and the transition toward an economy that relies less on physical currency.

Merely replacing cash with electronic money in the payment system is insufficient to eliminate the lower bound on interest rates. As long as physical cash remains in circulation, monetary policy will remain constrained by this lower bound. To completely remove this constraint, it would be necessary to completely suspend the convertibility of central bank reserves into cash. However, such a step would typically require legal measures in most countries, and public opinion may hinder

[19] For instance, it becomes feasible to set deposit and lending rates at significant negative levels when cash is not an option. If individuals and institutions had the ability to hold physical currency, it would result in a massive shift toward cash, rendering the targeted negative interest rates by the central bank ineffective as nobody would be willing to borrow or lend at such rates. However, the absence of cash eliminates this concern. Rogoff (2014) and Lilley and Rogoff (2020) have notably advocated for the elimination of cash as it would remove the lower bound on interest rates in a cashless monetary system. In addition to this argument, Rogoff (2014) case is also widely recognized for its emphasis on reducing the societal costs associated with illicit activities facilitated by cash usage (Ball et al., 2016, p. 63).

or delay the implementation even if cash is no longer necessary for transactions. Negative interest rates are not widely accepted or understood by the public, partly due to the concept of money illusion, which may lead individuals to hold on to cash as a safeguard against the introduction of negative interest rates by central banks. However, over time, perceptions and understanding may change as experiences with negative policy rates unfold. Effective communication by central banks can play a role in shaping these evolving perceptions and understanding.[20]

Actively promoting the transition to a cashless economy could serve as a long-term strategy for certain countries to mitigate the challenges posed by the lower bound constraint on monetary policy. However, it is important to recognize that phasing out cash and eliminating the lower bound are not viable solutions during times of crisis. Such a transition would require extensive changes to monetary and payment systems, as well as the fundamental nature of money, which cannot be implemented rapidly. As long as society is not fully equipped with inclusive cashless retail payment options that cater to all segments of the population, cash will continue to play a role. This implies the need for an interim period in the journey toward a cashless payment system, where alternative monetary policy tools must be employed to address situations when the lower bound on interest rates become binding. Potential interim measures may include temporarily raising the inflation target, implementing modestly negative interest rates, and utilizing quantitative easing.

An alternative temporary approach, suggested by Buiter (2007, 2009) and Agarwal and Kimball (2015), involves separating the value of cash from electronic money and allowing them to function as distinct currencies with a controlled exchange rate set by the central bank. Under this system, the central bank could gradually devalue cash in relation to electronic money, effectively generating a negative yield on cash compared to electronic money. This approach would eliminate the lower bound on interest rates while still maintaining cash as a medium of exchange. However, there are numerous unresolved issues associated with the implementation of such a system. Notably, it would require legal and structural modifications that typically fall outside the purview of the central bank's authority.[21]

---

[20] In a cashless economy, monetary policy can function below zero in the same manner as it operates above the lower bound. Central bank reserves would continue to serve as the anchor and reference currency, just as central bank reserves and cash currently constitute the reference currency. The existing frameworks for inflation targeting can remain in place if they are deemed suitable for achieving price and macroeconomic stability. However, the benefits and costs associated with a higher inflation target would undergo a change. While many of the benefits and costs outlined in Ball et al. (2016, Chap. 4) would still be relevant, the advantage of higher inflation in terms of circumventing the lower bound constraint on monetary policy would no longer exist. In fact, in cashless economies, future inflation targets may be even lower than the current targets, as the current low inflation targets may already account for a small but nonzero probability of encountering the lower bound. To accommodate such changes in optimal inflation targets, it would be advisable to adopt a periodic review process that ensures the inflation target remains aligned with the central bank's mandate over time.

[21] An instance of this is the issue of legal tender. The existing legal framework that governs financial contracts stipulates the accepted forms of payment, typically referring to the domestic legal tender.

To summarize, the widespread adoption of electronic payment systems driven by market forces, along with concerns over the rapid spread of COVID-19, is pushing many countries toward a nearly cashless state. In such fully cashless economies, there is no limit to how low interest rates can go, allowing monetary policy to function equally effectively above and below zero. Embracing a cashless approach would enable enhanced macroeconomic stability and potentially lower inflation targets compared to economies where the lower bound on interest rates poses a constraint on monetary policy.

The pace at which countries are transitioning to cashless systems and whether it is seen as a desirable goal from a public policy perspective are contingent upon how challenges related to social inclusion in electronic payment systems and privacy concerns are perceived and addressed. These considerations are influenced by varying social norms and preferences across countries. In most countries, cash is expected to remain a part of retail payment systems for a significant period, making it worthwhile to consider the proposal of raising the inflation target, as discussed earlier. Implementing a periodic review process for the inflation target would enable central banks to make adjustments over time while mitigating the potential risk of damaging their credibility.

8.5 So What Should Be Done?

The implementation of quantitative easing and negative nominal policy interest rates in advanced economies may seem unconventional and extraordinary. However, it is more accurate to view these measures as the application of a conventional approach to monetary policy within a postrecession context characterized by low inflation and sluggish economic recovery. Throughout history, adjusting the cost of financing by participating in asset markets has been the customary practice of central banks for many centuries. Central banks, driven by their commitment to achieving their mandates, have demonstrated that the lower bound of zero does not present an insurmountable obstacle for nominal interest rates. They have successfully utilized large-scale purchases of long-term or risky securities to reduce term and risk premiums, resulting in higher asset prices and stimulating overall economic demand. These measures have had a significant impact on the macroeconomy, leading to a greater degree of output and employment recovery compared to what would have been achieved without these policies. However, it is important to note that the pace of output and employment recovery has been relatively sluggish compared to previous severe recessions. Additionally, the recovery process remains unfinished in many economies, particularly in the Eurozone and Japan.

In the case of two domestic currencies coexisting, there would be two legal tenders with distinct values. Resolving this matter would necessitate contentious legal reforms.

While these tools have certain limitations and are not without their drawbacks, they are far from being depleted. The presence of a liquidity trap has indeed posed challenges to monetary policy, but it has not rendered it entirely ineffectual. The notion that monetary policy is inconsequential has been historically proven to be a highly erroneous and perilous belief (Romer & Romer, 2013). Prior to the emergence of inflation in mid-2021, it has been proposed that in the case of a central bank facing below-target inflation and inadequate aggregate demand, it has the ability to adhere to the following:

1. To lower nominal policy rates below zero is an option for the central bank in such circumstances. Rates can be reduced significantly, potentially even reaching as low as -2% on a temporary basis. By implementing lower rates, a more robust economic stimulus can be achieved, with any negative consequences being manageable. The duration of negative interest rates required would be shorter if the downturn can be reversed more swiftly.
2. Increase the magnitude and range of asset purchases, also known as quantitative easing (QE). Although the extent to which QE can be utilized may differ among economies due to factors such as financial market structure and legal constraints on central bank authority, the potential negative repercussions (such as potential financial losses for the central bank) are not as substantial as commonly believed. Implementing a forceful QE strategy could provide a macroeconomic stimulus equivalent to reducing the policy interest rate by a range of 2–6 percentage points and potentially even more.
3. Contemplate the possibility of adopting a higher inflation target, even if only for a temporary period. Simply announcing a higher target may not be seen as credible if the current target is consistently missed. However, if supported by the aforementioned measures of pushing nominal rates below zero and expanding asset purchases, it could enhance inflation expectations and consequently reduce the real interest rate in practice, given a fixed nominal rate.

We acknowledge that the central bank's role becomes more challenging in an environment of weak demand and low or negative inflation, particularly in the absence of sufficient utilization of fiscal policy. The resurgence of proposals like "helicopter money," which involve the central bank directly transferring spending power to households, presents a potential method to stimulate the economy in a liquidity trap. A more effective combination of policies would undoubtedly lead to improved economic performance overall.

However, the increasing prevalence of electronic payments is diminishing the necessity of cash in today's economy. The gradual transition toward a cashless society is almost certain to occur and will be a less significant transformation compared to the shift from commodity money to fiat money. While the complete elimination of cash is not an immediate possibility, even with the recent impact of COVID-19, ongoing technological advancements, which can be encouraged by regulatory measures, bring us closer to that eventual outcome while still ensuring social inclusion in the payment system. In a society without cash, the presence of a lower bound on nominal interest rates is not apparent, allowing monetary policy to more effectively respond to and reverse economic downturns.

8.6 Monetary Policy in Uncharted Waters: Implications of Uncertainty

The primary concern of a central bank when determining an appropriate approach to monetary policy is to ensure favorable financial conditions that promote high employment and low inflation in the future. To gain insight into the economic outlook, various tools are utilized, including macroeconometric models that aim to capture the interconnectedness of economic variables in the real world through systems of equations. These models come in different forms and sizes and, when provided with up-to-date information and assumptions, generate numerical predictions for factors such as income growth, inflation rates, and unemployment rates in the upcoming timeframe. The current concerns regarding macro models are significant and raise doubts on multiple fronts. Some of these concerns are linked to the state of the present economy, while others are emerging independently, adding to the overall scrutiny of these models. The accuracy of economic forecasts is generally highest when the real-world economic conditions align closely with the period from which the model's equations were derived. However, when the questions being asked fall outside the range of the model's structure, its ability to provide reliable answers diminishes significantly. As a result, the forecasts generated by these models are considerably less dependable than they would be in normal circumstances.

Given the heightened uncertainties surrounding macroeconometric models, including the reliability of their forecasts, as well as the questions surrounding the exploitable Phillips curve and the stability of the money demand equation, monetary policymakers face a challenging situation. In such circumstances, it becomes crucial for policymakers to exercise caution and consider alternative approaches to inform their decision-making.[22]

[22]Milton Friedman has fervently advocated for a consistent approach, suggesting that policymakers should maintain a steady course and refrain from intervention. However, proponents of the natural rate rational expectation hypothesis have emerged, challenging the notion that there exists a trade-off between inflation and unemployment even in the short run. They argued that unemployment is influenced by factors such as labor force characteristics, technological advancements, capital-output ratios, wage flexibility, and unexpected policy actions while contending that the choice of a policy rule cannot systematically impact unemployment. Additionally, supporters of "optimal control theory" (Brayton et al., 2014) echoed similar sentiments albeit with different reasoning, since, while acknowledging the existence of a trade-off, their viewpoint emphasized that in the face of increased uncertainty regarding economic relationships, an uncomplicated (non-feedback) rule advocating steady growth in monetary aggregates is more likely to yield optimal outcomes.

However, a significant challenge emerges as individuals become aware of the inherent uncertainties associated with model outcomes, and they understandably perceive the reliability of the estimates to diminish as the projections extend further into the future. Consequently, policymakers tend to discard or overlook values beyond a timeframe of four to six quarters. Yet it is precisely in the distant quarters that the price and wage impacts of policy stimuli become evident. These individuals are misusing the model by reacting inaccurately to heightened uncertainty regarding future forecasts. Instead of dismissing the projections and advocating for an active short-term policy, they should be contemplating a more measured policy approach (for a long-standing argument on this issue, see, for example, MacLaury, 1976).

Therefore, although the heightened uncertainties surrounding the accuracy and stability of macroeconometric models imply a more restrained approach to policymaking, there is still a lack of consensus regarding the most effective manner in which to fulfill these responsibilities.

References

Agarwal, R., & Kimball, M. S. (2015). Breaking through the zero lower bound. *IMF Working Paper* No. 15/224, International Monetary Fund, Washington DC, USA.

Ball, L., Gagnon, J., Honohan, P., & Krogstrup, S. (2016). *What Else can central banks do?* Geneva reports on the world economy 18, International Centre for Monetary and Banking Studies, Geneva Switzerland & CEPR-Centre for Economic Policy Research, London, UK.

Barro, R. J., & Gordon, D. B. (1983a). A positive theory of monetary policy in a natural rate model. *Journal of Political Economy, 91*(4), 589–610.

Barro, R. J., & Gordon, D. B. (1983b). Rules, discretion and reputation in a model of monetary policy. *Journal of Monetary Economics, 12*(1), 101–121.

Bartsch, E., Benassy-Queré, A., Corsetti, G., & Debrun, X. (2020). It's all in the mix: How can monetary and fiscal policies work or fail together. *Geneva reports on the world economy* 23, International Centre of Monetary and Banking Studies, Geneva, Switzerland, and Centre for Economic Policy Research, London, UK.

Bernanke, Ben (2003). A perspective on inflation targeting. Remarks the US Federal Reserve Governor at the Annual Washington Policy Conference of the National Association for Business Economics, Washington, DC, USA, March 25.

Bernanke, B. S. (2010). Central Bank Independence, transparency, and accountability. *Speech* delivered at the Institute for Monetary and Economic Studies International Conference, Bank of Japan, Tokyo, Japan, May 25.

Bernanke, B. S. (2016). What tools does the fed have left? Part 3: Helicopter money. Brookings advisory perspectives, 11 April.

Bernanke, B. S. (2017). Monetary policy in a new era. Speech, Brookings Institution, Hutchins Center on Fiscal and Monetary Policy, Washington, DC, USA, October 2nd.

Blanchard, O., & Pisani-Ferry, J. (2019). The euro area is not (yet) ready for helicopter money. Peterson Institute for International Economics, November, Peterson Institute for International Economics, Washington, DC, USA.

Blinder, A., Ehrmann, M., de Haan, J., & Jansen, D.-J. (2017). Necessity as the mother of invention: Monetary policy after the crisis. *ECB working paper series* no 2047, April, European Central Bank, Frankfurt Am Main, Germany.

Blinder, A. S. (1996). Central banking in a democracy. Federal Reserve Bank of Richmond. *Economic Quarterly, 82*, 1–14.

Board of Governors of the Federal Reserve System. (2023). Statement on longer-run goals and monetary policy strategy, adopted effective January 24, 2012; as reaffirmed effective January 31, 2023.

Borio, C., Disyatat, P., & Zabai, A. (2016). Helicopter money: The illusion of a free lunch. VoxeEU.org, 24 May.

Brayton, F., Laubach, T., & Reifschneider, D. (2014). Optimal-control monetary policy in the FRB/US model. In *FEDS notes*. Board of Governors of the Federal Reserve System.

Brunnermeier, M. K. (2023). Rethinking monetary policy in a changing world. *Finance & Development 'New Directions for Monetary Policy'*, 60(1), International Monetary Fund, March, pp 6–9.

Buiter, W. H. (2007). Is Numérairology the future of monetary economics? Unbundling numéraire and medium of exchange through a virtual currency with a shadow exchange rate. *Open Economies Review, 18*, 127–156.

Buiter, W. H. (2009). Negative nominal interest rates: Three ways to overcome the zero lower bound. *North American Journal of Economics and Finance, 20*(3), 213–238.

Buiter, W. H. (2014). The simple analytics of helicopter money: Why it works—always. *Economics, 8*(August).

Cecchetti, S. G., & Schoenholtz, K. L. (2020). Helicopters to the rescue? *Money and Banking Blogpost*. May 10. Available online: https://www.moneyandbanking.com/commentary/2020/5/10/helicopters-to-the-rescue

Coppola, F. (2019). *The case for People's quantitative easing* (Book series the case for). Polity.

Cukierman, A. (1992). *Central Bank strategy, credibility, and Independence: Theory and evidence*. MIT Press.

Debelle, G., & Fischer, S. (1994). How independent should a Central Bank be? *Proceedings* of the conference on '*Goals, Guidelines, and Constraints Facing Monetary Policymakers*', North Falmouth, Massachusetts, in June 1994 (pp. 195–221). Boston: Federal Reserve Bank of Boston.

ECB—European Central Bank. (2015). The Role of the Central Bank Balance Sheet in Monetary Policy. ECB Monthly Bulletin Issue 4, (pp. 61–77), ECB—European Central Bank, Frankfurt Am Main, Germany.

Fahr, S., Motto, R., Rostagno, M., & Smets, F. (2011). Lessons for monatary policy: Strategies from the recent past. In M. Jarociήki, F. Smets, & C. Thimann (Eds.), *Approaches to monetary policy revisited – lessons from the crisis, sixth ECB central banking conference proceedings* (pp. 26–66).

Friedman, M. (1968). "Should There Be an Independent Monetary Authority?" In Leland B. Yeager (Ed.), In Search of a Monetary Constitution, Harvard University Press, Cambridge, Massachusetts, 1962. Reprinted in Friedman, Milton, *Dollars and Deficits*, Prentice Hall, Englewood Cliffs, 1968.

Friedman, M. (1969). *The optimal quantity of money and other essays*. Aldine.

Gali, J. (2020). The effects of a money-financed fiscal stimulus. *Journal of Monetary Economics, 115*(C), 1–19.

James, H. (2015). "Dual Currencies". *Presentation* at the CEPR, Imperial College and SNB conference 'Removing the Zero Lower Bound On Interest Rates", London, 18 May.

Kokores, I. T. (2022). *Monetary policy and financial stability: Challenges before and after the global financial crisis*. Cambridge Scholars Publishing.

Kydland, F. E., & Prescott, E. C. (1977). Rules rather than discretion: The inconsistency of optimal plans. *Journal of Political Economy, 85*(3), 473–492.

Lilley, A., & Rogoff, K. (2020). The case for implementing effective negative interest rate policy. In J. H. Cochrane & J. B. Taylor (Eds.), *Strategies for monetary policy* (Vol. Chapter 2, pp. 27–69). Hoover Institution Press. Barnes & Noble.

MacLaury, B. K. (1976). *Monetary policy in uncharted waters* (pp. 11–16). Federal Reserve Bank of Minnesota.

Muellbauer, J. (2014). Combating Eurozone deflation: QE for the people. VoxEU. CEPR, December, 23.

Orphanides, A. (2014). The need for a price stability mandate. *Cato Journal, 34*(2), 265–279.

Orphanides, A. (2018). The boundaries of Central Bank independence: Lessons from unconventional times. *Bank of Japan Monetary and Economic Studies*, 35–56.

Powell, J. H. (2023). *Panel* on 'Central Bank Independence and the Mandate—Evolving Views'. Remarks. Symposium on Central Bank Independence, Sveriges Riksbank, Stockholm, Sweden, January 10.

Reichlin, L., Turner, A., & Woodford, M. (2013). Helicopter money as a policy option. VoxEU.org.

Rogoff, K. S. (1985). The optimal degree of commitment to an intermediate monetary target. *Quarterly Journal of Economics, 100*(4), 1169–1189.

Rogoff, K. S. (2014). Costs and benefits to phasing out paper currency. NBER working paper, no. 20126, Cambridge MA: National Bureau of Economic Research

Rogoff, K. S. (2015). Costs and benefits to phasing out paper currency. In J. A. Parker & M. Woodford (Eds.), *NBER macroeconomics annual 2014* (Vol. 29, pp. 445–456). University of Chicago Press.

Romer, C. D., & Romer, D. H. (2013). The Most dangerous idea in federal reserve history: Monetary policy doesn't matter. *American Economic Review, 103*, 55–60.

Thorbecke, W. (2002). A dual mandate for the federal reserve: The pursuit of price stability and full employment. *Eastern Economic Journal, 28*(2), 255–268.

Tucker, P. (2018a). The governance of monetary and financial stability policy. Banking perspectives. *The Clearing House. Quarter, 2*, 50–57.

Tucker, P. (2018b). *Unelected power: The quest for legitimacy in central banking and the regulatory state*. Princeton University Press.

Wood, J. H. (2015). *Central banking in a democracy: The Federal Reserve and its alternatives* (Routledge explorations in economic history). Routledge.

Wyplosz, C. (2021). The ECB's new definition of price stability: Better but short of specifics. Monetary dialogue. In-depth analysis PE 695.437 requested by the ECON Committee, Policy Department for Economic, Scientific and Quality of Life Policies Directorate-General for Internal Policies, European Parliament, November.

Chapter 9
Looking to the Future: Monetary Policy in Uncharted Waters

> I ask you to contemplate and think about what Paul Volcker did in 1982. This is the Paul Volcker who engineered, … policies from 1979 until 1982, to break the back of America's stagflation. He set us on the right course. … In the summer of 1982 Volcker saw that the recession was not ending when he thought it would; and he saw therefore in mid-summer a window of opportunity where, without unduly jeopardizing the gains on inflation, he could stimulate the recovery. … [T] here was an element of gamble in his move - but if you have to work with perfect certainty don't try to be a central banker".
> *[emphasis added].*
> *Paul, A. Samuelson (1997), op. cit., pp. 15–16*

9.1 Introduction

These findings primarily focus on recent crises such as the global financial crisis, Eurozone sovereign debt crisis, pandemic crisis, and energy crisis stemming from the war in Ukraine. However, there are additional significant challenges to consider. Firstly, the evolution of payment methods, ranging from physical coins and notes to checks, plastic cards, and electronic transfers, has been ongoing. The emergence of digital money and crypto currency use introduces new risks due to its utilization of open networks for communication and value transfer, contrasting with the closed nature of the interbank market. The efficiency of open networks relies on maintaining a critical mass of users, as their collapse can occur suddenly if potential users anticipate that the threshold will not be reached, leading to a self-perpetuating run from the network. In such a scenario, panic could spread through interconnections between networks. If digital money issuers were exempt from reserve and supervision requirements applicable to banks, the central bank's control over liquidity levels in the economy would be significantly impeded. Secondly, while there is widespread consensus that monetary policies have contributed to overall stabilization and inflation control since 1995 until the recent resurgence of inflation in mid-2021, this notable achievement may also be attributed to globalization (Aglietta & Mojon, 2010).

I. T. Kokores, *Monetary Policy in Interdependent Economies*, Financial and Monetary Policy Studies 55, https://doi.org/10.1007/978-3-031-41958-4_9

The global organization of production has the potential to reduce the conventional bottlenecks that previously led to localized inflationary pressures resulting from constraints in local factors of production. Consequently, central banks may need to reassess how they analyze inflation pressures by considering the geographical basis of supply and demand and exploring the possibility of international coordination of monetary policies. As demonstrated throughout this text, central banks continually face new challenges arising from structural changes, technological advancements, and the occurrence of novel crises. Therefore, we will now shift our focus to the key threats that central banks currently confront. Amidst the largest financial crisis since the 1930s, it has been crucial to recognize that the expansion of lender of last resort interventions implemented by central banks since August 2007 has prevented the collapse of banking systems, which highlights the lessons central bankers have learned from past financial crises, emphasizing the imperative of avoiding such collapses at any cost.

Despite the magnitude of the global financial crisis, it had been still reasonable to anticipate that the phase of deleveraging would result in a severe recession, albeit not as severe as the Great Depression. Unemployment was expected to increase by approximately 2–4%, which is comparable to the levels observed during the early 1990s and significantly lower than the staggering 25% unemployment rate witnessed during the Great Depression in the United States. However, the magnitude of the deleveraging process could not have been underestimated. It encompasses various sectors including banks, nonbank financial institutions, households, and nonfinancial companies, and, therefore, monetary authorities have been particularly vigilant in preventing the emergence of a self-perpetuating cycle of debt deflation outlined in Fisher (1933). Given the willingness of the private sector to reduce its debt burden, the risk of an increase in precautionary savings, which eventually led to downward pressures on prices resulting in a decrease in income and an increase in real interest rates, further exacerbates the situation by diverting a larger portion of income toward debt repayment. Ultimately, as the situation continued to deteriorate following the subsequent crises, bankruptcies became at several cases the only viable solution for individuals and firms burdened with excessive debt.

On the income front, there are two approaches to stimulating demand: The first involves transferring income to households with a higher propensity to spend, specifically targeting low-income households. The second approach focuses on implementing public investment programs that have the potential to enhance long-term productivity, such as investments in infrastructure and research. In terms of managing the debt dynamic, public policies should strive to reduce the effective interest rates on private debt, which, ideally, should be lower than the growth rate of nominal income. Failing to achieve this measure results in a prolonged deleveraging process or reliance on bankruptcies, both of which would carry significant social costs. These principles have influenced the formulation of recent crisis management policies since the advent of the GFC, and further measures have been implemented as the evolution of each crisis necessitated them.

Taking a long-term perspective, the financial crisis served as compelling proof that the economy is still susceptible to the self-perpetuating cycle of credit expansion and fluctuating asset prices reflecting an inherent instability (especially bullish) markets (Minsky, 1982). In light of this, the exclusive emphasis of monetary authorities on maintaining stability in the prices of goods and services, while asset prices experience significant volatility, may cause the former to deviate at times from their regulatory and policy objectives concerning nominal, financial, and real stability. In a broader sense, economists and central banks have eventually been facing the need to determine whether it is desirable to control asset price fluctuations and, if so, whether this can be achieved solely through traditional supervision policies or if it should also be incorporated as an objective of monetary policy; the latter scenario necessitates the development of an operational framework that considers the impact of asset price volatility (Aglietta & Mojon, 2010; Barrett et al., 2016, 2017). By redefining the objectives of central banks, the aim is to enhance the economy's ability to withstand the destabilizing effects of financial innovations. Previous financial crises, such as those in the 1990s and 2007–2009, have been driven by excessive credit expansion, often facilitated by various forms of financial innovations.

In the 2007–2009 GFC, the use of securitization and credit risk transfers hindered the effectiveness of bank supervision, resulting in a significant increase in leverage for both financial intermediaries and households. This surge in leverage was partly concentrated in a "shadow banking system" that operated outside the capital requirements imposed on traditional banks. For example, government-sponsored enterprises (as Fannie Mae and Freddie Mac) had leverage ratios exceeding 60, which were five times the maximum leverage allowed for commercial banks.

It is likely that future bank regulations will expand their scope to encompass shadow banks, considering the lessons learned from the past. However, looking at historical patterns, it is important to recognize that future financial innovations may introduce new methods of leveraging during the optimistic phase of the asset price and economic cycle. Therefore, it has become necessary to establish macroprudential policy principles that can implement proactive measures to counteract the rapid growth of credit deviating from its long-term trend. These policies act as a safeguard against the potential risks posed by the credit cycle.

Irrespective of ad hoc crisis management, if there is a consensus to entrust central banks with the task of addressing this form of financial instability, economists need to develop suitable policy tools. The recent crises have demonstrated that financial instability can occur even in the presence of a commendable track record of price stability. Additionally, traditional interest rate adjustments may be ineffective in curbing speculative behavior while simultaneously imposing significant costs on nonspeculative investment. Additional tool, such as contingent capital adequacy ratios (for the advancements in prudential policy measures, see Kokores, 2022, pp. 296–315), may have been required to enable central banks to pursue both objectives effectively. It is possible that central bankers will develop a more optimal solution to mitigate financial instability. However, it is important to note that financial and monetary crises have consistently reshaped the responsibilities of central banks and the recent crises that emerged since 2007 should be no different in this regard.

Nevertheless, while having an independent central bank focused on maintaining price stability is an attractive institutional arrangement for monetary policy, caution must be exercised in its design (Orphanides, 2018, p. 53). Concerns raised by economists like Friedman (1962) remain relevant and should be taken into account. Independence, accompanied by broad discretionary powers and a mandate lacking clear operational guidelines, could potentially be counterproductive, especially during challenging periods when coordination among monetary, fiscal, and other policies is crucial. The purpose of independence is to shield monetary policy from short-term political interference and ensure its consistency, independent of individual personalities. However, the delegated discretionary authority should not encourage a lack of accountability during difficult times. To achieve this, it is essential to establish transparent and well-defined goals that promote both accountability and democratic legitimacy.

9.2 Impact of the COVID-19 Pandemic Crisis, the Power of Central Bank Balance Sheets, and the Initial Policy Responses[1]

In response to the COVID-19 pandemic, policymakers worldwide swiftly implemented a wide range of fiscal and monetary measures to provide exceptional support in mitigating the profound impact on output and incomes caused by lockdowns and social distancing measures. This comprehensive policy mix exhibited significant alignment on a global scale. Central banks expanded their utilization of unconventional tools to alleviate liquidity strains affecting businesses and consumers due to disrupted cash flows. Targeted lending programs were implemented, often with implicit or explicit state guarantees. The fiscal policy response was equally remarkable, with measures such as enhancing automatic stabilizers through generous short-time work schemes; distributing checks to households, small and medium enterprises, and self-employed individuals; as well as implementing tax deferrals, cuts, and carryback provisions to mitigate income losses.[2] These policy measures were put into action at a time when policy tools were already strained and approaching their limits. Prior to the COVID-19 crisis, public debt levels in numerous countries had reached unprecedented levels during peacetime. Simultaneously, interest rates were historically low, and in many countries, conventional policy rates had reached or were near their minimum effective levels.

In fact, the COVID-19 pandemic has resulted in a significant increase in both public and private debt levels for most countries, surpassing the already elevated levels from the global financial crisis. Additionally, there has been a growing consensus that the so-called "equilibrium" interest rate, denoted as R*, which

[1] This section draws heavily from ECA (2020), pp. 50–58.

[2] A detailed and informative discussion of these measures is provided by BIS (2020).

represents the real riskless interest rate needed for economies to achieve full employment on average, has been steadily declining over the past few decades and may now be approaching or even falling below zero. With a low or potentially negative equilibrium interest rate (R*), central banks face limited room for maneuver in implementing monetary policy to counter even moderate negative shocks while maintaining inflation around the target level, typically set at 2%. In order to ease monetary policy, the central bank would need to push the actual real interest rate below R*, which becomes challenging when inflation remains persistently below target and nominal short-term interest rates are constrained by the zero lower bound. Although unconventional monetary policy tools like asset purchase programs can extend the reach of monetary policy within the realm of interest rates, there is often a call for fiscal policy to play a more significant role in stabilization efforts. This entails urging fiscal policy to contribute toward economic stability alongside monetary policy (Draghi, 2019; Bartsch et al., 2020).[3]

Since the occurrence of the global financial crisis and more prominently with the advent of the COVID-19 crisis in late 2019—taking global scale during early 2020—it has become evident that achieving stabilization necessitates a collaborative approach involving fiscal and monetary policies. This shift in perspective comes after years of institutional endeavors to establish legal and operational independence for central banks, as during the period of the Great Moderation the prevailing belief was that monetary policy alone would be adequate to ensure economic stability in terms of both business cycles and inflation. However, when confronted with crises, the constrained scope for monetary interventions has revitalized the concept of the "policy mix," highlighting the need for coordination between fiscal and monetary measures. In 2020, the global community faced a new crisis caused by the COVID-19 pandemic, which disrupted production, supply chains, and consumption, and created significant challenges for public finances. In response, policymakers implemented a range of monetary, fiscal, and prudential measures to protect the financial sector from the economic consequences, aiming to prevent the crisis from escalating into a financial crisis. During the early stages of the pandemic, the

[3]The underlying long-term structural factors that influence R*, such as population aging, low productivity growth, and financial imbalances, have not significantly diminished. Despite the possibility of inflated debt-to-GDP ratios leading to higher-risk premia in certain countries, the global "equilibrium" interest rate has been expected to remain very low as long as global savings remain abundant and productivity growth remains sluggish. This has two important implications for policy: Firstly, a low or negative R* adds complexity to assessing the sustainability of debt. While a negative or extremely low real interest rate may incentivize governments to pursue fiscal expansions, it should not be assumed that the debt will automatically repay itself. Accounting principles, historical experiences, and fiscal projections caution against relying on debt as a "magic" solution. Although negative interest rates may have allowed countries to sustain persistent deficits, these deficits cannot have been unlimited. Moreover, negative real interest rates in the past have not always prevented fiscal stress or crises. Secondly, besides explicit government liabilities, implicit and contingent liabilities continue to impact the fiscal outlook's stability. It is important to recognize that larger balance sheets are more vulnerable to market downturns and the existence of multiple equilibria (European Commission, 2018a; Mauro & Zhou, 2020; Bartsch et al., 2020).

European Central Bank, the Federal Reserve, and the Bank of Japan took swift and decisive action by utilizing their balance sheets. Unlike previous crisis cases, where interest rate policy was limited by the zero lower bound, these central banks acted promptly without hesitation. Their actions involved implementing monetary easing measures, which helped mitigate the economic impact of the crisis. Additionally, these central banks played a crucial role in providing support for government securities and private assets, thus averting a collapse in the financial markets. Furthermore, their interventions facilitated the necessary fiscal expansion by ensuring the availability of financing.

Certainly, central banks had a more enhanced set of tools to address the pandemic crisis. However, the COVID-19 crisis presented unique challenges. It had the potential to be larger in scale, depending on the extent and speed of the economic recovery, and it was accompanied by significant uncertainty regarding how to effectively overcome the health risks that underlie it. The *lessons learned from the 2008–2012 crisis show the following*: (1) The costs associated with a crisis are substantial and impose immense strain on government budgets, increasing the likelihood of interconnected repercussions among various sectors of the economy, the sovereign entities, and the financial industry. (2) Effective crisis management and successful recovery can be achieved through a robust and unified (among economically interconnected economies, as the EU) approach, which combines coordinated economic and fiscal measures with prudent monetary policies. This comprehensive strategy yields positive outcomes in navigating and surmounting crises while facilitating economic recovery. (3) The key factors for emerging from a crisis and re-establishing economic growth are a resilient single market, cohesion, solidarity, and balanced economic development. To prioritize the restoration of investment and provide substantial support to businesses in order to achieve these goals have remained vital as the COVID crisis progressed.

The economic landscape of the EU let alone several advanced economies underwent significant changes with the onset of the COVID-19 pandemic marked with most quarantine measures in March 2020 across several countries. The pandemic posed a significant risk to public health, and the subsequent implementation of containment measures resulted in a substantial economic shock. [4] During the COVID-19 crisis, banks exhibited stronger capitalization and more effective liquidity management than in previous crises. However, the implementation of lockdown measures resulted in a considerable decline in business revenue, along with an

[4] See ECA (2020) Annex III for the costs of the financial and sovereign debt crises over 2008–2017, as well as the initial cost (partially estimated—at the date of their publication) of the response to the COVID-19 pandemic. As the implementation of the pandemic health measures and lockdowns has resulted in significant disruptions in various sectors including production, services, and global supply chains, key sectors such as tourism, transport, and trade have been particularly affected. The European Commission (2020a) projected a decline in EU GDP by 7.4% (7.7% for the euro area) in 2020, surpassing the decline witnessed during the financial and sovereign debt crisis of 2008–2012. However, a rebound is expected in 2021, with GDP projected to grow by 6% (6.3% for the euro area).

upsurge in loan demand and a heightened risk of business defaults. Furthermore, the elevated unemployment rates had the potential to lead to defaults on private loans and mortgages, which could impact real estate prices. As a result, banks were likely to face an increased volume of nonperforming loans and incur losses due to the essential restructuring of private debt in the coming years.[5] In the context of the COVID-19 crisis, it is crucial that the relevant mechanisms are capable of performing their functions when needed. The impact of the crisis on banks largely depended on how the crisis developed and the subsequent recovery, as well as the capital resources banks had prior to the crisis, their exposure to the most affected sectors, and the level of support provided to the real economy by the public sector.[6] Within a span of 3 months, the Federal Reserve, the Bank of Japan (BOJ), and the European Central Bank (ECB) significantly increased the size of their balance sheets. This expansion was of an unprecedented scale, with the Fed alone creating as much high-powered money in that short period as it had in its first century of existence from 1913 to 2013.[7] The BOJ and ECB also implemented substantial balance sheet expansions (see Fig. 9.1). These central banks utilized their authority to create reserves from nothing, which is a capability inherent in a fiat currency system. The resulting growth in balance sheets amounted to a monetary stimulus equivalent to 15% to 25% of the respective countries' GDP, as in Fig. 9.2 (Orphanides, 2021, p. 36).

Typically, the unprecedented printing of money would raise concerns, as a misuse of central bank balance sheets can have detrimental effects on the economy. During a crisis, conventional approaches involve lowering policy rates as the primary course of action. However, when interest rate policy had been constrained by the zero lower bound, expanding the balance sheet became the appropriate response. The latter involves creating reserves and utilizing them to acquire assets or provide liquidity to encourage lending, effectively accommodating monetary conditions without

---

[5] Based on initial assessments that do not account for the effects of policy interventions, the European Banking Authority anticipated that the average ratio of nonperforming loan coverage will reach levels comparable to those observed during the period following the 2008–2012 crisis (EBA, 2020a).

[6] The COVID-19 pandemic resulted in significant capital market volatility and a further flattening of the euro swap curve, indicating expectations for interest rate developments. This led to a notable decline in the market value of financial assets and an increase in the market value of long-term insurance and defined benefit pension liabilities, which negatively affected the insurance and pensions sectors. Stress tests for the insurance sector indicated that the majority of insurers demonstrated sufficient solvency ratios under the tested stressed market scenarios, as stated in the "2018 insurance stress test report" by the European Insurance and Occupational Pensions Authority (EIOPA). Pension funds, also known as Institutions for Occupational Retirement Provision, experienced slightly improved cover ratios (assets covering liabilities) in 2019. However, they have faced challenges due to the persistently low interest rate and low yield environment, which impacted the profitability of their investments and the valuation of defined benefit obligations; see "2017 IORP Stress Test Report," December 13, 2017, para. 243 and 235, and 2019 IORP Stress Test Report 19/673, EIOPA, December 17, 2019, pp. 15–48.

[7] Between March and June 2020, the US Federal Reserve expanded its balance sheet by $3 trillion dollars.

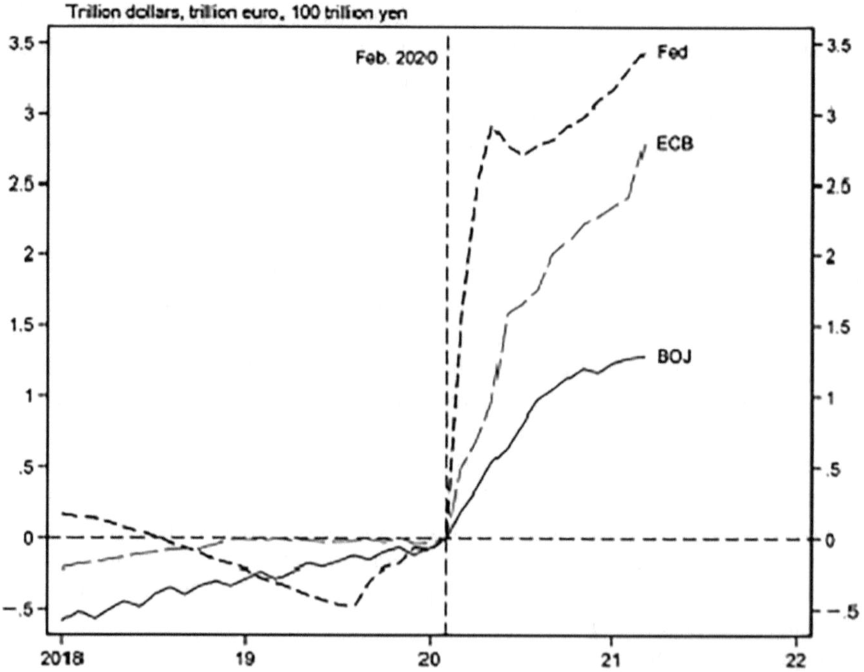

Fig. 9.1 Size of central bank balance sheet. Note: Monthly data relative to February 2020. Source: Orphanides (2021), p. 37

decreasing the overnight interest rate. Expanding the balance sheet aims to enable the narrowing of interest rate spreads, to decrease term premia, and to bolster asset prices, all of which can reduce financing costs for households and businesses while supporting overall demand.[8]

National authorities swiftly implemented measures to activate countercyclical and macroprudential capital buffers, enhancing banks' ability to provide loans to support the real economy and absorb unforeseen losses. These actions with reference to the EU, as detailed in the ECA (2020, Annexes IV and V), were accompanied by additional steps taken by EU and national authorities to bolster banks' lending capabilities. These measures included temporary alleviation of capital and liquidity requirements, extensions to transitional provisions to mitigate the effects of heightened provisioning under IFRS 9 on regulatory capital, and a more accommodating regulatory approach toward loans backed by public guarantees (European

[8] Since the late 1990s, an extensive literature has examined the monetary policy challenge at the ZLB, as, for example, Fuhrer and Madigan (1997) and Krugman (1998); reviews of alternative policy options include Goodfriend (2000). See Orphanides (2021) and the reviews suggested therein.

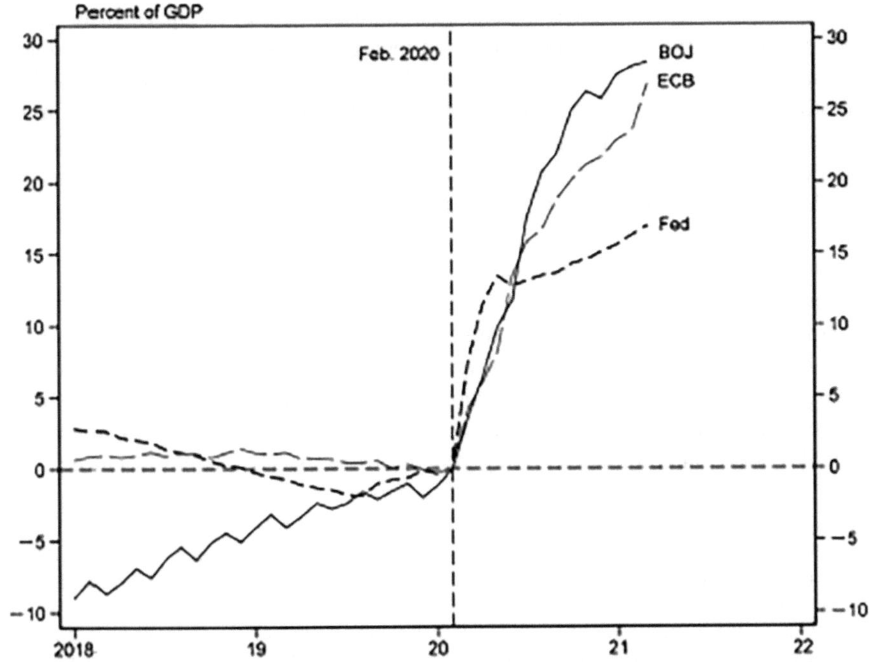

Fig. 9.2 Central bank balance sheet as ratio to GDP. Note: monthly data relative to February 2020. Ratio to average GDP over previous four quarters. Source: Orphanides (2021), p. 37

Commission, 2020b).[9] Supervisors also effected their crucial role of monitoring banks' credit risk, assessing impairments and nonperforming loans, and evaluating their potential impact. This ongoing oversight is deemed necessary to promptly identify banks that are experiencing difficulties or are at risk of failure. The COVID-19 pandemic led (as anticipated, see, for example, ECA, 2020, Fig. 9) to a substantial worsening of the fiscal deficit, and a significant increase in public debts, due to the considerable strain it puts on government expenditures and revenues across the EU member states.[10]

[9] To enhance their ability to withstand losses during the pandemic crisis, the ECB requested banks to refrain from distributing dividends until at least October 2020. European Commission (2020b) confirmed the flexibility in regulations, aligning with the Basel Committee. This flexibility encompassed provisions for public and private moratoria on loan repayments (see European Banking Association, 2020b), and supervisory measures were implemented, enabling banks to temporarily utilize liquidity and capital buffers.

[10] Governments implemented various measures to provide assistance to essential businesses, support enterprises, and offer social welfare programs in response to the crisis. Additionally, credit support programs for businesses, backed by guarantees from both member states and the European Union, may result in increased fiscal expenditures in the medium term. As a result, the crisis is likely to have varying impacts on different member states, potentially exacerbating their economic disparities. According to the Commission, these disparities will be reflected in the fact that certain

In response to this altered economic landscape, the European Union has implemented various fiscal and economic measures to support its member states. These measures aimed to bolster recovery efforts and stimulate economic growth.[11] In order to safeguard the unity of the EU's single market and promote fair competition, the Commission has put forward several proposals (European Commission, 2020c).[12] Additionally, various other measures that could support economic recovery have been endorsed and implemented. Several fiscal and economic measures have also been implemented at the national level.[13]

On April 15, 2020, the European Council and the European Commission Presidents presented a Joint European Roadmap toward lifting COVID-19 containment measures, a report that highlights four key areas for action as part of the way forward (see European Commission and European Council, 2020a, 2020b, 2020c), as follows: (1) measures to restore the functioning of the single market, (2) greater efforts to boost investment, and (3) global action, in particular in the EU's immediate neighborhood, namely, a functioning system of EU and national governance.

member states may experience a recession of nearly 10%, while the average decline in GDP is estimated to be around 6–7.5% (see European Commission, 2020c). The asset purchase program implemented by the ECB plays a crucial role in facilitating the transmission of monetary policy. Additionally, the confirmation of eligibility for all member states to access credit lines from the European Stability Mechanism provides reassurance that support will be available to alleviate some of the pressures faced by member states.

[11] At the advent of the pandemic crisis, important developments relevant to EU-level fiscal and economic coordination and the so-called European Semester include the following: (1) the activation of the "general escape" clause under the Stability and Growth Pact, enabling member states to deviate from the preventive arm requirements, such as the medium-term budgetary objective or the adjustment path toward it (This activation also grants the Commission the authority to recommend an extension of the deadline for member states to rectify excessive deficits under the corrective arm, known as the excessive deficit procedure. Additionally, member states have activated national escape clauses within their fiscal frameworks, allowing them to suspend the imposed restrictions in response to severe economic downturns and other exceptional circumstances.) and (2) new Commission guidelines for the 2020 Stability and Convergence Programmes—streamlining the format and content of the SCPs (in the 2020 cycle).

[12] Examples of these measures include the establishment of the Single Market Enforcement Task Force, the implementation of the Solvency Support Instrument, the adoption of the Pact on Migration and Asylum, the introduction of the Strategic Investment Facility, and the implementation of the pharmaceutical strategy. Furthermore, the EU has made adjustments to state aid rules by adopting a new State aid Temporary Framework on March 19, 2020 (see European Commission, 2020d, Temporary Framework for State aid measures to support the economy in the current COVID-19 outbreak. European Commission, 1863 final), which was subsequently extended on April 3 (see European Commission, 2020e, Amendment to the Temporary Framework for State aid measures to support the economy in the current COVID-19 outbreak, European Commission, 2215 final).

[13] The fiscal support measures implemented are projected to represent over 3% of the GDP of the European Union member states. Additionally, measures aimed at providing liquidity support to sectors and companies experiencing challenges are estimated to account for more than 16% of the EU GDP. The European Fiscal Monitor indicates that the majority of member states will increase their spending by approximately 1.6% of GDP and offer tax relief equivalent to another 1.4% of GDP as part of their fiscal response.

By expanding the *eligibility* boundaries for using the power of their balance sheets, the three central banks managed to stabilize markets very quickly and efficiently.[14] The willingness of central banks to utilize the potential of their balance sheets more extensively than before played a crucial role in the success of their policies in 2020. The Bank of Japan (BOJ), having already gained experience in utilizing its balance sheet to support government debt and private assets, utilized this knowledge to provide decisive assistance in March 2020. Recognizing the high risks of market collapse, the US Federal Reserve and the European Central Bank made similar decisions to expand the use of their balance sheets as a potential safeguard.

The Federal Reserve's turning point came on March 23, 2020, when it made corporate debt eligible for support through Section 13(3) facilities. As for the ECB, the pivotal moment arrived on April 22 when it suspended reliance on credit rating agencies to determine the eligibility of government debt, thereby putting an end to the recurring crises caused by this mechanism in the euro area during the previous decade (Orphanides, 2021, p. 47). Therefore, the effective utilization of central bank balance sheet policies at the start of the pandemic in March 2020 demonstrated a much more successful approach to tackling the economic difficulties compared to previous encounters with the zero lower bound (ZLB) over the past 25 years. It also highlighted the immense power that independent central banks possess during times of crisis. In an environment of low interest rates, central banks must be prepared to employ the power of their balance sheets to address crises and potential recessions. However, implementing balance sheet policies is more complex for central banks than interest rate policies and gives rise to challenging questions of governance. Such policies entail greater uncertainty and have more significant fiscal and distributional effects, which can attract political scrutiny and criticism.[15] As Orphanides

[14]The primary factor that played a crucial role in stabilizing markets was the issue of *eligibility*. Concerns regarding the ongoing eligibility of government debt in the euro area for monetary policy operations, driven by the ECB's reliance on credit rating agencies, had previously created instability in the markets. On April 22, the ECB addressed this vulnerability by making a significant announcement. It declared that the eligibility of marketable assets used as collateral in its credit operations, as well as for its asset purchase programs, would be preserved through grandfathering (European Central Bank, 2020). This decision, made by the ECB during the crisis, was of utmost importance. Essentially, the ECB suspended the practice of relying on credit rating agencies to determine the eligibility of government debt and other securities. Consequently, even if a member state's government debt were downgraded, it would still be considered eligible collateral and included in the asset purchase programs. With this decisive action, the ECB effectively utilized the power of its balance sheet as a safeguard, capable of preventing self-fulfilling adverse equilibria and avoiding another crisis episode in the euro area (Orphanides, 2021, p. 46).

[15]Whenever central banks showcase the extraordinary capabilities of their balance sheets, they inevitably invite unwanted attention and controversy, which in turn increases the likelihood of compromising their political independence. While this risk is present, it cannot be used as a justification for inaction. Choosing not to utilize the balance sheet powers of a central bank to avoid criticism would be a failure to fulfill their responsibilities in meeting the central bank's fundamental mandate. Central banks must be prepared to employ the power of their balance sheets when necessary, irrespective of the potential for political scrutiny and criticism and regardless of perceived risks to their political independence (Orphanides, 2021, p. 51).

(2021) remarks: "The successful activation of the power of central bank balance sheets in response to the pandemic was instrumental for fulfilling the mandate of central banks as independent institutions. The demonstration of this power also attracted attention to it, highlighting the challenge of maintaining central bank independence. Pursuing a systematic policy that achieves a central bank's core mandate can protect the central bank's institutional integrity and address this challenge" (p. 52).

The current discussion underscores the urgency of implementing an effective policy mix, which is now more crucial than ever before. Since the GFC, monetary policy has continuously sought to expand its range of unconventional tools but has been unable to achieve official inflation targets. The economic devastation caused by the COVID-19 pandemic has further intensified this issue. The focus of policy debates has shifted from questioning how far negative interest rates and quantitative easing can be pushed to emphasizing the imperative for robust collaboration between fiscal and monetary policies. The concept of the policy mix, which had largely disappeared from economics textbooks, has now resurfaced with great force and significance (Bartsch et al., 2020).[16] A crucial question that arises today is whether the combined impact of monetary and fiscal policies, necessary to tackle the aftermath of the GFC and the COVID-19 pandemic, can be sufficiently robust when both policies face limitations. Monetary policy is constrained by the zero lower bound on interest rates, while fiscal policy is hindered by historically high levels of public debt. Another way to phrase this question is whether even seemingly minor shocks, let alone the magnitude of the COVID-19 shock, could escalate into severe and unexpected events, considering the constraints on our economic policy options.

Given the experiences of the past decade, there is reason for cautious optimism in the short term regarding these questions. Firstly, the lower bound on interest rates, often referred to as the "liquidity trap," did not have as devastating an impact as anticipated. Monetary policy demonstrated its effectiveness by implementing unconventional measures that directly influenced financial conditions and had a more

[16] The concept of the policy mix can be traced back to Tinbergen's perspective on economic policy, which viewed it as a means to address an optimal control problem. In this framework, having an additional independent instrument enables the pursuit of an additional objective. Resolving the assignment problem involves aligning each instrument with the objective it can most effectively serve. In the early 1960s, Mundell put forward the idea that in a fixed exchange rate system like the Bretton Woods arrangement, monetary policy should focus on maintaining external balance, while fiscal policy should ensure internal balance, specifically full employment. While Tinbergen emphasized the independence of policy instruments, Tobin's research demonstrated that monetary and fiscal policies jointly influence output and prices by affecting aggregate demand. This concept, known as the "common funnel theorem," suggests that various combinations of monetary and fiscal policies can achieve the necessary impulse to maintain macroeconomic stability. In the short term, monetary and fiscal policies can serve as substitutes. While Mundell proposed that monetary and fiscal policies should push aggregate demand in opposite directions, known as a divergent policy mix, Tobin's funnel theory suggests the importance of implementing countercyclical policies together, known as a congruent mix, to achieve price stability and full employment. With the shift toward more flexible exchange rates, the common funnel approach has become the prevailing paradigm (Bartsch et al., 2020).

targeted impact. Secondly, extreme events prompted monetary and fiscal authorities to recognize the strong synergies between the two components of the policy mix. Central banks took measures to lower government financing costs and provide safeguards against market stress driven by perception, enabling public budgets to support economies despite the historically high levels of public debt. The common objective of achieving a higher R* represents a unique scenario where the advantages of global coordination should be evident to most nations. By increasing R*, the policy mix can be positioned toward a more balanced approach, which would significantly enhance countries' capacity for stabilization and enable them to better navigate major global shocks. Furthermore, the reduction in uncertainty regarding the impact of adverse shocks would, in itself, contribute to the sustainability of the R* increase by decreasing savings and fostering investment.

9.3 A Review of Inflation Expectations After the COVID-19 Crisis

Despite the significant uncertainty surrounding the measurement of output gaps during the pandemic, there continues to be a notable relationship between economic slack and inflation. During the pandemic crisis, long-term inflation expectations have remained relatively stable, and there has been limited evidence to suggest that the extraordinary policy measures undertaken have disrupted these expectations (IMF, 2021, Chap. 2). Since the beginning of 2021, advanced and emerging market economies have experienced an increase in headline consumer price index (CPI) inflation, driven by strengthening demand, shortages in inputs, and rapidly rising commodity prices. Given the unprecedented nature of the recovery, considerable uncertainty remained, particularly when assessing economic slack. Prolonged disruptions in the supply chain, unexpected shocks in commodity and housing prices, long-term commitments in expenditure, and a potential destabilization of inflation expectations could lead to significantly higher inflation compared to the baseline predictions. However, through clear communication and the implementation of appropriate monetary and fiscal policies tailored to specific country contexts, the risk of "inflation scares" derailing inflation expectations has readily been mitigated.

From a macroeconomic standpoint, if inflation in advanced economies rises consistently and catches policymakers off guard, it could disrupt financial markets and lead to an unexpected withdrawal of monetary support. This rise in inflation would primarily impact individuals who rely heavily on labor income, typically those with lower incomes, but it could also affect lenders negatively while benefiting debtors. The consequences of inflation can be intricate and have varying effects on different segments of the population. Understanding the inflation process requires considering inflation expectations and supply shocks. A critical concern is identifying the factors that both have triggered and could cause recent inflation surges to persist, potentially leading to unanchored expectations and a self-perpetuating cycle of inflation (for the United States, see Bernanke & Blanchard, 2023).

Policymakers have been concerned that the unprecedented policy measures implemented in response to the COVID-19 crisis may have limited the flexibility of monetary policy, thereby affecting the credibility of central banks and potentially leading to a detachment of inflation expectations from their desired targets. The Phillips curve relationship is a crucial component of central banks' policy frameworks. It illustrates a trade-off between low economic slack, such as low cyclical unemployment, and high inflation. According to the Phillips curve, inflation is influenced by both supply disturbances caused by disruptions in the supply chain and long-term inflation expectations. As inflation-targeting regimes have become more widespread, long-term inflation expectations have gained importance in explaining inflation outcomes. There are alternative approaches to understanding the inflation process, one of which involves considering monetary aggregates as potential indicators of future inflation.

Research by Pradhan and Goodhart (2021) provides a comprehensive review of these alternative approaches. In the current crisis, Agur et al. (2022) have found that despite significant increases in the money supply resulting from substantial fiscal and monetary stimulus, the short-term impact of money growth on inflation has been relatively modest, particularly in countries with credible central banks. Reifschneider and Wilcox (2022) argued that even if the increased fiscal spending were to have a greater impact on reducing unemployment than anticipated, the likelihood of a significant surge in inflation was still low. Numerous studies have found that the Phillips curve relationship (between inflation and labor market tightness) is relatively weak, indicating that inflation is not highly responsive to changes in the labor market. Moreover, considering the US history of low inflation spanning more than three decades, it has been expected that inflation expectations will remain firmly established and not easily influenced.

Nevertheless, to estimate the relationship between economic slack and inflation during the COVID-19 period is particularly challenging (IMF, 2021). The pandemic has introduced significant uncertainties surrounding unemployment levels and output gaps. The extraordinary fiscal and monetary policy measures implemented in response to the economic shock are also likely to obscure the relationship between slack and inflation to a greater extent than observed during a normal business cycle. In addition to the uncertainties surrounding economic slack, there are other factors that further complicate the measurement of this relationship. These include disruptions in global supply chains, sectoral disruptions caused by the pandemic, volatility in commodity prices, changes in the composition of consumer baskets (as highlighted by Cavallo, 2020; Reinsdorf, 2020), and the influence of extreme base effects. These factors introduce measurement challenges that go beyond the traditional considerations related to potential output.

Headline inflation rates have been pushed upward by increasing commodity prices and supply chain disruptions. Additionally, the unique nature of the current economic recovery has raised concerns about the duration it will take for supply to match the accelerating demand. These uncertainties have heightened worries that inflation might exceed central bank targets over a sustained period and cause inflation expectations to become unanchored. Such a scenario could trigger a self-reinforcing cycle of inflation.

The process of establishing policy credibility and shaping inflation expectations is complex and dynamic, making it challenging to pinpoint with precision. Furthermore, assessing inflation anchoring cannot solely rely on historical data relationships. Therefore, policymakers must be prepared to take action and ensure the existence of robust monetary frameworks that incorporate triggers for necessary interventions. These triggers could include early indications of inflation expectations becoming unanchored, identified through forward-looking surveys, unsustainable fiscal and current accounts, or significant movements in the exchange rate. Policymakers need to remain vigilant for potential triggers that could create a perfect storm of inflation risks. Although these risks may seem relatively benign when considered individually, their combined occurrence could lead to inflation levels significantly higher than predicted in baseline forecasts. Case studies demonstrate that effective policy measures have been successful in reducing inflation and anchoring expectations, but clear and credible communication has also played a vital role in maintaining expectations. Therefore, during periods of policy normalization, advanced economy central banks should provide transparent and state-contingent forward guidance and communication, including well-defined triggers for action, to prevent scenarios resembling market tantrums caused by uncertainty over policy adjustments.

Nevertheless, Bernanke and Blanchard (2023) argue that misjudgments of the economic effects of COVID era fiscal programs are one potential explanation of the failure to forecast the subsequent inflation. They stress that the Federal Open Market Committee projected a minor shift in inflation forecasts between September 2020 and June 2021 in the Survey of Economic Projections. Despite the passage of a bill in December 2020 that allocated $900 billion for COVID relief and the subsequent signing of the $1.9 trillion American Rescue Plan by President Biden in March 2021, the Committee maintained its expectation that inflation would return to the Federal Reserve's 2% target by 2023. These two programs were in addition to the $2.2 trillion CARES Act, passed in March 2020 and signed by US President Trump, which had already bolstered the financial positions of businesses and households and increased their future spending capacity. In terms of the proportion of the GDP, the total costs of these three fiscal packages related to the COVID pandemic were approximately 4 and 1/2 times larger than the American Recovery and Reinvestment Act, which was implemented in response to the 2008 financial crisis and subsequent recession.

As, for example, stressed in IMF (2021), central banks have the option to adopt a forward-looking approach by looking beyond temporary inflationary pressures and avoid excessive or untimely tightening of policies until there is greater clarity on the underlying dynamics of prices, as long as inflation expectations remain firmly anchored. However, central banks have been prepared and indeed undertook swift action as the necessary, and had to outline contingent plans that reflect their true preferences. Fiscal policies should adhere to sustainable medium-term frameworks.

Nevertheless, given the significant uncertainty surrounding medium-term output gaps, the optimal timing for withdrawing policy support during the recovery may be affected. Therefore, policies should take into account the unusual short-term dynamics and uncertainties related to potential output. *Policy recommendations should be adjusted based on the specific vulnerabilities and business cycle phases of each economy, and the potential spillovers of uncoordinated monetary and fiscal tightening should be a central topic in discussions on multilateral policy discussions.*

9.4 Monetary Policy Conduct Under Heightened Uncertainty: Inflation Diagnostics

The circumstances related to the war in Ukraine have been characterized by significant uncertainty, and it will take a considerable period before the repercussions can be fully assessed. However, in qualitative terms, the global economy will be influenced by three main factors as a result (Kuroda, 2022, pp. 3–6), namely, (1) an increase in international commodity prices, (2) a decline in trade activity and disruption of supply chains, and (3) a deterioration in the confidence of businesses and households.[17]

In an effort to address the monetary policy reaction, we admit that in theory when supply shocks lead to a significant increase in commodity prices, domestic prices rise. The general principle is that monetary policy does not directly address the "direct effects" of supply shocks, such as the price hikes in gasoline and electricity resulting from higher crude oil prices. The prices of commodities like crude oil and natural gas are determined by global market supply and demand and are beyond the control of monetary policy implemented by a national central bank. Similarly, the

[17] Among the various channels influencing economies, the increase in international commodity prices appears to have the most significant impact (Kuroda, 2022). Russia is a substantial producer of commodities, such as crude oil, natural gas, and coal, and it has experienced a surge in prices for these resources, which can be attributed to concerns regarding potential supply shortages caused by the war and economic sanctions imposed on Russia. The consequences of such higher commodity prices vary across economies, primarily determined by their trade balance in commodities. For example, since the United States is the largest global producer of crude oil and natural gas, it bounds to maintain a relatively balanced trade in these commodities through exports and imports, such that an increase in pertinent prices does not result in a net outflow of income from the US economy. Conversely, since Japan and the European Union member states heavily rely on imports for crude oil, natural gas, and coal (with the value of these imports accounting for a significant percentage of their GDP), higher pertinent prices lead to a net outflow of income. Thus, a burden is imposed on certain sectors within their respective economies, and the distribution of this cost depends on how the increase in commodity prices propagated. Notably, price hikes in crude oil and natural gas automatically translate to higher gasoline prices, electricity costs, and gas charges. Consequently, households experience a direct decline in real income. Since escalating energy prices result in increased production and operational expenses for companies, corporate profits decrease if firms are unable to fully pass on the extra cost to their selling prices.

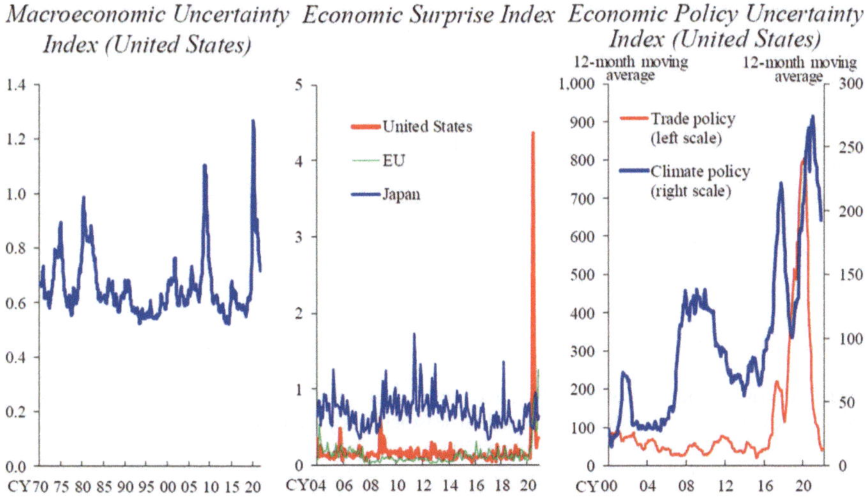

Fig. 9.3 Heightened economic uncertainty. Note: the latest period is December 2021 for the left-hand chart, November 2020 for the middle chart, January 2022 for trade policy, and December 2021 for climate policy in the right-hand chart. Source: Kuroda (2022), p. 11, Jurado et al. (2015), Scotti (2016), Baker (2016), Gavriilidis (2021)

central bank policy measures cannot resolve commodity shortages arising from the situation in Ukraine. Nevertheless, a central bank needs to address the hazard of the rise in commodity prices triggering inflation expectations through secondary effects and the potential to initiate an inflationary spiral driven by increasing wages and prices. In some cases, a central bank may need to respond by tightening monetary policy. In fact, central banks in the United States and the Eurozone have decided to adjust their accommodative monetary measures, as a precautionary measure against such secondary effects.

In recent years, uncertainties have increased substantially due to various noneconomic factors, including the COVID-19 pandemic, the war in Ukraine, and the long-term issue of climate change. As a result, central banks have encountered unprecedented challenges in carrying out monetary policy due to such changing circumstances. In the past, the economy was primarily influenced by demand shocks, and the situation was relatively stable during the period of the Great Moderation, while since the 2010s there have been frequent and *unpredictable* supply shocks, such as natural disasters, the pandemic, and the war in Ukraine. These events have been relatively uncommon in recent years, resulting in limited data on their economic impact. In times of heightened uncertainty, central banks must approach monetary policy with caution, carefully analyzing available data and avoiding preconceptions (Fig. 9.3).

The recent surge in inflation since mid-2021 can be interpreted as a result of significant relative price shocks in the current complex environment, which as mentioned includes high inflation, shocks related to high-energy prices and the pandemic, and the war in Ukraine. These shocks, combined with downward nominal

Fig. 9.4 HICP inflation and the HICP price level. Notes: left panel, annual percentage changes; right, index: December 1998 = 100, based on seasonally adjusted data. The latest observations are for October 2022. Sources: Eurostat, Lane (2022)

price and wage rigidities, initially contribute to an increase in the inflation rate, and the magnitude and scope of these shocks are influenced by the energy shock, the pandemic, and the war-related events. In such circumstances, conventional measures of current underlying inflation may not accurately reflect the persistent component of inflation (Lane, 2022). Therefore, supplementary indicators like forward-looking wage growth trackers can play a useful role in understanding the medium-term dynamics of inflation. Despite the current anchoring of long-term inflation expectations around, for example, the ECB's 2% target, there is a risk of de-anchoring if above-target inflation persists for an extended period. To address this risk and ensure inflation returns to the target in a timely manner, interest rates have been modestly raised to appropriate levels by major advanced economy central banks. Lane (2022), in an effort to outline the causes and patterns of current inflation with reference to the euro area, presents the following data visualizations as in Figs. 9.4, 9.5, 9.6, and 9.7., which provide a justification of the pattern of inflation surges in distinct sectors.

9.5 A Credible Macroeconomic Policy Is a Necessity

Implementing a strategy of gradually decreasing the growth of money supply and reducing the government budget deficit can effectively decrease and eventually eliminate inflation in an economy. It is advisable in this case to adopt a gradual approach due to various political and psychological considerations. Based on previous experience, skepticism arises regarding a government's determination to initiate and persist in a gradual process aimed at achieving price stability. Such skeptics, as well as those who may not fully comprehend the implications of the new policy approach, will be surprised by the change. This element of surprise may result in real costs, particularly in the early stages of the new approach. In fact, significant changes have the potential to shock the economy and trigger a recession. Previous

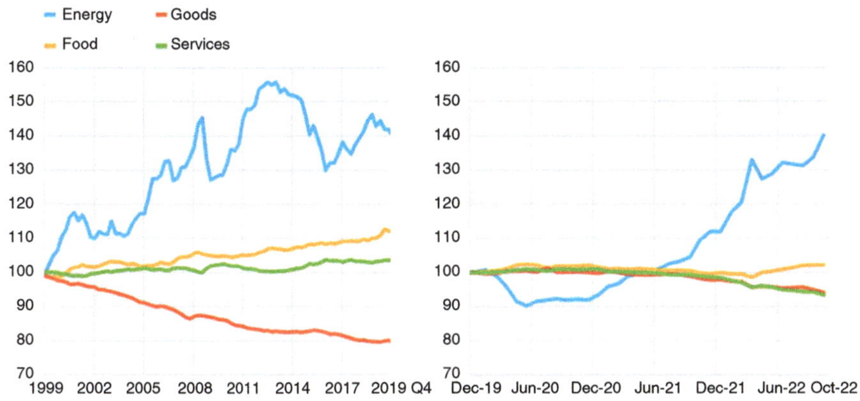

Fig. 9.5 Eurozone price developments relative to HICP for different sectors. Note: left panel, index, 1998 Q4 = 100. Right panel, index, December 2019 = 100. Seasonally adjusted data for HICP, food, goods, and services. Seasonally adjusted series for energy are not available. The goods category here only includes non-energy industrial goods. The latest observations are for October 2022. Sources: Eurostat, Lane (2022)

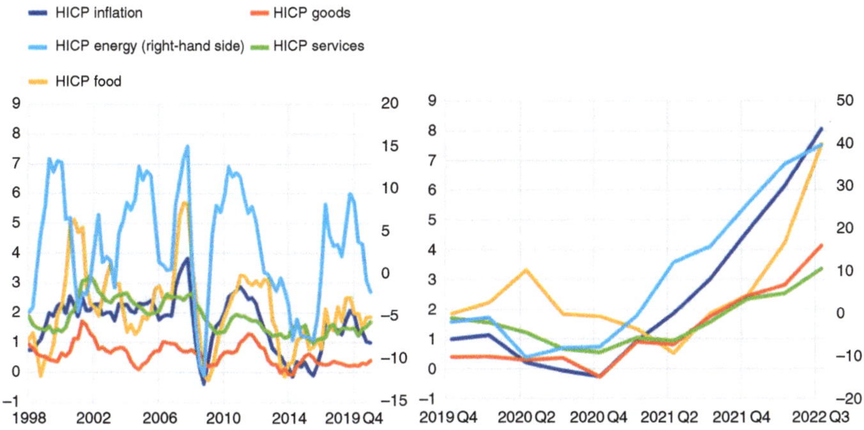

Fig. 9.6 Eurozone HICP inflation and inflation across HICP components. Note: annual percentage changes. HICP goods here only includes non-energy industrial goods. The latest observations are for Q3 2022. Sources: Eurostat, ECB staff calculations, Lane (2022)

experience has shown that a severe recession can lead to the abandonment of efforts to control inflation. Therefore, it is crucial to start with gradual initial steps. Larger initial steps could be taken without causing a shock or recession when the public has confidence that the government will undertake the necessary monetary and fiscal measures to control inflation and in the case they are not constrained by previous agreements. Once the process of gradually reducing aggregate demand has commenced and the government has clearly shown its commitment to implementing it, the costs associated with the program will decrease. As the new approach becomes

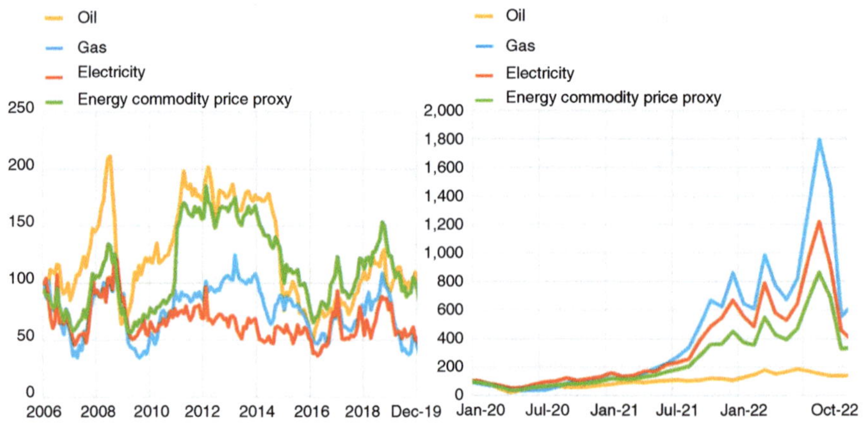

Fig. 9.7 Developments in energy commodity prices. Notes: left panel, index, January 2006 = 100; right panel, index, December 2019 = 100. The "energy commodity price proxy" represents a weighted average of oil, gas, and electricity prices indexed to January 2006 (left panel) and December 2019 = 100 (right panel), using weights based on the respective shares of oil, gas, and electricity in euro area final energy consumption (2006–2020 data). Electricity prices are calculated as a weighted average of wholesale electricity prices in the five largest euro area economies. The latest observations are for October 2022. Sources: Refinitiv, Eurostat, ECB staff calculations, Lane (2022)

familiar and comprehensible, even significant steps will not result in higher unemployment. As surprises diminish over time, the expenses of combating inflation through macroeconomic policies will also decrease.

9.5.1 Inflation Can Be Eliminated Without Creating High Unemployment

An illustration of *gradualist policy* is depicted in Fig. 9.8, with "full employment" unemployment rate denoted by U_F. Initially, the economy is at point P_0, characterized by an inflation rate of i_0 and an unemployment rate U_F. Subsequently, a minor contractionary adjustment in policy is implemented. As a result, the economy transitions to point P_1, leading to an increase in unemployment due to the lack of anticipation of the policy change by the public. However, once the policy change takes effect, some members of the public become convinced that future announcements of tighter policies should be given greater weight. As workers acknowledge and respond to the new policy measures, it becomes possible to simultaneously reduce both inflation and unemployment. Once the second step, involving an additional gradual tightening of policy, is communicated and implemented, workers start to moderate their wage demands. This adjustment is driven by their self-interest, as failing to lower wage expectations would render labor costs excessive and lead to layoffs. Consequently, the expected policy tightening not only reduces inflation but

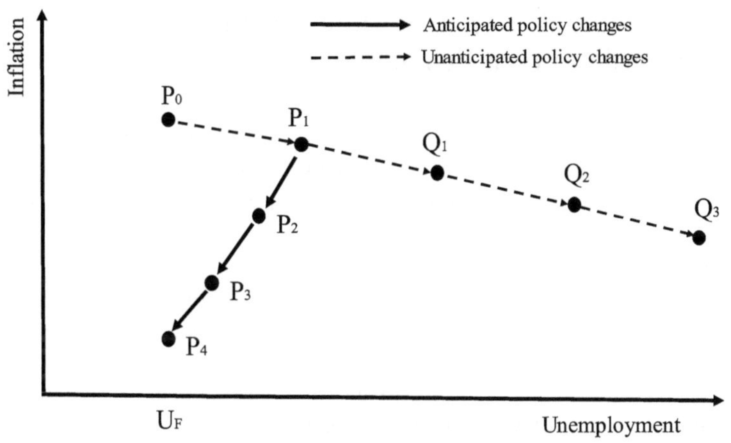

Fig. 9.8 A gradualist policy scenario. Source: Federal Res. Bank of Minneapolis (1978), p. 7

also decreases unemployment, as firms find it more feasible to hire additional workers when wage growth is more subdued.

Successive tightening policy measures lead to further reductions in both inflation and unemployment, as participants in the labor market adapt their wage demands to align with the lower inflation rate. As a result, fewer workers face job losses due to excessive labor costs. This process continues until point P_4 is reached, indicating full employment with significantly lower inflation. The growing awareness among a larger portion of the labor market about the consequences of the new policy mitigates the costs associated with achieving substantial inflation reduction, which become moderate and short-lived. However, if labor markets fail to adjust, the sequence of policy steps outlined above results in a series of points P_1 (Q_1, Q_2, and Q_3). This is the scenario that critics of tighter macroeconomic policies often refer to when arguing against their effectiveness, claiming that they are too costly in the fight against inflation.

Clearly, both firms and workers will comprehend the consequences of a policy shift for their respective markets. They will acquire knowledge and make necessary adjustments accordingly. Even those who may initially doubt the effectiveness of the policy change will ultimately realize that modifying their economic behavior is in their best interest, given the altered circumstances. This will lead to adjustments in wage demands, and any previous errors made by the public, due to misperceptions of government policy, will become less significant over time. Consequently, the subsequent policy measures in the sequence will not result in significant unemployment since decision-makers will accurately anticipate these steps.

9.6 Concluding Remarks on Monetary Policy in Interdependent Economies

Shortly after the collapse of the Bretton Woods system, concerns regarding the necessity of international coordination in bank regulation began to emerge.[18] The increasing efforts of international regulators to harmonize financial oversight have been paralleled by the growing significance of the *financial trilemma* (Schoenmaker, 2013), which differs from the previously discussed monetary policy trilemma (Obstfeld & Taylor, 2017, and current Chap. 5.7, footnote 20). In the financial trilemma, countries are faced with the choice between national financial policies, integration into global financial markets, or ensuring financial stability. For instance, if there is widespread integration into global financial markets and each nation retains control over its own financial policies, the possibility of regulatory arbitrage among jurisdictions could jeopardize financial stability.[19] On the other hand, a country that implements national financial rules may enhance financial stability by isolating itself from global market integration. However, many countries have been willing to relinquish a certain degree of sovereignty over financial regulation to maintain access to international capital markets while upholding financial stability. Although the financial trilemma is evidently applicable to currency zones with integrated payment systems, such as the euro area, it also applies to countries that have their own floating currencies.

The importance of enhancing the macrofinancial policy framework has emerged as a key lesson learned right from the advent of the global financial crisis. A key component of this macrofinancial policy framework is the inclusion of macroprudential policies, which aim to prevent the emergence of systemic risks within the financial system. From the perspective of monetary policy, this development is positive, but it also presents challenges. The positive aspect is that successful implementation of macroprudential policies can reduce the likelihood and severity of financial crises, thereby reducing the need for monetary policy to take unconventional measures to address the aftermath of such crises. However, the challenge lies in ensuring that the new institutional arrangements for macroprudential policy, in which central banks are likely to have a significant role, do not compromise the independence of monetary policy. Additionally, it is important to recognize that macroprudential policy should be seen as a complement to monetary policy, rather

[18] Over the years, the Basel Committee on Banking Supervision has expanded its influence and attracted emerging markets to its sphere of operation. Alongside the Basel Committee at the Bank for International Settlements, the Financial Stability Board has emerged, initially known as the Financial Stability Forum in 1999, with the purpose of overseeing the global financial system as a whole. The significance of the Financial Stability Board's role has increased due to the rise of "shadow banking" alongside the conventional banking, the expansion of financially influential and globally operating institutions, and the growing complexity of financial markets and traded instruments.

[19] For evidence on arbitrage channels, see Aiyar et al. (2014), Bayoumi (2017), and Cerutti et al. (2017).

than a substitute for it. The primary focus for maintaining financial stability should be on implementing prudential policies. However, the crisis has highlighted the need for monetary policy to also consider financial developments more comprehensively.

Current macroeconomic models utilized in the formulation of monetary policy exhibit a limited understanding of the connections between macroeconomics and finance, and they failed to incorporate important financial factors such as default risk, systemic liquidity risk, and the functioning of shadow banks. Addressing these gaps in a widely accepted manner still requires significant research and development.

Furthermore, even though, in an ideal scenario, prudential policies would be sufficient to ensure financial stability, under not so normal a time, monetary policy also plays a crucial role in supporting financial stability, which yet does not imply that monetary policy should expand its objectives to include financial stability explicitly. Rather, it suggests that in its pursuit of price stability, monetary policy should more explicitly consider the emergence of financial imbalances and take proactive measures to address them. In addition to monitoring indicators of price and output trends, monetary policy should also closely monitor variables such as credit growth and levels of indebtedness, especially when accompanied by rapid increases in asset prices and current account deficits. These factors often serve as strong signals of potential financial imbalances that could ultimately jeopardize both financial and price stabilities.

According to the findings of Brunnermeier and Schnabel (2016), historical evidence indicates that the occurrence of asset bubbles is often preceded or accompanied by expansionary monetary policy, surges in lending activities, capital inflows, and financial innovation or deregulation. Their research suggests that the severity of the subsequent economic crisis following the bursting of a bubble is less determined by the *type of asset* involved and more influenced by the *financing of the bubble* itself. Crises tend to be more severe when accompanied by a boom in lending and high levels of leverage among market participants, particularly when financial institutions actively participate in the speculative buying spree. Past experiences also demonstrate that adopting a purely passive approach of merely addressing the aftermath of bubble formation can be costly in many cases. Both monetary policy and macroprudential measures that actively counter the inflation of bubbles have the potential to deflate them and mitigate the resulting economic crises. However, effectively implementing such proactive policy approaches poses significant challenges. A favorable outcome is that monetary policy will exhibit greater symmetry throughout the economic cycle. This means that policymakers will be more inclined to act proactively during periods of economic prosperity, leaning against potential risks, and less reliant on reactive measures to address problems during downturns. However, it is important not to underestimate the challenges associated with empirically identifying the buildup of financial imbalances in real time.

One significant outcome of the recent crises is the substantial accumulation of public debt in many countries, reaching levels relative to GDP that were last seen in the aftermath of World War II, that jeopardizes the long-term viability of public finances in numerous advanced economies; this outcome will necessitate significant and sustained efforts for many years to come. It is evident that this undertaking presents considerable political challenges, despite being essential in order to prevent future episodes of instability. One crucial risk that needs to be addressed is the temptation to subtly influence the central bank into maintaining low interest rates, with the aim of generating slightly higher inflation in order to alleviate the burden of public debt. This underscores the ongoing importance of preserving the hard-earned independence of central banks to prevent the recurrence of "fiscal dominance," which could lead to highly detrimental macroeconomic and financial outcomes.

Systemic liquidity risk also arises from the interaction between financial markets and institutions. Prior to the crisis, this risk was significantly underestimated by both private sector and regulatory authorities, leading to banks relying heavily on short-term wholesale funding. When the crisis unfolded and liquidity dried up, central banks were left with no alternative but to inject massive amounts of systemic liquidity. The term "systemic risk" refers to the possibility of a disturbance occurring within the financial system that carries the potential for significant adverse effects on the real economy or, with reference to the EU, for one or more of its member states; these adverse effects hamper the smooth functioning of the internal market.[20] The significance of financial intermediaries, markets, and infrastructure in terms of systemic risk depends on factors such as their size, their interconnectedness with other components of the financial system, and the extent of the impact they would have on the overall system if they were to experience failure. For that reason, it is essential to give greater consideration to systemic liquidity risk.[21] The operating environment for monetary policy is also becoming increasingly complex due to the effects of globalization in both trade and finance.

Recent crises have underscored the importance of giving increased consideration to the global aspects of economic analysis, particularly in the context of highly interconnected international financial systems and closely linked production processes, as, for example, through global supply chains (Draghi, 2019).[22] While many

[20]In the EU, the ESRB, created in 2010 through Regulation (EU) No. 1092/2010 on European Union macroprudential oversight of the financial system and establishing a European Systemic Risk Board, plays a supervisory role in identifying systemic risks within the EU and proposing actions to prevent or reduce these risks.

[21]Possible measures in this regard include improving the transparency and availability of structural liquidity in systemic markets, such as derivatives. This can be facilitated by transitioning from over-the-counter markets to central counterparties and exchanges that facilitate the clearing and trading of standardized derivative contracts. Another approach is to utilize macroprudential tools to better incorporate the "pricing" of systemic liquidity risk by accounting for the broader costs associated with excessive reliance on continuous liquidity. For instance, the International Monetary Fund has recently suggested the implementation of a systemic liquidity surcharge on financial institutions (both banks and nonbanks) based on their incremental contribution to systemic liquidity risk (Vinals, 2012).

[22]One specific area of concern relates to trade. During the significant decline in global trade at the end of 2008, there was a noticeable decrease in the volume of goods being transported, such as those involved in shipping. This had consequences akin to an inventory adjustment, which was also occurring at that time. Therefore, it is crucial to gain a deeper comprehension of the dynamics surrounding trade flows, particularly in the event of a similar situation arising in the future.

of the deficiencies in international projections can be attributed to the same shortcomings observed in projections for the euro area, the crises have emphasized the specific requirement to place greater emphasis on understanding *the international transmission of both financial and confidence-related factors*. Pertinent research suggests a connection between confidence levels in the United States and the euro area, as confidence shocks originating in the United States can have a significant immediate impact on confidence indicators in the euro area (Dees & Soares Brinca, 2011; Kenny & Morgan, 2011). Additionally, the crisis revealed a substantial shift in the inflation outlook, largely influenced by sharp fluctuations in global commodity prices and the rapidly evolving global and regional—as, for example, the euro area—economic landscape.

This shift in inflation outlook underscores the importance of furthering our understanding of global inflation dynamics, specifically in relation to imbalances in global supply and demand, as well as fluctuations in commodity prices within the context of rapid changes in global economic activity. The current rise in inflation is to a great extent a result of the interaction between disruptions in supply chains and significant fiscal deficits. The COVID-19 pandemic, along with the war in Ukraine, disrupted supply chains and caused shortages. To address these shortages, wealthy industrial nations implemented substantial fiscal stimulus packages. However, this has led to a cycle where increased spending creates more demand, which in turn exacerbates the shortfalls. This dangerous cycle could potentially lead to further negative consequences (King, 2022; James, 2023). Escalating prices of essential goods like food and fuel have the potential to trigger discontent, protests, and even political upheavals and government instability worldwide.[23]

The commonly recognized initial phase of modern globalization emerged during the mid-nineteenth century amid widespread hunger crises. However, this era was disrupted by World War I and the subsequent Great Depression. Eventually, a different form of globalization emerged in the 1970s. Both of these pivotal moments in the emergence of globalization, namely, the 1840–1850s and the 1970s, were marked by shortages and periods of inflationary surges (James, 2023), as depicted in Fig. 9.9.

Following the inflationary surge set off by the 1970s oil shocks, new container shipping technology helped spur renewed expansion of world trade, while consumer price increases slowed dramatically. Additionally, during the 1970s, there was a pervasive and damaging skepticism regarding the feasibility of democracy. The world faced a multitude of intricate crises, much like the present day. However, a solution was found. Societies, voters, and subsequently political leaders began to draw comparisons and explore alternative approaches adopted elsewhere. It became

[23]The hunger crises of the mid-nineteenth century and the oil shocks of the 1970s at first ignited explosive rounds of worldwide inflation. In both cases, new technologies dramatically altered global supply systems, expanding globalization and leading to lengthy periods of disinflation. Thus, rampant inflation eventually drove the world to more rather than less globalization, with broad benefits (James, 2023, p. 64).

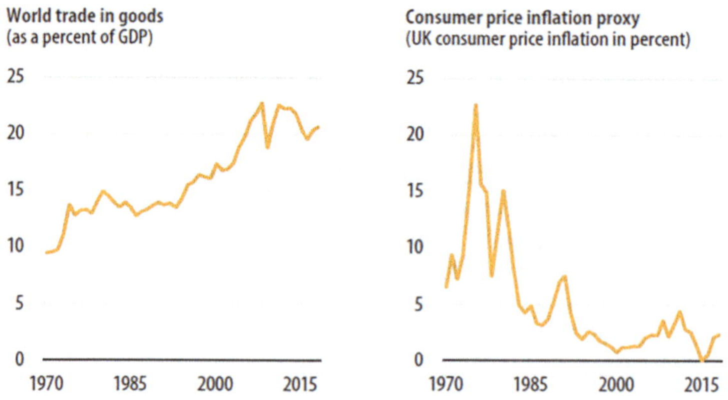

Fig. 9.9 Globalization and inflation. Source: James (2023), p. 66; Catão and Obstfeld (2019); Bank of England, "A Millennium of Economic Data" dataset; IMF, "World Economic Outlook" database

evident, as it did in the mid-nineteenth century and the 1970s, that governments that resisted global integration fared poorly in comparison.

Presently, we are witnessing an increase in protests targeting both autocratic regimes and democratic systems. A prevailing sentiment among these protests is dissatisfaction with the current methods of handling pandemics, conflicts, and even advancements in information technology. New technologies also emerge that have the potential to drive economic growth and provide enhanced solutions for various contemporary challenges, including healthcare, energy policy, climate change, and security. Addressing these issues effectively requires international collaboration and coordination. For instance, the possibilities offered by remote medicine and education existed prior to the pandemic, but their widespread adoption was accelerated out of necessity, leading to a revolution that could expand access and reduce costs. Remote work, transcending political boundaries, is akin to past communication revolutions. Information technology enables us to communicate more while reducing the need for physical movement. The globalization of the 1970s was primarily driven by intricate supply chains, while the crises are giving rise to a different form of globalization centered around information exchange. Societies will demonstrate varying degrees of competence in adapting to the new data revolution. The current dynamics of globalization hold the potential to revolutionize system optimization, making the outcomes of previous technological advancements more affordable and accessible. In this sense, globalization itself can be seen as the true Inflation Reduction Act (James, 2023).

In principle, central banks could prevent excessive tightening of monetary policy without explicit coordination by accurately predicting each other's policy actions and their global impact. However, highlighting this computational challenge demonstrates its difficulty compared to proactive direct consultation, which would offer more transparent guidance at the very least. Furthermore, coordinated efforts among central banks, accompanied by clear public communication, could effectively moderate global inflation expectations. Central banks have successfully coordinated their actions during financial crises that posed deflationary risks, and the current context of inflation equally warrants such an approach. It is positive that central banks have responded proactively to inflation by taking decisive actions that demonstrate their commitment to restoring price stability. Ideally, most central banks in advanced economies should have initiated these measures earlier, which would have allowed for a smoother increase in interest rates instead of the steep paths required due to delayed action. However, it is important to strike a balance as there can be too much of a good thing.

It is currently rendered crucial for monetary policymakers to assess the broader landscape and consider how the robust actions of other central banks will collectively reduce the global inflationary pressures they all face. Each economy will require varying degrees of monetary tightening moving forward. By collectively pursuing a more moderate tightening trajectory and effectively communicating their coordinated intentions to the public, central banks can avoid unnecessary output and employment sacrifices beyond what is necessary to bring inflation under control. The increased interconnectedness of the global economy amplifies the risks of excessive measures. To prevent an economic downturn that goes beyond the necessary steps to address inflation, central banks should collaborate to implement a more gradual tightening of monetary policy and provide clear communication about their plans (Obstfeld, 2022). The successful coordination of monetary policy during the global financial crisis highlights the effectiveness of such collective efforts, and the current challenges posed by inflation call for a similar collaborative approach. Since the GFC, central banks in advanced economies have increased their range of instruments but frequently fell short of achieving their official inflation targets.

The significant economic turmoil triggered by the COVID-19 pandemic has exacerbated this issue and emphasized the necessity for greater cooperation between monetary and fiscal policies. The notion of a "policy mix," which had largely faded from standard economic textbooks, has re-emerged as a crucial consideration. The advantages of raising the current low equilibrium real interest rate (R*) have also been put forward as a potential remedy; an elevated R* could play a crucial role in aligning the monetary and fiscal policy mix more effectively and enhancing countries' capacity to prevent extreme events (Bartsch et al., 2020). However, *in a financially interconnected world, individual nations have limited influence over R**. Therefore, the importance of global coordination is emphasized to complement for international policy initiatives that aim to increase R*.

The ongoing strategic reviews of monetary and fiscal frameworks in various countries present a distinctive chance to reconsider deliberated policy concerns. As, for example, Bartsch et al. (2020) argue it is essential to have not only effective coordination between monetary and fiscal policies but also coordination among policymakers in all major economies. It has been widely acknowledged that due to the increasing level of international interdependencies and the potential for greater cross-border connections in financial markets and intermediaries, public policy in banking and finance can no longer be developed and executed solely at the national level. In fact, the international dimension has likely become the primary policy factor in numerous areas, emphasizing its significance (Kokores, T. 1989, p. 31).

Nevertheless, as highlighted by the adverse effect of the GFC, it appears that significant macroeconomic vulnerabilities still persist within the Eurozone (European Commission, 2018b). If another crisis were to occur in the near future, the ability to respond effectively would be severely limited for several reasons: Firstly, the ECB is already facing limitations in its ability to further loosen monetary policy. Secondly, many countries have experienced a reduction in fiscal space to address adverse shocks. Lastly, there have been notable changes in the political landscape of various countries over the past decade. Another crisis, coupled with economic difficulties, could further erode political support for necessary reforms and international cooperation. Given these constraints in managing future crises, a crucial challenge lies in ensuring macroeconomic stability and building resilience to shocks within the Eurozone. Nevertheless, the ECB and Euro area governments have encountered numerous challenges in the past decade, leading to various modifications in the EMU framework. Although the ECB has faced criticism for its relatively delayed response to macroeconomic challenges, it has actually surpassed other prominent global central banks in developing novel and unconventional monetary policy instruments.[24] Following the previous crises, Eurozone governments reached an agreement to introduce several modifications concerning financial regulation and crisis management.

The key question is whether the existing institutional framework remains vulnerable and inadequate to handle the next crisis or if significant improvements have been made over the past decade, making a "muddling through" approach a potentially effective strategy (Gern et al., 2019, p. 25). In conclusion, despite facing challenges in its second decade, the euro project has achieved notable successes. The ECB has effectively maintained price stability, and the common currency enjoys popularity among citizens of the euro area, surpassing earlier expectations. Numerous enhancements have been implemented in the structure of Economic and Monetary Union over the past 15 crisis years. However, significant issues persist, such as fiscal capacity, sovereign default risks, and financial stability. Further challenges

[24] In addition to employing asset purchase programs similar to those of the Federal Reserve and the Bank of England, the ECB has also implemented a negative deposit rate on reserves. This rate, combined with the substantial increase in bank reserves resulting from the Eurosystem's asset purchases, has likely played a significant role in reducing bond yields in the euro area in recent years. Evidence suggests that individual euro area banks have adjusted their balance sheets in response to negative rates and the rise in reserves (Ryan & Whelan, 2021). Furthermore, the ECB has introduced a new tool known as Outright Monetary Transactions (OMT), which was developed following the Draghi (2012) declaration to do "whatever it takes" to defend the euro. Although the announcement of the OMT instrument had a notable impact on mitigating pessimistic sentiment surrounding peripheral sovereign bond yields during the peak of the euro crisis in 2012, it had not been utilized thus far, and practical implementation details remain uncertain. Considering the ongoing energy crisis triggered by the war in Ukraine, the recent inflation surge, and the likelihood of another economic downturn in the future, it is probable that the ECB will need to utilize all of its newly developed tools, and potentially develop additional ones, to combat any severe recession that may arise. With these tools in place, there is a possibility of a quicker policy response to future crises.

persist in a monetary union, as the euro area, than national economies, since to ensure the cohesion of the euro, European policymakers must strive to reduce the likelihood of crises and create a more resilient environment for future economic downturns. The economics profession has proposed various plans for further improvements, and it falls upon Europe's politicians to enact them. A crucial lesson learned from the global financial crisis of 2007–2009 and its subsequent crises was that traditional macroeconomic models did not adequately account for the role of finance and financial markets. A similar gap exists in models of international monetary relations as, over the centuries, policymakers and scholars have grappled with the challenge of addressing financial stability concerns, and this remains a pressing issue (Obstfeld, and Taylor, p. 24). The urgency has increased in recent decades as financial markets have rapidly evolved, often seeking to circumvent regulations by engaging in risky activities. Economic analysis must incorporate the risks of financial instability more prominently within its frameworks, spanning from the study of business cycles to the examination of international economic interactions.

Globally, there is a renewed debate, particularly in the United States and continental Europe, about the appropriate limits of central bank authority. This discussion is not an isolated occurrence but reflects a broader unease with the expanding influence and scope of technocratic governance. It is important for those who express concerns about populism to also consider how to establish appropriate boundaries and constraints on technocracy to ensure its proper functioning and prevent excessive concentration of power (Tucker, 2018, p. 57). Addressing this issue will require establishing mechanisms that allow for the integration of the advantages of credible commitment, which is a significant societal benefit of delegated decision-making, while also implementing limitations on functions, goals, and procedures that acknowledge our fundamental political values and customs. Recognizing that every branch of government is prone to error over time and considering people's potentially strong negative reactions when disappointed by unelected officials, it is imperative to invest in such efforts. To address such concerns will primarily require rediscovering political norms that align the motivations of lawmakers with our democratic principles. Ultimately, it revolves around our expectations of elected officials.

Furthermore, the crisis taught us that maintaining price and output stability alone does not guarantee financial stability. Despite experiencing a period of low inflation, stable output, and well-anchored inflation expectations during the Great Moderation, significant risks to financial stability emerged in the form of excessive leverage, credit expansion, vulnerable funding systems, shared exposures, and lax lending practices. This prompts us to consider whether a different monetary policy approach could have potentially averted the crisis. Enhancing the effectiveness of microprudential and macroprudential policies and supervision would have been the preferred course of action in addressing the crisis. Furthermore, these policies hold promise in terms of their ability to better mitigate financial stability risks in the future. However, it remains important to consider the possibility that prudential measures may not be fully effective. If these policies can be easily bypassed or exploited, are slow to respond to changing conditions, narrowly focused and fail to address emerging risks, or come with unintended consequences, the question arises whether monetary policy should step in to safeguard financial stability.

There are three main perspectives on the matter (see Viñals, 2016, p. 122): The first viewpoint suggests that monetary policy can be utilized, but only as a secondary measure, once prudential policies have been fully utilized. The second perspective argues against the use of monetary policy to address financial imbalances, even as a secondary measure, as interest rates are considered too broad in their impact and impose significant costs on the economy. The third school of thought disagrees and asserts that monetary policy should always be combined with prudential policies, continuously working to counteract financial imbalances. Due to its broad influence, interest rates affect all aspects of the financial system. However, the ongoing discussion needs to move beyond mere disagreements between these schools of thought, which are often based on principles. To provide concrete policy recommendations to central banks, it is crucial to conduct a comprehensive cost-benefit analysis of the overall effects of using monetary policy to support financial stability. This analysis consists of three key aspects: the benefits of monetary policy in promoting financial stability, the costs incurred by deviating from inflation and output goals in pursuit of financial stability, and the reciprocal impact of inflation and output deviations on financial stability. Among these aspects, only the second one is well understood and accurately quantified. *Without further research to estimate the effects of the other two aspects, policymakers will not have a secure foundation on which to base their decisions.*

During the COVID-19 pandemic, there was a significant shift in circumstances. Developed economies experienced a sharp increase in government spending. In the United States, for example, the federal government provided substantial and concentrated support through direct payments to households known as "stimulus checks." European countries initially implemented more modest programs, primarily focused on preventing job losses and supporting green and digital transitions. The expansionary fiscal policies implemented in both the United States and Europe played a significant role in driving inflation. However, as spending was on the rise, countries also faced unprecedented supply shocks caused by pandemic-related issues, including disruptions in supply chains. These supply shocks further added to the inflationary pressures experienced.

The COVID-19 pandemic highlighted that controlling inflation cannot solely rely on monetary policy, as fiscal policy also plays a significant role, as, additionally, the increase in public debt raised concerns about *fiscal dominance*, where fiscal deficits do not respond to monetary policy measures. In the aftermath of the global financial crisis, monetary and fiscal authorities could work together due to low debt levels and the need for stimulus. However, the risk of fiscal dominance currently creates a potential conflict between these authorities (Brunnermeier, 2023, p. 6). Central banks may prefer to raise interest rates to combat inflation, while governments are averse to higher interest expenses. Governments would rather have central banks cooperate by monetizing their debt, meaning purchasing government securities that private investors are unwilling to buy. However, the independence of central banks can only be maintained if they commit to not giving in to government pressures to monetize excessive debt. In such cases, authorities would be compelled to reduce spending or raise taxes, or possibly both, as part of fiscal consolidation efforts.

Above all, it is crucial for the central bank to maintain the support and trust of the public, as they are the ultimate foundation of its authority and autonomy. To achieve this, the central bank should communicate its actions effectively, explaining the reasoning behind its decisions, particularly when faced with inflation driven by fiscal factors. The central bank can maintain its preeminence by establishing a credible commitment to refrain from monetizing public debt in the event of a default, thereby avoiding any perception of bailing out the government. To tackle such concerns, central banks should adopt a monetary strategy that places a strong emphasis on stabilizing inflation expectations (Brunnermeier, 2023, p. 9). It is not sufficient for policy to tighten only after inflation has already emerged. Instead, central banks should be proactive and respond promptly when early indicators signal potential inflationary pressures. In doing so, central banks need to consider and incorporate the expectations of both households and financial markets regarding future inflation. These expectations play a crucial role in shaping overall demand conditions and asset prices.

To conclude, as Mishkin (2011a, 2011b) adds, "there is one other piece of good news that has emerged from the GFC. The field of macro/monetary economics has become considerably more exciting" (p. 104). It has presented a novel research agenda that will engage scholars in the field for a substantial period of time. Moreover, central bankers now face a broader array of policy issues to consider, making their work more stimulating. Although it may be tiring, central banking has transformed into a more stimulating profession as a consequence.

As a Corollary

In a context of increased uncertainty caused by various noneconomic factors such as the COVID-19 pandemic, the war in Ukraine, and long-term climate changes, policymakers face the challenge of effectively combating inflation. To achieve this, it is crucial to minimize unexpected changes in both monetary and fiscal policies. *Policymakers should aim to establish a consistent and trustworthy set of policies that the public can rely on when forming expectations about future inflation and spending. In essence, policy credibility is rendered essential. The credibility of policy can only be achieved by announcing it clearly, faithfully implementing it, and avoiding sudden shifts in direction.*

References

Aglietta, M., & Mojon, B. (2010). Central banking. In A. N. Berger, P. Molyneux, & J. O. S. Wilson (Eds.), *The Oxford handbook of banking* (pp. 233–256). Oxford University Press.

Agur, I., Capelle, D., Dell'Ariccia, G., & Sandri, D. (2022). Monetary finance: Do not touch or handle with care? *IMF departmental paper* no. 2022-001, Research Department, International Monetary Fund, Washington, DC, January 13th.

Aiyar, S., Calomiris, C. W., & Wieladek, T. (2014). Does macro-prudential regulation leak? Evidence from a UK policy experiment. *Journal of Money, Credit, and Banking, 46*(S1), 181–214.

Baker, S., Bloom, N., & Davis, S. J. (2016). Measuring economic policy uncertainty. *Quarterly Journal of Economics, 131*(4), 1593–1636.

Barrett, C. R., Kokores, I. T., & Sen, S. (2016). Monetary policy games, financial instability and incomplete information. *Annals of Finance, 12*(2), 161–178.

Barrett, C. R., Kokores, I. T., & Sen, S. (2017). Financial instability and monetary policy: Rules or discretion? *Theoretical Economics Letters, Special Issue on Fiscal and Monetary Policy, 7*(4), 1043–1065.

Bartsch, E., Benassy-Queré, A., Corsetti, G., & Debrun, X. (2020). It's all in the mix: How can monetary and fiscal policies work or fail together. *Geneva reports on the world economy* 23, International Centre of Monetary and Banking Studies, Geneva, Switzerland, and Centre for Economic Policy Research, London, UK.

Bayoumi, T. (2017). *Unfinished business: The unexplored causes of the financial crisis and the lessons yet to be learned.* Yale University Press.

Bernanke, B. S., & Blanchard, O. (2023). What caused the U.S. pandemic-era inflation? Paper presented at the conference *'the fed: Lessons learned from the past three years'*, Brookings Institution, Hutchins Center on Fiscal & Monetary Policy, Washington, DC, USA, May 23.

BIS—Bank for International Settlements (2020). Annual economic report, Basel, Switzerland.

Brunnermeier, M. K. (2023). Rethinking monetary policy in a changing world. *Finance & Development 'New Directions for Monetary Policy'*, 60(1), International Monetary Fund, March, pp 6–9.

Brunnermeier, M. K., & Schnabel, I. (2016). Bubbles and central banks: Historical perspectives. In M. Bordo, Ø. Eitrheim, M. Flandreau, & J. Qvigstad (Eds.), *Central banks at a crossroads: What can we learn from history? Studies in macroeconomic history* (pp. 493–562). Cambridge University Press.

Catão, L. A. V., & Obstfeld, M. (2019). Introduction. In L. A. V. Catão & M. Obstfeld (Eds.), *Meeting Globalization's challenges: Policies to make trade work for all* (pp. 1–40). Princeton University Press.

Cavallo, A. (2020). Inflation with COVID consumption baskets. *NBER Working Paper* 27352, National Bureau of Economic Research, Cambridge, MA, USA.

Cerutti, E., Claessens, S., & Laeven, L. (2017). The use and effectiveness of macroprudential policies: New evidence. *Journal of Financial Stability, 28*, 203–224.

Dees, S., & Soares Brinca, P. (2011). Consumer confidence as a predictor of consumption spending: Evidence for the United States and the euro area. *ECB Working Paper* No. 1349, European Central Bank, Frankfurt Am Main, Germany.

Draghi, M. (2019). Stabilisation policies in a monetary union. *Speech* of the President of the European Central Bank -ECB at the Academy of Athens, Athens, Greece, October 1st.

European Banking Association—EBA. (2020a). The EU banking sector: First insights into the COVID-19 impacts. European Banking Association, May 25.

European Banking Association—EBA. (2020b). EBA guidelines on treatment of public and private moratoria in light of COVID-19 measures. European Banking Association, April 2.

European Commission. (2018a). The 2018 ageing report: Economic and budgetary projections for the EU member states, Brussels.

European Commission. (2018b). Eurobarometer: Support for the euro steady at all-time high levels. November 2018. https://ec.europa.eu/info/news/eurobarometer-2018-nov-20_en

European Commission. (2020a). *Spring 2020 economic forecast* 'A deep and uneven recession, an uncertain recovery, European Commission, May 6.

European Commission. (2020b). Banking package to facilitate lending to households and businesses in the EU. European Commission, April 28.

European Commission. (2020c). Europe's moment: Repair and prepare for the next generation. European Commission Press Release, European Commission, May 27.

European Court of Auditors. (2020). How the EU took account of lessons learned from the 2008-2012 financial and sovereign debt crises. *Review* no 5, European Court of Auditors, European Union, Luxembourg.

Fisher, I. (1933). The debt-deflation theory of great depressions. *Econometrica, 1*, 337–357.

Friedman, M. (1962). Should there be an independent monetary authority? In L. B. Yeager (Ed.), *Search of a monetary constitution*. Harvard University Press. Reprinted in Friedman, M. (1968). Dollars and deficits, Englewood Cliffs: Prentice Hall.

Fuhrer, J., & Madigan, B. (1997). Monetary policy when interest rates are bounded at zero. *The Review of Economics and Statistics, 79*(4), 573–585.

Gavriilidis, K. (2021). Measuring climate policy uncertainty. SSRN.

Gern, K. J., Kooths, S., & Stolzenburg, U. (2019). Euro at 20: The monetary union from a bird's-eye view. In *Depth analysis*, PE 631.038, European Parliament, January.

Goodfriend, M. (2000). Overcoming the zero bound on interest rate policy. *Journal of Money, Credit, and Banking, 32*(4), 1007–1035.

IMF—International Monetary Fund. (2021). *World economic outlook: Recovery during a pandemic—health concerns, supply disruptions*. Price Pressures.

James, H. (2023). In defense of globalisation. Finance & Development 'New Directions for Monetary Policy', vol. 60(1), International Monetary Fund, pp. 64–66.

Jurado, K., Ludvigson, S., & Ng, S. (2015). Measuring uncertainty. *American Economic Review, 105*(3), 1177–1216.

Kenny, G., & Morgan, J. (2011). Some lessons from the financial crisis for economic analysis. ECB occasional paper no. 130, October, European Central Bank, Frankfurt Am Main, Germany.

King, M. (2022). Monetary policy in a world of radical uncertainty. *Conference Paper* 1, Institute of International Monetary Research, University of Buckingham, UK, January.

Kokores, I. T. (2022). *Monetary policy and financial stability: Challenges before and after the global financial crisis*. Cambridge Scholars Publishing.

Krugman, P. R. (1998). It's Baaack: Japan's slump and the return of the liquidity trap. *Brookings Papers on Economic Activity, 29*(2), 137–206.

Kuroda, H. (2022). *Japan's inflation dynamics and the role of monetary policy* (p. 22). Speech at Columbia University.

Lane, P. R. (2022). Inflation diagnostics. *The ECB Blog*, European Central Bank, Frankfurt Am Main, Germany, 25 November.

Mauro, P., & Zhou, J. (2020). R minus g negative: Can we sleep more soundly? *IMF working paper* No 20/52, International Monetary Fund, Washington, DC.

Mishkin, F. S. (2011a). Over the cliff: From the subprime to the global financial crisis. *Journal of Economic Perspectives, 25*(1), 49–70.

Mishkin, F. S. (2011b). Monetary policy strategy: Lessons from the crisis. In M. Jarocińki, F. Smets, & C. Thimann (Eds.), *Approaches to monetary policy revisited—lessons from the crisis, sixth ECB central banking conference proceedings* (pp. 67–118).

Minsky, H. (1982). *Can "It" happen again? Essays on instability and finance*. M.E. Sharpe, Inc.

Obstfeld, M. (2022). Uncoordinated monetary policies risk a historic global slowdown. *Realtime Economics Blogpost*. Peterson Institute for International Economics. 12 Sept.

Obstfeld, M., & Taylor, A. M. (2017). International monetary relations: Taking finance seriously. *Journal of Economic Perspectives, 31*(3), 3–28.

Orphanides, A. (2018). The boundaries of Central Bank independence: Lessons from unconventional times. *Bank of Japan Monetary and Economic Studies*, 35–56.

Orphanides, A. (2021). The power of central Bank balance sheets. Keynote Speech, Bank of Japan Institute of Monetary Studies Conference on 'Adapting to the New Normal: Perspectives and Policy Challenges after the COVID-19 Pandemic', May 24–25. *Monetary and Economic Studies*, Bank of Japan, November.

Pradhan, M., & Goodhart, C. (2021). Friedman vs Phillips: A historic divide. *VoxEU*.

Reifschneider, D., & Wilcox, D. (2022). The case for a cautiously optimistic outlook for US inflation. Peterson Institute for International Economics, *Policy Brief* 22-3, March.

Reinsdorf, M. (2020). COVID-19 and the CPI: Is inflation underestimated? IMF working paper 20/224, Washington, DC: International Monetary Fund.

Ryan, E., & Whelan, K. (2021). Quantitative easing and the hot potato effect: Evidence from euro area banks. *Journal of International Money and Finance, 115*, 102354.

Samuelson, P. A. (1997). Wherein do the European and American models differ? *Banca d'Italia Temi di Discussione, 320*, Banca d' Italia.

Schoenmaker, D. (2013). *Governance of international banking: The financial trilemma*. Oxford University Press.

Scotti, C. (2016). Surprise and uncertainty indexes: Real-time aggregation of real-activity macro-surprises. *Journal of Monetary Economics, 82*, 1–19.

Tucker, P. (2018). The governance of monetary and financial stability policy. Banking perspectives. *The Clearing House. Quarter, 2*, 50–57.

Vinals, J. (2012). Monetary policy and financial stability: Challenges in the wake of the crisis. *International Journal of Central Banking, 8*(S1), 297–300.

Viñals, J. (2016). Introduction to the monetary policy section. In O. J. Blanchard, K. Rogoff, & R. Rajan (Eds.), *Progress and confusion: The state of macroeconomic policy* (pp. 121–127). MIT Press.

MIX
Papier aus verantwortungsvollen Quellen
Paper from responsible sources
FSC® C105338

If you have any concerns about our products,
you can contact us on
ProductSafety@springernature.com

In case Publisher is established outside the EU,
the EU authorized representative is:
Springer Nature Customer Service Center GmbH
Europaplatz 3, 69115 Heidelberg, Germany

Printed by Libri Plureos GmbH
in Hamburg, Germany